Quantile Regression

Quantile regression is gradually emerging as a unified statistical methodology for estimating models of conditional quantile functions. By complementing the exclusive focus of classical least-squares regression on the conditional mean, quantile regression offers a systematic strategy for examining how covariates influence the location, scale, and shape of the entire response distribution. This monograph is the first comprehensive treatment of the subject, encompassing models that are linear and nonlinear, parametric and nonparametric. The author has devoted more than 25 years of research to this topic. The methods are illustrated with a variety of applications from economics, biology, ecology, and finance. The treatment will find its core audiences in econometrics, statistics, and biostatistics.

Roger Koenker is McKinley Professor of Economics and Professor of Statistics at the University of Illinois at Urbana-Champaign. From 1976 to 1983 he was a member of the technical staff at Bell Laboratories. He has held visiting positions at The University of Pennsylvania; Charles University, Prague; Nuffield College, Oxford; University College London; and Australian National University. He is a Fellow of the Econometric Society.

Econometric Society Monographs No. 38

Editors:
Andrew Chesher, University College London
Matthew Jackson, California Institute of Technology

The Econometric Society is an international society for the advancement of economic theory in relation to statistics and mathematics. The Econometric Society Monograph Series is designed to promote the publication of original research contributions of high quality in mathematical economics and theoretical and applied econometrics.

Quantile Regression

Roger Koenker
University of Illinois

CAMBRIDGE
UNIVERSITY PRESS

CAMBRIDGE UNIVERSITY PRESS
Cambridge, New York, Melbourne, Madrid, Cape Town, Singapore,
São Paulo, Delhi, Dubai, Tokyo, Mexico City

Cambridge University Press
32 Avenue of the Americas, New York, NY 10013-2473, USA

www.cambridge.org
Information on this title: www.cambridge.org/9780521608275

First published 2005

A catalog record for this publication is available from the British Library

Library of Congress Cataloging in Publication data

Koenker, Roger, 1947–
Quantile regression / Roger Koenker.
    p. cm. – (Econometric Society monographs ; no. 38)
Includes bibliographical references and index.
ISBN 0-521-84573-4 (hardcover) – ISBN 0-521-60827-9 (pbk.)
1. Regression analysis.   2. Mathematical statistics.   I. Title.   II. Series.

QA278.2.K64   2005
519.5′36 – dc22   2004027656

ISBN 978-0-521-84573-1 Hardback
ISBN 978-0-521-60827-5 Paperback

To Emma, in memoriam

Contents

Contents

Preface

Francis Galton in a famous passage defending the "charms of statistics" against its many detractors, chided his statistical colleagues

> [who] limited their inquiries to Averages, and do not seem to revel in more comprehensive views. Their souls seem as dull to the charm of variety as that of a native of one of our flat English counties, whose retrospect of Switzerland was that, if the mountains could be thrown into its lakes, two nuisances would be got rid of at once (*Natural Inheritance,* p. 62).

It is the fundamental task of statistics to bring order out of the diversity – at times the apparent chaos – of scientific observation. And this task is often very effectively accomplished by exploring how *averages* of certain variables depend on the values of other "conditioning" variables. The method of least squares, which pervades statistics, is admirably suited for this purpose. And yet, like Galton, one may question whether the exclusive focus on conditional mean relations among variables ignores some "charm of variety" in matters statistical.

As a resident of one of the flattest American counties, my recollections of Switzerland and its attractive nuisances are quite different from the retrospect described by Galton. Not only the Swiss landscape, but also many of its distinguished statisticians have in recent years made us more aware of the charms and perils of the diversity of observations and the consequences of too blindly limiting our inquiry to averages.

Quantile regression offers the opportunity for a more complete view of the statistical landscape and the relationships among stochastic variables. The simple expedient of replacing the familiar notions of sorting and ranking observations in the most elementary one-sample context by *optimization* enables us to extend these ideas to a much broader class of statistical models. Just as minimizing sums of squares permits us to estimate a wide variety of models for conditional mean functions, minimizing a simple asymmetric version of absolute errors yields estimates for conditional quantile functions. For linear parametric models, computation is greatly facilitated by the reformulation of the optimization problem as a parametric linear program. Formal duality results for linear programs yield a new approach to rank statistics and rank-based inference for linear models.

I hope that this book can provide a comprehensive introduction to quantile regression methods and that it will serve to stimulate others to explore and further develop these ideas in their own research. Because ultimately the test of any statistical method must be its success in applications, I have sought to illustrate the application of quantile regression methods throughout the book wherever possible. Formal mathematical development, which plays an indispensable role in clarifying precise conditions under which statistical methods can be expected to perform reliably and efficiently, are generally downplayed, but Chapter 4 is devoted to an exposition of some of the basic asymptotic theory of quantile regression, and other chapters include technical material that provides further mathematical details.

Statistical software for quantile regression is now widely available in many well-known statistical packages. Fellow R users will undoubtedly recognize by the graphics that I am an R-ophile. I have devoted considerable research energy over the years to the development of software for quantile regression, first while I was at Bell Laboratories in the S language of John Chambers, later in S's commercial manifestation Splus, and in recent years in its splendid open-source embodiment R.

I am extremely grateful to many colleagues who have, over the years, collaborated on various aspects of the work described here. Gib Bassett, first and foremost, whose Ph.D. thesis on l_1-regression served as a springboard for much of our subsequent work on this subject, has been a continuing source of insight and enthusiastic support. Jana Jurečková, who took an early interest in this line of research, has made an enormous contribution to the subject, especially in developing the close connection between quantile regression ideas and rank statistics in work with Cornelius Gutenbrunner. Recently, I have had the pleasure of working with Zhijie Xiao and Ivan Mizera on time-series and multivariate smoothing problems, respectively. Independent work by David Ruppert, Ray Carroll, Alan Welsh, Tertius Dewet, Jim Powell, Gary Chamberlain, Xuming He, Keith Knight, Probal Chaudhuri, Hira Koul, Marc Hallin, Brian Cade, Moshe Buchinsky, Berndt Fitzenberger, Victor Chernozhukov, and Andrew Chesher, among others, has also played a crucial role in the development of these ideas.

Continuing collaboration over the past decade with a number of Ph.D. students including José Machado, Pin Ng, Quanshui Zhao, Yannis Bilias, Beum-Jo Park, M. N. Hasan, Daniel Morillo, Ted Juhl, Olga Geling, Gregory Kordas, Lingjie Ma, Ying Wei, Roberto Perrelli, and Carlos Lamarche has been especially rewarding.

Some of the material was originally prepared for short courses offered at the 1997 Brazilian Statistical Association meeting at Campos do Jordão, the 2001 South African Statistical Association Annual Conference in Goudini Spa, in the spring of 2003 at University College London, and in the fall of 2003 at the NAKE Workshop in Groningen. I would like to express my appreciation to organizers and participants for their comments and suggestions.

I would like to specially thank Steve Portnoy, with whom I have collaborated over many years on many aspects of quantile regression. He has been a great source of encouragement and inspiration from our earliest discussions in the mid-1970s. Originally, we had planned to write this book together, but in the end Steve's impatience with revisiting the scenes of old research and his eagerness to get on with the new proved even greater than my own, and I have had to fend for myself; readers are the poorer for it.

I would also like to express my appreciation to various institutions that have provided hospitable environments for this research: Bell Laboratories, Australian National University, Charles University, University College London, and my academic home for most of my career, the University of Illinois. Research support by the National Science Foundation over an extended period has contributed significantly and is deeply appreciated.

And finally, my most heartfelt thanks – to my wife Diane and daughter Hannah.

Urbana, July 2, 2004

CHAPTER 1

Introduction

1.1 MEANS AND ENDS

Much of applied statistics may be viewed as an elaboration of the linear regression model and associated estimation methods of least squares. In beginning to describe these techniques, Mosteller and Tukey (1977), in their influential text, remark:

> What the regression curve does is give a grand summary for the averages of the distributions corresponding to the set of xs. We could go further and compute several different regression curves corresponding to the various percentage points of the distributions and thus get a more complete picture of the set. Ordinarily this is not done, and so regression often gives a rather incomplete picture. Just as the mean gives an incomplete picture of a single distribution, so the regression curve gives a correspondingly incomplete picture for a set of distributions.

My objective in the following pages is to describe explicitly how to "go further." Quantile regression is intended to offer a comprehensive strategy for completing the regression picture.

Why does least-squares estimation of the linear regression model so pervade applied statistics? What makes it such a successful tool? Three possible answers suggest themselves. One should not discount the obvious fact that the computational tractability of linear estimators is extremely appealing. Surely this was the initial impetus for their success. Second, if observational noise is normally distributed (i.e., Gaussian), least-squares methods are known to enjoy a certain optimality. But, as it was for Gauss himself, this answer often appears to be an *ex post* rationalization designed to replace the first response. More compelling is the relatively recent observation that least-squares methods provide a general approach to estimating conditional mean functions.

And yet, as Mosteller and Tukey suggest, the mean is rarely a satisfactory end in itself, even for statistical analysis of a single sample. Measures of spread, skewness, kurtosis, boxplots, histograms, and more sophisticated density estimation are all frequently employed to gain further insight. Can something similar be done in regression? A natural starting place for this would be to supplement the conditional mean surfaces estimated by least squares with several estimated conditional quantile surfaces. In the chapters that follow, methods are described to accomplish this task. The basic ideas go back to the earliest work on regression by Boscovich in the mid-18th century to Edgeworth at the end of the 19th century.

1.2   THE FIRST REGRESSION: A HISTORICAL PRELUDE

It is ironic that the first faltering attempts to *do* regression are so closely tied to the notions of quantile regression. Indeed, as I have written on a previous occasion, the present enterprise might be viewed as an attempt to set statistics back 200 years, to the idyllic period before the discovery of least squares.

If least squares can be dated to 1805 by the publication of Legendre's work on the subject, then Boscovich's initial work on regression was half a century prior. The problem that interested Boscovich was the ellipticity of the earth. Newton and others had suggested that the earth's rotation could be expected to make it bulge at the equator with a corresponding flattening at the poles, making it an oblate spheroid, more like a grapefruit than a lemon. On the early history of regression and the contribution of Boscovich in particular, Stigler (1986) is the definitive introduction. Smith (1987) gives a detailed account of the development of geodesy, focusing attention on the efforts that culminated in the data appearing in Table 1.1.

To estimate the extent of this effect, the five measurements appearing in Table 1.1 had been made. Each represented a rather arduous direct measurement of the arc-length of $1°$ of latitude at five quite dispersed points – from Quito on the equator to a site in Lapland at $66°19'$N. It was clear from these measurements that arc length was increasing as one moved toward the pole from the equator, thus qualitatively confirming Newton's conjecture. But how the five measurements should be combined to produce one estimate of the earth's ellipticity was unclear.

For short arcs, the approximation

$$y = a + b \sin^2 \lambda, \tag{1.1}$$

Table 1.1. *Boscovich ellipticity data*

Location	Latitude	$\sin^2$ (Latitude)	Arc Length
Quito	$0°\ 0'$	0	56,751
Cape of Good Hope	$33°\ 18'$	0.2987	57,037
Rome	$42°\ 59'$	0.4648	56,979
Paris	$49°\ 23'$	0.5762	57,074
Lapland	$66°\ 19'$	0.8386	57,422

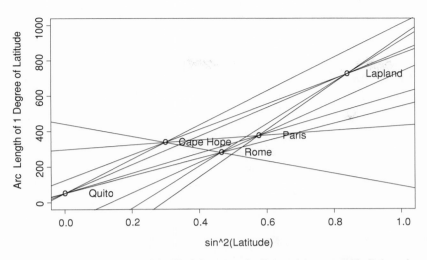

Figure 1.1. Boscovich ellipticity example. Boscovich computed all the pairwise slopes and initially reported a trimmed mean of the pairwise slopes as a point estimate of the earth's ellipticity. Arc length is measured as the excess over 56,700 toise per degree where one toise $\approx$ 6.39 feet, or 1.95 meters.

where y is the length of the arc and λ is the latitude, was known to be satisfactory. The parameter a could be interpreted as the length of a degree of arc at the equator and b as the exceedence of a degree of arc at the pole over its value at the equator. Ellipticity could then be computed as $1/\text{ellipticity} = \eta = 3a/b$. Boscovich, noting that any pair of observations could be used to compute an estimate of a and b, hence of η, began by computing all ten such estimates. These lines are illustrated in Figure 1.1. Some of these lines seemed quite implausible, especially perhaps the downward-sloping one through Rome and the Cape of Good Hope. Boscovich reported two final estimates: one based on averaging all ten distinct estimates of b, the other based on averaging all but two of the pairwise slopes with the smallest implied exceedence. In both cases the estimate of a was taken directly from the measured length of the arc at Quito. These gave ellipticities of 1/155 and 1/198, respectively. A modern variant on this idea is the median of pairwise slopes suggested by Theil (1950), which yields the somewhat lower estimate of 1/255.

It is a curiosity worth noting that the least-squares estimator of (a, b) may also be expressed as a weighted average of the pairwise slope estimates. Let h index the ten pairs, and write

$$b(h) = X(h)^{-1}y(h), \tag{1.2}$$

where, for the simple bivariate model and $h = (i, j)$,

$$X(h) = \begin{pmatrix} 1 & x_i \\ 1 & x_j \end{pmatrix} \quad y(h) = \begin{pmatrix} y_i \\ y_j \end{pmatrix}; \tag{1.3}$$

then we may write the least-squares estimator as

$$\hat{b} = \sum_h w(h)b(h), \tag{1.4}$$

where $w(h) = |X(h)|^2 / \sum_h |X(h)|^2$. As shown by Subrahmanyam (1972) and elaborated by Wu (1986), this representation of the least-squares estimator extends immediately to the general p-parameter linear regression model. In the bivariate example the weights are obviously proportional to the distance between each pair of design points, a fact that, in itself, portends the fragility of least squares to outliers in either x or y observations.

Boscovich's second attack on the ellipticity problem formulated only two years later brings us yet closer to quantile regression. In effect, he suggests estimating (a, b) in (1.1) by minimizing the sum of absolute errors subject to the constraint that the errors sum to zero. The constraint requires that the fitted line pass through the centroid of the observations, $(\bar{x}, \bar{y})$. Boscovich provided a geometric algorithm, which was remarkably simple, to compute the estimator. Having reduced the problem to regression through the origin with the aid of the constraint, we may imagine rotating a line through the new origin at $(\bar{x}, \bar{y})$ until the sum of absolute residuals is minimized. This may be viewed algebraically, as noted later by Laplace, as the computation of a *weighted median*. For each point we may compute

$$b_i = \frac{y_i - \bar{y}}{x_i - \bar{x}} \tag{1.5}$$

and associate with each slope the weight $w_i = |x_i - \bar{x}|$. Now let $b_{(i)}$ be the ordered slopes and $w_{(i)}$ the associated weights, and find the smallest j, say j^*, such that

$$\sum_{i=1}^{j} w_{(i)} > \frac{1}{2} \sum_{i=1}^{n} w_{(i)} \tag{1.6}$$

The Boscovich estimator, $\hat{\beta} = b_{(j^*)}$, was studied in detail by Laplace in 1789 and later in his monumental *Traite de Méchanique Céleste*. Boscovich's proposal, which Laplace later called the "method of situation," is a curious blend of mean and median ideas; in effect, the slope parameter b is estimated as a median, while the intercept parameter a is estimated as a mean.

This was clearly recognized by Edgeworth, who revived these ideas in 1888 after nearly a century of neglect. In his early work on index numbers and weighted averages, Edgeworth had emphasized that the putative optimality of the sample mean as an estimator of location was crucially dependent on the assumption that the observations came from a common normal distribution. If the observations were "discordant," say from normals with different variances, the median, he argued, could easily be superior to the mean. Indeed, anticipating the work of Tukey in the 1940s, Edgeworth compares the asymptotic variances of the median and mean for observations from scale mixtures of normals, concluding that, for equally weighted mixtures with relative scale greater than 2.25, the median had smaller asymptotic variance than the mean.

Edgeworth's work on median methods for linear regression brings us directly to quantile regression. Edgeworth (1888) discards the Boscovich–Laplace constraint that the residuals sum to zero and proposes to minimize the sum of absolute residuals in both intercept and slope parameters, calling it a "double median" method and noting that it could be extended, in principle, to a "plural median" method. A geometric algorithm was given for the bivariate case, and a discussion of conditions under which one would prefer to minimize absolute error rather than the by-then well-established squared error is provided. Unfortunately, the geometric approach to computing Edgeworth's new median regression estimator was rather awkward, requiring, as he admitted later, "the attention of a mathematician; and in the case of many unknowns, some power of hypergeometrical conception." Only considerably later did the advent of linear programming provide a conceptually simple and efficient computational approach.

Once we have a median regression estimator it is natural to ask, "are there analogs for regression of the other quantiles?" The answer to this question is explored in the next section.

1.3 QUANTILES, RANKS, AND OPTIMIZATION

Any real-valued random variable X may be characterized by its (right-continuous) distribution function

$$F(x) = P(X \leq x), \tag{1.7}$$

whereas for any $0 < \tau < 1$,

$$F^{-1}(\tau) = \inf\{x : F(x) \geq \tau\} \tag{1.8}$$

is called the τth quantile of X. The median, $F^{-1}(1/2)$, plays the central role.

The quantiles arise from a simple optimization problem that is fundamental to all that follows. Consider a simple decision theoretic problem: a point estimate is required for a random variable with (posterior) distribution function F. If loss is described by the piecewise linear function illustrated in Figure 1.2

$$\rho_\tau(u) = u(\tau - I(u < 0)) \tag{1.9}$$

for some $\tau \in (0, 1)$, find $\hat{x}$ to minimize expected loss. This is a standard exercise in decision theory texts (e.g., Ferguson, 1967, p. 51). The earliest reference that I am aware of is Fox and Rubin (1964), who studied the admissibility of the quantile estimator under this loss function. We seek to minimize

$$E\rho_\tau(X - \hat{x}) = (\tau - 1) \int_{-\infty}^{\hat{x}} (x - \hat{x}) dF(x) + \tau \int_{\hat{x}}^{\infty} (x - \hat{x}) dF(x). \tag{1.10}$$

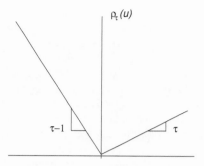

Figure 1.2. Quantile regression ρ function.

Differentiating with respect to $\hat{x}$, we have

$$0 = (1 - \tau) \int_{-\infty}^{\hat{x}} dF(x) - \tau \int_{\hat{x}}^{\infty} dF(x) = F(\hat{x}) - \tau. \qquad (1.11)$$

Since F is monotone, any element of $\{x : F(x) = \tau\}$ minimizes expected loss. When the solution is unique, $\hat{x} = F^{-1}(\tau)$; otherwise, we have an "interval of τth quantiles" from which the smallest element must be chosen – to adhere to the convention that the empirical quantile function be left-continuous.

It is natural that an optimal point estimator for asymmetric linear loss should lead us to the quantiles. In the symmetric case of absolute value loss it is well known to yield the median. When loss is linear and asymmetric, we prefer a point estimate more likely to leave us on the flatter of the two branches of marginal loss. Thus, for example, if an underestimate is *marginally* three times more costly than an overestimate, we will choose $\hat{x}$ so that $P(X \le \hat{x})$ is three times greater than $P(X > \hat{x})$ to compensate. That is, we will choose $\hat{x}$ to be the 75th percentile of F.

When F is replaced by the empirical distribution function

$$F_n(x) = n^{-1} \sum_{i=1}^{n} I(X_i \le x), \qquad (1.12)$$

we may still choose $\hat{x}$ to minimize expected loss:

$$\int \rho_\tau(x - \hat{x}) dF_n(x) = n^{-1} \sum_{i=1}^{n} \rho_\tau(x_i - \hat{x}) \qquad (1.13)$$

and doing so now yields the τth *sample* quantile. When τn is an integer there is again some ambiguity in the solution, because we really have an interval of solutions, $\{x : F_n(x) = \tau\}$, but we shall see that this is of little practical consequence.

Much more important is the fact that we have expressed the problem of finding the τth sample quantile, a problem that might seem inherently tied to the notion of an ordering of the sample observations, as the solution to a simple optimization problem. In effect we have replaced *sorting* by *optimizing*. This will prove to be the key idea in generalizing the quantiles to a much richer class of models in subsequent chapters. Before doing this, though, it is worth examining the simple case of the ordinary sample quantiles in a bit more detail.

The problem of finding the τth sample quantile, which may be written as

$$\min_{\xi \in \mathbf{R}} \sum_{i=1}^{n} \rho_\tau(y_i - \xi), \tag{1.14}$$

may be reformulated as a linear program by introducing $2n$ artificial, or "slack," variables $\{u_i, v_i : 1, \ldots, n\}$ to represent the positive and negative parts of the vector of residuals. This yields the new problem

$$\min_{(\xi, u, v) \in \mathbb{R} \times \mathbb{R}_+^{2n}} \left\{ \tau 1_n^\top u + (1 - \tau) 1_n^\top v \mid 1_n \xi + u - v = y \right\}, \tag{1.15}$$

where 1_n denotes an n-vector of 1. Clearly, in (1.15) we are minimizing a linear function on a polyhedral constraint set consisting of the intersection of the $(2n + 1)$-dimensional hyperplane determined by the linear equality constraints and the set $\mathbb{R} \times \mathbb{R}_+^{2n}$.

Figure 1.3 illustrates the most elementary possible version of the median linear programming problem. We have only one observation, at $y = 1$, and we wish to solve

$$\min_{(\xi, u, v) \in \mathbb{R} \times \mathbb{R}_+^2} \left\{ u + v \mid \xi + u - v = y \right\}.$$

The constraint set is the triangular region representing the intersection of the plane $\{(\xi, u, v) \mid \xi + u - v = 1\}$ with the cone $\{(\xi, u, v) \in \mathbb{R}^3 \mid u \geq 0, v \geq 0\}$. The long edge of this triangle extends off into the deeper regions of the figure. The objective function is represented by a series of vertical planes perpendicular to the $45°$ line in the (u, v) (horizontal) plane. Moving toward the origin reduces $u + v$, thus improving the objective function. It is apparent that any feasible point (ξ, u, v) that has both u and v strictly positive can be improved by reducing v and increasing u to compensate. But with only one observation we can move further. Reducing u and increasing ξ to compensate – that is, moving along the interior edge of the constraint set – allows us to reduce the objective function to zero, setting $\xi = 1$, coming to rest at the upper-left corner of the constraint set. Now, if we try to imagine increasing the number of observations, we have contributions to the objective function from each observation like the one illustrated in Figure 1.3. Given a trial value of the parameter ξ, we can consider a feasible point that sets each u_i equal to the positive part of the residual $y_i - \xi$ and v_i equal to the negative part of the ith residual. But, as in Figure 1.3, such solutions can always be improved by moving ξ closer to one of the sample observations.

Many features of the solution are immediately apparent from these simple observations. To summarize, $\min\{u_i, v_i\}$ must be zero for all i, because otherwise the objective function may be reduced without violating the constraint

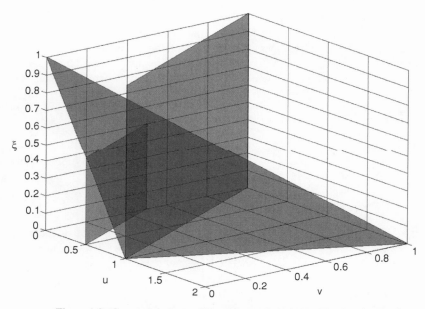

Figure 1.3. Computing the median with one observation. The figure illustrates the linear programming formulation of the median problem. The triangular region represents the constraint set; the vertical planes represent two different contours of the objective function, which decreases as ones moves toward the origin in the (u, v)-plane.

by shrinking such a pair toward zero. This is usually called complementary slackness in the terminology of linear programming. Indeed, for essentially the same reason we can restrict attention to "basic solutions" of the form $\xi = y_i$ for some observation i. Figure 1.4 depicts objective function (1.14) for three different random samples of varying sizes. The graph of the objective function is convex and piecewise linear with kinks at the observed y_is. When ξ passes through one of these y_is, the slope of the objective function changes by exactly 1 since a contribution of $\tau - 1$ is replaced by τ or vice versa.

Optimality holds at a point $\hat{\xi}$ if the objective function

$$R(\xi) = \sum_{i=1}^{n} \rho_\tau(y_i - \xi)$$

is increasing as one moves away from $\hat{\xi}$ to either the right or the left. This requires that the right and left derivatives of R are both nonnegative at the point $\hat{\xi}$. Thus,

$$R'(\xi+) \equiv \lim_{h \to 0}(R(\xi + h) - R(\xi))/h = \sum_{i=1}^{n}(I(y_i < \xi + 0) - \tau)$$

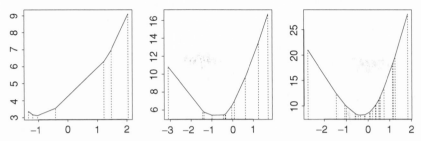

Figure 1.4. Quantile objective function with random data. The figure illustrates the objective function for the optimization problem defining the ordinary $\tau = 1/3$ quantile for three different random problems with y_is drawn from the standard normal distribution and sample sizes 7, 12, and 23. The vertical dotted lines indicate the position of the observations in each sample. Note that because 12 is divisible by 3, the objective function is flat at its minimum in the middle figure, and we have an interval of solutions between the fourth- and fifth-largest observations.

and

$$R'(\xi-) \equiv \lim_{h \to 0}(R(\xi - h) - R(\xi))/h = \sum_{i=1}^{n}(\tau - I(y_i < \xi - 0))$$

must both be nonnegative, and so $n\tau$ lies in the closed interval $[N^-, N^+]$, where N^+ denotes the number of y_i less than or equal to ξ and N^- denotes the number of y_i strictly less than ξ. When $n\tau$ is not an integer, there is a unique value of ξ that satisfies this condition. Barring ties in the y_is, this value corresponds to a unique order statistic. When there are ties, ξ is still unique, but there may be several y_i equal to ξ. If $n\tau$ *is* an integer then $\hat{\xi}_\tau$ lies between two adjacent order statistics. It is unique only when these order statistics coalesce at a single value. Usually, we can dismiss the occurrence of such ties as events of probability zero.

The duality connecting the sample quantiles and the ranks of the order statistics is further clarified through the formal duality of linear programming. While the primal problem, (1.15), may be viewed as generating the sample quantiles, the corresponding dual problem may be seen to generate the order statistics, or perhaps more precisely the *ranks* of the observations. This approach to ranks generalizes naturally to the linear model, yielding an elegant generalization of rank tests for the linear model.

1.4   PREVIEW OF QUANTILE REGRESSION

The observation developed in Section 1.3 that the quantiles may be expressed as the solution to a simple optimization problem leads, naturally, to more general methods of estimating models of conditional quantile functions. Least squares offers a template for this development. Knowing that the sample mean solves the problem

$$\min_{\mu \in \mathbb{R}} \sum_{i=1}^{n} (y_i - \mu)^2 \tag{1.16}$$

suggests that, if we are willing to express the *conditional* mean of y given x as $\mu(x) = x^\top \beta$, then β may be estimated by solving

$$\min_{\beta \in \mathbb{R}^p} \sum_{i=1}^{n} \left(y_i - x_i^\top \beta \right)^2. \tag{1.17}$$

Similarly, since the τth sample quantile, $\hat{\alpha}(\tau)$, solves

$$\min_{\alpha \in \mathbb{R}} \sum_{i=1}^{n} \rho_\tau (y_i - \alpha), \tag{1.18}$$

we are led to specifying the τth *conditional* quantile function as $Q_y(\tau|x) = x^\top \beta(\tau)$, and to consideration of $\hat{\beta}(\tau)$ solving

$$\min_{\beta \in \mathbb{R}^p} \sum_{i=1}^{n} \rho_\tau \left(y_i - x_i^\top \beta \right). \tag{1.19}$$

This is the germ of the idea elaborated by Koenker and Bassett (1978).

Quantile regression problem (1.19) may be reformulated as a linear program as in (1.15):

$$\min_{(\beta,u,v) \in \mathbb{R}^p \times \mathbb{R}_+^{2n}} \left\{ \tau 1_n^\top u + (1 - \tau) 1_n^\top v | X\beta + u - v = y \right\}, \tag{1.20}$$

where X now denotes the usual n by p regression design matrix. Again, we have split the residual vector $y - X\beta$ into its positive and negative parts, and so we are minimizing a linear function on a polyhedral constraint set, and most of the important properties of the solutions, $\hat{\beta}(\tau)$, which we call "regression quantiles," again follow immediately from well-known properties of solutions of linear programs.

We can illustrate the regression quantiles in a very simple bivariate example by reconsidering the Boscovich data. In Figure 1.5 we illustrate all of the *distinct* regression quantile solutions for this data. Of the ten lines passing through pairs of points in Figure 1.1, quantile regression selects only four. Solving (1.19) for any τ in the interval $(0, 0.21)$ yields as a unique solution the line passing through Quito and Rome. At $\tau = 0.21$, the solution jumps, and throughout the interval $(0.21, 0.48)$ we have the solution characterized by the line passing through Quito and Paris. The process continues until we get to $\tau = 0.78$, where the solution through Lapland and the Cape of Good Hope prevails up to $\tau = 1$.

In contrast to the ordinary sample quantiles that are equally spaced on the interval $[0,1]$, with each distinct order statistic occupying an interval of length exactly $1/n$, the lengths of the regression quantile solution intervals for $\tau \in [0, 1]$ are irregular and depend on the configuration of the design as well as the realized values of the response variable. *Pairs of points now play the role*

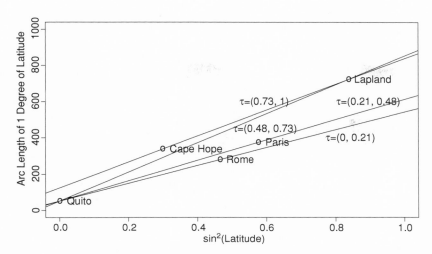

Figure 1.5. Regression quantiles for Boscovich ellipticity example. Only four of the full ten pairs of points form quantile regression solutions. The subintervals of (0, 1) for which each pair solves (1.19) are given in the figure.

of order statistics and serve to define the estimated linear conditional quantile functions. Again, in the terminology of linear programming, such solutions are "basic" and constitute extreme points of the polyhedral constraint set. If we imagine the plane represented by the objective function of (1.19) rotating as τ increases, we may visualize the solutions of (1.19) as passing from one vertex of the constraint set to another. Each vertex represents an exact fit of a line to a pair of sample observations. At a few isolated τ points, the plane will make contact with an entire edge of the constraint set and we will have a set-valued solution. It is easy to see, even in these cases, that the solution is characterized as the convex hull of its "basic" solutions.

One occasionally encounters the view that quantile regression estimators must "ignore sample information" since they are inherently determined by a small subset of the observations. This view neglects the obvious fact that all the observations participate in which "basic" observations are selected as basic.

We shall see that quantile regression does preserve an important robustness aspect of the ordinary sample quantiles: if we perturb the order statistics above (or below) the median in such a way that they *remain* above (or below) the median, the position of the median is unchanged. Similarly, for example, if we were to perturb the position of the Lapland observation upward, this would not affect the solutions illustrated in the figure for any τ in the interval (0, 0.48).

The Boscovich example is a bit too small to convey the full flavor of quantile regression even in the bivariate setting, so I will conclude this section with two other examples that exhibit various aspects of quantile regression in the bivariate context where pictures are easily available to illustrate the results.

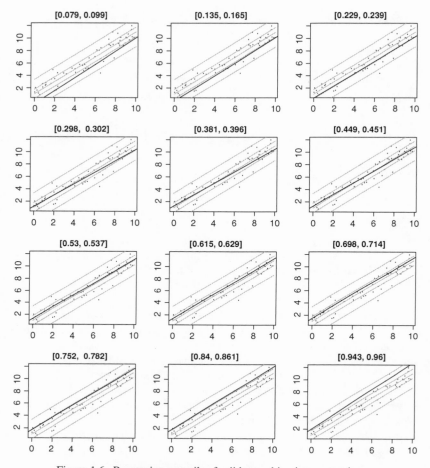

Figure 1.6. Regression quantiles for iid-error bivariate regression.

Consider an artificial sample in which we have a simple bivariate regression model with independent and identically distributed (iid) errors:

$$y_i = \beta_0 + x_i \beta_1 + u_i$$

and so the conditional quantile functions of y are

$$Q_y(\tau|x) = \beta_0 + x\beta_1 + F_u^{-1}(\tau),$$

where F_u denotes the common distribution function of the errors. In this simple case the quantile functions are simply a vertical displacement of one another and $\hat{\beta}(\tau)$ estimates the population parameters, $(\beta_0 + F^{-1}(\tau), \beta_1)^\top$.

In Figure 1.6 we illustrate data and several fitted regression quantile lines from such a model. The dots indicate 60 observations generated from the iid

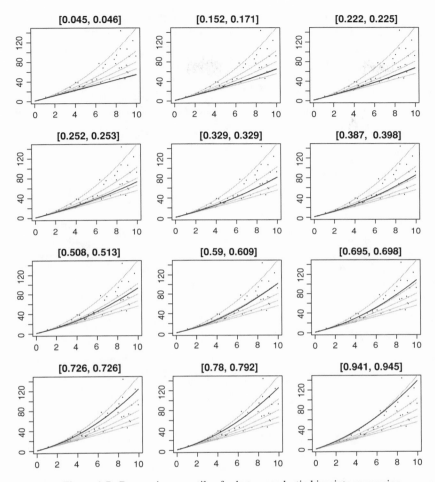

Figure 1.7. Regression quantiles for heteroscedastic bivariate regression.

error model with F selected to be Gaussian. The gray lines represent the *true* {0.05, 0.25, 0.50, 0.75, 0.95} conditional quantile lines. The black line in each panel depicts the estimated conditional quantile line for the τ interval indicated above the panel. As τ increases, we see that these estimated lines move up through the data, retaining in most cases a slope reasonably close to that of the family of true conditional quantile functions. In this example there are 66 distinct regression quantile solutions. Rather than illustrate *all* of them, we have chosen to illustrate only 12, spaced roughly evenly over the interval [0, 1]. Above each panel we indicate the τ interval for which the illustrated solution is optimal.

If real data analysis were always as well behaved as the iid linear model depicted in Figure 1.6, there would be little need for quantile regression. The least-squares estimate of the conditional mean function and some associated measure of dispersion would (usually) suffice. Robust alternatives to least squares could be used to accommodate situations in which errors exhibited long tails.

In Figure 1.7 we illustrate a somewhat more complicated situation. The model now takes the heteroscedastic form,

$$y_i = \beta_0 + x_i\beta_1 + \sigma(x_i)u_i,$$

where $\sigma(x) = \gamma x^2$ and the $\{u_i\}$ are again iid. The conditional quantile functions of y are now

$$Q_y(\tau|x) = \beta_0 + x\beta_1 + \sigma(x)F^{-1}(\tau)$$

and can be consistently estimated by minimizing

$$\sum \rho_\tau(y_i - \beta_0 - x_i\beta_1 - x_i^2\beta_2)$$

so that $\hat{\beta}(\tau)$ converges to $(\beta_0, \beta_1, \gamma F^{-1}(\tau))^\top$. Figure 1.7 illustrates an example of this form. Again, the *population* conditional quantile functions are shown as gray lines with the observed sample of 60 points superimposed and a sequence of estimated quantile regression curves appearing as black lines. The estimated quantile regression curves provide a direct empirical analog for the family of conditional quantile functions in the population.

1.5   THREE EXAMPLES

A simple bivariate example and two somewhat more elaborate multivariate examples are used to motivate quantile regression methods.

1.5.1   Salaries versus Experience

In Figure 1.8 we illustrate a p-sample version of the basic quantile regression problem with results of the 1995 survey of academic salaries in statistics conducted by the American Statistical Association (ASA). The figure is based on data from 99 departments in U.S. colleges and universities on 370 full professors of statistics. The data are grouped into three-year experience categories defined as years since promotion to the rank of full professor. The boxes appearing in the figure represent the interquartile range of salaries for each experience group. The upper limit of the box represents the 75th percentile of the salary distribution in each experience group from the survey, while the lower limit represents the 25th percentile. Thus, the central half of the surveyed salaries would fall within the boxes. Median salary for each group is depicted by the horizontal line drawn in each box. The width of the boxes is proportional to the square root of the respective sample sizes of the groups.

What can we conclude from the boxes? There clearly seems to be a tendency for salary to increase at a decreasing rate with "years in rank," with some suggestion that salary may actually decline for the oldest group. There

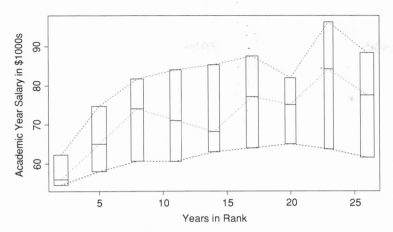

Figure 1.8. Boxplots of 1995 ASA academic salary survey for full professors of statistics in U.S. colleges and universities.

is also a pronounced tendency for the dispersion of the salary distribution to increase with experience. None of these findings is particularly surprising, but taken together they constitute a much more complete description than would be available from conventional least-squares regression analysis. The boxplot takes us much further than we are able to go with only the conditional mean function. Of course we would like to go still further: to estimate more quantiles of the distribution, to introduce additional covariates, to disaggregate the experience groups, and so forth. However, each of these steps diminishes the viability of the boxplot approach, which relies on adequate sample sizes for each of the groups, or cells, represented by the boxes. What could we do if the sample size of the salary survey were only 96 points, as it was in 1973–74, rather than the 370 observations of 1995?

Hogg (1975) provides an answer to this question, an answer that constituted an elaboration of a much earlier proposal by Brown and Mood (1951) for median regression. Hogg suggested dividing the observations (x_i, y_i) into two groups according to whether $x_i \leq \text{median}\{x_j\}$ or $x_i > \text{median}\{x_j\}$ and then estimating linear conditional quantile functions,

$$Q_Y(\tau|x) = \alpha + \beta x,$$

by choosing $(\hat{\alpha}, \hat{\beta})$ so that the number of observations in both groups had (approximately) the same proportion, τ, of their observations below the line. This can be accomplished relatively easily "by eye" for small data sets using a method Hogg describes. A more formal version of Hogg's proposal may be cast as a quantile regression version of the Wald (1940) instrumental variables estimator for the errors-in-variable model. This connection is developed more fully in Section 8.8. Based on the 1973–74 ASA data for full professor salaries, he obtains the estimates reported in Table 1.2. Since the estimated slope parameters

Table 1.2. *Hogg's (1975) linear quantile regression results for the 1973–74 ASA academic salary survey of full professors of statistics in U.S. colleges and universities. The monotone relation of the slope estimates indicates heteroscedasticity (i.e., increasing salary dispersion with experience)*

Quantile τ	Initial Professorial Salary $\hat{\alpha}$	Annual Increment $\hat{\beta}$
0.75	21,500	625
0.50	20,000	485
0.25	18,800	300

$\hat{\beta}$ increase with the quantile, these estimates reflect the same increasing dispersion, or heteroscedasticity, that we saw in the boxplots of Figure 1.8 for the more recent salary data. In this case, with so few data, it does not seem prudent to venture an opinion about the curvature of the salary profile.

We could probably agree that the dotted curves connecting the boxplot salary quartiles of Figure 1.8 appear somewhat undersmoothed. A parametric model for the conditional quartiles might improve the appearance of the plot, if we could agree on a transformation that would adequately capture the curvature of the salary profile. One attempt to do this is illustrated in Figure 1.9, where we have chosen the parametric model

$$Q_{\log(y)}(\tau|x) = \alpha + \beta \log x$$

for each of the quartiles, $\tau \in \{1/4, 1/2, 3/4\}$. The curves shown in Figure 1.9 have been estimated by median (ℓ_1) regression using only the respective grouped

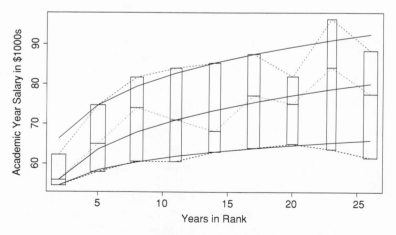

Figure 1.9. Boxplots of 1995 ASA academic salary survey for full professors of statistics in U.S. colleges and universities.

quartile data. (The individual data collected by the ASA are protected by confidentiality assurances.) These curves, and the parameters that characterize them, have a straightforward interpretation. The slope parameter in the log-linear quantile regression is simply a rate of growth of salary with respect to experience. In this example, the first quartile of the salary distribution has an estimated growth rate of 7.3% per year of tenure, whereas the median and the upper quartile grow at 14 and 13% respectively. As for Hogg's linear specification, higher coefficients at the higher quantiles imply increasing dispersion in salaries for more experienced faculty. However, in this case, the tendency is pronounced only in the left tail of the distribution and there is actually a slight narrowing of the gap between the median and the upper quartile for older faculty.

As this example illustrates, the specification and interpretation of quantile regression models is very much like that of ordinary regression. However, unlike ordinary regression, we now have a family of curves to interpret, and we can focus attention on particular segments of the conditional distribution, thus obtaining a more complete view of the relationship between the variables. If the slope parameters of the family of estimated quantile regression models seem to fluctuate randomly around a constant level, with only the intercept parameter systematically increasing with τ, we have evidence for the iid error hypothesis of classical linear regression. If, however, some of the slope coefficients are changing with τ, then this is indicative of some form of heteroscedasticity. The simplest example of this kind of heteroscedasticity is what we have called the linear location-scale model,

$$y_i = x_i^\top \beta + \left(x_i^\top \gamma \right) u_i,$$

with $\{u_i\}$ iid from F. In this case the coefficients of the τth quantile regression, $\hat{\beta}(\tau)$, converge to $\beta + \gamma F_u^{-1}(\tau)$, and so all of the parameters would share the same monotone behavior in τ, governed by the quantile function of the errors $F_u^{-1}(\tau)$. Clearly, this too is an extremely restrictive model, and we often find very different behavior (in τ) across slope coefficients. Such findings should remind us that the theory of the linear statistical model and its reliance on the hypothesis of a scalar iid error process is only a convenient fiction; life can be stranger, and more interesting.

1.5.2   Student Course Evaluations and Class Size

Our second example illustrates several advantages of the optimization approach to quantile regression. The data consist of mean course evaluation scores for 1482 courses offered by a large public university over the period 1980–94. We are primarily concerned with the effect of class size on course evaluation questionnaire (CEQ) score, but also of interest is the possibility of a time trend in the scores and any special effects due to the nature of particular types of courses.

In Figure 1.10 we illustrate the data for this example and plot five estimated quantile regression curves. These curves are specified as quadratic in the number

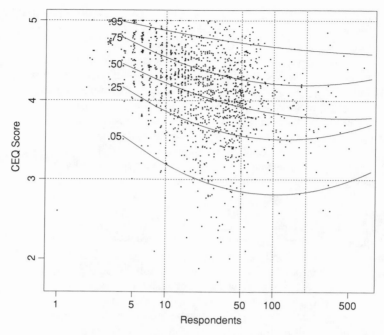

Figure 1.10. Course evaluation scores. Solid lines indicate estimated quantiles of CEQ response for an undergraduate course in 1992 as a function of the class size measured by number of CEQ respondents.

of CEQ respondents, which can be taken as the relevant measure of class size. In addition to the class size effect, we have included a linear time trend and an indicator variable that takes the value 1 for graduate courses and 0 for undergraduate courses. The model may thus be written as

$$Q_Y(\tau|x) = \beta_0(\tau) + \text{Trend}\,\beta_1(\tau) + \text{Grad}\,\beta_2(\tau) + \text{Size}\,\beta_3(\tau) + \text{Size}^2\beta_4(\tau)$$

and can be estimated for any $\tau \in (0, 1)$ by solving the problem

$$\min_{b\in\mathbb{R}^p} \sum_{i=1}^{n} \rho_\tau(y_i - x_i^\top b). \tag{1.21}$$

The estimated quantile regression parameters and their confidence intervals are given in Table 1.3. Details on the construction of the confidence intervals appear in the next chapter.

From Table 1.3 it can be seen that there is some evidence for a downward trend in CEQ scores for the lower quantiles, on the order of 0.01 to 0.02 rating points per year, but no evidence of a trend in the upper tail of the ratings distribution. One tentative conclusion from this is that ornery students are getting ornerier. Graduate courses have a fairly consistent tendency to be rated higher by about 0.10 rating points than undergraduate courses.

Table 1.3. *Quantile regression estimates for a model of student course evaluation scores. Numbers in parentheses give a 95% confidence interval for each reported coefficient.*

τ	Intercept	Trend	Graduate	Size	Size^2
0.050	4.749	−0.032	0.054	−0.642	0.069
	(4.123,5.207)	(−0.041,−0.016)	(−0.065,0.169)	(−0.930,−0.233)	(0.013,0.104)
0.250	5.003	−0.014	0.132	−0.537	0.056
	(4.732,5.206)	(−0.023,−0.008)	(0.054,0.193)	(−0.604,−0.393)	(0.034,0.066)
0.500	5.110	−0.014	0.095	−0.377	0.031
	(4.934,5.260)	(−0.018,−0.008)	(0.043,0.157)	(−0.484,−0.274)	(0.014,0.050)
0.750	5.301	−0.001	0.111	−0.418	0.040
	(5.059,5.379)	(−0.005,0.005)	(0.027,0.152)	(−0.462,−0.262)	(0.015,0.050)
0.950	5.169	0.001	0.054	−0.159	0.010
	(5.026,5.395)	(−0.004,0.006)	(−0.001,0.099)	(−0.323,−0.085)	(−0.005,0.035)

In order to plot the curves illustrated in Figure 1.10, we have set the indicator variable to zero to represent an undergraduate course and the trend variable to represent the last year in the sample, 1994. The curves clearly show a tendency for larger classes to receive lower ratings by students, with this decline occurring at a decreasing rate. The apparent tendency for scores to increase slightly for courses with more than 100 respondents may be entirely an artifact of the quadratic specification of the curves, but it may also be partially attributed to a departmental policy of trying to allocate its best teachers to the larger courses.

In the course evaluation example we have seen that the downward time trend in student evaluations is apparent at the median and lower quantiles but there is essentially no trend in the upper conditional quantile estimates. In contrast, the estimated disparity between graduate and undergraduate course ratings is positive and quite large (0.1 rating points) for the central quantiles, but negligible in the tails. This ∩-shape for $\hat{\beta}_j(\tau)$ may seem strange at first, but it is easily reconciled by considering a very simple two-sample quantile regression problem.

Suppose, to continue the course evaluation example, that sample one of undergraduate scores, supported on the interval $[1, 5]$, was quite symmetric around its median, while sample two of graduate ratings was skewed toward the upper bound of 5. If the two distributions have similar tail behavior, then the quantile regressions, which in the two-sample case simply connect the corresponding quantiles of the two distributions, would also display a ∩-shaped pattern – central quantiles with a significant positive slope, extreme quantiles with negligible slope. The effect of class size on the quantile regressions for CEQ scores is illustrated in Figure 1.10. There is some tendency for these curves to be initially more steeply sloped and to exhibit more curvature at lower quantiles.

Taken together, it is difficult to reconcile these observations with a conventional scalar-error linear model, but they do offer a much richer view of the data than the one provided by a least-squares analysis.

1.5.3   Infant Birth Weight

The third example reconsiders an investigation by Abreveya (2001) of the impact of various demographic characteristics and maternal behavior on the birth weight of infants born in the United States. Low birth weight is known to be associated with a wide range of subsequent health problems and has even been linked to educational attainment and labor market outcomes. Consequently, there has been considerable interest in factors influencing birth weight and public policy initiatives that might prove effective in reducing the incidence of low-birth-weight infants.

Although most of the analysis of birth weight has employed conventional least-squares regression methods, it has been recognized that the resulting estimates of various effects on the conditional mean of birth weights were not necessarily indicative of the size and nature of these effects on the lower tail of the birth-weight distribution. In an effort to focus attention more directly on the lower tail, several studies have recently explored binary response (e.g., probit) models for the occurrence of low birth weights – conventionally defined to be infants weighing less than 2500 grams. Quantile regression offers a natural complement to these prior modes of analysis. A more complete picture of covariate effects can be provided by estimating a family of conditional quantile functions.

The analysis will be based on the June 1997 Detailed Natality Data published by the National Center for Health Statistics. Like Abreveya's study, the sample is restricted to singleton births, with mothers recorded as either black or white, between the ages of 18 and 45, resident in the United States. Observations with missing data for any of the variables described in the following were also dropped from the analysis. This process yielded a sample of 198,377 babies. Education of the mother is divided into four categories: less than high school, high school, some college, and college graduate. The omitted category is "less than high school," so coefficients must be interpreted relative to this category. The prenatal medical care of the mother is also divided into four categories: those with no prenatal visit, those whose first prenatal visit was in the first trimester of the pregnancy, those with the first visit in the second trimester, and those with the first visit in the last trimester. The omitted category is the group with a first visit in the first trimester; they constitute almost 85 percent of the sample. The other variables are, hopefully, self-explanatory.

Figure 1.11 presents a concise summary of the quantile regression results for this example. Each plot depicts one coefficient in the quantile regression model. The solid line with filled dots represents the point estimates, $\{\hat{\beta}_j(\tau) : j = 1, \ldots, 16\}$, with the shaded gray area depicting a 90% pointwise confidence band. Superimposed on the plot is a dashed line representing the ordinary least-squares estimate of the mean effect, with two dotted lines again representing a 90% confidence interval for this coefficient.

In the first panel of the figure, the intercept of the model may be interpreted as the estimated conditional quantile function of the birth-weight distribution of

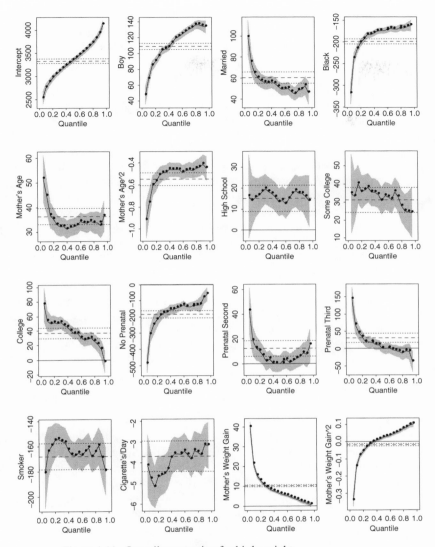

Figure 1.11. Quantile regression for birth weight.

a girl born to an unmarried, white mother with less than a high school education, who is 27 years old and had a weight gain of 30 pounds, did not smoke, and had her first prenatal visit in the first trimester of the pregnancy. The mother's age and weight gain are chosen to reflect the means of these variables in the sample. Note that the $\tau = 0.05$ quantile of this distribution is just at the margin of the conventional definition of a low-birth-weight baby.

Boys are obviously bigger than girls, about 100 grams bigger according to the ordinary least-squares (OLS) estimates of the mean effect, but, as is clear from the quantile regression results, the disparity is much smaller in the lower quantiles of the distribution and somewhat larger than 100 grams in the upper tail of the distribution. At any chosen quantile we can ask how different the corresponding weights of boys and girls are, given a specification of the other conditioning variables. The second panel answers this question.

Perhaps surprisingly, the marital status of the mother seems to be associated with a rather large positive effect on birth weight, especially in the lower tail of the distribution. The public health implications of this finding should, of course, be viewed with caution, however.

The disparity between birth weights of infants born to black and white mothers is very large, particularly at the left tail of the distribution. The difference in birth weight between a baby born to a black mother and a white mother at the 5th percentile of the conditional distribution is roughly one-third of a kilogram.

Mother's age enters the model as a quadratic. At the lower quantiles the mother's age tends to be more concave, increasing birth weight from age 18 to about age 30, but tending to decrease birth weight when the mother's age is beyond 30. At higher quantiles there is also this optimal age, but it becomes gradually older. At the third quantile it is about 36, and at $\tau = 0.9$ it is almost 40. This is illustrated in Figure 1.12.

Education beyond high school is associated with a modest increase in birth weight. High school graduation has a quite uniform effect over the whole range of the distribution of about 15 grams. This is a rare example of an effect that really does appear to exert a pure location shift effect on the conditional distribution. Some college education has a somewhat more positive effect in the lower tail than in the upper tail, varying from about 35 grams in the lower tail to 25 grams in the upper tail. A college degree has an even more substantial positive effect, but again much larger in the lower tail and declining to a negligible effect in the upper tail.

The effect of prenatal care is of obvious public health policy interest. Since individuals self-select into prenatal care, results must be interpreted with considerable caution. Those receiving no prenatal care are likely to be at risk in other dimensions as well. Nevertheless, the effects are sufficiently large to warrant considerable further investigation. Babies born to mothers who received no prenatal care were on average about 150 grams lighter than those who had a prenatal visit in the first trimester. In the lower tail of the distribution this effect is considerably larger – at the 5th percentile it is nearly half a kilogram! In contrast, mothers who delayed prenatal visits until the second or third trimester have substantially *higher* birth weights in the lower tail than mothers who had a visit in the first trimester. This might be interpreted as the self-selection effect of mothers confident about favorable outcomes. In the upper three quarters of the distribution there seems to be no significant effect.

Smoking has a clearly deleterious effect. The indicator of whether the mother smoked during the pregnancy is associated with a decrease of about 175 grams in birth weight. In addition, there is an effect of about 4 to 5 grams per cigarette per day. Thus, a mother smoking a pack per day appears to induce a birth-weight

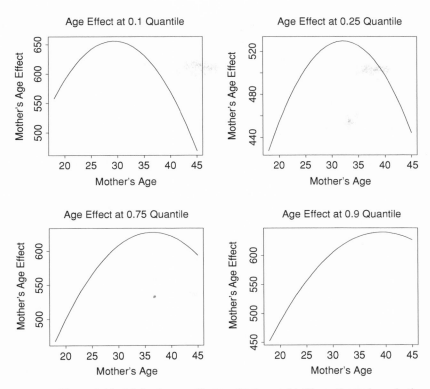

Figure 1.12. Mother's age effect on Birth weight. The estimated quadratic effect of mother's age on infant birth weight is illustrated at four different quantiles of the conditional birth-weight distribution. In the lower tail of the conditional distribution, mothers who are roughly 30 years of age have the largest children, but in the upper tail it is mothers who are 35–40 who have the largest children.

reduction of about 250 to 300 grams, or from about one-half to two-thirds of a pound. In contrast to some of the other effects, the effect of smoking is quite stable over the entire distribution, as indicated by the fact that the least-squares point estimates of the two smoking effects are (nearly) covered by the quantile regression confidence band.

Lest this smoking effect be thought to be attributable to some associated reduction in the mother's weight gain, one should hasten to point out that the weight gain effect is explicitly accounted for with a quadratic specification. Not surprisingly, the mother's weight gain has a very strong influence on birth weight, and this is reflected in the very narrow confidence band for both linear and quadratic coefficients. Figure 1.13 illustrates the marginal effect of weight gain by evaluating over the entire range of quantiles for four different levels of weight gain. At low weight gains by the mother, the marginal effect of another

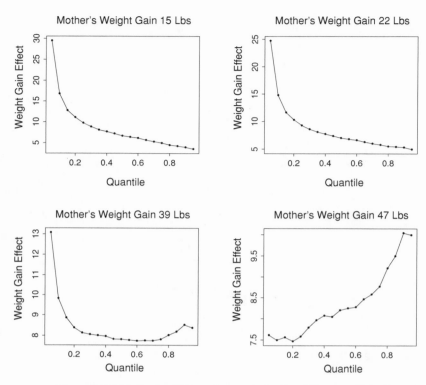

Figure 1.13. Mother's weight gain marginal effect. The marginal effect of the mother's weight gain, again parameterized as a quadratic effect, tends to decrease over the entire range of the conditional distribution of birth weight. Thus, incremental weight gain is most influential in increasing the weight of low-birth-weight infants. But for mothers with unusually large weight gains, this pattern is reversed and the effect is largest in the upper tail of the conditional birth-weight distribution.

pound gained is about 30 grams at the lowest quantiles and declines to only about 5 grams at the upper quantiles. This pattern of declining marginal effects is maintained for large weight gains, until we begin to consider extremely large weight gains, at which point the effect is reversed. For example, another pound gained by the mother who has already gained 50 pounds has only a 7-gram effect in the lower tail of the birth-weight distribution, and this increases to about 10 grams at the upper quantiles. The quadratic specification of the effect of mother's weight gain offers a striking example of how misleading the OLS estimates can be. Note that the OLS estimates strongly suggest that the effect is linear with an essentially negligible quadratic effect. However, the quantile regression estimates give a very different picture, one in which the quadratic effect of the weight gain is very significant except where it crosses the zero axis at about $\tau = 0.33$.

1.6 CONCLUSION

Although much more could be drawn out of the foregoing analyses, it may suffice to conclude here with the comment that the quantile regression results offer a much richer, more focused view of the applications than could be achieved by looking exclusively at conditional mean models. In particular, it provides a way to explore sources of heterogeneity in the response that are associated with the covariates. The next chapter delves more deeply into the interpretation of quantile regression models and their estimation.

CHAPTER 2

Fundamentals of Quantile Regression

In this chapter, we seek to provide a basic conceptual guide to quantile regression, illustrating the ideas with a number of examples and stressing various aspects of the interpretation of quantile regression. We begin with a discussion of quantile treatment effects in the two-sample treatment-control model. In this context, the difference between the empirical quantile functions of the treatment and control observations provides a natural generalization of conventional mean measures of the treatment effect. This "quantile treatment effect" is precisely what is delivered by the the quantile regression estimator of a model with a single binary indicator variable. We describe some basic characteristics of the quantile regression estimator, its equivariance properties, and robustness. The interpretation of estimated quantile regression parameters is described in the context of several applications. Some issues of misspecification are raised, and the chapter concludes with an interpretation of the quantile regression model as a random coefficient model.

2.1 QUANTILE TREATMENT EFFECTS

The simplest formulation of regression is the classical two-sample treatment-control model. We begin by reconsidering a general model of two-sample treatment response introduced by Lehmann and Doksum in the 1970s. This model provides a natural introduction to the interpretation of quantile regression models in more general settings.

Lehmann (1974) proposed the following model of treatment response:

> Suppose the treatment adds the amount $\Delta(x)$ when the response of the untreated subject would be x. Then the distribution G of the treatment responses is that of the random variable $X + \Delta(X)$ where X is distributed according to F.

Special cases obviously include the location shift model, $\Delta(X) = \Delta_0$, and the scale shift model, $\Delta(x) = \Delta_0 X$. If the treatment is beneficial in the sense that

$$\Delta(x) \geq 0 \quad \text{for all } x,$$

then the distribution of treatment responses, G, is stochastically larger than the distribution of control responses, F. Thus, in the context of survival analysis for clinical trials, for example, we could say that the treatment was unambiguously beneficial. However, if we encounter a crossing of the survival functions, the benefit of the treatment must be regarded as ambiguous.

Doksum (1974) shows that if we define $\Delta(x)$ as the "horizontal distance" between F and G at x so that

$$F(x) = G(x + \Delta(x)),$$

then $\Delta(x)$ is uniquely defined and can be expressed as

$$\Delta(x) = G^{-1}(F(x)) - x. \tag{2.1}$$

Thus, on changing variables so $\tau = F(x)$, we have the *quantile treatment effect*:

$$\delta(\tau) = \Delta(F^{-1}(\tau)) = G^{-1}(\tau) - F^{-1}(\tau).$$

Note that we can recover the mean treatment effect by simply integrating the quantile treatment effect over τ; that is,

$$\bar{\delta} = \int_0^1 \delta(\tau)d\tau = \int G^{-1}(\tau)d\tau - \int F^{-1}(\tau)d\tau = \mu(G) - \mu(F),$$

where $\mu(F)$ is the mean of the distribution F.

Doksum provides a thorough axiomatic analysis of this formulation of treatment response. Figure 2.1 illustrates the basic idea. At the median there is a positive treatment effect that becomes larger as we move upward into the right tail of the distribution. However, in the left tail, the treatment is actually disadvantageous. Figure 2.2 illustrates several variants of the quantile treatment effect for location, scale, and location-scale shifts of the normal distribution. In the upper panels of the distribution functions, the control distribution appears as black and the treatment as gray. In the middle panels we have the corresponding density functions, and in the lower panels we show the quantile treatment effects. In the location model, the quantile treatment effect is obviously constant, but in the scale and location-scale models the quantile treatment effect is an affine transformation of the control distribution and actually crosses the zero axis, indicating that the treatment is not always advantageous. A less-conventional example is illustrated in Figure 2.3, where the treatment alters the skewness of the distribution from highly left-skewed to highly right-skewed; this results in a $\cup$-shaped quantile treatment effect.

In the two-sample setting, the quantile treatment effect is naturally estimable by

$$\hat{\delta}(\tau) = \hat{G}_n^{-1}(\tau) - \hat{F}_m^{-1}(\tau),$$

where G_n and F_m denote the empirical distribution functions of the treatment and control observations, based on n and m observations, respectively. If we

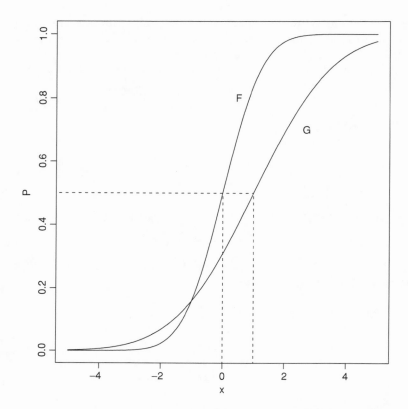

Figure 2.1. Lehmann quantile treatment effect. Horizontal distance between the treatment and control (marginal) distribution functions.

formulate the quantile regression model for the binary treatment problem as

$$Q_{Y_i}(\tau | D_i) = \alpha(\tau)(1 - D_i) + \beta(\tau)D_i, \tag{2.2}$$

where D_i denotes the treatment indicator, with $D_i = 1$ indicating treatment and $D_i = 0$ the control, we obtain the estimates $\hat{\alpha}(\tau) = \hat{F}_m^{-1}(\tau)$ and $\hat{\beta}(\tau) = \hat{G}_n^{-1}(\tau)$. However, if we consider

$$Q_{Y_i}(\tau | D_i) = \alpha(\tau) + \delta(\tau)D_i, \tag{2.3}$$

then we may estimate the quantile treatment effect directly.

To illustrate, Doksum reconsiders a study by Bjerkedal (1960) of the effect of injections of tubercle bacilli on guinea pigs. Survival times, following injection, were recorded (in days) for 107 control subjects and 60 treatment subjects. Of the control subjects, 42 lived longer than the experimental censoring threshold of 736 days. None of the treatment subjects survived more than 600 days.

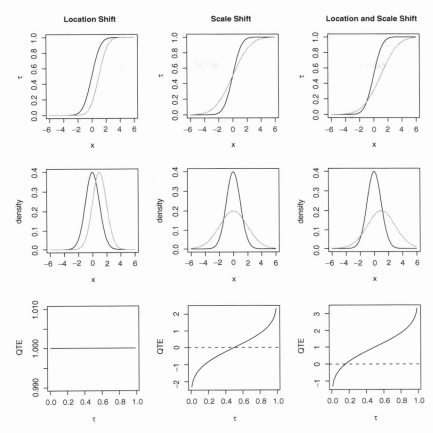

Figure 2.2. Lehmann quantile treatment effect for three examples. Location shift, scale shift, and location-scale shift.

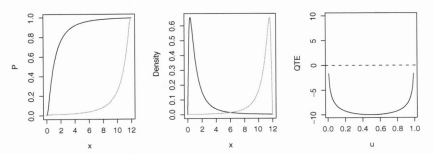

Figure 2.3. Lehmann quantile treatment effect for an asymmetric example. The treatment reverses the skewness of the distribution function.

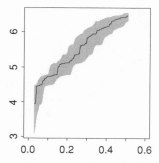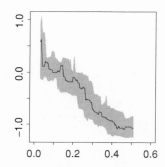

Figure 2.4. Quantile regression results for the guinea pig example analyzed by Doksum and taken from Bjerkedal. Fitted model (2.3) for log survival times is based on a sample of 107 controls and 60 treatment subjects injected with the tubercle bacilli. In the left-hand panel we plot the function $\hat{\alpha}(\tau)$, representing the empirical quantiles of the log survival time distribution for the control sample. In the right-hand panel we depict $\hat{\delta}(\tau)$, the estimated quantile treatment effect. In this simple two-sample setting, the quantile treatment effect $\hat{\delta}(\tau)$ is just the horizontal distance between the empirical distribution functions of the control and treatment samples. Note that the treatment has a positive effect on survival in the left tail, thus improving survival prospects for the weakest subjects. But the treatment has a very adverse effect on survival times in the right tail, dramatically reducing survival times for the stronger subjects. The shaded region illustrates a 90% confidence band for the estimated effects.

In Figure 2.4 we plot the estimated functions $\hat{\alpha}(\tau)$ and $\hat{\delta}(\tau)$. The plots are "censored" beyond $\tau = 0.6$ due to the censoring of the survival times of the control subjects. Confidence bands are indicated by the lightly shaded regions. The treatment effect in this example, depicted in the right-hand panel, is evidently neither a location shift, which would appear as a horizontal line, nor a scale shift, which would appear as a proportional dilation of the "control effect" depicted in the left-hand (intercept) panel. Here, animals receiving the treatment injection of bacilli appear to benefit from the treatment in the lower tail of the distribution, whereas the treatment shows a strongly significant adverse effect on survival in the upper tail. The treatment thus appears to have an advantageous effect on survival in the short run but seems very disadvantageous in the longer run.

Doksum suggests that we may wish to interpret control subjects in terms of a latent characteristic. Control subjects may be called frail if they are prone to die at an early age and robust if prone to die at an advanced age. This characteristic is thus implicitly indexed by τ, the quantile of the survival distribution at which the subject would appear if untreated; that is, $(Y_i | D_i = 0) = \alpha(\tau)$. And the treatment, under the Lehmann–Doksum model, is assumed to alter the subjects' control response, $\alpha(\tau)$, making it $\alpha(\tau) + \delta(\tau)$ under the treatment. If the latent characteristic, say, propensity for longevity, were observable *ex ante*, then we might view the treatment effect $\delta(\tau)$ as an explicit interaction with this observable variable. However, in the absence of such an observable variable, the quantile treatment effect may be regarded as a natural measure of the treatment response. Of course, there is no way of knowing whether the treatment actually operates in the manner described by $\delta(\tau)$. In fact, the treatment may miraculously make weak subjects especially robust and turn the strong into jello. All we can observe from experimental evidence, however, is the difference in the two marginal survival distributions, and it is natural to associate the treatment effect with the difference in the corresponding quantiles of these two distributions. This is what the quantile treatment effect does.

When the treatment variable takes more than two values, this interpretation requires only slight adaptation. In the case of p distinct treatments, we can write

$$Q_{Y_i}(\tau | D_{ij}) = \alpha(\tau) + \sum_{j=1}^{p} \delta_j(\tau) D_{ij},$$

where $D_{ij} = 1$ if observation i received the jth treatment and $D_{ij} = 0$ otherwise. Here $\delta_j(\tau)$ constitutes the quantile treatment effect connecting the distribution of control responses to the responses of subjects under treatment j. If the treatment is continuous, as, for example, in dose-response studies, then it is natural to consider the assumption that the effect is linear and to write

$$Q_{Y_i}(\tau | x_i) = \alpha(\tau) + \beta(\tau) x_i.$$

We assume thereby that the treatment effect, $\beta(\tau)$, of changing x from x_0 to $x_0 + 1$ is the same as the treatment effect of an alteration of x from x_1 to $x_1 + 1$. Interpreted in this fashion, the quantile treatment effect offers a natural extension to continuously varying treatments of the Lehmann–Doksum formulation for the discrete case.

In economics, a common application of this type involves investigations of the effect of years of schooling on observed wages. In this literature, it is common to identify latent components of wage determination with unobserved characteristics such as "spunk" or "ability"; thus, these terms play the same role as "propensity for longevity" in survival examples. The quantile treatment effect, $\beta(\tau)$, may be interpreted as an interaction effect between unobserved "ability" and the level of education. This interpretation has been recently explored in work of Arias, Hallock, and Sosa-Escudero (2001) in a study of the earnings of identical twins.

Finally, it may be noted that quantile treatment effect (2.1) is intimately tied to the traditional two-sample QQ-plot, which has a long history as a graphical diagnostic device. Following Parzen (1979), there is an extensive related literature on the issue of the "comparison density function"

$$\frac{d}{du} G(F^{-1}(u)) = \frac{g(F^{-1}(u))}{f(F^{-1}(u))},$$

an approach that is closely related to the PP-plot. Note that the function $\hat{\Delta}(x) = G_n^{-1}(F_m(x)) - x$ is exactly what is plotted in the traditional two-sample QQ-plot. This connection between the Lehmann–Doksum treatment effect and the

QQ-plot is explored by Doksum and Sievers (1976) and Nair (1982) for the p-sample problem. Quantile regression may be viewed as a method of extending the two-sample QQ-plot and related methods to general regression settings with continuous covariates. We will return to this observation and its implications for inference in Chapter 3.

2.2 HOW DOES QUANTILE REGRESSION WORK?

Much of our intuition about how ordinary regression "works" comes from the geometry of least-squares projection. The idea of minimizing the Euclidean distance $\| y - \hat{y} \|$ over all $\hat{y}$ in the linear span of the columns of X is very appealing. We may just imagine inflating a beach ball centered at y until it touches the subspace spanned by X. The quantile-regression ρ_τ "distance,"

$$d_\tau(y, \hat{y}) = \sum_{i=1}^{n} \rho_\tau(y_i - \hat{y}_i),$$

has diamond-shaped polyhedral contours. Replacing Euclidean beach balls with polyhedral diamonds raises some new problems, but many nice features and insights persist. We do not obtain an elegant "closed-form" solution such as

$$\hat{y} = X(X^\top X)^{-1} X^\top y,$$

but the algorithm that leads to the quantile regression estimates is really no more esoteric than, say, the sequence of Householder transformations, which are employed to produce the standard QR decomposition of X and lead eventually to the closed-form least-squares estimate.

To minimize

$$\| y - \hat{y}(\beta) \|^2 = (y - X\beta)^\top (y - X\beta),$$

we differentiate to obtain the "normal equations"

$$\nabla_\beta \| y - \hat{y}(\beta) \|^2 = X^\top (y - X\beta) = 0$$

and solve for $\hat{\beta}$. These normal equations yield a unique solution provided that the design matrix X has full column rank.

In quantile regression we proceed similarly, but we need to exercise some caution about the differentiation step. The objective function,

$$R(\beta) = d_\tau(y, \hat{y}(\beta)) = \sum_{i=1}^{n} \rho_\tau \left(y_i - x_i^\top \beta \right),$$

is piecewise linear and continuous. It is differentiable except at the points at which one or more residuals, $y_i - x_i^\top \beta$, are zero. At such points, $R(\beta)$ has *directional* derivatives in all directions, depending, however, on the direction of evaluation. The directional derivative of R in direction w is given by

$$\nabla R(\beta, w) \equiv \frac{d}{dt} R(\beta + tw) \mid_{t=0}$$

$$= \frac{d}{dt} \sum_{i=1}^{n} (y_i - x_i^\top \beta - x_i^\top tw)[\tau - I(y_i - x_i^\top \beta - x_i^\top + tw) < 0)] \mid_{t=0}$$

$$= - \sum \psi_\tau^*(y_i - x_i^\top \beta, -x_i^\top w) x_i^\top w,$$

where

$$\psi_\tau^*(u, v) = \begin{cases} \tau - I(u < 0) & \text{if } u \neq 0 \\ \tau - I(v < 0) & \text{if } u = 0. \end{cases}$$

If, at a point $\hat{\beta}$, the directional derivatives are all nonnegative (i.e., $\nabla R(\hat{\beta}, w) \geq 0$ for all $w \in \mathbb{R}^p$ with $\| w \| = 1$), then $\hat{\beta}$ minimizes $R(\beta)$. This is a natural generalization of simply setting $\nabla R(\beta) = 0$ when R is smooth. It simply requires that the function is increasing as we move away from the point $\hat{\beta}$ regardless of the direction in which we decide to move. We can visualize the nature of such solutions by imagining a polyhedral constraint set with flat faces connected by straight edges meeting at vertices like a cut-glass bowl. Minimizing a linear function subject to such a constraint set typically yields a solution at a vertex; to verify the optimality of such a vertex solution, one needs only to verify that the objective function is nondecreasing along all edges emanating from the vertex.

These vertex solutions, as we will show in more detail in Chapter 6, correspond to points in parameter space at which p observations are interpolated when p parameters are being estimated. This "exact-fit" property of the solution is sometimes regarded with suspicion: "Aren't all the other observations being 'ignored'?" Of course, all observations participate equally in determining which ones are eventually interpolated. Just as the median identifies one middle observation, the median regression estimator identifies a group of p observations that define a hyperplane that best represents the conditional median function. This property was already recognized by Gauss (1809):

> Laplace made use of another principle for the solution of linear equations the number of which is greater than the number of the unknown quantities, which had been previously proposed by Boscovich, namely, that the sum of the errors themselves taken positively, be made a minimum. It can be easily shown, that a system of values of unknown quantities derived from this principle alone, must necessarily (except in the special cases in which the problem remains, to some extent, indeterminate) exactly satisfy as many equations out of the number proposed, as there are unknown quantities so that the remaining quantities come under consideration only so far as they help to determine the choice.

2.2.1 Regression Quantiles Interpolate p Observations

In the terminology of linear programming, these p-element subsets are called basic solutions. They may be seen as extreme points of the polyhedral constraint set: vertices of the polyhedron that constitutes the constraint set. Minimizing a linear function with respect to a constraint set of this form *is* the task of linear programming. It is clear from the geometry that solutions must either occur uniquely, when the plane representing the objective function touches only a single vertex of the constraint set, or occur multiply, when the objective function happens to come to rest on an edge or an entire facet of the constraint set. We will have more to say about nonuniqueness later; for now, it will suffice to observe that, even when multiple solutions occur, the basic solutions play a fundamental role because any element of the solution set can be constructed as a linear combination of solution of this form. They necessarily constitute the vertices of the full solution set and thus must constitute a polyhedral, convex set themselves. This is already familiar from the elementary case of the median.

To facilitate consideration of these p-element subsets of observations, we require a bit more notation. Let $h \in \mathcal{H}$ index p-element subsets of the first n integers, $\mathcal{N} = \{1, 2, \ldots, n\}$, and let $X(h)$ denote the submatrix of X with rows $\{x_i : i \in h\}$. Likewise, let $y(h)$ be a p vector with coordinates $\{y_i : i \in h\}$. The complement of h with respect to $\mathcal{N}$ will be written as $\bar{h}$, and $X(\bar{h})$ and $y(\bar{h})$ may be defined accordingly.

With this notation in mind, we can express any basic solution that passes through the points $\{(x_i, y_i), i \in h\}$ as

$$b(h) = X(h)^{-1} y(h),$$

presuming, of course, that the matrix $X(h)$ is nonsingular. There are obviously too many of these basic solutions, $\binom{n}{p} = O(n^p)$, to simply search through them as one searches through a drawer of old socks. What the simplex algorithm of linear programming finally provided was an efficient way to conduct this search, essentially by traversing from vertex to vertex of the constraint set, always taking the direction of steepest descent.

2.2.2   The Subgradient Condition

We are now ready to introduce the basic optimality condition for the quantile regression problem:

$$\min_{b \in \mathbb{R}^p} \sum_{i=1}^{n} \rho_\tau(y_i - x_i^\top b). \tag{2.4}$$

We have seen that we can restrict attention to candidate solutions of the "basic" form:

$$b(h) = X(h)^{-1} y(h).$$

For some h, $X(h)$ may be singular. This need not worry us; we can restrict attention to $b(h)$ with $h \in \mathcal{H}^* = \{h \in \mathcal{H} : |X(h)| \neq 0\}$. We have also seen that our optimality condition entails verifying that the directional derivatives are nonnegative in all directions. To check this at $b(h)$, we must consider

$$\nabla R(b(h), w) = -\sum_{i=1}^{n} \psi_\tau^*(y_i - x_i^\top b(h), -x_i^\top w)x_i^\top w.$$

Reparameterizing the directions so that $v = X(h)w$, we have optimality if and only if

$$0 \leq -\sum_{i=1}^{n} \psi_\tau^*(y_i - x_i^\top b(h), -x_i^\top X(h)^{-1}v)x_i^\top X(h)^{-1}v$$

for all $v \in \mathbb{R}^p$. Now note that, for $i \in h$, and by adopting a convenient convention for the ordering of the elements of h, we have $e_i^\top = x_i^\top X(h)^{-1}$, the ith unit basis vector of $\mathbb{R}^p$, and so we may rewrite this as

$$0 \leq -\sum_{i \in h} \psi_\tau^*(0, -v_i)v_i - \xi^\top v = -\sum_{i \in h}(\tau - I(-v_i < 0))v_i - \xi^\top v,$$

where

$$\xi^\top = \sum_{i \in \bar{h}} \psi_\tau^*(y_i - x_i^\top b(h), -x_i^\top X(h)^{-1}v)x_i^\top X(h)^{-1}.$$

Finally, note that the space of "directions," $v \in \mathbb{R}^p$, is spanned by the directions $v = \pm e_k (k = 1, \ldots, p)$. That is, the directional derivative condition holds for all $v \in \mathbb{R}^p$ if and only if it holds for the $2p$ canonical directions $\{\pm e_i : i = 1, \ldots, p\}$. Thus, for $v = e_i$, we have the p inequalities

$$0 \leq -(\tau - 1) - \xi_i(h) \qquad i = 1, \ldots, p,$$

whereas for $v = -e_i$ we have

$$0 \leq \tau + \xi_i(h) \qquad i = 1, \ldots, p.$$

Combining these inequalities, we have our optimality condition in its full generality. If none of the residuals of the nonbasic observations, $i \in \bar{h}$, is zero, as would be the case with probability one if the ys had a density with respect to Lebesgue measure, then the dependence of ξ on v disappears and we may combine the two sets of inequalities to yield

$$-\tau 1_p \leq \xi(h) \leq (1 - \tau)1_p.$$

Summarizing the foregoing discussion, we may slightly reformulate Theorem 3.3 of Koenker and Bassett (1978) with the aid of the following definition introduced by Rousseeuw and Leroy (1987).

Definition 2.1. *We say that the regression observations (y, X) are in general position if any p of them yield a unique exact fit; that is, for any $h \in \mathcal{H}$,*

$$y_i - x_i^\top b(h) \neq 0 \qquad \text{for any } i \notin h.$$

Note that if the y_i's have a density with respect to Lesbesgue measure then the observations (y, X) will be in general position with probability one.

Theorem 2.1. *If (y, X) are in general position, then there exists a solution to quantile-regression problem (2.4) of the form $b(h) = X(h)^{-1}y(h)$ if and only if, for some $h \in \mathcal{H}$,*

$$-\tau 1_p \leq \xi(h) \leq (1 - \tau)1_p, \tag{2.5}$$

where $\xi^\top(h) = \sum_{i \in \bar{h}} \psi_\tau(y_i - x_i^\top b(h))x_i^\top X(h)^{-1}$ and $\psi_\tau = \tau - I(u < 0)$. Furthermore, $b(h)$ is the unique solution if and only if the inequalities are strict; otherwise, the solution set is the convex hull of several solutions of the form $b(h)$.

Remark 2.1. Several comments on degeneracy and multiple optimal solutions may be useful at this point. Primal degeneracy in the quantile regression problem refers to circumstances in which (y, X) are not in general position; therefore, we have more than p zero residuals – either at a solution or, more generally, in exterior point algorithms like a simplex on the path to a solution. This is unusual, unless the y_i's are discrete. On the other hand, multiple optimal solutions occur when inequalities (2.5) are satisfied only weakly. This occurs, typically, when the xs are discrete, so that sums of the x_is, weighted by τ or $(\tau - 1)$, sum exactly to τ or $\tau - 1$. If the xs have a component that has a density with respect to Lesbesgue measure, then for any given τ this occurs with probability zero. In the dual problem, the roles of degeneracy and multiple optimal solutions are reversed: degeneracy arises from discrete xs and multiple optimal solutions from discrete ys.

It might be thought that such *inequalities* could not offer the same essential analytical services provided by the more conventional gradient conditions of smooth (quasi-) maximum likelihood theory. Fortunately, as we shall see, that pessimism is not justified. Indeed, as we have already seen in Figure 1.4, the graph of the objective function actually appears quite smooth as long as n is moderately large, relative to p.

An important finite sample implication of optimality condition (2.5) is the following result that shows, provided the design matrix "contains an intercept," there will be roughly $n\tau$ negative residuals and $n(1 - \tau)$ positive ones.

Theorem 2.2. *Let P, N, and Z denote the proportion of positive, negative, and zero elements of the residual vector $y - X\hat{\beta}(\tau)$. If X contains an intercept, that is, if there exists $\alpha \in \mathbb{R}^p$ such that $X\alpha = 1_n$, then for any $\hat{\beta}(\tau)$, solving (1.19), we have*

$$N \leq n\tau \leq N + Z$$

and

$$P \leq n(1 - \tau) \leq P + Z.$$

Proof. We have optimality of $\hat{\beta}(\tau)$ if and only if

$$-\sum_{i=1}^{n} \psi_{\tau}^{*}(y_i - x_i^{\top}\hat{\beta}(\tau), -x_i^{\top}w)x_i^{\top}w \geq 0$$

for all directions $w \in \mathbb{R}^p$. For $w = \alpha$, such that $X\alpha = 1_n$, we have

$$-\sum \psi_{\tau}^{*}(y_i - x_i^{\top}\hat{\beta}(\tau), -1) \geq 0,$$

which yields

$$\tau P - (1 - \tau)N - (1 - \tau)Z \leq 0.$$

Similarly, for $w = -\alpha$, we obtain

$$-\tau P + (1 - \tau)N - \tau Z \leq 0.$$

Combining these inequalities and using the fact that $n = N + P + Z$ completes the proof. ∎

Corollary 2.1. *As a consequence, if $Z = p$, which occurs whenever there is no degeneracy, then the proportion of negative residuals is approximately τ*

$$\frac{N}{n} \leq \tau \leq \frac{N + p}{n},$$

and the number of positive residuals is approximately $(1 - \tau)$,

$$\frac{P}{n} \leq 1 - \tau \leq \frac{P + p}{n}.$$

Remark 2.2. In the special case that $X \equiv 1_n$, this result fully characterizes the τth sample quantile. If τn is an integer, then we will have only weak satisfaction of the inequalities, and consequently there will be an interval of τth sample quantiles between two adjacent order statistics. If τn is not an integer, then the τth sample quantile is unique.

The foregoing remark can be extended to the two-sample problem in the following manner.

Corollary 2.2. *Consider the two-sample model where X takes the form*

$$X = \begin{bmatrix} 1_{n_1} & 0 \\ 0 & 1_{n_2} \end{bmatrix}$$

and write $y = (y_1^{\top}, y_2^{\top})^{\top}$ to conform to X. Denote any τth sample quantile of the subsample y_i by $\hat{\beta}_i(\tau)$; then any regression quantile solution for this problem takes form

$$\hat{\beta}(\tau) = (\hat{\beta}_1(\tau), \hat{\beta}_2(\tau))^{\top};$$

that is, the line characterizing a τth regression quantile solution in the two-sample problem simply connects two corresponding ordinary sample quantiles from the two samples.

Proof. The result follows immediately by noting that the optimality condition

$$-\sum_{i=1}^{n} \psi_\tau^*(y_i - b, -x_i^\top w)x_i^\top w \geq 0$$

for $b \in \mathbb{R}^2$ and $w \in \mathbb{R}^2$ separates into two independent conditions,

$$-\sum_{i=1}^{n_j} \psi_\tau^*(y_{ij} - b_j, -w_j)w_j \geq 0 \quad j = 1, 2,$$

where y_{ij} denotes the ith element of the jth sample. ∎

Remark 2.3. Our formulation of the optimality conditions for quantile regression in this section is fully equivalent to the approach based on the subgradient described by Rockafellar (1970). To make this connection more explicit, recall that the subgradient of a function $f: X \to \mathbb{R}$, at x, denoted $\partial f(x)$, is the subset of the dual space X^* given by

$$\partial f(x) = \{\xi \in X^* | \nabla f(x, v) \geq \xi^\top v \text{ for all } v \in X\}.$$

It is then clear that $\nabla f(x, v) \geq 0$ for all $v \in \mathbb{R}^p$ if and only if $0 \in \partial f(x)$.

2.2.3   Equivariance

Several important features of the least-squares regression estimator are sometimes taken for granted in elementary treatments of regression, but they play an important role in enabling a coherent interpretation of regression results. Suppose we have a model for the temperature of a liquid, y, but we decide to alter the scale of our measurements from Fahrenheit to Centigrade, or we decide to reparameterize the effect of two covariates to investigate the effect of their sum and their difference. We expect such changes to have no fundamental effect on our estimates. When the data are altered in one of these entirely predictable ways, we expect the regression estimates also to change in a way that leaves our interpretation of the results *invariant*. Several such properties can be grouped together under the heading of *equivariance* and treated quite explicitly because they are often an important aid in careful interpretation of statistical results. To facilitate this treatment, we will explicitly denote a τth regression quantile based on observations (y, X) by $\hat{\beta}(\tau; y, X)$. Four basic equivariance properties of $\hat{\beta}(\tau; y, X)$ are collected in the following result.

Theorem 2.3 (Koenker and Bassett, 1978). *Let A be any $p \times p$ nonsingular matrix, $\gamma \in \mathbb{R}^p$, and $a > 0$. Then, for any $\tau \in [0, 1]$,*

> *(i) $\hat{\beta}(\tau; ay, X) = a\hat{\beta}(\tau; y, X)$*
> *(ii) $\hat{\beta}(\tau; -ay, X) = -a\hat{\beta}(1 - \tau; y, X)$*

> (iii) $\hat{\beta}(\tau; y + X\gamma, X) = \hat{\beta}(\tau; y, X) + \gamma$
> (iv) $\hat{\beta}(\tau; y, XA) = A^{-1}\hat{\beta}(\tau; y, X).$

Remark 2.4. Properties (i) and (ii) imply a form of scale equivariance, property (iii) is usually called shift or regression equivariance, and property (iv) is called equivariance to reparameterization of design.

Presuming that X "contains an intercept" (i.e., there exists $\gamma \in \mathbb{R}^p$ such that $X\gamma = 1_n$), the effect of our temperature scale change is simply to shift $\hat{\beta}(\tau; y, X)$ to $5/9(\hat{\beta}(\tau; y, X) - 32\gamma)$. Typically, in this example, γ would be the first unit basis vector e_1 and so the first column of X would be 1_n. The first coordinate of $\hat{\beta}$ would be shifted by 32 and all the coordinates would be then rescaled by the factor $5/9$. In the second example, the situation is even simpler. The result of reparameterizing the xs is that the new coefficients are now one-half the sum and one-half the difference of the old pair of coefficients, respectively. These equivariance properties are shared by the least-squares estimator, but this is not universally true for other regression estimators.

Quantiles enjoy another equivariance property, one much stronger than those already discussed. This property, which we may term *equivariance to monotone transformations*, is critical to an understanding of the full potential of quantile regression. Let $h(\cdot)$ be a nondecreasing function on $\mathbb{R}$. Then, for any random variable Y,

$$Q_{h(Y)}(\tau) = h(Q_Y(\tau)); \tag{2.6}$$

that is, the quantiles of the transformed random variable $h(Y)$ are simply the transformed quantiles of the original Y. Of course, the mean does not share this property:

$$Eh(Y) \neq h(E(Y)),$$

except for affine h, as we considered earlier, or other exceptional circumstances. Condition 2.6 follows immediately from the elementary fact that, for any monotone h,

$$P(Y \leq y) = P(h(Y) \leq h(y)),$$

but the property has many important implications.

It is common in considering least-squares regression to posit a model of the form

$$h(y_i, \lambda) = x_i^\top \beta + u_i,$$

where $h(y, \lambda)$ denotes a transformation of the original response variable y, which (*mirabile dictu!*) achieves three objectives simultaneously:

   (i) it makes $E(h(y_i, \lambda)|x)$ linear in the covariates, x;
   (ii) it makes $V(h(y_i, \lambda)|x)$ independent of x (i.e., homoscedastic); and
   (iii) it makes $u_i = h(y_i, \lambda) - x_i\beta$ Gaussian.

Frequently, in practice however, these objectives are conflicting, and we need a more sophisticated strategy. There is certainly no *a priori* reason to expect that a single transformation, even the celebrated Box–Cox transformation

$$h(y, \lambda) = (y^\lambda - 1)/\lambda,$$

which is the archetypical choice in this context, would be capable of so much. There is also an associated difficulty that, having built a model for $E(h(y, \lambda)|x)$, we may still wish to predict or interpret the model as if it were constructed for $E(y|x)$. One often sees $h^{-1}(x^\top \hat{\beta})$ used in place of $E(y|x)$ in such circumstances – $\exp(x^\top \hat{\beta})$ when the model has been specified as $\log(y) = x^\top \beta$, for example – but this is difficult to justify formally. Of course, the linearity of the expectation operator is also a particularly convenient property and is not shared by the quantiles except under very special circumstances (see Section 2.6).

Transformations are rather more straightforward to interpret in the context of quantile regression than they are for ordinary, mean regression. Because of the equivariance property, having estimated a linear model, $x^\top \hat{\beta}$, for the conditional median of $h(y)$ given x, we are perfectly justified in interpreting $h^{-1}(x^\top \hat{\beta})$ as an appropriate estimate of the conditional median of y given x.

Furthermore, because we have focused on estimating a local feature of the conditional distribution rather than a global feature like the conditional mean, we may concentrate on the primary objective of the transformation – achieving linearity of the conditional quantile function – and leave the other objectives aside for the moment.

2.2.4   Censoring

A particularly instructive application of the foregoing equivariance results, and one which has proven extremely influential in the econometric application of quantile regression, involves censoring of the observed response variable. The simplest model of censoring may be formulated as follows. Let y_i^* denote a latent (unobservable) response assumed to be generated from the linear model

$$y_i^* = x_i^\top \beta + u_i \quad i = 1, \ldots, n, \tag{2.7}$$

where $\{u_i\}$ is independently and identically distributed (iid) from a distribution function F with density f. Due to censoring, we do not observe the y_i^*s directly, but instead we see

$$y_i = \max\{0, y_i^*\}.$$

This model may be estimated by maximum likelihood:

$$\hat{\beta} = \operatorname{argmin}_\beta \left\{ \prod_{i=1}^n (1 - F(x_i^\top \beta))^{\Delta_i} f(y_i - x_i^\top \beta)^{1-\Delta_i} \right\}$$

where Δ_i denotes the censoring indicator, $\Delta_i = 1$ if the ith observation is censored, and $\Delta_i = 0$ otherwise. For F Gaussian, this leads to an estimate of the conditional mean function and has received intense scrutiny by Heckman (1979) and many subsequent authors. However, another F yields another functional in place of the conditional mean and consequently leads to a specification bias for the Gaussian maximum likelihood estimator. See Goldberger (1983) for a discussion of this bias in some typical cases.

Powell (1986) observed that the equivariance of the quantiles to monotone transformations implies that in this model the conditional quantile functions of the response depend only on the censoring point but are independent of F. Formally, we may express the τth conditional quantile function of the observed response, y_i, in model (2.7) as

$$Q_{y_i}(\tau | x_i) = \max\{0, x_i^\top \beta + F_u^{-1}(\tau)\}. \tag{2.8}$$

The censoring transformation, by the prior equivariance result, becomes, transparently, the new conditional quantile function. The parameters of the conditional quantile functions may now be estimated by replacing

$$\min_b \sum_{i=1}^n \rho_\tau(y_i - x_i^\top b)$$

by

$$\min_b \sum_{i=1}^n \rho_\tau(y_i - \max\{0, x_i^\top b\}), \tag{2.9}$$

where we assume, as usual, that the design vectors x_i contain an intercept to absorb the additive effect of $F_u^{-1}(\tau)$.

Generalizing model (2.8) slightly to accommodate a linear scale (heteroscedasticity) effect,

$$y_i^* = x_i^\top \beta + (x_i^\top \gamma)u_i \quad i = 1, \ldots, n \tag{2.10}$$

with u_i iid F_u, it is clear that the new conditional quantile functions

$$Q_{y_i}(\tau | x_i) = \max\{0, x_i^\top \beta + x_i^\top \gamma F_u^{-1}(\tau)\} \tag{2.11}$$

can also be estimated by solving (2.9). Because heteroscedasticity of this form is also a source of specification bias for the iid error maximum likelihood estimator, even in the Gaussian case, its straightforward accommodation within the conditional quantile formulation must be counted as a significant advantage.

A constant censoring point is typical of many econometric applications where 0 is a natural lower bound or institutional arrangements dictate, for example, top-coding of a specified amount. However, it is also straightforward to accommodate observation-specific censoring from the right and left. Suppose that we observe

$$y_i = \begin{cases} \bar{y}_i & \text{if } y_i^* > \bar{y}_i \\ y_i^* & \text{otherwise;} \\ \underline{y}_i & y_i^* < \underline{y}_i \end{cases}$$

then, by the same argument that led to (2.9) (see Fitzenberger, 1996), we would now have

$$\min_{b} \sum_{i=1}^{n} \rho_\tau(y_i - \max\{\underline{y}_i, \min\{\bar{y}_i, x_i^\top b\}\}). \tag{2.12}$$

This framework provides a quite general treatment of fixed censoring for linear model applications. We will defer the discussion of computational aspects of solving problems (2.9) and (2.12) until Chapter 6. For computational purposes, the nonlinear "kinks" in the response function created by the censoring require careful attention because they take us out of the strict linear programming formulation of the original quantile regression problem. The linear equality constraints become, under censoring, nonlinear equality constraints.

Censoring is also typical in survival analysis applications. Random censoring, in which the censoring points are only observed for the censored observations, has recently been considered within the quantile-regression framework by Ying, Jung, and Wei (1995) and Powell (1994). Powell (1986) deals with the truncated regression situation in which only the uncensored observations are available to the investigator. It is an elementary point that censoring beyond a fixed threshold has no effect on the uncensored quantiles, but the extension of this idea to regression has proven to be one of the most compelling rationales for the use of quantile regression in applied work.

2.3 ROBUSTNESS

The comparison of the relative merits of the mean and median in statistical applications has a long, illustrious history. Since Gauss, it has been recognized that the mean enjoys a strong optimality if the density of the "law of errors" happens to be proportional to e^{-x^2}. On the other hand, if there are occasional, very large errors, as was commonly the case in early astronomical calculations, for example, the performance of the median can be superior, a point stressed by Laplace and many subsequent authors including, remarkably, Kolmogorov (1931).

2.3.1   The Influence Function

The modern view of robustness of statistical methods, strongly influenced by Tukey (see, e.g., Andrews, Bickel, Hampel, Huber, Rogers, and Tukey, 1974), is framed by the sensitivity curve, or influence function of the estimators, and perhaps to a lesser degree by their finite sample breakdown points. The influence function, introduced by Hampel (1974), is a population analog of Tukey's empirical sensitivity curve. It offers a concise description of how an estimator $\hat{\theta}$ evaluated at a distribution F is affected by "contaminating" F. Formally, we may view $\hat{\theta}$ as a functional of F and write $\hat{\theta}(F)$, and we may consider contaminating F by replacing a small amount of mass ε from F by an equivalent mass concentrated at y, allowing us to write the contaminated distribution function as

$$F_\varepsilon = \varepsilon \delta_y + (1 - \varepsilon)F,$$

where δ_y denotes the distribution function that assigns mass 1 to the point y. Now we may express the influence function of $\hat\theta$ at F as

$$IF_{\hat\theta}(y, F) = \lim_{\varepsilon \to 0} \frac{\hat\theta(F_\varepsilon) - \hat\theta(F)}{\varepsilon}.$$

For the mean,

$$\hat\theta(F_\varepsilon) = \int y\,dF_\varepsilon = \varepsilon y + (1 - \varepsilon)\hat\theta(F)$$

and so

$$IF_{\hat\theta}(y, F) = y - \hat\theta(F),$$

whereas for the median (see Problem 2.5),

$$\tilde\theta(F_\varepsilon) = F_\varepsilon^{-1}(1/2)$$

$$IF_{\tilde\theta}(y, F) = \text{sgn}\,(y - \tilde\theta(F))/f(F^{-1}(1/2)), \qquad (2.13)$$

presuming, of course, the existence and positivity of the density term in the denominator.

There is a dramatic difference between the two influence functions. In the case of the mean, the influence of contaminating F at y is simply proportional to y, implying that a little contamination, *however small*, at a point y sufficiently far from $\theta(F)$ can take the mean arbitrarily far away from its initial value at F. In contrast, the influence of contamination at y on the median is *bounded* by the constant $s(1/2) = 1/f(F^{-1}(1/2))$ which, following Tukey, we will call the "sparsity" at the median, because it is simply the reciprocal of the density function evaluated at the median. The sparsity is low where the density is high and vice versa.

The comparison of the influence functions of the mean and median graphically illustrates the fragility of the mean and the robustness of the median in withstanding the contamination of outlying observations. Much of what has already been said extends immediately to the quantiles generally, and from there to quantile regression. The influence function of the τth quantile is obtained simply by replacing the $1/2$ in (2.13) by τ. The boundedness of the quantile influence function is obviously maintained, provided that the sparsity at τ is finite. Extending the *IF* to median regression is straightforward, but we now need F to represent the joint distribution of the pairs (x, y). Writing dF in the conditional form

$$dF = dG(x)f(y|x)dy$$

and again assuming that f is continuous and strictly positive when needed, we have

$$IF_{\hat{\beta}_F(\tau)}((y, x), F) = Q^{-1}x \, \text{sgn} \, (y - x^\top \hat{\beta}_F(\tau)),$$

where

$$Q = \int xx^\top f(x^\top \hat{\beta}_F(x))dG(x).$$

Again, we see that the estimator has bounded influence in y because y only appears clothed by the protective $\text{sgn} \, (\cdot)$ function. However, the naked x appearing in IF should be a cause of some concern. It implies that introducing contamination at (x, y) with x sufficiently deviant can have extremely deleterious consequences. We could illustrate this effect with an example in which we gradually move a single outlier farther and farther from the mass of the data until eventually all of the quantile regression lines are forced to pass through this same offending point. There is nothing surprising or unusual here; similar behavior of the least-squares estimator is well known. We will consider several proposals to robustify the behavior of quantile regression to influential design observations in Section 8.5, where we deal with the breakdown point of quantile regression estimators.

The robustness of the quantile regression estimator to outlying ys can be seen clearly in the following thought experiment. Imagine a data cloud with the fitted τth quantile regression plane slicing through it. Now consider taking any point, say y_i, above that plane and moving it farther way from the plane *in the y direction*. How is the position of the fitted plane affected? A moment's reflection on the subgradient condition reveals that the contribution of the point to the subgradient is independent of y_i as long as $\text{sgn} \, (y_i - x_i^\top \hat{\beta}(\tau))$ does not change. In other words, we are free to move y_i up and down at will *provided we do not cross the fitted plane* without altering the fit. This clarifies somewhat the earlier remarks that (i) the influence function is constant above the fitted quantile and (ii) observations are never "neglected," rather they participate equally in electing the representative points. Unlike the sample mean where influence is increasing in the discrepancy, $y - \hat{\theta}_F$, quantile influence depends on y only through the sign of this discrepancy.

This feature of quantile regression can be restated more formally as follows.

Theorem 2.4. *Let D be a diagonal matrix with nonnegative elements d_i, for $i = 1, \ldots, n$; then*

$$\hat{\beta}(\tau; y, X) = \hat{\beta}(\tau; X\hat{\beta}(\tau; y, X) + D\hat{u}, X),$$

where $\hat{u} = y - X\hat{\beta}(\tau; y, X)$.

As long as we do not alter the sign of the residuals, *any* of the y observations may be altered without altering the initial solution. Although this may, at first thought, appear astonishing, even bizarre, a second thought assures us that without it we could not have a quantile. It is a crucial aspect of interpreting quantile regression. When a mean dog wags its tail even its essential center moves. When the kinder, median dog wags its tail its soul remains at rest.

2.3.2 The Breakdown Point

The influence function is an indispensable tool exquisitely designed to measure the sensitivity of estimators to infinitesimal perturbations of the nominal model. But procedures can be infinitesimally robust, and yet still highly sensitive to small, finite perturbations. Take, for example, the α-trimmed mean, which is capable of withstanding a proportion $0 < \epsilon < \alpha$ of contamination but also capable of breaking down completely when $\epsilon > \alpha$.

The finite sample breakdown point of Donoho and Huber (1983) has emerged as the most successful notion of *global* robustness of estimators. Essentially, it measures the smallest fraction of contamination of an initial sample that can cause an estimator to take values arbitrarily far from its value at the initial sample. This concept has played a crucial role in recent work on robust estimation and inference. It offers an appealing, yet tractable, global quantification of robustness, complementing the local assessment captured by the influence function. Indeed a primary goal of recent research in robustness has been the construction of so-called high-breakdown methods exemplified by Rousseeuw's (1984) least-median-of-squares estimator for the linear regression model, which achieves asymptotic breakdown point one-half. Despite the attention lavished on the breakdown point of estimators in recent years, it remains a rather elusive concept. In particular, its nonprobabilistic formulation poses certain inherent difficulties. He, Jurečková, Koenker, and Portnoy (1990) showed that the breakdown point of regression estimators is closely tied to a measure of tail performance introduced by Jurečková (1981) for location estimators.

Let $T_n = T_n(X_1, \ldots, X_n)$ be an estimator of a location parameter θ_0, where $X_1, \ldots, X_n$ are iid with common symmetric-about-zero distribution function $F(x)$. Jurečková considered the measure of performance,

$$B(a, T_n) = \frac{-\log P_\theta(|T_n - \theta_0| > a)}{-\log(1 - F(a))},$$

for fixed n as $a \to \infty$, and she showed that this rate is controlled by the tail behavior of F. For any (reasonable) translation equivariant T_n, she showed that

$$1 \leq \liminf_{a \to \infty} B(a, T_n) \leq \limsup_{a \to \infty} B(a, T_n) \leq n.$$

For the sample mean, $T_n = \bar{X}_n$, and F has exponential tails, so that

$$\lim_{a \to \infty} \frac{-\log(1 - F(a))}{ca^r} = 1$$

for some $c > 0$ and $r > 0$. In this case, $\bar{X}_n$ attains optimal tail performance, with log of the probability of a large error tending to zero n times faster than the log of the probability that a single observation exceeds the bound a. Whereas, on the contrary, for F with algebraic tails, so

$$\lim_{a \to \infty} \frac{-\log(1 - F(a))}{m \log a} = 1$$

for some $m > 0$, and $B(a, T_n)$ tends to one. In contrast, the sample median has much better tail behavior with the log $P(|T_n - \theta| > a)$ tending to zero as $a \to \infty$ at least $n/2$ times faster than the tails of the underlying error distribution, for either exponential or algebraic tailed errors.

For location equivariant estimators, $T_n(X_1, \ldots, X_n)$, that are monotone in each argument, it can be shown (Theorem 2.1 of (He, Jurečková, Koenker, and Portnoy, 1990) that T_n has a universal breakdown point m^*, independent of the initial sample, and for any symmetric absolutely continuous F having density, $f(z) = f(-z) > 0$, for $z \in \mathbb{R}$, and such that $\lim_{a \to \infty} \log(1 - F(a + c)) / \log(1 - F(a)) = 1$ for any $c > 0$,

$$m^* \le \liminf B(a, T_n) \le \limsup B(a, T_n) \le n - m^* + 1.$$

This close link between breakdown and tail performance extends to regression, where the least-squares estimator is found to have $\lim B(a, T_n) = \bar{h}^{-1}$, with $\bar{h} = \max_i h_{ii}$ and $h_{ii} = x_i^\top (X^\top X)^{-1} x_i$, for iid Gaussian errors, but again $\lim B(a, T_n) = 1$ for Fs with algebraic tails. For quantile regression estimators, a trivial upper bound on tail performance and breakdown is given by $\lim B(a, \hat{\beta}(\tau)) \le [\min\{\tau, 1 - \tau\}n] + 1$, but the corresponding lower bound is more challenging.

Of course, $\hat{\beta}(\tau)$ has breakdown point $m^* = 1$ if we consider contamination of (x, y) pairs; a single observation judiciously pulled to infinity in both x and y directions can force *all* of the quantile-regression hyperplanes to pass through it. This sensitivity to contamination of design observations is a well-known defect of the entire class of M-estimators. Before addressing this issue directly, it is revealing to consider briefly the question of breakdown and tail performance in the context of fixed design observations.

For the regression median, $\hat{\beta}(1/2)$, the quantities

$$g_i = \sup_{\|b\|=1} \frac{|x_i^\top b|}{\sum_{i \in N} |x_i^\top b|}$$

play the role of influence diagnostics analogous to the $h_{ii} = x_i^\top (X^\top X)^{-1} x_i$ in conventional least-squares theory. Define m_* to be the largest integer m such that, for any subset M of $N = \{1, 2, \ldots, n\}$ of size m,

$$\inf_{\|b\|=1} \frac{\sum_{i \in N \setminus M} |x_i^\top b|}{\sum_{i \in N} |x_i^\top b|} > 1/2.$$

Then $\lim B(a, \hat{\beta}(1/2)) \ge m_* + 1$ for algebraic tailed F, and the breakdown point m^* of $\hat{\beta}(1/2)$ satisfies $m_* + 1 \le m^* \le m_* + 2$. Although it is somewhat difficult to compute precisely the value of m_* for general designs in higher dimensions, for scalar regression through the origin it is quite easy. In this case, with x_i iid $U[0, 1]$, for example, m_*/n tends to $1 - 1/\sqrt{2} \approx 0.29$, a quite respectable breakdown point. For regression quantiles other than the median, breakdown is determined by similar considerations. Section 8.5 describes some proposals for high-breakdown quantile regression methods.

2.4 INTERPRETING QUANTILE REGRESSION MODELS

In the classical linear regression model, where

$$E(Y|X = x) = x^\top \beta,$$

we are used to interpreting the coefficients β in terms of the partial derivatives:

$$\frac{\partial E(Y|X = x)}{\partial x_j} = \beta_j.$$

Of course there are many caveats that must accompany this interpretation. For instance, we may have several coefficients associated with a single covariate in a model with quadratic effects or interaction terms. In this case, changes in a single covariate induce changes in several coordinates of the vector x, and derivatives must be computed accordingly. For example, if we have

$$E(Y|Z = z) = \beta_0 + \beta_1 z + \beta_2 z^2,$$

it is clear that

$$\frac{\partial E(Y|Z = z)}{\partial z} = \beta_1 + 2\beta_2 z$$

and therefore the "effect" of a change in z on the conditional expectation of y now depends on both β_1 and β_2 and perhaps the effect depends more significantly on the value of z, at which we choose to evaluate the derivative. This is illustrated in the birth-weight analysis of Chapter 1.

In the transformation model,

$$E(h(Y)|X = x) = x^\top \beta,$$

there is a strong temptation to write

$$\frac{\partial E(Y|X = x)}{\partial x_j} = \frac{\partial h^{-1}(x^\top \beta)}{\partial x_j}.$$

This is a common practice in logarithmic models, that is, where $h(Y) = \log(Y)$, but this practice is subject to the famous Nixon dictum, "You can do it, but it would be wrong." The difficulty is obviously that $Eh(Y)$ is not the same as $h(EY)$ except in very exceptional circumstances, and this makes interpretation of mean regression models somewhat trickier in practice than one might gather from some applied accounts.

As we have already noted, the situation is somewhat simpler in this respect in the case of quantile regression. Since

$$Q_{h(Y)}(\tau|X=x) = h(Q_Y(\tau|X=x))$$

for any monotone transformation $h(\cdot)$, we have immediately that, if

$$Q_{h(Y)}(\tau|X=x) = x^\top \beta(\tau),$$

then

$$\frac{\partial Q_Y(\tau|X=x)}{\partial x_j} = \frac{\partial h^{-1}(x^\top \beta)}{\partial x_j}.$$

So, for example, if we specify

$$Q_{\log(Y)}(\tau|X=x) = x^\top \beta(\tau),$$

then it follows that

$$\frac{\partial Q_Y(\tau|X=x)}{\partial x_j} = \exp(x^\top \beta)\beta_j,$$

subject, of course, to our initial qualifications about the possible interdependence among the components of x.

The interpretation of the partial derivative itself, $\partial Q_Y(\tau|X=x)/\partial x_j$, often requires considerable care. We emphasized earlier in the context of the two-sample problem that the Lehmann–Doksum quantile treatment effect is simply the response necessary to keep a respondent at the same quantile under both control and treatment regimes. Of course, this is not to say that a particular subject who happens to fall at the τth quantile initially, and then receives an increment Δx_j, say, another year of education, will necessarily fall on the τth conditional quantile function following the increment. Indeed, as much of the recent literature on treatment effects has stressed (see, e.g., Angrist, Imbens, and Rubin, 1996), we are typically unable to identify features of the joint distribution of control and treatment responses because we do not observe responses under both regimes for the same subjects. With longitudinal data one may be able to explore in more detail the dynamics of response, but in many applications this will prove impossible. This is certainly also the case in conventional mean regression, where we are able to estimate the average response to treatment but its dynamics remain hidden.

2.4.1   Some Examples

At this stage it is useful to consider some examples in an effort to clarify certain issues of interpretation.

Table 2.1. *The union wage premium. Quantile regression estimates of the union wage premium in the U.S. as estimated by Chamberlain (1994) based on 5358 observations from the 1987 CPS data on workers with 20–29 years of experience*

Sector	0.1	0.25	0.5	0.75	0.9	OLS
Manufacturing	0.281	0.249	0.169	0.075	−0.003	0.158
	(0.12)	(0.12)	(0.11)	(0.1)	(0.11)	(0.14)
Nonmanufacturing	0.47	0.406	0.333	0.248	0.184	0.327
	(0.14)	(0.14)	(0.13)	(0.16)	(0.18)	(0.16)

The Union Wage Premium

Chamberlain (1994) considers the union wage premium – that is, the percentage wage premium that union workers receive over comparable nonunion employees. Based on 1987 data from the U.S. Current Population Survey (CPS), Chamberlain estimated a model of log hourly wages for 5338 men with 20–29 years of work experience. In addition to union status, the model included several other covariates that are conventionally included in earnings models of this type: years of schooling, years of potential work experience, indicators of whether the respondent was married or living in a metropolitan area, and indicators of regional, occupational, and industrial categories.

The results for the union wage effect are summarized in Table 2.1 for manufacturing and nonmanufacturing employees separately. In the last column of the table, the conditional mean effect estimated by least squares is reported. It shows nearly a 16% wage premium for union workers in manufacturing and almost a 33% premium for non-manufacturing employees. But is important to ask, how is this premium distributed? Is the union wage premium shared equally by all strata of workers, as would be the case if union membership induced a pure location shift in the distribution of log wages? Or do some strata benefit more than others from union status?

The results clearly indicate that, conditional on other labor market characteristics, it is the lowest wage workers that benefit most from union membership. If there were a pure location shift effect, as we implicitly assume in the mean regression model, we would expect to see that the coefficients at each of the five estimated quantiles would be the same as the 15.8% mean effect for manufacturing. Instead, we see that workers at the first decile of the conditional wage distribution receive a 28% boost in wages from union membership, and this figure declines steadily as one moves up through the conditional wage distribution until, at the upper decile, the union wage premium has vanished. For nonmanufacturing workers, the picture is quite similar; the mean shift of 32.7% is strongest at the lower quantiles and essentially disappears in the upper tail of the conditional wage distribution.

These findings should not, as Chamberlain comments, surprise students of unionism. Prior work had shown that the dispersion of wages conditional on covariates similar to those used by Chamberlain was considerably smaller for union workers than for nonunion workers. And the pattern of observed quantile regression union effects can be roughly anticipated from this dispersion effect. But the precise nature of the pattern, its asymmetry, and the effect of other covariates on aspects of the conditional distribution other than its location are all revealed more clearly by the quantile regression analysis.

An important aspect of the union wage premium problem, one that is quite explicitly neglected in Chamberlain's work, involves the causal interpretation of the estimated model. There is much econometric literature on this aspect of the interpretation, which stresses the endogoneity of union status. Individuals are obviously not randomly assigned to union or nonunion status; they are selected in a rather complicated procedure that makes causal interpretation of estimated union effects fraught with difficulties. We shall return to this important issue in Section 8.8.

Demand for Alcohol

Manning, Blumberg, and Moulton (1995) estimate a model for the demand for alcohol based on a sample of 18,844 observations from the U.S. National Health Interview Survey. The model is a conventional log-linear demand equation:

$$\log q_i = \beta_0 + \beta_1 \log p_i + \beta_2 \log x_i + u_i,$$

where q_i denotes annual alcohol consumption as reported by individual i, $\log p_i$ is a price index for alcohol computed on the basis of the place of residence of individual i, and x_i is the annual income of the ith individual. Roughly 40% of the respondents reported zero consumption, and so for quantiles with $\tau < 0.4$, we have no demand response to either price or income. The income elasticity is fairly constant at about $\hat{\beta} \approx 0.25$, with some evidence of a somewhat less elastic response near $\tau = .4$ and $\tau = 1$. More interesting is the pattern of the price elasticity, $\beta_1(\tau)$, which is most elastic at moderate consumption levels with $\tau \approx 0.7$ and becomes very inelastic (unresponsive to price changes) for individuals with either very low levels of consumption ($\tau = 0.4$), or very high levels of consumption ($\tau = 1$). This seems quite consistent with prior expectations. Given income, individuals with very low levels of demand could be expected to be quite insensitive to price, as would those with very high levels of demand – those for whom demand is dictated more by physiological considerations. Again, the presumption that price and income act as a pure location shift effect on log consumption appears to be a very inadequate representation of the actual state of affairs. Certainly, from a policy standpoint it is important to have a clear indication of how the mean response to changes in prices is "allocated" to the various segments of the conditional distribution of demand, and this is what the quantile regression analysis provides.

Daily Melbourne Temperatures

The third example reconsiders a semiparametric AR(1) model for daily temperature in Melbourne, Australia. Hyndman, Bashtannyk, and Grunwald (1996) recently analyzed these data using a modal regression approach. The quantile regression approach is strongly complementary and offers a somewhat more complete view of the data. Figure 2.5 provides an AR(1) scatterplot of 10 years of daily temperature data. Today's maximum daily temperature is plotted against yesterday's maximum. Not surprisingly, one's first impression from the plot suggests a "unit-root" model in which today's forecasted maximum is simply yesterday's maximum. But closer examination of the plot reveals that this impression is based primarily on the left-hand side of the plot, where the central tendency of the scatter follows the 45-degree line quite closely. On the right-hand side, however, corresponding to summer conditions, the pattern

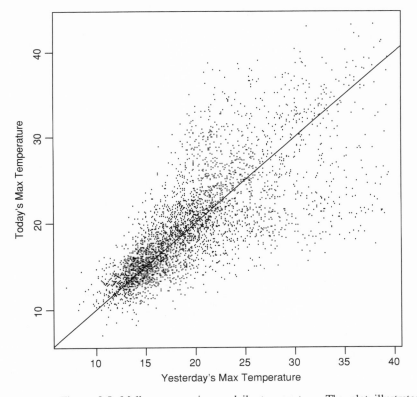

Figure 2.5. Melbourne maximum daily temperature. The plot illustrates 10 years of daily maximum (Centigrade) temperature data for Melbourne, Australia as an AR(1) scatterplot. Note that, conditional on hot weather on the prior day, the distribution of maximum temperature on the following day appears to be bimodal.

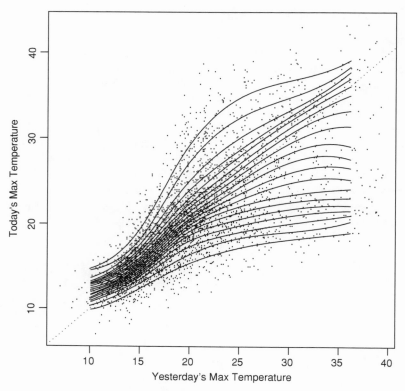

Figure 2.6. Melbourne daily maximum temperature. Superimposed on the AR(1) scatterplot of daily maximum temperatures are 12 estimated conditional quantile functions. These functions support the view that the conditional density of maximum temperature conditional on prior warm weather is bimodal.

is more complicated. There, it appears that *either* there is another hot day, falling again along the 45-degree line, *or* there is a dramatic cooling off. But a mild cooling off appears to be quite rare. In the language of conditional densities, if today is hot, tomorrow's temperature appears to be bimodal with one mode roughly centered at today's maximum and the other mode centered at about 20°C.

Figure 2.6 superimposes 19 estimated quantile regression curves on the scatterplot. Each curve is specified as a linear B-spline of the form

$$Q_{Y_t}(\tau | Y_{t-1}) = \sum_{i=1}^{p} \phi_i(Y_{t-1})\beta_i(\tau),$$

where $\{\phi_i(\cdot) : i = 1, \ldots, p\}$ denote the basis functions of the spline. Once the knot positions of the spline have been selected, such models are linear in

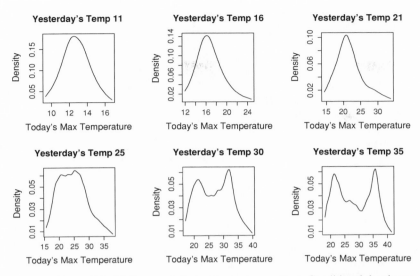

Figure 2.7. Melbourne daily maximum temperature. Conditional density estimates of today's maximum temperature for several values of yesterday's maximum temperature, based on the Melbourne data. Note that today's temperature is bimodal when yesterday was hot. When yesterday was cold, the density of today's temperature is unimodal and concentrated at somewhat warmer temperatures.

parameters and thus can be easily estimated by the methods already introduced. Related smoothing spline methods are discussed later in Chapter 7.

Given a family of estimated conditional quantile functions, it is straightforward to estimate the conditional density of the response at various values of the conditioning covariate. Figure 2.7 illustrates this approach with several density estimates based on the Melbourne data. In the last panel of this figure, we clearly see the bimodal form of the conditional density for the summer days in which we are conditioning on a high value of yesterday's temperature.

The particular form of mean reversion illustrated in this example has a natural meteorological explanation: high-pressure systems bringing hot weather from the interior of the continent must eventually terminate with a cold front generated over the Tasman Sea, generating a rapid drop in temperature. This sort of dynamic does not seem entirely implausible in other time-series settings, including those in economics and finance, and yet the conventional time-series models that we usually consider are incapable of accommodating behavior of this type. Clearly, models in which the conditioning covariates affect only the location of the response distribution are inadequate, and the recent wave of models for conditional scale, variance, and so on also are unsatisfactory. We must allow the entire shape of the conditional density to change with x, and this is readily done within the scope of the quantile regression formulation.

Glacier Lilies, Gophers, and Rocks

Cade, Terrell, and Schroeder (1999) consider a model of the viability of the glacier lily (*Erythronium grandiflorum*) as a function of several ecological covariates. They argue generally that in ecology it is often of interest to formulate models for maximum sustainable population densities, and they suggest that it may therefore be more informative to estimate the effect of certain covariates on upper quantiles of the response rather than focus on models of conditional central tendency. Cade *et al.* explore several models for the prevalence of lily seedlings as a function of the number of flowers observed in 256 contiguous 2×2 m quadrats of subalpine meadow in western Colorado. An index of rockiness of the terrain and an index of gopher burrowing activity are also used as explanatory variables.

As in the alcohol demand example, there is a preponderance of observations with zero response, making conventional least-squares estimation of mean regression models problematic. In a simple bivariate model in which the number of seedlings depends solely on the number of flowers observed, we illustrate several fitted log-linear quantile regression models in Figure 2.8. As can be seen in these figures, the relationship is very weak until we reach the upper tail. Only the 0.95 and 0.99 quantile regression estimates exhibit a significant slope. Note that in fitting the log-linear model it was necessary to deal with the fact that nearly half of the response observations were zero. In mean regression it is occasionally suggested that one transform by $\log(y + \epsilon)$ to account for this, but it is clear that the least-squares fit can be quite sensitive to the choice of epsilon. In contrast for the quantile regression model, as long as we are interested in quantiles such that all the zero-response observations fall below the fitted relationship, the choice of ϵ has no effect.

Regarding the strong *negative* relationship between the number of seedlings and the number of observed flowers in the upper tail of the conditional distribution, Cade *et al.*, comment:

> Negative slopes for upper regression quantiles were consistent with the explanation provided by Thompson et al. that sites where flowers were most numerous because of lack of pocket gophers (which eat lilies), were rocky sites that provided poor moisture conditions for seed germination; hence seedling numbers were lower.

Here we risk missing the primary relationship of interest by focusing too much attention on the conditional central tendency. Fitting the upper quantile regressions reveals a strong relationship posited in prior work. Cade *et al.* go on to explore the effect of other covariates and find that their measure of the rockiness of the terrain plays a significant role. After the inclusion of the index of rockiness, the number of observed flowers exerts a more natural, statistically significant, *positive* effect on the presence of seedlings at the upper quantiles of the conditional distribution. This reversal of sign for the flower effect further supports the view cited earlier.

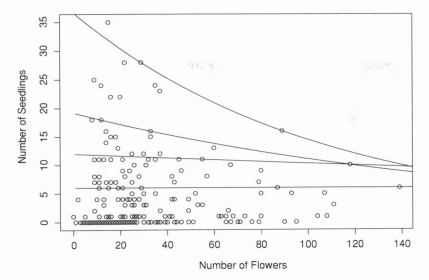

Figure 2.8. Glaciar lily seedling counts. Plotted observations on flower and seedling counts for 256 contiguous 2×2 m quadrats of subalpine meadow in western Colorado. As in Cade *et al.*'s (1999) study, one outlying count of 72 seedlings in a region with 16 flowers was omitted from the plot but included in the fitting. The four plotted curves are estimates of the $\tau \in \{0.75, 0.9, 0.95, 0.99\}$ conditional quantile functions. Note that almost half – 127 of 256 – of the observations have zero seedling counts.

It is common in many disciplines that theory offers predictions about upper or lower bounds of stochastic processes conditional on observable covariates. In these cases it is valuable to be able to estimate these extreme regression quantiles directly, as suggested in the foregoing example. Of course the theory of the most extreme regression quantiles is considerably more complicated than the theory for more central quantile regression, and we must balance considerations of robustness and efficiency. Section 4.7 offers a more extensive review of the literature on extreme quantile regression estimation.

A somewhat unsettling feature of Figure 2.8 is the crossing of the fitted conditional quantile functions at the extreme right-hand side of the figure. Given the sparsity of data in this region, this might be viewed as inevitable: the fit of a globally quadratic model determined by the data to the left of the crossing cannot anticipate problems in regions without any observations. Some further consideration of this problem is provided in the next section.

2.5   CAUTION: QUANTILE CROSSING

An attractive feature of quantile regression that has been repeatedly emphasized is that it enables us to look at slices of the conditional distribution without any reliance on global distributional assumptions. Only local information near the specified quantile is employed. This can be seen in Theorem 2.4 in the insensitivity of the fit to perturbations of the observations above and below the fit. It is also apparent in the asymptotic behavior described in the next chapter. But even the most appealing mathematical features can occasionally assume a more malevolent aspect. The virtues of independently estimating a family of conditional quantile functions can sometimes be a source of serious embarrassment when we find that estimated quantile functions cross, thus violating the basic principle that distribution functions and their associated inverse functions should be monotone increasing.

It is of some comfort to recognize that such crossing is typically confined to outlying regions of the design space. The following result shows that at the centroid of the design, $\bar{x} = n^{-1} \sum x_i$, the estimated conditional quantile function

$$\hat{Q}_Y(\tau|\bar{x}) = \bar{x}^\top \hat{\beta}(\tau)$$

is monotone in τ.

Theorem 2.5. *The sample paths of $\hat{Q}_Y(\tau|\bar{x})$ are nondecreasing in τ on* $[0, 1]$.

Proof. We will show that $\tau_1 < \tau_2$ implies $\bar{x}^\top \hat{\beta}(\tau_1) \le \bar{x}^\top \hat{\beta}(\tau_2)$. For any $b \in \mathbb{R}^p$,

$$\sum_{i=1}^{n} \left[\rho_{\tau_2}(Y_i - x_i^\top b) - \rho_{\tau_1}(Y_i - x_i^\top b) \right] = n(\tau_2 - \tau_1)(\bar{Y} - \bar{x}^\top b).$$

$$(2.14)$$

This equation follows directly from the definition of ρ_τ:

$$
\begin{aligned}
\rho_{\tau_2}(Y_i - x_i^\top t) &- \rho_{\tau_1}(Y_i - x_i^\top t) \\
&= (\tau_2 - \tau_1)(Y_i - x_i^\top t)^+ + \left[(1 - \tau_2) - (1 - \tau_1) \right](Y_i - x_i^\top t)^- \\
&= (\tau_2 - \tau_1)\left[(Y_i - x_i^\top t)^+ - (Y_i - x_i^\top t)^- \right] \\
&= (\tau_2 - \tau_1)(Y_i - x_i^\top t).
\end{aligned}
$$

$$(2.15)$$

Now, using the definition of $\hat{\beta}(\tau)$ as a minimizer of ρ_τ, and applying (2.14) with $b = \hat{\beta}(\tau_k)$ for $k = 1, 2$, we have

$$
\begin{aligned}
\sum_{i=1}^{n} \rho_{\tau_1}&\left(Y_i - x_i^\top \hat{\beta}(\tau_1)\right) + n(\tau_2 - \tau_1)\left(\bar{Y} - \bar{x}^\top \hat{\beta}(\tau_2)\right) \\
&\le \sum_{i=1}^{n} \rho_{\tau_1}\left(Y_i - x_i^\top \hat{\beta}(\tau_2)\right) + n(\tau_2 - \tau_1)\left(\bar{Y} - \bar{x}^\top \hat{\beta}(\tau_2)\right) \\
&= \sum_{i=1}^{n} \rho_{\tau_2}\left(Y_i - x_i^\top \hat{\beta}(\tau_2)\right)
\end{aligned}
$$

$$(2.16)$$

$$\leq \sum_{i=1}^{n} \rho_{\tau_2}\left(Y_i - x_i^\top \hat{\beta}(\tau_1)\right)$$

$$= \sum_{i=1}^{n} \rho_{\tau_1}\left(Y_i - x_i^\top \hat{\beta}(\tau_1)\right) + n(\tau_2 - \tau_1)\left(\bar{Y} - \bar{x}^\top \hat{\beta}(\tau_1)\right).$$

Simplifying, we see that this is equivalent to

$$n(\tau_2 - \tau_1)\left(\bar{x}^\top \hat{\beta}(\tau_2) - \bar{x}^\top \hat{\beta}(\tau_1)\right) \geq 0, \qquad (2.17)$$

from which the result follows immediately. ∎

Of course monotonicity at $x = \bar{x}$ is not a guarantee that $\hat{Q}_Y(\tau|x)$ will be monotone in τ at other values of x. Indeed it is obvious that if $\hat{Q}_Y$ is linear in variables then there must be crossing sufficiently far away from $\bar{x}$. It may be that such crossing occurs outside the convex hull of the x observations, in which case the estimated model may be viewed as an adequate approximation within this region. But it is not unusual to find that crossing has occurred inside this region as well. It is easy to check whether $\hat{Q}_Y(\tau|x)$ is monotone at particular x points. If there is a significant number of observed points at which this condition is violated, then this can be taken as evidence of misspecification of the covariate effects.

To illustrate the consequences of such misspecification, consider the simple location-scale shift model:

$$y_i = \beta_0 + x_i \beta_1 + (\gamma_0 + \gamma_1 x_i) v_i. \qquad (2.18)$$

Suppose that the v_i are iid with distribution function F. When the scale parameter $\gamma_1 = 0$, then we have a pure location shift model and the family of conditional quantile functions are parallel. When $\gamma_0 = 0$ and $\gamma_1 > 0$, we have a family of conditional quantile functions that all pass through the point $(0, \beta_0)$. This is fine as long as we contemplate using the model only in the region of positive xs. If, however, venturing into more dangerous territory, we let x_is take both positive and negative values, then the quantile functions are no longer linear. If v has quantile function $F^{-1}(\tau)$ then $-v$ has quantile function $-F^{-1}(1 - \tau)$, and so the quantile quantile functions for our location-scale model may be written in piecewise linear form:

$$Q_Y(\tau|x_i) = \begin{cases} \beta_0 + x_i \beta_1 + (\gamma_0 + \gamma_1 x_i) F^{-1}(\tau) & \text{if } \gamma_0 + \gamma_1 x_i \geq 0 \\ \beta_0 + x_i \beta_1 + (\gamma_0 + \gamma_1 x_i) F^{-1}(1 - \tau) & \text{otherwise.} \end{cases}$$

If we persist in fitting linear models in the face of this nonlinearity of the true model, we can be badly misled. In Figure 2.9 we illustrate two cases: in the left panel the quantile functions are kinked at the point $x = 0$ and we observe xs uniformly distributed on the interval $[-0.1, 5]$. In this case there is very little bias introduced by the kinks in the conditional quantile functions. The gray lines represent the fitted linear approximations to the piecewise linear conditional quantile functions, and there is little distortion except at the 0.01

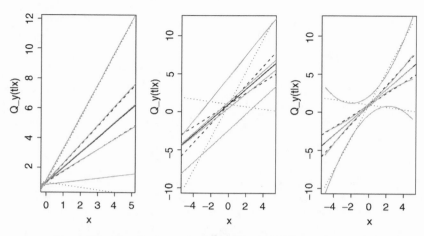

Figure 2.9. Quantile regression under misspecification. In model (2.18), with $\beta_0 = 1, \beta_1 = 1, \gamma_0 = 0, \gamma_1 = 1$, and v_is iid $\mathcal{N}(0, 0.5^2)$, the conditional quantile functions depicted as dashed and dotted lines appear to cross but are actually kinked at the point $x = 0$. When linear conditional quantile functions are estimated, the degree of distortion, or bias, depends on the location of the kink relative to the support and density of the x observations. In the left-most panel, x is uniform on the interval $[-0.1, 5]$. The gray lines show the fitted conditional quantile lines for $\tau \in \{0.01, 0.3, 0.5, 0.7, 0.99\}$. There is little distortion except for the $\tau = 0.01$ fit. In the middle panel, we repeat the exercise with $x \sim [-5, 5]$, and so the kink occurs in the middle of the domain. Now all the fitted lines are distorted except the median, and the fitted quantile functions mimic an iid error model with parallel quantile functions even though the true conditional quantile functions are highly nonlinear. In the right-most panel, the fitted conditional quantile functions are respecified as quadratic in x and now quite accurately mimic the piecewise linear form of the true functions, except in the most extreme x regions.

quantile. In the middle panel, the xs are now uniform on $[-5, 5]$, and we see that the attempt to fit the piecewise linear truth with a strictly linear model completely misrepresents reality, except at the median where reality is still really linear. The true ∨-shaped and ∧-shaped quantile functions appear, due to the symmetry of the xs, to produce parallel quantile functions as if there were iid error. In the rightmost panel of the figure, the fitted curves are respecified as quadratic, and it is apparent that they now provide a somewhat more accurate representation of the model.

In some applications we may wish to impose monotonicity in some stronger form across the quantile functions. One strategy for accomplishing this has been proposed by He (1997), who adopts the location-scale shift model,

$$y_i = x_i^\top \beta + (x_i^\top \gamma) u_i, \tag{2.19}$$

with u_i iid. He suggests estimating this model in three steps:

1. a median regression of y_i on x_i to obtain $\hat{\beta}$ and associated residuals, $\hat{u}_i = y_i - x_i^\top \hat{\beta}$,
2. a median regression of $|\hat{u}_i|$ on x_i to obtain $\hat{\gamma}$ and associated fitted values, $s_i = x_i^\top \hat{\gamma}$; and
3. a bivariate quantile regression of $\hat{u}_i$ on s_i constrained through the origin to determine scalar coefficients $\hat{\alpha}(\tau)$.

Provided that the scale estimates s_i are nonnegative, we may take

$$\hat{Q}_Y(\tau|x) = x^\top(\hat{\beta} + \hat{\alpha}(\tau)\hat{\gamma})$$

as an estimate of the conditional quantile functions. It is guaranteed to be monotone in τ at all x since $\hat{\alpha}$ must be monotone by Theorem 2.5. We cannot be sure that the s_is will be nonnegative, and so it might be useful to consider constraining step 2 to produce nonnegative fitted values. This could be relatively easily accomplished using the approach described by Koenker and Ng (2004). However, He suggests quite sensibly that the unconstrained approach is preferable – if it produces negative fitted values, this may be taken as diagnostic evidence of misspecification of the model.

Location-scale model (2.19) imposes quite stringent restrictions on the family of conditional quantile functions. In Section 3.8 we will consider testing the plausibility of these restrictions.

2.6 A RANDOM COEFFICIENT INTERPRETATION

When we write the linear quantile regression model as

$$Q_Y(\tau|x) = x^\top \beta(\tau), \tag{2.20}$$

and claim that the model holds for all $\tau \in (0, 1)$, we have specified a complete stochastic mechanism for generating the response variable Y. Recall that a random variable, Y with distribution function F, can be simulated by generating a standard uniform random variable, $U \sim U[0, 1]$, and then setting $Y = F^{-1}(U)$. Thus, in model (2.20), Y conditional on $X = x$ can be simulated by setting $Y = x^\top \beta(U)$ for $U \sim U[0, 1]$. Given a mechanism for generating a sequence of design vectors $(x_1, \ldots, x_n)$, we can draw independent random uniforms $(u_1, \ldots, u_n)$ and generate sample responses as

$$y_i = x_i^\top \beta(u_i), \quad i = 1, \ldots, n. \tag{2.21}$$

Note that this procedure allows us to generate xs as a dependent sequence, perhaps recursively, depending on the σ-field generated by the lagged y_is.

This strategy for simulating observations from the linear quantile regression model also suggests a new random coefficient interpretation of the model. The vector $\beta(U)$ has the special feature that all its coordinates are determined by a single draw of the uniform variable U. Thus, in contrast to most of the literature on random coefficient models – typically those employing multivariate Gaussian structure – marginal distributions of the coefficients $\beta_j(U)$ from (2.20) can take a quite arbitrary form but are tied together by a strong form of dependence. Implicit also in the formulation of model (2.20) is the requirement that $Q_Y(\tau|x)$ is monotone increasing in τ for all x. In some circumstances, this necessitates restricting the domain of x; in other cases, when the coordinates of x are themselves functionally dependent, monotonicity may hold globally.

To illustrate, consider the quadratic model

$$Q_Y(\tau|x(z)) = \beta_0(\tau) + \beta_1(\tau)z + \beta_2(\tau)z^2. \tag{2.22}$$

If $\beta_2(\tau) = 0$, and $\beta_0(\tau)$ and $\beta_1(\tau)$ are monotone increasing, then $Q_Y(\tau|x(z))$ is monotone in τ for any $z \geq 0$. However, under these conditions, unless $\beta_1(\tau)$ is a constant function, monotonicity will fail for some sufficiently negative values of z. This need not be considered a fatal flaw of the model, particularly in circumstances under which z is expected to be positive. The linear specification may provide a perfectly adequate approximation over the relevant domain. When $\beta_2(\tau)$ is nonzero, it is easy to find open neighborhoods of the parameter space for which monotonicity of $Q_Y(\tau|x(z))$ holds globally for all $z \in \mathbb{R}$. The distinction between specifications that are linear in parameters and those that are linear in variables needs to be kept in mind.

Evaluation of the monotonicity of a fitted function

$$\hat{Q}_Y(\tau|x) = x^\top \hat{\beta}(\tau) \tag{2.23}$$

at the observed design points $\{x_i : i = 1, \ldots, n\}$ is relatively straightforward and provides a useful check on model adequacy. At one central design point, monotonicity is assured by Theorem 2.5.

Of course if the coordinates of x are functionally related, as in the quadratic example, then $\bar{x}$ itself needs not be a valid design point. But the fact that $Q_Y(\tau|x)$ is monotone in τ at $\bar{x}$ means that it will also be monotone in τ *near* $\bar{x}$, and consequently we can reparameterize the model so that the random coefficients are comonotone. Comonotonicity was introduced by Schmeidler (1986) and plays an important role in variants of expected utility theory based on the Choquet integral discussed in Section 3.9.

Definition 2.2. *Two random variables $X, Y : \Omega \to \mathbb{R}$ are said to be comonotonic if there exists a third random variable $Z : \Omega \to \mathbb{R}$ and increasing functions f and g such that $X = f(Z)$ and $Y = g(Z)$.*

A crucial property of comonotonic random variables is the behavior of the quantile functions of their sums. For comonotonic random variables X, Y, we have

$$F_{X+Y}^{-1}(u) = F_X^{-1}(u) + F_Y^{-1}(u).$$

This is because, by comonotonicity, we have $U \sim U[0, 1]$ such that $g(U) = F_X^{-1}(U) + F_Y^{-1}(U)$, where g is left-continuous and increasing, and so by monotone invariance of the quantile function we have $F_{g(U)}^{-1} = g \circ F_U^{-1} = F_X^{-1} + F_Y^{-1}$. In the language of classical rank correlation, comonotonic random variables are perfectly concordant (i.e., have rank correlation 1). The classical Fréchet bounds for the joint distribution function H of two random variables, X and Y, with univariate marginals F and G is given by

$$\max\{0,\, F(x) + G(y) - 1\} \leq H(x, y) \leq \min\{F(x), G(y)\}.$$

Comonotonic X and Y achieve the upper bound. The extremal nature of comonotonicity is further clarified by the following result.

Theorem 2.6 (Major, 1978). *Let X, Y be random variables with marginal distribution functions F and G, respectively, and finite first absolute moments. Let $\rho(x)$ be a convex function on the real line; then*

$$\inf E\rho(X - Y) = \int_0^1 \rho(F^{-1}(t) - G^{-1}(t))dt,$$

where the inf is over all joint distributions, H, for (X, Y) having marginals F and G.

It is easy to see that the bound is achieved when X and Y are comonotonic because, in this case, for $U \sim U[0, 1]$, we have

$$E\rho(X - Y) = E\rho(F^{-1}(U) - G^{-1}(U)) = \int_0^1 \rho(F^{-1}(u) - G^{-1}(u))du.$$

Mallows (1972) formulates Major's result for the special case of $\rho(u) = u^2$ and notes that it implies, among other things, that the maximal Pearson correlation of X and Y occurs at the Fréchet bound, where

$$\max \int xy\, dF(x, y) = \int_0^1 F^{-1}(t)G^{-1}(t)dt.$$

It is dangerous to leap immediately to the conclusion that the random coefficient vector in quantile regression model (2.20), $\beta(U)$, should be comonotonic. In fact, in most parameterizations of the model there is no reason to expect that the functions $\beta_i(\tau)$ will be monotone. What is crucial is that there exists a reparameterization that does exhibit comonotonicity. Recall from Theorem 2.3 that we can always reparameterize (2.20) as

$$Q_Y(\tau|x) = x^\top A A^{-1} \beta(\tau) = z^\top \gamma(\tau). \tag{2.24}$$

Suppose that we now choose $p = \dim(\beta)$ design points $\{x^k : k = 1, \ldots, p\}$ where model (2.20) holds. This is always possible for x^ks sufficiently close to $\bar{x}$. The matrix A can be chosen so that $Ax^k = e^k$, the kth unit basis vector. Then for any x^k we have that, conditional on $X = x^k$,

$$Y = (e^k)^\top \gamma(U) = \gamma_k(U). \tag{2.25}$$

Inside the convex hull of the x^k points, that is, conditioning on a point $x = \sum w_k x^k$ for $0 \le w_k \le 1$ with $\sum w_k = 1$, we have

$$Y = \sum w_k \gamma_k(U) \tag{2.26}$$

and we have a comonotonic random coefficient representation of the model. In effect, we have done nothing more than reparameterize the model so that the coordinates

$$\gamma_k(\tau) = F_{Y|X}^{-1}(\tau | x^k) \quad k = 1, \ldots, p$$

are the conditional quantile functions of Y at the points x^k. The fact that quantile functions of weighted sums of comonotonic random variables with nonnegative weights are weighted sums of the marginal quantile functions allows us to interpolate linearly between the chosen x^k. Of course, linear extrapolation is also possible, but, as usual, with extrapolation we should be cautious.

The simplest example of the foregoing theory is the two-sample treatment-control model. If we write the model to estimate the Lehmann treatment effect as in (2.3), then there is no particular reason to expect that the parameter $\delta(\tau) = G^{-1}(\tau) - F^{-1}(\tau)$ will be monotone increasing. However, if we reparameterize the model as in (2.2), then we clearly have monotonicity in both coordinates of the population parameter vector.

2.7   INEQUALITY MEASURES AND THEIR DECOMPOSITION

The extensive literature on the measurement of inequality has devoted considerable attention to the problem of decomposing, or attributing, changes in inequality to various causal factors. An important class of inequality measures for this purpose is based on Gini's mean difference,

$$\gamma = (2\mu)^{-1} E|X - Y|.$$

Gini's γ measures inequality in the distribution of wealth by computing the expected disparity in two random draws, X and Y, from the prevailing distribution of wealth, normalized by mean wealth μ. This might be interpreted as a measure of "expected envy" for two randomly selected members of the society. A more convenient definition for present purposes for the Gini coefficient is formulated by considering the Lorenz curve.

Let Y be a positive random variable with distribution function F_Y and mean $\mu < \infty$; then the Lorenz curve may be written in terms of the quantile function of Y, $Q_Y(\tau) = F_Y^{-1}(\tau)$, as

$$\lambda(t) = \mu^{-1} \int_0^t Q_Y(\tau) d\tau.$$

The Lorenz curve describes the proportion of total wealth owned by the poorest proportion t of the population. Gini's mean difference may be expressed as

$$\gamma = 1 - 2 \int_0^1 \lambda(t)dt,$$

that is, as twice the area between the $45°$ line and the Lorenz curve.

A family of such inequality measures allowing the investigator to accentuate the influence of certain ranges of wealth can be formulated by considering monotone transformations of Y. Let $\mu_h = Eh(Y)$, and write

$$\lambda_h(t) = \mu_h^{-1} \int_0^t Q_{h(Y)}(\tau)d\tau = \mu_h^{-1} \int_0^t h(Q_Y)(\tau)d\tau.$$

Thus, for example, by considering log wealth rather than wealth itself, we can downplay the influence of the upper tail and focus more attention on the lower tail of the distribution.

The advantages of the Gini/Lorenz formulation of inequality measurement for exploring decompositions based on quantile regression is apparent if we consider the model

$$Q_{h(Y)}(\tau|x) = x^\top \beta(\tau)$$

for the conditional quantile functions of wealth. As a consequence, we have an immediate additive decomposition of the Lorenz curve,

$$\lambda_h(t|x) = \mu_h^{-1} \int_0^t Q_{h(Y)}(\tau|x)d\tau = \mu_h^{-1} \sum_{j=1}^p x_j \int_0^t \beta_j(\tau)d\tau,$$

and this yields an additive decomposition of the Gini coefficient as well. Such decompositions allow the investigator to explore the evolution of aggregate changes in Gini's coefficient over time: a portion of the change may be attributed to change in the distribution of the covariates, and another portion to changes in the "structure of wealth" as represented by the evolution over time of $\beta(\tau)$.

Doksum and Aaberge (2002) consider the decomposition of the Gini coefficient in somewhat more detail, and Machado and Mata (2001) have investigated related decompositions in the context of applications to wage inequality in labor economics. The asymptotic behavior of the Lorenz curve and related statistics has been extensively studied by Goldie (1977) and subsequent authors. A multivariate extension of the Lorenz/Gini approach is explored by Mosler (2002).

2.8 EXPECTILES AND OTHER VARIATIONS

We have seen that minimizing sums of asymmetrically weighted absolute errors yields the sample quantiles. What if we try to minimize asymmetrically weighted sums of squared errors, or use some other asymmetrically weighted loss function? This question has been explored by several authors, including

Aigner, Amemiya, and Poirier (1976), Newey and Powell (1987), Efron (1992), and Jones (1994). Minimizing the asymmetrically weighted least-squares criterion,

$$R(\xi) = \sum_{i=1}^{n} \tau(y_i - \xi)_+^2 + (1 - \tau)(y_i - \xi)_-^2, \qquad (2.27)$$

where u_+ and u_- denote the positive and negative parts of u; this yields what Newey and Powell (1987) call the expectiles. The central case, $\tau = 1/2$, gives the sample mean. This centering around the mean can be viewed as a virtue, as Efron has argued in the context of count data. But it also raises some concern about the robustness of estimation procedures designed for the expectiles and their interpretation. In contrast to the quantiles, which depend only on local features of the distribution, expectiles have a more global dependence on the form of the distribution. Shifting mass in the upper tail of a distribution has no impact on the quantiles of the lower tail, but it does have an impact on *all* the expectiles.

In location-scale settings, linear conditional quantile functions imply linear conditional expectile functions, and so there is a convenient rescaling of the expectiles to obtain the quantiles. But in more complicated settings, the relationship between the two families is more opaque. Figure 2.10 illustrates a

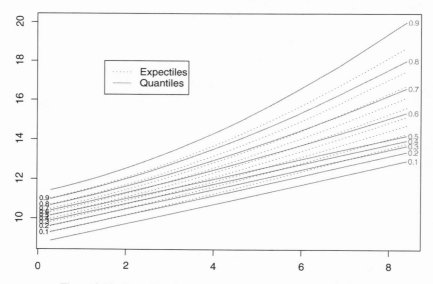

Figure 2.10. Quantiles and expectiles. Families of conditional quantile functions and their associated conditional expectile functions are illustrated. The model has linear quantile functions in the lower tail (i.e., with $\tau < 1/2$ and quadratic conditional quantile functions for $\tau > 1/2$. Note that all of the (dotted) expectile functions exhibit a nonlinearity that is induced by the nonlinearity of the (gray) quantiles in the upper tail.

family of conditional quantile functions that are linear in the lower tail, that is, for $\tau < 1/2$, but the quantile functions are quadratic functions of the covariate in the upper tail. The conditional expectile functions for this example, shown as dotted lines, exhibit nonlinearity throughout the entire range. See Problems 2.5 and 2.6.

2.9   INTERPRETING MISSPECIFIED QUANTILE REGRESSIONS

In the classical least-squares setting, if we consider the model

$$y_i = \theta(z_i) + u_i \tag{2.28}$$

with the $\{u_i\}$ iid from the distribution F, and independent of the z_i, but, mistakenly, we estimate the linear model,

$$y_i = \sum_{j=1}^{p} x_j(z_i)\beta_j + v_i, \tag{2.29}$$

then the least-squares estimator, $\hat{\beta} = (X^\top X)^{-1} X^\top y$, has the property that

$$\hat{\beta} \to E_Z(x(Z)x(Z)^\top)^{-1}x(Z)\theta(Z)$$

Thus, we can view the population version of the misspecified least-squares projection as occurring in two steps: in the first, the response y is projected to obtain the correct conditional mean response θ. In the second step, θ is projected into the linear subspace spanned by the columns of X. We may thus interpret the least-squares estimator $\hat{\beta}$ as an estimator of the best $\mathcal{L}_2$ approximation of the true conditional mean vector θ by a vector lying in the column space of X. This approximation is clearly dependent on the distribution of design points, because it minimizes the quantity $(\theta(Z) - x(Z)^\top b)^2$.

In quantile regression, the analysis of the consequences of misspecification is somewhat more complicated, but there is still a sense in which we have an $\mathcal{L}_2$ approximation of the true conditional quantile function by a function linear in parameters. The following result is due to Angrist, Chernozhukov, and Fernandez (2003) who provide a somewhat different proof.

Theorem 2.7. *Suppose Y has τth conditional quantile function $Q_Y(\tau|Z)$ and conditional density function $f_Y(\cdot|Z)$; then*

$$\beta(\tau) \equiv \mathrm{argmin}_{b \in \mathbb{R}^p} E\rho_\tau(Y - x(Z)^\top b)$$
$$= \mathrm{argmin}_{b \in \mathbb{R}^p} E_Z w(Z, b)\Delta^2(Z, b),$$

where $\Delta(Z, b) = x(Z)^\top b - Q_Y(\tau|Z)$ and

$$w(Z, b) = \int_0^1 (1 - u)f_Y(Q_Y(\tau|Z) + u\Delta(Z, b)|Z)du.$$

Proof. Let $U = Y - Q_Y(\tau|Z)$ and write

$$\beta(\tau) = \mathrm{argmin}_{b \in \mathbb{R}^p} E(\rho_\tau(U - \Delta) - \rho_\tau(U)).$$

Taking expectations of Y conditional on Z and then with respect to Z, and using Knight's (1998) identity (4.3), yields

$$E(\rho_\tau(U - \Delta) - \rho_\tau(U)) = E\left[\int_0^\Delta (I(U \le s) - I(U \le 0))ds - \Delta\psi_\tau(U)\right]$$

$$= E_Z\left[\int_0^\Delta (F_Y(Q_Y(\tau|Z) + s|Z) - \tau)ds\right]$$

$$= E_Z[R_Y(Q_Y(\tau|Z) + \Delta|Z) - R_Y(Q_Y(\tau|Z)|Z) - \tau\Delta)],$$

where $\psi_\tau(u) = \tau - I(u < 0)$ and $R_Y(s|Z) = \int_{-\infty}^s F_Y(t|Z)dt$. Now recall that for twice-differentiable functions g we have

$$g(b) = g(a) + (b - a)g'(a) + \int_a^b (b - x)g''(x)dx;$$

therefore, setting $b = a + \Delta$ and transforming $x \to a + u\Delta$, we have

$$g(a + \Delta) - g(a) = \Delta g'(a) + \Delta^2 \int_0^1 (1 - u)g''(a + u\Delta)du.$$

Setting $a = Q_Y(\tau|Z)$ and $g(s) = R_Y(s|Z)$ completes the proof. ■

Therefore, in misspecified situations the usual quantile regression estimator *does* minimize a quadratic measure of discrepancy between the true conditional quantile function and the best linear predictor thereof, but this measure of discrepancy must be weighted by a factor that depends on the conditional density of the response. When the discrepancy is small so that the conditional density is locally almost constant in the interval between $x(Z)^\top\beta(\tau)$ and $Q_Y(\tau|Z)$, then the weighting is simply proportional to $f_Y(Q_Y(\tau|Z)|Z)$, thus assigning more weight to regions of design space where the density is large, and estimation is consequently more accurate. It is interesting to contrast this weighting with the use of unweighted least squares estimation criteria in repeated measurement applications by, for example, Chamberlain (1994) and Bassett, Tam, and Knight (2002).

2.10   PROBLEMS

Problem 2.1. The quantile treatment effect described in Section 2.1 assumes that subjects at the τth quantile of the control distribution will also fall at the τth quantile of the treatment distribution. Suggest some alternative models of the joint distribution of the control and treatment outcomes, *given fixed* *marginals*, and explain how knowledge of the joint distribution might be relevant to treatment assignment.

Problem 2.2. In many randomized treatment settings, *the copula is unidentified*. Explain the slogan in light of the preceeding problem and suggest ways that might be used to circumvent it by enriching the experimental setup.

Problem 2.3. Extend Corollary 2.2 to the p-sample problem with design matrix

$$X = \begin{bmatrix} 1_{n_1} & 0 & \cdots & 0 \\ 0 & 1_{n_2} & & \\ \vdots & & \ddots & \\ 0 & & & 1_{n_p} \end{bmatrix}.$$

Problem 2.4. Suppose we have the reformulated p-sample design matrix

$$X = \begin{bmatrix} 1_{n_1}, & 0 & \cdots & 0 \\ 1_{n_2} & 1_{n_2} & \vdots & \\ \vdots & \vdots & & 0 \\ 1_{n_p} & 0 & & 1_{n_p} \end{bmatrix};$$

express the regression quantile estimator $\hat{\beta}(\tau)$ in this case as

$$\hat{\beta}(\tau) = (\hat{\beta}_1(\tau), \hat{\delta}_2(\tau), \ldots, \hat{\delta}_p(\tau))',$$

where $\hat{\delta}_i(\tau) = \hat{\beta}_i(\tau) - \hat{\beta}_1(\tau)$, and interpret.

Problem 2.5. Show that, if the real-valued random variable Y has distribution function F with finite expectation μ, then the τth expectile of Y is the unique root of the equation

$$G(y) \equiv \frac{P(y) - yF(y)}{2(P(y) - yF(y)) + y - \mu} = \tau,$$

where $P(y) = \int_{-\infty}^{x} y \, dF(y)$. (Jones, 1994)

Problem 2.6. Because the expectiles and the quantiles in Figure 2.10 are quite different, one may ask: Are there distributions for which the quantiles and expectiles coincide? Show that the distribution function

$$F(y) = 1/2(1 + \text{sgn}(y)\sqrt{1 + 4/(4 + y^2)})$$

satisfies this requirement. Would minimizing $R(\xi)$ in (2.27) yield a consistent estimator of the expectiles for this distribution?

CHAPTER 3

Inference for Quantile Regression

This chapter provides a practical guide to statistical inference for quantile regression applications. In the earlier chapters, we have described a number of applications of quantile regression and provided various representations of the precision of these estimates; in this chapter and the one to follow, we will describe a variety of inference methods more explicitly. There are several competing approaches to inference in the literature and some guidance will be offered on their advantages and disadvantages. Ideally, of course, we would aspire to provide a finite-sample apparatus for statistical inference about quantile regression like the elegant classical theory of least-squares inference under independently and identically distributed (iid) Gaussian errors. But we must recognize that even in the least-squares theory it is necessary to resort to asymptotic approximations as soon as we depart significantly from idealized Gaussian conditions.

Nevertheless, we will begin by briefly describing what is known about the finite-sample theory of the quantile regression estimator and its connection to the classical theory of inference for the univariate quantiles. The asymptotic theory of inference is introduced with a heuristic discussion of the asymptotic behavior of the ordinary sample quantile; then a brief overview of quantile regression asymptotics is given. A more detailed treatment of the asymptotic theory of quantile regression is deferred to Chapter 4. Several approaches to inference are considered: Wald tests and related problems of direct estimation of the asymptotic covariance matrix, rank tests based on the dual quantile regression process, likelihood-ratio-type tests based on the value of the objective function under null and alternative models, and, finally, several resampling methods are introduced. The chapter concludes with a description of a small Monte Carlo experiment designed to evaluate and compare the foregoing methods.

3.1 THE FINITE-SAMPLE DISTRIBUTION OF REGRESSION QUANTILES

Suppose $Y_1, \ldots, Y_n$ are iid random variables with common distribution function F, and assume that F has a continuous density f in a neighborhood of

$\xi_\tau = F^{-1}(\tau)$ with $f(\xi_\tau) > 0$. The objective function of the τth sample quantile,

$$\hat{\xi}_\tau \equiv \inf_\xi \left\{ \xi \in \mathbb{R} \mid \sum_{i=1}^n \rho_\tau(Y_i - \xi) = \min! \right\},$$

is the sum of convex functions and, hence, is itself convex. Consequently, by the monotonicity of the gradient,

$$g_n(\xi) = \sum_{i=1}^n (I(Y_i < \xi) - \tau),$$

we have

$$\begin{aligned}
P\{\hat{\xi}_\tau > \xi\} &= P\{g_n(\xi) < 0\} \\
&= P\left\{ \sum I(Y_i < \xi) < n\tau \right\} \\
&= P\{B(n, F(\xi)) < n\tau\},
\end{aligned}$$

where $B(n, p)$ denotes a binomial random variable with parameters (n, p). Thus, letting $m = \lceil n\tau \rceil$ denote the smallest integer $\geq n\tau$, we may express the distribution function, $G(\xi) \equiv P\{\hat{\xi}_\tau \leq \xi\}$, of $\hat{\xi}(\tau)$, using the incomplete beta function, as

$$\begin{aligned}
G(\xi) &= 1 - \sum_{k=m}^n \binom{n}{k} F(\xi)^k (1 - F(\xi))^{n-k} \\
&= n \binom{n-1}{m-1} \int_0^{F(\xi)} t^{m-1} (1 - t)^{n-m} dt.
\end{aligned}$$

Differentiating yields the density function for $\hat{\xi}(\tau)$;

$$g(\xi) = n \binom{n-1}{m-1} F(\xi)^{m-1} (1 - F(\xi))^{n-m} f(\xi). \tag{3.1}$$

This form of the density can be deduced directly by noting that the event $\{x < Y_{(m)} < x + \delta\}$ requires that $m - 1$ observations lie below x, $n - m$ lie above $x + \delta$, and one lies in the interval $(x, x + \delta)$. The number of ways that this arrangement can occur is

$$\frac{n!}{(m-1)!1!(n-m)!} = n \binom{n-1}{m-1},$$

and each arrangement has the probability $F(\xi)^{m-1} (1 - F(\xi))^{n-m} [F(\xi + \delta) - F(\xi))]$. Thus,

$$P\{x < Y_{(m)} < x + \delta\} = n \binom{n-1}{m-1} F(\xi)^{m-1} (1 - F(\xi))^{n-m} f(\xi)\delta + o(\delta^2),$$

and we obtain (3.1) by dividing both sides by δ and letting it tend to zero.

This approach may also be used to construct confidence intervals for ξ_τ of the form

$$P\{\hat{\xi}_{\tau_1} < \xi_\tau < \hat{\xi}_{\tau_2}\} = 1 - \alpha,$$

where τ_1 and τ_2 are chosen to satisfy

$$P\{n\tau_1 < B(n, \tau) < n\tau_2\} = 1 - \alpha.$$

In the case of continuous F, these intervals have the remarkable property that they are distribution free; that is, they hold irrespective of F. In the case of discrete F, closely related distribution-free *bounds* for $P\{\hat{\xi}_{\tau_1} < \xi_\tau < \hat{\xi}_{\tau_2}\}$ and $P\{\hat{\xi}_{\tau_1} \leq \xi_\tau \leq \hat{\xi}_{\tau_2}\}$ may be constructed.

The finite-sample density of the regression quantile estimator, $\hat{\beta}(\tau)$, may be derived under iid errors from subgradient condition (2.5) introduced in the previous chapter in a manner much like the derivation of the density in the one-sample case given earlier.

Theorem 3.1 (Koenker and Bassett 1978). *Consider the linear model*

$$Y_i = x_i^\top \beta + u_i \quad i = 1, \ldots, n$$

with iid errors $\{u_i\}$ having a common distribution function F and strictly positive density f at $F^{-1}(\tau)$. Then the density of $\hat{\beta}(\tau)$ takes the form

$$g(b) = \sum_{h \in \mathcal{H}} P\{\xi_h(b) \in \mathcal{C}\} |X(h)| \prod_{i \in h} f\left(x_i^\top(b - \beta(\tau)) + F^{-1}(\tau)\right),$$

$$(3.2)$$

where $\xi_h(b) = \sum_{i \in \bar{h}} \psi_\tau(y_i - x_i b) x_i^\top X(h)^{-1}$ and $\mathcal{C}$ denotes   the   cube $[\tau - 1, \tau]^p$.

Proof. From Theorem 2.1, $\hat{\beta}(\tau) = b(h) \equiv (X(h))^{-1} Y(h)$ if and only if $\xi_h(b(h)) \in \mathcal{C}$. For any $b \in \mathbb{R}^p$, let $B(b, \delta) = b + [-\delta/2, \delta/2]^p$ denote the cube centered at b with edges of length δ and write

$$P\{\hat{\beta}(\tau) \in B(b, \delta)\} = \sum_{h \in \mathcal{H}} P\{b(h) \in B(b, \delta), \xi_h(b(h)) \in \mathcal{C}\} \quad (3.3)$$

$$= \sum_{h \in \mathcal{H}} E I(b(h) \in B(b, \delta)) P\{\xi_h(b(h)) \in \mathcal{C}|Y(h)\},$$

where the expectation is taken with respect to the vector $Y(h)$. The preceding conditional probability is defined from the distribution of $\xi_h(b(h))$, which is a discrete random variable (taking on 2^{n-p} values for each $h \in \mathcal{H}$). As $\delta \to 0$, this conditional probability tends to $P\{\xi_h(b) \in \mathcal{C}\}$; this probability is independent of $Y(h)$.

Now, divide both sides by Volume$(B(b, \delta)) = \delta^p$, and let $\delta \to 0$ to put things in density form. The conditional probability tends to $P\{\xi_h(b) \in \mathcal{C}\}$, which no longer depends on $Y(h)$. The other factor tends to the joint density of the vector $X(h)^{-1}Y(h)$ which, since

$$f_{Y(h)}(y) = \prod_{i \in h} f(y_i - x_i^\top \beta),$$

can be written as

$$f_{(X(h))^{-1}Y(h)}(b) = |X(h)| \prod_{i \in h} f\left((X(h)b)_i - x_i^\top \beta(\tau) + F^{-1}(\tau)\right)$$

$$= |X(h)| \prod_{i \in h} f\left(x_i^\top (b - \beta(\tau)) + F^{-1}(\tau)\right). \qquad (3.4)$$

Note that h, for which $X(h)$ is singular, contributes nothing to density. The result now follows by reassembling the pieces. ∎

Unfortunately, from a practical standpoint, the $\binom{n}{p}$ summands of (3.2) are not very tractable in most applications and, as in the least-squares theory, we must resort to asymptotic approximations for a distribution theory adaptable to practical statistical inference. In the next section, we try to provide a heuristic introduction to the asymptotic theory of quantile regression. A more detailed formal treatment of the asymptotic theory of quantile regression may be found in Chapter 4.

3.2 A HEURISTIC INTRODUCTION TO QUANTILE REGRESSION ASYMPTOTICS

The optimization view of the sample quantiles also affords an elementary approach to their asymptotic theory. Suppose $Y_1, \ldots, Y_n$ are iid from the distribution F and for some quantile $\xi_\tau = F^{-1}(\tau)$ assume that F has a continuous density f at ξ_τ with $f(\xi_\tau) > 0$. The objective function of the τth sample quantile,

$$\hat{\xi}_\tau \equiv \inf_\xi \{\xi \in \mathbb{R} | n^{-1} \sum \rho_\tau(Y_i - \xi) = \min!\},$$

as we have already noted, is the sum of convex functions and, hence, is itself convex. Consequently, its gradient

$$g_n(\xi) = n^{-1} \sum_{i=1}^n (I(Y_i < \xi) - \tau)$$

is monotone in ξ. Of course, when ξ equals one of the Y_i then this "gradient" needs the subgradient interpretation discussed earlier, but this is not crucial to the argument that follows.

The function g_n is clearly monotonically increasing in ξ and, by monotonicity, $\hat{\xi}_\tau$ is greater than ξ if and only if $g_n(\xi) < 0$, and so

$$P\{\sqrt{n}(\hat{\xi}_\tau - \xi_\tau) > \delta\} = P\{g_n(\xi_\tau + \delta/\sqrt{n}) < 0\}$$
$$= P\{n^{-1} \sum (I(Y_i < \xi_\tau + \delta/\sqrt{n}) - \tau) < 0\}.$$

Thus, we can reduce the asymptotic behavior of $\hat{\xi}_\tau$ to a DeMoivre–Laplace central limit theorem problem in which we have a triangular array of Bernoulli random variables. The summands take the values $(1 - \tau)$ and $-\tau$ with probabilities $F(\xi_\tau + \delta/\sqrt{n})$ and $1 - F(\xi_\tau + \delta/\sqrt{n})$, respectively. Expanding F, we have

$$Eg_n(\xi_\tau + \delta/\sqrt{n}) = (F(\xi_\tau + \delta/\sqrt{n}) - \tau) \to f(\xi_\tau)\delta/\sqrt{n}$$

and

$$V(g_n(\xi_\tau + \delta/\sqrt{n})) = F(\xi_\tau + \delta/\sqrt{n})(1 - F(\xi_\tau + \delta/\sqrt{n}))/n \to \tau(1 - \tau)/n,$$

and so we may set $\omega^2 = \tau(1 - \tau)/f^2(\xi_\tau)$ and write

$$P\{\sqrt{n}(\hat{\xi}_\tau - \xi_\tau) > \delta\} = P\left\{ \frac{g_n(\xi_\tau + \delta/\sqrt{n}) - f(\xi_\tau)\delta/\sqrt{n}}{\sqrt{\tau(1 - \tau)/n}} < -\omega^{-1}\delta \right\}$$

$$\to 1 - \Phi(\omega^{-1}\delta).$$

Therefore, we conclude that

$$\sqrt{n}(\hat{\xi}_\tau - \xi_\tau) \rightsquigarrow \mathcal{N}(0, \omega^2). \tag{3.5}$$

There are two influences on the precision of the τth sample quantile. The $\tau(1 - \tau)$ effect tends to make $\hat{\xi}_\tau$ more precise in the tails, but this would be typically dominated by the effect of the density term, which tends to make $\hat{\xi}_\tau$ less precise in regions of low density.

Extending the foregoing argument to consider the limiting form of the joint distribution of several quantiles, set $\hat{\zeta}_n = (\hat{\xi}_{\tau_1}, \ldots, \hat{\xi}_{\tau_m})$ with $\zeta_n = (\xi_{\tau_1}, \ldots, \xi_{\tau_m})$ and we obtain (see Problem 3.1)

$$\sqrt{n}(\hat{\zeta}_n - \zeta) \rightsquigarrow \mathcal{N}(0, \Omega), \tag{3.6}$$

where Ω is an $m \times m$ matrix composed of the following elements:

$$(\omega_{ij}) = (\tau_i \wedge \tau_j - \tau_i \tau_j)/(f(F^{-1}(\tau_i))f(F^{-1}(\tau_j))).$$

This result is the starting point of the large-sample theory for finite linear combinations of order statistics.

3.2.1   Confidence Intervals for the Sample Quantiles

Given an estimate of the nuisance parameter, ω, one can easily make confidence interval estimates for the parameter $\xi(\tau)$ based on the asymptotic approximation given in (3.5). But there is a more direct route to confidence intervals. Suppose we were interested in testing the hypothesis $H_0 : \xi(\tau) = \xi_0(\tau)$. Under this null hypothesis, the statistic

$$Z_n = \sum_{i=1}^{n} I(Y_i - \xi_0(\tau))$$

is binomial, $B(n, \tau)$, and so a test could be based on Z_n, rejecting H_0, if

$$T_n = n^{-1}Z_n - \tau$$

was too large in absolute value. Of course, we need to be able to evaluate how large "too large" is. A nice feature of this test is that it requires no auxiliary estimation of nuisance parameters and the null distribution of the test statistic is independent of the original distribution, F, of the observations. Note that T_n is precisely our gradient $g_n(\xi_0(\tau))$ evaluated at the hypothesized parameter $\xi_0(\tau)$.

To convert our test based on T_n to a procedure for constructing a confidence interval, we need to look for the set

$$C_\alpha = \{\xi : T_n(\xi) \text{ does not reject at level } \alpha\}.$$

Because $T_n(\xi)$ is piecewise constant and monotone increasing, we are restricted to a finite number of distinct confidence levels. Such intervals take a particularly simple form – they are intervals between two order statistics:

$$C_\alpha = [Y_{(L)}, Y_{(U)}],$$

where $Y_{(i)}$ denotes the ith-order statistic from the sample: $Y_1, Y_2, \ldots, Y_n$. The choice of the integers L and U can be determined directly from the exact binomial theory of T_n or may be approximated in large samples as

$$\{L, U\} = n\tau \pm c_{\alpha/2}\sqrt{n\tau(1 - \tau)},$$

where $c_{\alpha/2} = \Phi^{-1}(1 - \alpha/2)$. Zhou and Portnoy (1996) discuss extensions of these procedures for contructing prediction intervals for general quantile regression models. Prediction intervals based on estimated inter-quantile ranges are particularly well-suited to applications in which the predictive density is thought to be asymmetric. The rank test inversion procedures of Section 3.5.5 are also closely related to these procedures.

3.2.2   Quantile Regression Asymptotics with IID Errors

These results for the ordinary sample quantiles in the one-sample model generalize nicely to the classical linear regression model,

$$y_i = x_i^\top \beta + u_i,$$

with iid errors $\{u_i\}$. Suppose that $\{u_i\}$ have a common distribution function F with associated density f, with $f(F^{-1}(\tau_i)) > 0$ for $i = 1, \ldots, m$, and $n^{-1}\sum x_i x_i^\top \equiv Q_n$ converges to a positive definite matrix Q_0. Then the joint asymptotic distribution of the mp-variate quantile regression estimators $\hat{\xi}_n = (\hat{\beta}_n(\tau_1)^\top, \ldots, \hat{\beta}_n(\tau_m)^\top)^\top$ takes the form

$$\sqrt{n}(\hat{\xi}_n - \zeta) = (\sqrt{n}(\hat{\beta}_n(\tau_j) - \beta(\tau_j)))_{j=1}^m \leadsto \mathcal{N}(0, \Omega \otimes Q_0^{-1}). \qquad (3.7)$$

A formal discussion of this result is deferred until Section 4.3. In the iid error regression setting, the form of the $\beta(\tau_j)$ is particularly simple. The conditional quantile planes are parallel, and so, presuming that the first coordinate of β corresponds to the "intercept" parameter, we have $\beta(\tau) = \beta + \xi_\tau e_1$, where $\xi_\tau = F^{-1}(\tau)$ and e_1 is the first unit basis vector of $\mathbb{R}^p$. Because Ω takes the same form as in the one-sample setting, many of the classical results on L-statistics can be directly carried forward to iid error regression using this result. This result, which is essentially the content of Theorem 4.1 of Koenker and Bassett (1978), affords considerable scope for Wald-type inference in the quantile regression setting. Hypotheses that may be formulated as linear restrictions of the vector ζ are immediately subject to test using the limiting normal theory and its χ^2 adaptations.

3.2.3   Quantile Regression Asymptotics in Non-IID Settings

The classical iid error linear regression model yields a particularly simple form for the limiting distribution of the quantile regression estimator $\hat{\beta}(\tau)$. However, it might be argued that, in the location shift form of the iid error model, quantile regression is really superfluous; in this case any reasonable estimator of the conditional central tendency of the response, given the covariates, is perfectly adequate. In non-iid error settings like the conditional location-scale model introduced in Section 2.5, the asymptotic theory of $\hat{\beta}(\tau)$ is somewhat more complicated. As we shall show in Section 4.3, the limiting covariance matrix of $\sqrt{n}(\hat{\beta}(\tau) - \beta(\tau))$ takes the form of a Huber (1967) sandwich:

$$\sqrt{n}(\hat{\beta}(\tau) - \beta(\tau)) \rightsquigarrow \mathcal{N}\left(0, \tau(1 - \tau)H_n^{-1}J_n H_n^{-1}\right),$$

where

$$J_n(\tau) = n^{-1} \sum_{i=1}^n x_i x_i^\top$$

and

$$H_n(\tau) = \lim_{n \to \infty} n^{-1} \sum_{i=1}^n x_i x_i^\top f_i(\xi_i(\tau)).$$

The term $f_i(\xi_i(\tau))$ denotes the conditional density of the response, y_i, evaluated at the τth conditional quantile. In the iid case, these f_is are identical, and the sandwich collapses to the expression we have already considered. We are then faced with the relatively simple problem of estimating a density, or its reciprocal, at a point. However, in the non-iid case, we face a somewhat more challenging task.

The preceding approach may be extended easily to the problem of estimating asymptotic covariance matrices for distinct vectors of quantile regression parameters. In these cases we would like to estimate, the asymptotic covariance matrix for $\hat{\beta}(\tau_1), \ldots, \hat{\beta}(\tau_m)$ has blocks

$$\text{Acov}(\sqrt{n}(\hat{\beta}(\tau_i) - \beta(\tau_i)), \sqrt{n}(\hat{\beta}(\tau_j) - \beta(\tau_j)))$$
$$= [\tau_i \wedge \tau_j - \tau_i \tau_j]H_n(\tau_i)^{-1}J_n H_n(\tau_j)^{-1},$$

where i and j run from 1 to m. Thus, Wald tests, like the heteroscedasticity tests described earlier, that involve linear restrictions across several quantile regression parameter vectors can be easily carried out with the same machinery. It should be emphasized that this approach is computationally extremely efficient and, thus, is particularly attractive for large problems where bootstrapping and the rank test inversion approaches (discussed later) are computationally demanding.

3.3 WALD TESTS

The classical theory of linear regression *assumes* that the conditional quantile functions of the response variable, y, given covariates x, are all parallel to one another, implying that the slope coefficients of distinct quantile regressions will be identical. Covariate effects shift the location of the response distribution but do not change its scale or shape. In applications, however, as we have seen, quantile regression slope estimates often vary considerably across quantiles, and so an immediate and fundamental problem of inference in quantile regression involves testing for equality of slope parameters across quantiles. Some simple tests designed for this purpose were suggested by Koenker and Bassett (1982a). We will first introduce a simple version of these tests for the two-sample problem and then generalize to more complicated settings.

3.3.1   Two-Sample Tests of Location Shift

For the two-sample problem, these Wald tests correspond to tests of equality between the interquantile ranges of the two samples. Thus, they may be considered to be tests of homogeneity of scale or tests for heteroscedasticity. Consider the two-sample model

$$Y_i = \alpha_1 + \alpha_2 x_i + u_i,$$

where $x_i = 0$ for n_1 observations in the first sample and $x_i = 1$ for n_2 observations in the second sample. The τth regression quantile estimate of the "slope" parameter α_2 in this model is simply the difference between the τth sample quantiles of the two samples (see Problem 2.2). Thus, a test of the equality of the slope parameters across quantiles τ_1 and τ_2 is just a test of the hypothesis

$$\begin{aligned}
\alpha_2(\tau_2) - \alpha_2(\tau_1) &= (Q_2(\tau_2) - Q_1(\tau_2)) - (Q_2(\tau_1) - Q_1(\tau_1)) \\
&= (Q_2(\tau_2) - Q_2(\tau_1)) - (Q_1(\tau_2) - Q_1(\tau_1)) \\
&= 0,
\end{aligned}$$

that is, that the $(\tau_2 - \tau_1)$ interquantile ranges are identical for the two samples. By (3.7) the asymptotic variance of $\hat{\alpha}_2(\tau_2) - \hat{\alpha}_2(\tau_1)$ is given by

$$\sigma^2(\tau_1, \tau_2) = \left[\frac{\tau_1(1 - \tau_1)}{f^2(\xi_1)} - 2\frac{\tau_1(1 - \tau_2)}{f(\xi_1)f(\xi_2)} + \frac{\tau_2(1 - \tau_2)}{f^2(\xi_2)} \right] \left[\frac{n}{nn_2 - n_2^2} \right],$$

where $\xi_i = F^{-1}(\tau_i)$ and a test of the null hypothesis can be based on the asymptotic normality of the statistic,

$$T_n = (\hat{\alpha}_2(\tau_2) - \hat{\alpha}_2(\tau_1))/\hat{\sigma}(\tau_1, \tau_2).$$

Of course, it is obvious from the form of $\sigma^2(\tau_1, \tau_2)$ that it is necessary to estimate the nuisance parameters, $1/f(F^{-1}(\tau_1))$ and $1/f(F^{-1}(\tau_2))$, a topic which will be deferred to Section 3.4.1.

A variety of other tests are immediately suggested by this construction. For example, we can test that the symmetry of the response distribution under the treatment with the following hypothesis:

$$H_0: \qquad \alpha_2\left(\frac{1}{2} + \delta\right) - \alpha_2\left(\frac{1}{2} - \delta\right) - 2\alpha_2\left(\frac{1}{2}\right) = 0$$

for some $\delta \in (0, \frac{1}{2})$. The hypothesis

$$H_0: \qquad \alpha_1\left(\frac{1}{2} + \delta\right) - \alpha_1\left(\frac{1}{2} - \delta\right) - 2\alpha_1\left(\frac{1}{2}\right) = 0$$

focuses attention solely on the symmetry of the control distribution. Combining the two linear restrictions yields a test of the joint hypothesis that both the control and treatment distributions are symmetric. This leads us to the general linear hypotheses of the next section.

3.3.2   General Linear Hypotheses

More general hypotheses are easily accommodated by the Wald approach. For example, as Koenker and Bassett (1982b), we may consider a general linear hypothesis on the vector $\zeta = (\beta(\tau_1)^\top, \dots, \beta(\tau_m)^\top)^\top$ of the form

$$H_0: \ R\zeta = r$$

and test statistic

$$T_n = n(R\hat{\zeta} - r)^\top [RV^{-1}R^\top]^{-1}(R\hat{\zeta} - r),$$

where V_n is the $mp \times mp$ matrix with ijth block

$$V_n(\tau_i, \tau_j) = [\tau_i \wedge \tau_j - \tau_i\tau_j]H_n(\tau_i)^{-1}J_n(\tau_i, \tau_j)H_n(\tau_j)^{-1}, \qquad (3.8)$$

as at the end of the previous section. The statistic T_n is asymptotically χ_q^2 under H_0, where q is the rank of the matrix R. This formulation accommodates a wide variety of testing situations, from simple tests on a single quantile regression coefficient to joint tests involving several covariates and several distinct quantiles. Thus, for example, we might test for the equality of several slope coefficients across several quantiles; such tests provide a robust alternative to conventional least-squares-based tests of heteroscedasticity because they can be constructed to be insensitive to outlying response observations. The same formulation can, of course, be adopted to accommodate nonlinear hypotheses on the vector ζ by interpreting H_0 as the Jacobian of the nonlinear hypothesis. Newey and Powell (1987) discuss tests for symmetry employing this approach.

3.4 ESTIMATION OF ASYMPTOTIC COVARIANCE MATRICES

In this section we consider the problem of estimating the asymptotic covariance matrix. We begin with the iid error setting and then consider more general conditions.

3.4.1 Scalar Sparsity Estimation

It is a somewhat unhappy fact of life that the asymptotic precision of quantile estimates in general, and quantile regression estimates in particular, depend on the reciprocal of a density function evaluated at the quantile of interest – a quantity Tukey (1965) has termed the "sparsity function" and Parzen (1979) calls the quantile-density function. It is perfectly natural that the precision of quantile estimates should depend on this quantity because it reflects the density of observations near the quantile of interest; if the data are very sparse at the quantile of interest they will be difficult to estimate. On the other hand, when the sparsity is low, so that there are many observations near the quantile of interest, then the quantile will be more precisely estimated. Thus, to estimate the precision of the τth quantile regression estimate directly, the nuisance quantity

$$s(\tau) = [f(F^{-1}(\tau))]^{-1}$$

must be estimated, and this leads us into the realm of density estimation and smoothing. We shall see that it is possible to pull ourselves out of this swamp by the bootstraps, or related statistical necromancy, but we defer the exploration of these strategies a bit and begin by exploring the more direct approach of estimating the asymptotic covariance matrix.

Differentiating the identity $F(F^{-1}(t)) = t$, we find that the sparsity function is simply the derivative of the quantile function; that is,

$$\frac{d}{dt}F^{-1}(t) = s(t).$$

Therefore, just as differentiating the distribution function F yields the density function f, differentiating the quantile function F^{-1} yields the sparsity function s. It is therefore natural, following Siddiqui (1960), to estimate $s(t)$ by using a simple difference quotient of the empirical quantile function:

$$\hat{s}_n(t) = [\hat{F}_n^{-1}(t + h_n) - \hat{F}_n^{-1}(t - h_n)]/2h_n,$$

where $\hat{F}^{-1}$ is an estimate of F^{-1} and h_n is a bandwidth that tends to zero as $n \to \infty$. Choice of the bandwidth is discussed in Section 4.10.1.

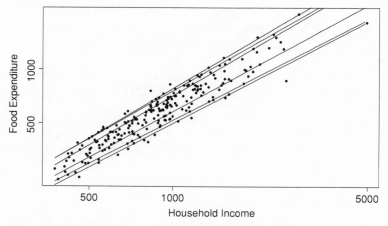

Figure 3.1. Engel curves for food. This figure plots data taken from Ernst Engel's (1857) study of households' expenditure on food versus annual income. The data consist of 235 observations on European working-class households. Superimposed on the plot are six estimated quantile regression lines corresponding to the quantiles $\tau \in \{0.05, 0.1, 0.25, 0.75, 0.9, 0.95\}$.

To illustrate the application of this approach, consider the data depicted in Figure 3.1. This is a classical data set in economics and is based on 235 budget surveys of 19th century working-class households. Household expenditure on food is measured vertically, and household income is measured horizontally. The data were originally presented by Ernst Engel (1857) to support his hypothesis that food expenditure constitutes a declining share of household income. Following established custom, we have transformed both variables to the logscale, so that a slope less than unity is evidence for Engel's law. We have superimposed six estimated linear conditional quantile functions for these data. The fitted lines look roughly parallel, but we might like a formal test of the hypothesis of equality of slopes. Focusing on the inner two lines, which represent the fit for the first ($\tau = 0.25$) and third ($\tau = 0.75$) quantiles, we find that the difference in the slopes is

$$\hat{\beta}_2(3/4) - \hat{\beta}_2(1/4) = 0.915 - 0.849 = 0.0661.$$

In Figure 3.2 we illustrate the function $\hat{Q}_Y(\tau|\bar{x})$ for this data set. The vertical scale is the natural logarithm of food expenditure. The dotted lines forming triangles illustrate the estimation of the sparsity function at the first and third quartiles. The Hall–Sheather bandwidth for both estimates is 0.097, yielding sparsity estimates of $\hat{s}(1/4) = 0.543$ and $\hat{s}(3/4) = 0.330$. The lower diagonal element of $(X^\top X)^{-1}$ is 0.022, and so the test statistic for the equality of the two slopes is 1.93, which has a p-value of 0.03 for a one-tailed test of the hypothesis of equality of the slopes. This result offers very weak evidence of increasing dispersion in the logarithm of food expenditure with income, a finding that may

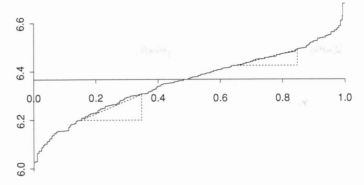

Figure 3.2. Sparsity estimation for the Engel data. This figure plots $\hat{Q}_Y(\tau|\bar{x}) = \bar{x}'\hat{\beta}(\tau)$ for the Engel data. The vertical scale is logarithmic in expenditure on food. The estimation of the sparsity function by the Siddiqui method is illustrated by the dotted triangles that depict the difference quotient estimator of the sparsity at the first and third quartiles. The estimate of the sparsity is given by the slope of the hypotenuse of the triangles. The Hall–Sheather bandwidth is 0.097 for this example.

seem surprising in view of Figure 3.1. In large samples, the formal statistical significance of such tests is extremely common. The substantive significance of such heteroscedasticity is, of course, completely open to question, too. It would be very surprising if such a small difference in slopes could be viewed as "economically significant."

There are obviously many other possible approaches to the estimation of the sparsity parameter. Welsh (1987) considers a kernel approach that may be interpreted as a weighted average of Siddiqui estimates in which those with narrow bandwidth are given greater weight. Another approach is suggested by simply fitting a local polynomial to $\hat{F}^{-1}(t)$ in the neighborhood of τ and using the slope of this fitted function at τ as an estimate of sparsity. Koenker and Bassett (1982a) employed the histospline methods of Boneva, Kendall, and Stefanov (1971) to estimate the sparsity function.

3.4.2   Covariance Matrix Estimation in Non-IID Settings

Two approaches to the estimation of the matrix H_n will be described. One is the natural extension of sparsity estimation methods described earlier, suggested by Hendricks and Koenker (1991). The other, which is based on kernel density estimation ideas, was proposed by Powell (1991).

The Hendricks–Koenker Sandwich

Provided that the τth conditional quantile function of $y|x$ is linear, then for $h_n \to 0$ we can consistently estimate the parameters of the $\tau \pm h_n$ conditional quantile functions by $\hat{\beta}(\tau \pm h_n)$. And the density $f_i(\xi_i)$ can thus be estimated by the difference quotient

$$\hat{F}_i(\xi_i(\tau)) = 2h_n/x_i^\top(\hat{\beta}(\tau + h_n) - \hat{\beta}(\tau - h_n)),$$

using the same choice of bandwidth mentioned earlier. Substituting this estimate in the expression for H_n preceding yields an easily implementable estimator for the asymptotic covariance matrix of $\hat{\beta}(\tau)$ in the non-iid error model. Note that the matrix J_n involves no nuisance parameters and thus is immediately computable.

A potential difficulty with the proposed estimator $\hat{F}_i(\xi_i(\tau))$ is that there is no guarantee of positivity for every observation in the sample. Indeed, as we have already seen, the quantity

$$d_i = x_i^\top(\hat{\beta}(\tau + h_n) - \hat{\beta}(\tau - h_n))$$

is *necessarily* positive only at $x = \bar{x} = n^{-1}\sum x_i$. Nevertheless, in practice we find that problems due to "crossing" of the estimated conditional quantile planes occur only infrequently and in the most extreme regions of the design space. In the implementation of this approach, we simply replace $\hat{F}_i$ by its positive part; that is, we use

$$\hat{F}_i^+ = \max\{0, 2h_n/(d_i - \varepsilon)\},$$

where $\varepsilon > 0$ is a small tolerance parameter intended to avoid dividing by zero in the (rare) cases in which $d_i = 0$ because the ith observation is basic at both $\tau \pm h_n$.

The Powell Sandwich

Powell has suggested an alternative, and in some respects even simpler, way to estimate the quantile regression sandwich. Noting that in estimating the matrix $H_n(\tau)$ we are really after a matrix weighted density estimator, he proposes a kernel estimator of the form

$$\hat{H}_n(\tau) = (nh_n)^{-1}\sum K(\hat{u}_i(\tau)/h_n)x_i x_i^\top,$$

where $\hat{u}_i(\tau) = y_i - x_i^\top\hat{\beta}(\tau)$ and h_n is a bandwidth parameter satisfying $h_n \to 0$ and $\sqrt{n}h_n \to \infty$. He shows that, under certain uniform continuity requirements on the f_i, $\hat{H}_n(\tau) \to H_n(\tau)$ in probability. In practice, of course, there remains a number of nettlesome questions about the choice of the kernel function K and the bandwidth parameter h_n. We will have more to say about this later when we describe a small Monte Carlo experiment designed to compare the performance of various confidence interval strategies for quantile regression.

Powell (1991) uses

$$\hat{H} = \frac{1}{2nc_n}\sum I(|\hat{u}_i| < c_n)x_i x_i^\top,$$

where $c_n \to 0$ and $\sqrt{n}c_n \to \infty$. In the R implementation of this approach, I use the default bandwidth

$$c_n = \kappa(\Phi^{-1}(\tau + h_n) - \Phi^{-1}(\tau - h_n)),$$

where κ is a robust estimate of scale. The bandwidth $h_n = \mathcal{O}(n^{-1/3})$, so $c_n = \mathcal{O}(n^{-1/3})$ and Powell's conditions are satisfied. Note that, as $h_n \to 0$,

$$\frac{\Phi^{-1}(\tau + h_n) - \Phi^{-1}(\tau - h_n)}{2h_n} \to \frac{1}{\phi(\Phi^{-1}(\tau))}.$$

3.5 RANK-BASED INFERENCE

The Wald approach to inference starts from the vantage point of the alternative hypothesis and asks the following question: Is it plausible that certain linear restrictions hold? Alternatively, we may consider starting at the null hypothesis and asking: Is there a direction to move in the space of alternative hypotheses that leads to more plausible estimates? This is the "score" approach of Rao (1947). Application of the score approach to quantile regression inference results in a remarkable confluence of statistical theory: score tests for quantile regression are, in effect, a class of generalized rank tests for the linear regression model. This observation was first made by Gutenbrunner and Jurečková (1992), who linked the dual quantile regression process to the classical Hájek (1965) rankscore functions, and was elaborated by Gutenbrunner, Jurečková, Koenker, and Portnoy (1993).

The works of Spearman (1904), Hotelling and Pabst (1936), Friedman (1937), and Kendall (1938) are generally credited with initiating the rank-based approach to statistical inference. The appearance of the work of Wilcoxon (1945), Mann and Whitney (1947), and Hoeffding (1948) on tests for location shift based on ranks, and the subsequent analysis of these tests by Hodges and Lehmann (1956) and Chernoff and Savage (1958), firmly established the subject as a precocious challenger to classical likelihood-based methods of inference. The rigorous reformulation of the asymptotic theory of rank tests introduced by Hájek (1965) and developed by Hájek and Šidák (1967) and others, in conjunction with the emergence of robustness as a major theme of statistical research in the late 1960s gave a significant impetus to the growth of rank-based methods.

3.5.1 Rank Tests for Two-Sample Location Shift

As an introduction to rank tests in an elementary setting, we may begin by comparing the performance of the Wilcoxon–Mann–Whitney test for location shift with the classical two-sample t-test. Let $X_1, \ldots, X_n$ be a random sample of "control" observations from the distribution function $F(x)$ and let $Y_1, \ldots, Y_m$ denote a random sample of "treatment" observations from $F(x - \theta)$. We assume at the outset that the treatment constitutes a pure location shift. Suppose we wish to test the hypothesis of "no treatment effect," $H_0 : \theta = 0$, against the alternative, $H_1 : \theta > 0$.

If F were known to be Gaussian, we would immediately compute the sample means $\bar{X}_n$ and $\bar{Y}_m$ and then compute the test statistic

$$T = (\bar{X}_n - \bar{Y}_m)/s,$$

where $s^2 = \sigma^2(n^{-1} + m^{-1})$, replacing σ^2 by

$$\hat{\sigma}^2 = (n + m - 2)^{-1} \left[\sum_{i=1}^{n}(X_i - \bar{X}_n)^2 + \sum_{i=1}^{m}(Y_i - \bar{Y}_m)^2 \right]$$

if necessary. If T exceeded $\Phi^{-1}(1 - \alpha)$, we would reject H_0 at level α if σ^2 were known, replacing the normal critical value by its corresponding t_{n+m-2} value if σ^2 needed to be estimated.

Mann and Whitney (1947) proposed an alternative to the two-sample t-test is based on the statistic

$$S_1 = \sum_{i=1}^{m} \sum_{j=1}^{n} I(Y_i > X_j).$$

We simply count the number of pairs of observations – one from each sample – for which the treatment observation exceeds the control observation. If S_1 is large, it suggests that treatment observations are generally larger than controls and H_0 should be rejected.

How is this connected to ranks? Wilcoxon (1945) suggests an alternative formulation: pool the two samples and compute the rank of each observation in the pooled sample. Let S_0 denote the sum of the treatment observation ranks; again, if S_0 is large, it suggests rejection of H_0. It is easy to show that, in the absence of ties,

$$S_1 = S_0 - m(m + 1)/2,$$

and so the Mann–Whitney and Wilcoxon forms of the test are actually equivalent. Efron (1967) suggests a very nice interpretation of a normalized version of the Wilcoxon statistic as an estimate of the probability associated with the region over which $G(x)$ exceeds $F(x)$. One of the most attractive features of this test is that its null distribution is independent of the form of F generating the original observations. To see this, let $Z_1, \ldots, Z_n$ denote $X_1, \ldots, X_n$ and let $Z_{n+1}, \ldots, Z_{n+m}$ denote $Y_1, \ldots, Y_m$. Under H_0, the Z_i are iid. Thus, for any permutation $(i_1, \ldots, i_{n+m})$ of $(1, \ldots, n + m)$, $(Z_{i_1}, \ldots, Z_{i_{n+m}})$ has the same distribution as $(Z_1, \ldots, Z_{n+m})$. Therefore, in the absence of "ties,"

$$\{R_1 = r_1, \ldots, R_{n+m} = r_{n+m}\} = \{Z_{i_1} < \cdots < Z_{i_{n+m}}\},$$

where R_i is the rank of the ith observation in the pooled sample and $r_{i_j} \equiv j$. It follows that the $(n + m)!$ possible events $\{R_1 = r_1, \ldots, R_{n+m} = r_{n+m}\}$ are equally likely. Because S_0 is a function solely of these ranks, its distribution under H_0 is also independent of F. For modest n, m we can compute exact critical values for the test based on combinatorial considerations (see, e.g., Lehmann, 1974, for details). For large n, m we can rely on the fact that, under H_0,

$$\tilde{S}_1 = (S_1 - \mu_1)/\sigma_1 \rightsquigarrow \mathcal{N}(0, 1),$$

where $\mu_1 = mn/2$ and $\sigma_1^2 = nm(n + m - 2)/12$. Even for modest sample sizes this approximation is quite good.

It is tempting to think that the main reason for preferring the Wilcoxon test to the t-test is the fact that it has a guaranteed probability of Type I error for quite arbitrary distributions of F, whereas the exact theory of the t-statistic depends on the normality of the observations. However, as long as F has a finite second moment and n and m are reasonably large, the critical values of the t distribution are also reasonably accurate for the t-statistic. It is power considerations that constitute the most compelling case for the Wilcoxon test under non-Gaussian conditions.

Exact power comparisons are rather impractical, but asymptotic results are very revealing. In the late 1940s Pitman proposed considering sequences of local alternatives of the form

$$H_n : \theta_n = \theta_0/\sqrt{n}$$

for precisely this problem, and showed that, at the normal model $F = \Phi$, the limiting ratio of sample sizes required to achieve the same size and power with the Wilcoxon and the t-test is $3/\pi \approx 0.955$. This ratio takes the general form

$$\mathrm{ARE} = \frac{12\sigma^2(F)}{\omega^2(F)},$$

where $\sigma^2(F)$ denotes the variance of the distribution F and

$$\omega^2(F) = \int_0^1 f(F^{-1}(t))dt = \int_{-\infty}^{\infty} f^2(x)dx,$$

which is usually referred to as the asymptotic relative efficiency, or ARE, of the two tests. It provides a natural measure of their relative performance. If, for example, at the normal model, 1000 observations are required to achieve power 0.95 at level 0.05 for a given alternative with the Wilcoxon test, this implies that the same power and level would be achievable with the t-test with roughly 955 observations. Therefore, transforming to ranks has "wasted" about 5% of the observations. This loss of information is hardly surprising because the optimality of the t-test at the normal model is a cornerstone of statistical thinking.

What happens in non-Gaussian situations? Table 3.1 presents the asymptotic relative efficiency of the Wilcoxon test relative to the t-test in the location shift problem for eight well-known Fs.

The striking feature of this table is not the modest loss of information at the normal model but the enormous gains achieved by transforming to ranks in

Table 3.1. *ARE of Wilcoxon and t-tests of location shift*

F	Normal	Uniform	Logistic	Exp	t_3	Exp	LNormal	t_2
ARE	.955	1.0	1.097	1.5	1.9	3	7.35	∞

certain non-Gaussian situations. We would need 50% more observations if we foolishly used the t-test instead of the Wilcoxon test at the double exponential distribution, and *seven times* as many observations at the lognormal distribution. In the latter case, note that, if we were clever enough to do the log transformation to get back to normality, the Wilcoxon test is unaffected, because ranks are invariant to monotone transformations. But the transformation to ranks achieves most of what we could have achieved had we known that the log transformation was appropriate. For extremely heavy-tailed distributions, the advantage for the rank test is even more pronounced.

The message of Table 3.1 is a familiar one from robust statistics: if we are willing to pay a small insurance premium (5% efficiency loss) at the Gaussian model we can protect ourselves against the extremely poor performance of least-squares-based methods in heavy-tailed situations. The 5% premium seems very modest, particularly in view of the huge improvement in the log-normal case, but one may wonder whether there are other plausible distributions for which the asymptotic relative efficiency of the two tests is even worse than 0.955 in the Gaussian case. This question was answered originally by Hodges and Lehmann (1956). To find the f that minimizes ARE, one must minimize the L_2 norm of the density subject to the constraint that the density has variance one. This turns out to be isomorphic to a standard problem in kernel density estimation. The least favorable density turns out to be the one generating the Epanechnikov kernel, and this solution gives a lower bound to the ARE of about 0.864. Thus, even in non-Gaussian cases, the t-test can never be more than about 15% better than the Wilcoxon test of location shift, but *can be arbitrarily worse* as indicated in the table.

3.5.2   Linear Rank Statistics

A more general approach to two-sample rank tests is suggested by considering the distribution of the ranks when the Xs are generated from $f(x)$ and the Ys from $f(y - \theta)$. Let R denote the vector of ranks from the combined sample $Z = (X_1, \ldots, X_n, Y_1, \ldots, Y_m)$:

$$f_R(r; \theta) = \int_{z_j = z_{(r_j)}} \prod_{k=1}^{n} f(z_k) \prod_{k=n+1}^{n+m} f(z_k - \theta) dz$$

$$= \int_{\xi_1 < \ldots < \xi_{n+m}} \prod_{j=1}^{n+m} f(\xi_{r_j}) \prod_{k=1}^{m} \frac{f(\xi_{r_k} - \theta)}{f(\xi_{r_k})} d\xi,$$

where $\xi_{r_j} = z_{(r_j)}$, $j = 1, \ldots, n + m$. But the density of the order statistics $Z_{(1)}, \ldots Z_{(n+m)}$ when $Z_1, \ldots Z_{n+m}$ are iid with density $f(z)$ is $(n+m)! \prod f(\xi_{r_k})$, and so

$$f_R(r; \theta) = ((n+m)!)^{-1} E_0 \prod_{k=1}^{m} \frac{f(\xi_{r_k} - \theta)}{f(\xi_{r_j})},$$

where E_0 designates that the expectation is taken with respect to the density $f(x)$, that is, under the null hypothesis that $\theta = 0$. For any fixed alternative θ, the optimal rank test could be computed as the likelihood ratio based on this expression for the density. A more practical option involves computing a locally most powerful test based on the score function

$$\frac{\partial \log f_R(R; \theta)}{\partial \theta} = - \sum_{j=1}^{n} E_0 \frac{f'(Z_{(R_j)})}{f(Z_{(R_j)})}.$$

To illustrate, suppose f is logistic, so that

$$f(z) = e^z/(1 + e^z)^2 = F(z)(1 - F(z)).$$

Then, $-f'(x)/f(x) = 2F(x) - 1$ and $F(Z(i)) = i/(n + m + 1)$, and so the locally most powerful rank test of $H_0 : \theta = 0$ is based on the sum of the ranks and hence *is* the Wilcoxon–Mann–Whitney test. In contrast, if f were Gaussian, so that $-f'(x)/f(x) = x$, we may approximate the optimal rank test by using the statistic

$$T_n = \sum_{i=1}^{n} \Phi^{-1}(R_i/(n + m + 1))$$

proposed by van der Waerden. Alternative approximations for $EZ_{(i)}$ with Z_i Gaussian have also been suggested (see, e.g., Hettmansperger, 1984). In general the approximate test statistic

$$T_n = \sum_{i=1}^{m} f'(F^{-1}(R_i/(n + m + 1)))/f(F^{-1}(R_i/(n + m + 1)))$$

may be used since $Z_{(i)} = F^{-1}(U_{(i)})$ where $U_1, \ldots, U_{n+m}$ are iid uniform on $(0, 1)$, and $EU_{(i)} = i/(n + m + 1)$.

3.5.3 Asymptotics of Linear Rank Statistics

The monograph of Hájek and Šidák (1967) constituted a complete reappraisal of the theory of rank statistics and provided an elegant general approach to the study of the asymptotic theory of linear rank statistics. For any sample $\{Y_1, Y_2, \ldots, Y_n\}$, and associated ranks $\{R_1, R_2, \ldots, R_n\}$, Hájek and Šidák introduced the rank-generating functions:

$$\hat{a}_i(t) = \begin{cases} 1 & \text{if } t \leq (R_i - 1)/n \\ R_i - tn & \text{if } (R_i - 1)/n \leq t \leq R_i/n \\ 0 & \text{if } R_i/n \leq t. \end{cases} \tag{3.9}$$

These functions "generate the ranks" of the Ys in the sense that, integrating with respect to Lebesgue measure,

$$\hat{b}_i = \int_0^1 \hat{a}_i(t)\, dt = (R_i - 1/2)/n,$$

and so the $\hat{b}_i$s *are* the ranks normalized to lie in the $(0, 1)$ interval. More general notions of "ranks" may be obtained by replacing Lebesgue measure by alternative score functions $\varphi(t)$. For example, $\varphi(t) = 1/2 sgn(t - 1/2)$ generates sign scores:

$$\hat{b}_i = \int \hat{a}_i(t)\, d\varphi(t) = \hat{a}_i(1/2) - 1/2 = \begin{cases} +1/2 & \text{if } R_i \geq n/2 + 1 \\ 0 & \text{otherwise} \\ -1/2 & \text{if } R_i \leq n/2. \end{cases}$$

The invariance of the ranks to monotone transformations of the Y_is means that the R_is may also be viewed as the ranks of the uniform random sample $\{U_1, \ldots, U_n\}$ with $U_i = F(Y_i)$, and the rank-generating functions $\hat{a}_i(t)$ may be seen as replacing the indicator functions $I(Y_i > F^{-1}(t)) = I(U_i > t)$ by the smoother "trapezoidal" form given by (3.9). The rank-generating functions behave like an empirical process as the following result shows.

Theorem 3.2 (Hájek and Šidák 1967, Theorem V.3.5). *Let* $c_n = (c_{11}, c_{21}, \ldots, c_{nn})$ *be a triangular array of real numbers satisfying*

$$\max(c_i - \bar{c})^2 / \sum_{i=1}^n (c_i - \bar{c})^2 \to 0 \tag{3.10}$$

and assume that $\{Y_1, \ldots, Y_n\}$ *constitute a random sample from an absolutely continuous distribution* F. *Then the process*

$$Z_n(t) = \left[\sum_{i=1}^n (c_i - \bar{c})^2 \right]^{-1/2} \sum_{i=1}^n (c_i - \bar{c})\hat{a}_i(t)$$

converges weakly to a Brownian bridge process on $C[0, 1]$.

In the two-sample problem, the c_{in}s may be taken simply as the indicator of which sample the observations belong to, and the "Lindeberg condition," (3.10), is satisfied as long as n_1/n stays bounded away from 0 and 1. A limiting normal theory for a broad class of linear rank statistics of the form

$$S_n = \left[\sum (c_{ni} - \bar{c}_n)^2 \right]^{-1/2} \sum (c_{ni} - \bar{c}_n)\hat{b}_i,$$

where $\hat{b}_i = \int \hat{a}_i(t) d\varphi(t)$, is immediate. In particular, for any square integrable $\varphi : [0, 1] \to \mathbb{R}$, we have the linear representation

$$S_n = \left[\sum (c_{ni} - \bar{c}_n)^2 \right]^{-1/2} \sum (c_{ni} - \bar{c}_n)\varphi(U_i) + o_p(1). \tag{3.11}$$

The score function φ can be chosen to target a variety of hypotheses, notably that the two samples differ by a location or scale shift. It follows that S_n is asymptotically Gaussian under the null with mean 0 and variance $A^2(\varphi) = \int (\varphi(t) - \bar{\varphi})^2 dt$, where $\bar{\varphi} = \int \varphi(t) dt$. Behavior under sequences of local alternatives can be studied using standard contiguity results.

Thus, for example, in the two-sample location shift model with local alternatives $H_n : \theta_n = \theta/\sqrt{n}$, we have S_n asymptotically Gaussian with mean $\omega(\varphi, F)(\sum(c_{in} - \bar{c}_n)^2)^{1/2}\theta$ and variance $A^2(\varphi)$, where

$$\omega^2(\varphi, F) = \int f(F^{-1}(t))d\varphi(t).$$

In the Wilcoxon case, φ is Lebesgue measure, and so $A^2(\varphi) = 1/12$ and $\omega^2 = \int f^2(x)dx$. Evaluating this expression yields Table 3.1. An important virtue of such rank tests is that the test statistic and its limiting behavior under the null hypothesis are independent of the distribution F generating the observations. The power of the test is obviously dependent on F, but the statistic itself does not require estimation of a nuisance parameter like the sparsity parameter required for the Wald tests or the error variance in the case of least-squares procedures.

3.5.4   Rank Tests Based on Regression Rankscores

How can these ideas be extended to general regression settings when, under the null, a nuisance regression parameter is present? This question was answered by Gutenbrunner and Jurečková (1992), who observed that the Hájek–Šidák rankscores may be viewed as a special case of a more general formulation for the linear model in which the functions $\hat{a}_{ni}(\tau)$ are defined as solutions of the linear program

$$\max\{y'a \mid X^\top a = (1 - \tau)X^\top 1_n, \ a \in [0, 1]^n\}, \tag{3.12}$$

where $[0, 1]^n$ is the n-dimensional unit cube and 1_n is an n-vector of ones. This problem is formally dual to linear program (1.15) defining the regression quantiles.

Whereas the primal quantile regression problem may be viewed as generating the sample quantiles, the dual problem may be seen to generate the order statistics or perhaps more precisely the *ranks* of the observations. What does the solution $\hat{a}(\tau)$ look like for the simplest dual problem? Clearly, at $\tau = 0$, feasibility requires that all of the $\hat{a}_i(0) = 1$, and similarly at $\tau = 1$, $\hat{a}_i(1) = 0$ for all $i = 1, \ldots, n$. Starting at $\tau = 0$, consider increasing τ. How should we modify the $\hat{a}_i$s? Initially we should focus on $y_{(1)} = \min\{y_1, \ldots, y_n\}$ because decreasing its weight has the least impact on the sum $y'a$. Thus, if $y_{(1)} = y_j$, then as τ increases a_j must decrease linearly to satisfy the equality constraint. This is fine until τ reaches $1/n$, but at this point a_j has been driven to 0 and it is allowed to go no further. Now $y_{(2)}$, being the smallest available response, is gradually downweighted, and the process continues until all the observations have achieved weight $a_i = 0$, at which point $\tau = 1$.

Thus, as we observed in Section 1.3, when X is simply an n-vector of ones, the Hájek rankscores $\hat{a}_i(\tau)$ take the value one for $\tau \leq (R_i - 1)/n$, where R_i is the rank of y_i in the sample $y_1, \ldots, y_n$ and $\hat{a}_i(\tau) = 0$ for $\tau > R_i/n$. In the interval $[(R_i - 1)/n, R_i/n)$, $\hat{a}_i(\tau) = R_i/n - \tau$, and so we have linear interpolation. More generally, in regression the rankscore functions need not be monotone decreasing, but $\hat{a}_i(\tau) = 1$ when (x_i, y_i) is below the fitted plane, $H(x) = x^\top \hat{\beta}(\tau)$, and $\hat{a}_i(\tau) = 0$ when $y_i > x_i^\top \hat{\beta}(\tau)$. For $\tau \in (0, 1)$ such that $y_i = x_i^\top \hat{\beta}(\tau)$, $\hat{a}_i(\tau)$ lies somewhere between zero and one.

In Figure 3.3 we illustrate the regression rankscores for the well-known stackloss data of Brownlee (1965). There are 21 daily observations on a plant designed for the oxidation of ammonia to produce nitric acid. There are three covariates and so four parameters are being estimated at each quantile. A curious feature of the data is that 8 of the 21 observations, numbers $\{6, 7, 13, 14, 16, 17, 18, 19\}$, have zero residuals at the $\tau = 0.25$ fit. The "rank" given above each subplot is the Wilcoxon "score," that is, the integral of the regression rankscore function with respect to Lebesgue measure.

Asymptotically, the quantile regression rankscore process, $\hat{a}_n(\tau)$, behaves like a weighted empirical process based on the "true" rankscores:

$$\tilde{a}_{ni}(\tau) = I\left(y_i > x_i^\top \beta(\tau)\right).$$

To explore this further, we consider the location-scale linear quantile regression model,

$$Q_{Y_i}(\tau|x_i) = x_i^\top \beta + \left(x_i^\top \gamma\right) F_u^{-1}(\tau),$$

arising from the iid error model

$$Y_i = x_i^\top \beta + \left(x_i^\top \gamma\right) u_i$$

with $\{u_i\}$ iid from distribution function F_u. Following Gutenbrunner and Jurečková (1992), we will denote the diagonal matrix with entries $x_i^\top \gamma$ by Γ_n and introduce a triangular array $\{v_{ni} : i = 1, \ldots, n\}$ of q-dimensional vectors. The residuals from the *weighted* least-squares projection of $V_n = (v_{ni})$ into the space spanned by $X_n = (x_{ni})$ will be written as

$$\tilde{V}_n = V_n - X_n \left(X_n^\top \Gamma_n^{-1} X_n\right)^{-1} X_n^\top \Gamma_n^{-1} V_n.$$

Linear rank statistics based on the regression rankscore process are obtained by simply integrating to obtain the "score" vector,

$$\hat{b}_{ni} = -\int_0^1 \varphi(\tau) d\hat{a}_{ni}(\tau),$$

where φ is a function of bounded variation that we will assume is constant outside $\mathcal{T} = [\varepsilon, 1 - \varepsilon]$ for some $\varepsilon \in (0, 1/2)$. Asymptotically, these rank statistics behave exactly as the corresponding statistics based on the original Hájek rankscores.

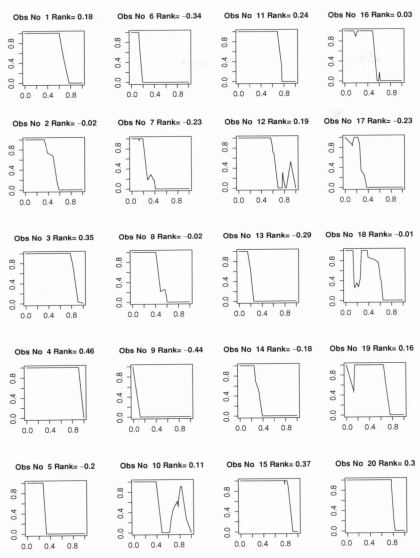

Figure 3.3. Regression rankscores for the stackloss data. For each of the 21 observations, the regression rankscore plots indicate the region of the unit interval for which response lies above the fitted quantile regression hyperplane ($\hat{a}_i(\tau) = 1$), below the fitted hyperplane ($\hat{a}_i(\tau) = 0$), and the region in which the response lies on the fitted hyperplane ($\hat{a}_i(\tau) \in (0, 1)$). Integrating the rankscore functions with respect to Lebesgue measure and subtracting $1/2$ yields the normalized "ranks" indicated above each panel of the plot.

For the classical Wilcoxon score function $\varphi(\tau) = \tau - 1/2$ centered at zero, integration by parts yields

$$\hat{b}_{ni} = -\int_0^1 (s - 1/2) d\hat{a}_{ni}(s)$$

$$= \int_0^1 \hat{a}_{ni}(s) ds - 1/2$$

$$= \sum_{j=1}^{J} \frac{1}{2}(\hat{a}_{ni}(\tau_{j+1}) - \hat{a}_{ni}(\tau_j)) - 1/2,$$

where the last sum is over the J breakpoints $\{\tau_j\}$ of the quantile regression process. As we see, this is just a recentered form of the rescaled ranks introduced earlier.

Regression rankscore tests play the role of Lagrange multiplier, or score, tests in quantile regression. Consider the model

$$Q_{Y_i}(\tau | x_i, z_i) = x_i^\top \beta(\tau) + z_i^\top \zeta(\tau)$$

with the associated null hypothesis,

$$H_0 : \zeta(\tau) = 0,$$

and local alternatives,

$$H_n : \zeta_n(\tau) = \zeta_0(\tau)/\sqrt{n}.$$

Estimating the restricted form of the model, we obtain

$$\hat{a}_n(\tau) = \text{argmax}\{y'a | X^\top a = (1 - \tau)X^\top 1_n, \ a \in [0, 1]^n\},$$

from which we can compute the test statistic,

$$T_n = S_n^\top M_n^{-1} S_n / A^2(\varphi), \tag{3.13}$$

where

$$S_n = n^{-1/2}(Z - \hat{Z})^\top \hat{b}_n$$
$$\hat{Z} = X(X^\top \Psi X)^{-1} X^\top \Psi Z$$
$$\Psi = \text{diag}(f_i(Q_{Y_i}(\tau | x_i, z_i)))$$
$$M_n = (Z - \hat{Z})(Z - \hat{Z})^\top / n$$
$$\hat{b}_n = \int_0^1 \hat{a}_n(s) d\varphi(s).$$

Koenker and Machado (1999) show under mild conditions on the score function φ that T_n has a limiting central χ_q^2 theory under the null, where q denotes the dimension of the parameter ζ. Under the local alternatives, T_n has a noncentral χ_q^2 theory with noncentrality parameter, $\eta(\varphi, \zeta) = \xi^\top M_n^{-1} \xi / A^2(\varphi)$, and $\eta(\varphi, \zeta, F) = \int_0^1 \zeta(s) f(F^{-1}(s)) d\varphi(s)$. Thus, T_n can be used either to explore a global effect of the covariates, Z, on the response Y, or by choosing the φ

to focus exclusively on a single τ as a purely local, quantile-specific test. We describe the latter strategy in more detail in the next subsection.

The choice of the score function φ should obviously be tailored to the plausible forms of the alternatives $\zeta_0(\cdot)$. In the simplest case that $\zeta_0(t) \equiv \zeta_0$, a fixed q-vector, z_i exerts a pure location shift effect; there is a large literature on classical rank tests for location shift to guide this selection. In this case, power is optimized as we have seen by choosing

$$\varphi(s) = \frac{-f'(F^{-1}(s))}{f(F^{-1}(s))}$$

so that $\int f(F^{-1}(s))d\varphi(s) = \int \varphi^2 ds = \mathcal{I}(F)$, the Fisher information for location of the innovation distribution. Similarly, we can consider tailoring the score function to the hypothesis that the z_is exert a pure scale shift. In either case, fully efficient tests can be designed under the (somewhat implausible) preconception that the innovation density is known.

There is a natural tendency to think that such rank tests sacrifice efficiency in comparison to conventional likelihood-based testing methods; however, as we have noted, this need *not* be the case. Indeed, it is worth recalling in this context the celebrated Chernoff–Savage result that the normal scores two-sample rank test of location shift has the same asymptotic power as the two-sample Student t-test at the Gaussian model and strictly *better* asymptotic power than the t-test for local alternatives with non-Gaussian innovations. This result generalizes to efficiency comparisons of the T_n tests described earlier with the classical regression F test in the location shift mode (see, e.g., Koenker, 1996; Hallin and Jurečková, 1999).

3.5.5 Confidence Intervals Based on Regression Rankscores

An important application of the foregoing general theory of rank tests involves the construction of confidence intervals for individual parameters of the quantile regression model. The score function

$$\varphi_\tau(t) = \tau - I(t < \tau)$$

enables us to focus the attention of the test entirely at the τth quantile. The median case

$$\varphi_{1/2}(t) = \frac{1}{2} \operatorname{sgn}\left(t - \frac{1}{2}\right)$$

is an important special case that is usually referred to as sign-scores.

Specializing to the scalar ζ case and using the τ-quantile score function

$$\varphi_\tau(t) = \tau - I(t < \tau)$$

and proceeding as before, we find that

$$\hat{b}_{ni} = -\int_0^1 \varphi_\tau(t)d\hat{a}_{ni}(t) = \hat{a}_{ni}(\tau) - (1 - \tau) \tag{3.14}$$

with $\bar{\varphi} = \int_0^1 \varphi_\tau(t)dt = 0$ and $A^2(\varphi_\tau) = \int_0^1 (\varphi_\tau(t) - \bar{\varphi})^2 dt = \tau(1 - \tau)$. A test of the hypothesis $H_0 : \zeta = \zeta_0$ may be based on $\hat{a}_n$ from solving

$$\max\{(y - z\zeta_0)^\top a | X^\top a = (1 - \tau)X^\top 1, a \in [0, 1]^n\} \qquad (3.15)$$

and the fact that

$$S_n(\zeta_0) = n^{-1/2} x_2^\top \hat{b}_n(\zeta_0) \rightsquigarrow \mathcal{N}\left(0, A^2(\varphi_\tau)q_n^2\right) \qquad (3.16)$$

under H_0, where $q_n^2 = n^{-1} z^\top (I - X(X^\top X)^{-1} X^\top) z$. That is, we may compute

$$T_n(\zeta_0) = S_n(\zeta_0)/(A(\varphi_\tau)q_n)$$

and reject H_0 if $|T_n(\zeta_0)| > \Phi^{-1}(1 - \alpha/2)$.

If we would like a confidence interval for ζ, we can invert this rank test, that is, find the values ζ_0 such that the test fails to reject. This takes us back to linear program (3.15), which may now be viewed as a one-parameter parametric linear programming problem in ζ. In ζ the dual vector $\hat{a}_n(\zeta)$ is piecewise constant; ζ may be altered without compromising the optimality of $\hat{a}_n(\zeta)$ as long as the signs of the residuals in the primal quantile regression problem do not change. When ζ gets to such a boundary, the solution does change, but optimality may be restored by taking one simplex pivot. The process may continue in this way until $T_n(\zeta)$ exceeds the specified critical value. Since $T_n(\zeta)$ is piecewise constant, linearly interpolating in ζ may be used to obtain the desired level for the confidence interval. See Beran and Hall (1993) for a detailed analysis of the salutary effect of interpolation like this in the case of confidence intervals for ordinary quantiles. This interval, unlike the Wald-type sparsity intervals, is not symmetric, but it *is* centered on the point estimate $\hat{\beta}_2(\tau)$ in the sense that $T_n(\hat{\beta}_2(\tau)) = 0$. This follows immediately from the constraint $X^\top \hat{a} = (1 - \tau)X^\top 1$ in the full problem.

The primary virtue of this approach is that it inherits the scale invariance of the test statistic T_n and therefore circumvents the problem of estimating the sparsity function. Implemented in R, using an adaptation of the algorithm described by Koenker and d'Orey (1993), it has essentially the same computational efficiency as the sparsity methods. A more detailed description of the computational aspects of the parametric programming problem is provided in Section 6.3.

3.6 QUANTILE LIKELIHOOD RATIO TESTS

Having now introduced variants of the Wald and score test for quantile regression, it is natural to investigate analogs of the likelihood ratio test as well. Koenker and Bassett (1982b) have shown that for median regression a test of the hypothesis

$$H_0 : R\beta = r \qquad (3.17)$$

in the iid-error linear model,

$$y_i = x_i^\top \beta + u_i, \tag{3.18}$$

could be based on the statistic

$$L_n = 8 \left(\tilde{V} \left(\frac{1}{2} \right) - \hat{V} \left(\frac{1}{2} \right) \right) / s \left(\frac{1}{2} \right), \tag{3.19}$$

where we will denote the value of the objective function at the unrestricted minimizer $\hat{\beta}(\frac{1}{2})$ by

$$\hat{V}(\tau) = \min_{\{b \in \mathbb{R}^p\}} \sum \rho_\tau \left(y_i - x_i^\top b \right) \tag{3.20}$$

and

$$\tilde{V}(\tau) = \min_{\{b \in \mathbb{R}^p | Rb = r\}} \sum \rho_\tau \left(y_i - x_i^\top b \right) \tag{3.21}$$

denotes the value under the restricted estimator $\tilde{\beta}(\tau)$. It was shown that under H_0, T_n is asymptotically χ_q^2 where $q = \text{rank}(R)$. That this statistic is related to a likelihood ratio is easy to see. Consider the standard Laplace (double exponential) density,

$$f(u) = \frac{1}{4} \exp \left(-\frac{1}{2} |u| \right).$$

Under the assumption that $\{u_i\}$ in (3.18) comes from this density, we have the log-likelihood

$$\ell(\beta) = -n \log(4) - \frac{1}{2} \sum_{i=1}^n \left| y_i - x_i^\top \beta \right|,$$

and the likelihood ratio statistic for testing H_0 would be

$$2(\ell(\hat{\beta}) - \ell(\tilde{\beta})) = 2(\tilde{V}(1/2) - \hat{V}(1/2)),$$

which we would expect to have a χ_q^2 asymptotic distribution under H_0. How does this relate to statistic (3.19)? Where does the factor 8 come from? Note that in the standard Laplace case $s(1/2) = (f(0))^{-1} = 4$, and so the usual theory of the likelihood ratio is vindicated – for this very special case, twice the log-likelihood ratio converges in distribution to χ_q^2 under H_0. However, when the standard Laplace assumption fails to hold, $s(1/2)$ may be quite different from 4 and the likelihood ratio statistic needs to be modified accordingly.

The simplest example of this, an example that yields another variant of the likelihood ratio, is the Laplace density with free scale parameter σ. Now,

$$f(u) = \frac{1}{4\sigma} \exp \left\{ -\frac{1}{2\sigma} |u| \right\},$$

and so the log-likelihood is

$$\ell(\beta, \sigma) = -n \log(4\sigma) - \frac{1}{2\sigma} \sum |y_i - x_i^\top \beta|.$$

It is easily seen that the maximum likelihood estimator of σ is

$$\hat{\sigma} = n^{-1} \hat{V}\left(\frac{1}{2}\right) = \frac{1}{2n} \sum |y_i - x_i^\top \hat{\beta}|$$

for the unrestricted model and, similarly, $\tilde{\sigma} = n^{-1} \tilde{V}(\frac{1}{2})$ is the maximum likelihood estimator under H_0. Concentrating the likelihood with respect to β we have

$$\ell(\hat{\beta}, \hat{\sigma}) = -n \log \hat{\sigma} - n - n \log 4,$$

and with an analogous definition of $\ell(\tilde{\beta}, \tilde{\sigma})$ the likelihood ratio statistic becomes

$$2(\ell(\hat{\beta}, \hat{\sigma}) - \ell(\tilde{\beta}, \tilde{\sigma})) = 2n \log(\tilde{\sigma}/\hat{\sigma}).$$

Again, we are entitled to expect that the likelihood ratio statistic will have a limiting χ_q^2 behavior. This can be easily checked using the earlier result by writing

$$\log(\tilde{\sigma}/\hat{\sigma}) = \log(1 + (\tilde{\sigma} - \hat{\sigma})/\hat{\sigma}) \approx (\tilde{\sigma} - \hat{\sigma})/\hat{\sigma}, \tag{3.22}$$

an approximation whose validity is easy to establish under the null. Dividing numerator and denominator by $\sigma \equiv E|u|$, and arguing that $\hat{\sigma}/\sigma \to 1$, we have

$$2n \log(\tilde{\sigma}/\hat{\sigma}) = 2n(\tilde{\sigma} - \hat{\sigma})/\sigma + o_p(1)$$
$$= 2(\tilde{V}(1/2) - \hat{V}(1/2))/\sigma + o_p(1). \tag{3.23}$$

Noting that $s(1/2) = 4\sigma$ in this case completes the argument.

Although the unknown-scale form of the Laplace model is certainly preferable to the original fixed-scale form, it is still unsatisfactory in that any departure from the condition $s = 4\sigma$ wreaks havoc with the asymptotic behavior of the test statistic under the null. As long as the errors are iid, this is easily rectified by defining the modified likelihood ratio statistics,

$$L_n(1/2) = 8(\tilde{V}(1/2) - \hat{V}(1/2))/s(1/2), \tag{3.24}$$

or again, using (3.22),

$$\Lambda_n(1/2) = 8n\sigma \log(\tilde{\sigma}/\hat{\sigma})/s(1/2), \tag{3.25}$$

which may be shown to be asymptotically equivalent with limiting χ_q^2 behavior. By directly evaluating the effect of the restriction on the mean absolute deviation from the median regression estimate, this result provides a useful complement to alternative Wald and score formulations of tests of H_0. The modified likelihood ratio tests obviously require estimation of the nuisance parameters σ and s, but this is quite straightforward. For σ we may simply use $n^{-1} \hat{V}(1/2)$, whereas for s we may use the sparsity estimation methods described earlier. It should be emphasized, however, that the foregoing theory for the likelihood ratio form of the test requires that the conditional density of the response be constant along the conditional median function. This would be true in the classical iid error model, where the covariates have a pure location-shift effect, but in more general settings one would need to reweight the terms in the objective function to obtain limiting χ^2 behavior.

The same approach we have elaborated for the median may be extended immediately to other quantiles. Define $\hat{V}(\tau)$ and $\tilde{V}(\tau)$ as in Section 3.2, let $\hat{\sigma}(\tau) = n^{-1}\hat{V}(\tau)$, $\tilde{\sigma}(\tau) = n^{-1}\tilde{V}(\tau)$, and for the τth quantile consider the test statistics

$$L_n(\tau) = \frac{2}{\lambda^2(\tau)s(\tau)}[\tilde{V}_n(\tau) - \hat{V}_n(\tau)]$$

and

$$\Lambda_n(\tau) = \frac{2n\hat{\sigma}(\tau)}{\lambda^2(\tau)s(\tau)} \log(\tilde{\sigma}(\tau)/\hat{\sigma}(\tau)),$$

where $\lambda^2(\tau) = \tau(1 - \tau)$. Tests of this sort based on the drop in the optimized value of the objective function of an M-estimator when relaxing the restriction imposed by the hypothesis are termed ρ-tests by Ronchetti (1985). Following this terminology, we will refer to tests based on $L_n(\tau)$ and $\Lambda_n(\tau)$ as quantile ρ-tests, although the phrase quasi-likelihood-ratio tests would also be appropriate.

3.7 INFERENCE ON THE QUANTILE REGRESSION PROCESS

We have seen that the regression rankscore process can be employed to construct regression analogs of the well-established rank tests of the location–scale-shift hypotheses developed for the p-sample model. They can also be adapted, using the quantile score function, to test the hypothesis that particular covariates exert no effect at selected quantiles. This ability to focus attention on particular quantiles is especially valuable because inference based on global hypotheses risks averaging out important effects. A finding that a covariate has no location-shift effect is sometimes taken to imply that it has no effect whatsoever. But it is not unusual to find situations in which a covariate exerts significant negative effects in one tail of the conditional distribution while exerting a positive effect in the other tail. These effects may cancel out in an evaluation of the "average" location effect but still be of substantial interest.

Classical goodness-of-fit tests offer a natural way to expand inference for the quantile regression model. Rather than asking, in the two-sample model, if the treatment distribution differs from the control distribution by a location shift, we ask instead if it differs in any way at all. This leads us to variants of the two-sample Kolmogorov–Smirnov and Cramér–von Mises tests. Rather than formulating tests based on the difference in empirical distribution functions, however, we can formulate tests based on differences in the empirical quantile functions. In the simplest two-sample setting we can consider the test statistic

$$T_n = \sup_{\tau \in \mathcal{T}} \left| G_m^{-1}(\tau) - F_n^{-1}(\tau) \right|,$$

where F_n and G_m denote the control and treatment empirical distribution functions, respectively. We will take $\mathcal{T}$ to be a closed subinterval of $(0, 1)$, typically $[\epsilon, 1 - \epsilon]$, for some $\epsilon \in (0, 1/2)$. Other forms of the test statistic based on L_p norms, for example,

$$T_n = \int_{\mathcal{T}} \left| G_m^{-1}(\tau) - F_n^{-1}(\tau) \right| d\tau$$

or

$$T_n = \left(\int_{\mathcal{T}} \left(G_m^{-1}(\tau) - F_n^{-1}(\tau) \right)^2 d\tau \right)^{-1/2},$$

may also be considered. The latter L_2 form of the test is closely related to Wasserstein distance; see, for example the discussion by Shorack and Wellner (1986) in their Section 2.6.

As we have seen in Chapter 2, the quantile treatment effect in the two-sample model,

$$\delta(\tau) = G^{-1}(\tau) - F^{-1}(\tau),$$

may be estimated by solving the bivariate quantile regression problem

$$(\hat{\alpha}(\tau), \hat{\delta}(\tau)) = \operatorname{argmin} \sum_{i=1}^{n} \rho_\tau(y_i - \alpha - x_i \delta),$$

where x_i is an indicator of the treatment; that is, $x_i = 1$ if y_i is a treatment response, and $x_i = 0$ if y_i is a control observation.

Under the null hypothesis that the treatment and control distributions are identical, tests based on the large sample theory of the rankscore, Wald, and ρ-processes just introduced can be constructed. Critical values of the tests can be evaluated by simulation of the underlying Brownian bridge approximations. Quantile regression offers a natural extension of these testing principles to the general linear regression setting. Covariates need not be binary, or even discrete. Given the standard model,

$$Q_{y_i}(\tau | x_i) = x_i^\top \beta(\tau), \tag{3.26}$$

we can formulate the null hypothesis,

$$H_0: R\beta(\tau) = r(\tau) \qquad \tau \in \mathcal{T}, \tag{3.27}$$

and consider tests of H_0 against the sequence of alternatives:

$$H_n: R\beta(\tau) - r(\tau) = \zeta(\tau)/\sqrt{n} \qquad \tau \in \mathcal{T}. \tag{3.28}$$

This might entail, for instance, the assertion that some subset of the covariates exert no influence on the conditional quantiles of the response over a specified range of quantiles, $\tau \in \mathcal{T}$. Such exclusion restrictions may be expressed by setting $R = [0 \vdots I_q]$ and $r(\tau) = 0$ for an appropriate partitioning of the parameter vector.

To investigate the asymptotic behavior of such statistics, we require some rather basic theory and notation regarding Bessel processes. Let $W_q(\tau)$ denote a q-vector of independent Brownian motions and, thus, for $\tau \in [0, 1]$,

$$B_q(t) = W_q(t) - \tau W_q(1)$$

will represent a q-vector of independent Brownian bridges. Note that, for any fixed $\tau \in (0, 1)$,

$$B_q(\tau) \sim \mathcal{N}(0, \tau(1 - \tau)I_q).$$

The normalized Euclidean norm of $B_q(\tau)$,

$$\mathcal{B}_q(\tau) = \| B_q(\tau) \| / \sqrt{\tau(1 - \tau)},$$

is generally referred to as a Bessel process of order q. Critical values for $\sup \mathcal{B}_q^2(\tau)$ have been tabled by DeLong (1981) and, more extensively, by Andrews (1993) using simulation methods. The seminal work on Bessel processes and their connection to K-sample goodness-of-fit tests is Kiefer's (1959). Again, for any fixed $\tau \in (0, 1)$ we have that $\mathcal{B}_q^2(\tau) \sim \chi_q^2$. Thus, we may interpret $\mathcal{B}_q^2(\tau)$ as a natural extension of the familiar univariate χ^2 random variable with q degrees of freedom. Note that, in the special case $q = 1$, $\sup \mathcal{B}_1^2(\cdot)$ behaves asymptotically like a squared Kolmogorov–Smirnov statistic.

To characterize the behavior of the test statistic under local alternatives, it is helpful to define a noncentral version of the squared Bessel process as an extension of the noncentral χ^2 distribution. Let $\mu(\tau)$ be a fixed, bounded function from $[0, 1]$ to $\mathbb{R}^q$. The standardized squared norm

$$\| \mu(\tau) + B_q(\tau) \|^2 / (\tau(1 - \tau))$$

will be referred to as a noncentral Bessel process of order q with noncentrality function $\eta(\tau) = \mu(\tau)^\top \mu(\tau) / (\tau(1 - \tau))$ and will be denoted by $\mathcal{B}_{q,\eta(\tau)}^2$. Of course, for any fixed $\tau \in (0, 1)$, $\mathcal{B}_{q,\eta(\tau)}^2 \sim \chi_{q,\eta(\tau)}^2$, a noncentral χ_q^2 random variable with q degrees of freedom and noncentrality parameter $\eta(t)$.

3.7.1 Wald Processes

Under null hypothesis (3.27), the Wald process,

$$v_n(\tau) = \sqrt{n}[RV(\tau, \tau)R^\top]^{-1}(R\hat{\beta}(\tau) - r(\tau)),$$

with $V(\tau, \tau)$ as in (3.8), converges weakly to a q-dimensional Brownian bridge. And under the sequence of local alternatives, the statistic

$$\mathcal{B}_n(\tau) = \| v_n(\tau) \| / \sqrt{\tau(1 - \tau)}$$

behaves asymptotically like a noncentral Bessel process with noncentrality parameter $\eta = \zeta^\top [RV(\tau, \tau)R^\top]^{-1}\zeta/(\tau(1 - \tau))$. Variants of this theory are considered in more detail by Koenker and Machado (1999).

3.7.2   Quantile Likelihood Ratio Processes

The quantile likelihood ratio, or ρ-tests, considered earlier can also be adapted to test hypothesis (3.27). However, as has been already emphasized, some reweighting of the terms in the objective function may be necessary to accommodate variation in the conditional density over the design space.

3.7.3   The Regression Rankscore Process Revisited

The regression rankscore process can also be used to formulate tests of null hypothesis (3.27). Reparameterizing, we can reduce the hypothesis to an exclusion restriction. Let P be a matrix such that $A = [P \vdots R]^\top$ is nonsingular and $R^\top P = 0$. Transforming

$$\tilde{y} = y - XR(R^\top R)^{-1}R^\top r(\tau)$$
$$\tilde{X} = XP(P^\top P)^{-1}$$
$$Z = XR(R^\top R)^{-1}$$

allows us to use test statistic (3.13) with the quantile score function $\varphi_\tau(t) = \tau - I(t < \tau)$. As shown by Koenker and Machado (1999), the resulting rankscore process,

$$T_n(\tau) = S_n^\top(\tau)M_n^{-1}S_n(\tau)/A^2(\varphi_\tau),$$

has the same noncentral Bessel process representation as the Wald process described earlier in this section.

3.8 TESTS OF THE LOCATION-SCALE HYPOTHESIS

At various stages we have considered the linear location–scale model

$$y_i = x_i^\top \alpha + \left(x_i^\top \gamma\right) u_i,$$

where the u_i are assumed to be iid from some distribution F_0. In this case, the conditional quantile functions of the response can be written as

$$Q_{y_i}(\tau|x_i) = x_i^\top \beta(\tau),$$

where $\beta(\tau) = \alpha + \gamma F_0^{-1}(\tau)$. Thus, all p components of the vector function β are – under the location-scale hypothesis – identical up to an affine transformation. Alternatively, we may wish to test the more restrictive hypothesis that we have a pure location-shift model so that $x_i^\top \gamma = 1$. In this section we will describe a general strategy designed to test such hypotheses. In the two-sample treatment control model, these hypotheses have the interpretation that the treatment and control distributions differ either by a location shift or by a location–scale shift. It is natural to consider tests of the Kolmogorov–Smirnov type; however, the introduction of unknown nuisance parameters into the null hypothesis raises some new and rather challenging issues.

The problem posed in this section is closely related to the classical problem of one-sample goodness-of-fit tests based on the empirical distribution function when there are unknown nuisance parameters under the null hypothesis. Rather than testing that observations arose from a *standard* normal distribution, we may wish to test that they arose from *some* normal distribution with unspecified mean and variance parameters. If, proceeding naively, we compute $\hat{\theta}_n = (\hat{\mu}_n, \hat{\sigma}_n)$, then construct the parametric empirical process

$$U_n(y) = \sqrt{n}(F_n(y) - F_{\hat{\theta}_n}(y)),$$

where $F_{\hat{\theta}_n}(y) = \Phi((y - \hat{\mu}_n)/\hat{\sigma}_n)$, and compute the Kolmogorov–Smirnov statistic,

$$K_n = \sup \| U_n(y) \|,$$

close examination of the limiting theory shows that U_n under mild conditions has a limiting Gaussian process, but with covariance function that depends on the estimation of the parameter θ. Consequently, K_n does not have the desired Kolmogorov–Smirnov distribution. There has been considerable discussion of various approaches to deal with this problem, notably the work of Durbin (1973).

Khmaladze (1981) offered the first general approach to these one-sample goodness-of-fit problems with estimated parameters. Fortunately, Khmaladze's general approach extends naturally to the related problems in the quantile regression setting. This has been explored by Koenker and Xiao (2002).

As we have seen, in the location-scale model, the process

$$\sqrt{n}\varphi_0(\tau)\Omega^{-1/2}(\hat{\beta}(\tau) - \beta(\tau))$$

converges on compact sets; $\mathcal{T} \subset (0, 1)$ to a p-dimensional independent Brownian bridge process. Here, $\varphi_0(\tau) = f_0(F_0^{-1}(\tau))$ and $\Omega = H_0^{-1} J_0 H_0^{-1}$ with $J_0 = \lim n^{-1} \sum x_i x_i^\top$ and $H_0 = \lim n^{-1} \sum x_i x_i^\top /(\gamma^\top x_i)$. And so it follows that a test of the hypothesis

$$R\beta(\tau) = r(\tau)$$

can be based on the process

$$v_n(\tau) = \sqrt{n}\varphi_0(t)(R\Omega R^\top)^{-1/2}(R\hat{\beta}(\tau) - r(\tau)),$$

provided that R and r are completely specified. Nuisance parameters involving φ_0 and Ω can be replaced without jeopardizing the first-order asymptotics of the tests. However, the location-scale shift hypothesis is not so straightforward.

Consider the problem of testing the pure location-shift hypothesis that all the slope coefficients of the quantile regression model are constant over $\tau \in \mathcal{T}$. We can write this in $R\beta = r$ form by taking $R = [0 \vdots I_{p-1}]$ and $r = (\alpha_2, \ldots, \alpha_p)^\top$: a fixed, but unknown vector. The natural expedient of replacing the unknown r in the test statistic by estimates introduces some fundamental difficulties. The process

$$\hat{v}_n(\tau) = \sqrt{n}\varphi_0(\tau)(R\Omega R^\top)^{-1/2}(R\hat{\beta}(\tau) - \hat{r}(\tau))$$

remains asymptotically Gaussian; however, the estimation of r introduces a new drift component that complicates the covariance kernel of the process and disrupts the asymptotically distribution-free character of the limiting theory. One way to resolve this difficulty, described in more detail in the next chapter, employs the Khmaladze (1981) martingale transformation. In effect, this involves replacing $\hat{v}(t)$ by the residual process obtained by a continuous time recursive least-squares regression of $\hat{v}_n(t)$ on the score functions defining the estimator of $\hat{r}$. After transformation, we have

$$\tilde{v}_n = Q_g \hat{v}_n \Rightarrow w_0,$$

a standard Brownian motion, with $p - 1$ independent coordinates. Tests based on the Kolmogorov–Smirnov-type statistic

$$K_n = \sup_{\tau \in \mathcal{T}} \|\tilde{v}_n(\tau)\|$$

then have easily simulated critical values.

The choice of the norm used in the definition of K_n is obviously also an issue. Koenker and Xiao (2002) suggested that the ℓ_1-norm avoids accentuating the effect of one or two extreme coordinates and therefore may be preferable to the usual Euclidean norm. The index set $\mathcal{T}$ is typically chosen to be an interval of the form $[\epsilon, 1 - \epsilon]$, but may be chosen to focus attention on one tail or some other feature of the distribution if this better suits the application. In some situations it is desirable to restrict the interval of estimation to a closed subinterval $[\tau_0, \tau_1]$ of $(0, 1)$. This can be easily accommodated by considering the renormalized test statistic

$$K_n = \sup_{\tau \in \mathcal{T}} \|\tilde{v}_n(\tau) - \tilde{v}_n(\tau_0)\| / \sqrt{\tau_1 - \tau_0}.$$

Koenker and Xiao (2002) illustrate the role of the foregoing tests in an application to model the effect of unemployment insurance rules on the duration of spells of unemployment. The data are taken from the Pennsylvania unemployment bonus experiments conducted in 1988–89. In this period, new claimants for unemployment insurance were randomized into one of several treatment groups or a control group. Control participants abided by the usual rules of the unemployment insurance system; treatment participants were offered a cash bonus to be awarded if the claimant was certifiably reemployed within a specified qualification period. For simplicity we will focus on only one of the treatment groups: those offered a bonus of six times their weekly benefit provided reemployment was established within 12 weeks. For this group the bonus averaged about $1000 for those collecting it. For a more detailed analysis incorporating the other treatments, see Koenker and Bilias (2001).

The model proposed to analyze the experimental data is the quantile regression model of the well-known accelerated failure time (AFT) model. Conditional quantiles of the logarithm of the unemployment durations (in weeks) are assumed to take the linear form

$$Q_{\log(T)}(\tau, x) = x^\top \beta(\tau).$$

There is an extensive set of covariates associated with each participant, but these were reduced to the following:

- Indicator for the treatment group.
- Indicators for female, black, and Hispanic respondents.
- Number of dependents, with 2 indicating two or more dependents.
- Indicators for the five quarters of entry to the experiment.
- Indicator for whether the claimant "expected to be recalled" to a previous job.
- Indicators for whether the respondent was "young" – less than 35 – or "old" – indicating age greater than 54.
- Indicator for whether claimant was employed in the durable goods industry.
- Indicator for whether the claimant was registered in one of the low unemployment short-unemployment-duration districts: Coatesville, Reading, or Lancaster.

The choice of the log transformation was dictated primarily by the desire to achieve linearity of the parametric specification and its convenience of interpretation. When the covariate effects influence only the location of the response $\log(T)$, we can write the restricted model as

$$\log(T_i) = x_i^\top \beta + u_i$$

with u_i iid, yielding the classical form of the AFT. Furthermore, if the distribution function of the errors takes the particular form $F(u) = 1 - e^{-e^u}$, then we have the Cox proportional hazard model with Weibull baseline hazard. It is natural to ask whether it is possible to formulate tests of these restrictions.

In Figure 3.4 we present the results from estimating model. We restrict the estimation to the interval [0.20, 0.80] because roughly 20% of the sample are immediately reemployed within the first week, and another 20% of the sample do not find work within the 26-week follow-up window of the experiment. These proportions depend to some degree on the nontreatment covariates of the model, but they are not dependent on the treatment, and so little is lost by treating them as fixed. The intercept plot in the upper left can be interpreted as the estimated quantiles of unemployment duration (in log weeks) for a white, middle-aged male entering the experiment in the first quarter, not expected to be recalled to his prior job, not previously employed in the durable

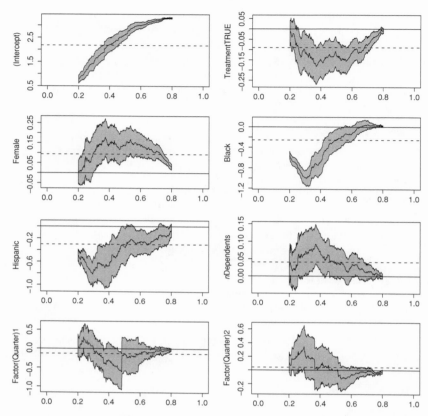

Figure 3.4. Quantile regression process for log duration model. A 90% point-wise confidence band for the quantile regression parameters is indicated by the shaded region. The solid horizontal line indicates $\beta = 0$, the null effect. The least-squares estimate is represented by the dashed line in each of the panels.

goods sector, and not from one of the low-unemployment counties. The treatment effect is not at all what we should expect from a location-shift model: there is essentially no treatment effect near the 0.2 and 0.8 cutoffs, but a rather substantial, almost 15% reduction in durations in the central region of the distribution. This is certainly as we might have expected to see, because the bonus should not have much effect on the extreme outcomes where the bonus is not at issue.

Glossing briefly over the other covariate effects, we find that women and older workers are generally slower to return to work than their younger male counterparts. Blacks and Hispanics also have significantly shorter durations than whites throughout most of the distribution. An expectation to be recalled to a previous job seems to exert a strong disincentive to return to work quickly, but

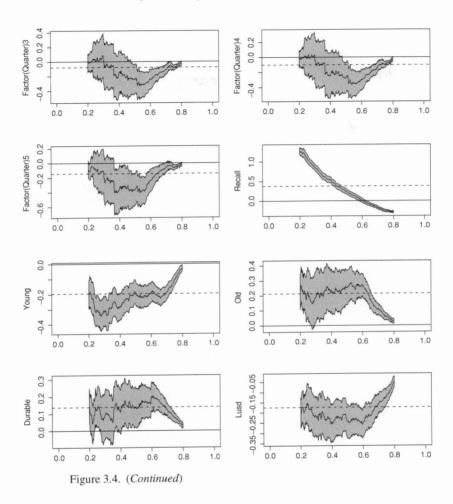

Figure 3.4. (*Continued*)

in the upper tail this reverses itself and there are a significant shorter durations above the 0.6 quantile.

Our tests of the location-and location–scale-shift hypotheses are based on a discretization of the quantile regression process to 301 equally spaced points on the interval [0.20, 0.80]. Recall that if the location-shift hypothesis holds then we would expect to see all the covariate plots in Figure 3.4 looking like random variation around a constant level. Whereas, if the location-scale shift model is appropriate, all the plots should appear as affine shifts of the intercept plot, and so all the coefficients should have roughly the same shape viewed as functions of τ. Neither of these visual impressions appears to be very promising based on Figure 3.4, but we may wish to have a more formal evaluation.

We will try to briefly describe the steps involved in computing the relevant test statistics. We begin by computing the estimates of the nuisance parameters: these are obtained for the location case by simply averaging over the set T, and for the location–scale case by regressing the slope components $\hat{\beta}_i(t), i = 2, \ldots, p$, on $\hat{\beta}_1(t)$ over the 301 "observations" in the set T. We then compute the difference between each coefficient and its prediction under the hypothesis and standardize the resulting $(p - 1)$-dimensional process to obtain $\hat{v}_n(t)$. To perform the transformation

$$\tilde{v}_n = Q_g \hat{v}_n,$$

we need to estimate the score functions $\dot{g} = (1, \dot{f}/f, 1 + F^{-1}\dot{f}/f)$. There is a moderately large literature dealing with the estimation of score functions. Koenker and Xiao (2002), following Portnoy and Koenker (1989), employ a variant of Silverman's (1986) adaptive kernel density estimator for the separate numerator and denominator components. Given the estimate of $\dot{g}$ based on the first (intercept) coordinate $\hat{\beta}_1$, the martingale transformation is just a recursive least-squares procedure whose residuals constitute the process $\tilde{v}_n$. At this point we can compute the test statistic K_n.

In this application we take $T = [0.25, 0.75]$ so that there is an additional 5% trimming designed to mollify the erratic behavior of the transformed process in the tails where the recursive estimation is least reliable. The norm is chosen to be $\|a\| = \sum |a_i|$, and we take $\tau_0 = 0.20$ and $\tau_1 = 0.80$. There are 15 slope coefficients under test, and so according to Table B.2 the 1% critical value for the test statistics is 16.00. Table 3.2 reports test statistics of 122.44 and 380.01 for the location–scale- and location-shift hypotheses, respectively. In both cases the superficial implausibility of the hypotheses suggested by the first plot is strongly confirmed by the formal test. Note that these values for the joint test differ slightly from those appearing in the original paper; the tests on the individual coefficients are unchanged.

It is of some independent interest to investigate which of the coordinates contribute "most" to the joint significance of the K_n statistic. This inquiry is fraught with all the usual objections to multiple testing because the coordinates are not independent; but we plunge ahead, nevertheless. In place of the joint hypothesis, we can consider univariate subhypotheses of the form

$$\beta_i(\tau) = \mu_i + \sigma_i \beta_1(\tau)$$

for each "slope" coefficient. In effect, this approach replaces the matrix standardization used for the joint test by a scalar standardization. The martingale transformation is then applied just as in the previous case. Table 3.2 reports the test statistics,

$$K_{ni} = \sup_{\tau \in T} |\tilde{v}_{ni}(\tau) - \tilde{v}_{ni}(\tau_0)|/\sqrt{\tau_1 - \tau_0},$$

for each of the covariates. Effects for the five quarters of entry are not reported. The critical values for these coordinatewise tests are 1.923 at 0.05 and 2.420 at 0.01, and so the treatment, race, gender, and age effects are highly significant.

Table 3.2. *Tests of the location–scale-shift hypothesis*

Variable	Location–scale shift	Location shift
Treatment	5.41	5.48
Female	4.47	4.42
Black	5.77	22.00
Hispanic	2.74	2.00
N-Dependents	2.47	2.83
Recall effect	4.45	16.84
Young effect	3.42	3.90
Old effect	6.81	7.52
Durable effect	3.07	2.83
Lusd effect	3.09	3.05
Joint effect	122.44	380.01

Also reported in Table 3.2 are the corresponding test statistics for the pure location-shift hypothesis. Not surprisingly, we find that the more restrictive hypothesis of constant $\beta_i(\tau)$ effects is considerably less plausible than the location–scale hypothesis. The joint test statistic is now 380.01, with 0.01 critical value of 16.00, and all of the reported covariate effects are significant at level 0.05, with the exception of the Hispanic effect.

3.9 RESAMPLING METHODS AND THE BOOTSTRAP

Assessing the accuracy of the sample quantiles was one of the earliest success stories for the bootstrap. As noted by Efron (1982), the classical delete-one jacknife estimate of the sampling variance fails for sample quantiles. Suppose $\hat{\theta}_n$ is the median of the sample $\{X_1, \ldots, X_n\}$ and let $\hat{\theta}_{(i)}$ denote the median with the ith observation deleted; then the jacknife estimate of the variance of the median is

$$v_n = \frac{n-1}{n} \sum_{i=1}^{n} \left(\hat{\theta}_{(i)} - \hat{\theta}_{(\cdot)} \right)^2,$$

with $\hat{\theta}_{(\cdot)} = n^{-1} \sum \hat{\theta}_{(i)}$. As we have seen, the asymptotic variance of $\sqrt{n}(\hat{\theta}_n - F^{-1}(1/2))$ should equal $1/(2f^2(F^{-1}(1/2)))$; but for $n = 2m$,

$$v_n = \frac{n-1}{4}(x_{m+1} - x_m)^2,$$

and, thus,

$$nv_n \rightsquigarrow \frac{1}{4f^2(F^{-1}(1/2))} \left(\frac{\chi_2^2}{2} \right)^2,$$

where $(\chi_2^2/2)^2$ is a random variable with mean 2 and variance 20. Thus, v_n markedly overstates the sampling variability of the median "on average" and fails to converge to the correct asymptotic variance. In such cases, the delete-one distributions are too close to the empirical distribution of the original sample; the bootstrap rectifies this. By resampling from the empirical, with replacement, the bootstrap distributions differ from the original empirical by $\mathcal{O}(1/\sqrt{n})$, whereas the delete-one distributions differ only by $\mathcal{O}(1/n)$. In this case, this leads to a difference quotient estimate of the density that has too narrow a bandwidth, thus exaggerating its variability.

There is quite an extensive literature on the use of the bootstrap and related resampling schemes for quantile regression. Efron (1982, pp. 35–6) suggested the residual bootstrap for a nonlinear median regression problem, and this form of the bootstrap has been considered by De Angelis, Hall, and Young (1993a), Buchinsky (1994), Hahn (1995), and several others. In the linear quantile regression setting, let

$$\hat{\beta}(\tau) = \operatorname{argmin} \sum \rho_\tau \left(y_i - x_i^\top b \right)$$

and let $\hat{F}_n$ denote the empirical distribution of the residuals, $\hat{u}_i = y_i - x_i \hat{\beta}(\tau)$, with respect to this fit:

$$\hat{F}_n(u) = n^{-1} \sum_{i=1}^n I(\hat{u}_i < u).$$

Now, consider drawing bootstrap samples $u_i^*, \ldots, u_n^*$ from $\hat{F}_n(u)$; with replacement, set $y_i^* = x_i \hat{\beta}(\tau) + u_i^*$ and compute

$$\beta_n^*(\tau) = \operatorname{argmin} \sum \rho_\tau \left(y_i^* - x_i^\top b \right).$$

DeAngelis *et al.* show that under iid error conditions the distribution of the bootstrapped β_n^*s,

$$\hat{G}(z) = P(\sqrt{n}(\beta_{nj}^*(\tau) - \hat{\beta}_{nj}(\tau)) \le z_j, \ j = 1, \ldots, p | \mathcal{X}),$$

conditional on the initial sample $\mathcal{X} = \{(x_i, Y_i) : i = 1, \ldots, n\}$ converges to the limiting distribution of $\sqrt{n}(\hat{\beta}_n(\tau) - \beta(\tau))$ and, furthermore, that the error of this approximation is of order $O(n^{-1/4})$ as $n \to \infty$.

To contrast this with the conventional strategy of directly estimating the asymptotic covariance matrix $\omega^2 D_0$, where $\omega^2 = \tau(1-\tau)/f^2(F^{-1}(\tau))$ and $D_0 = \lim n^{-1} \sum x_i x_i^\top$, they observe that $f(F^{-1}(\tau))$ can be estimated nonparametrically to $O(n^{-2/5})$ accuracy. Consequently, the error of approximation of the $\mathcal{N}(0, \hat{\omega}^2 D_0)$ approximation is also of order $O(n^{-2/5})$. This leads to the question of whether the residual bootstrap approximation can be improved by some further smoothing. DeAngelis *et al.* show that sampling from a smoothed version of $\hat{F}_n$ can yield improvement to $O(n^{-2/5})$ for the bootstrap. Knight (2002) provides an explicit form for the distribution of the $n^{1/4}$ normalized discrepancy between $\sqrt{n}(\beta_n^*(\tau) - \hat{\beta}_n(\tau))$ and the bootstrap form of its Bahadur representation.

In applications, we are rarely confident about the iid error, location-shift model and so the residual bootstrap is of limited practical interest for quantile regression. Fortunately, the (x, y) pair form of the bootstrap provides a simple, effective alternative for independent but not identically distributed settings. Instead of drawing bootstrap samples from the empirical distribution of the residuals as we have just described, we may draw samples of the (x_i, y_i) pairs from the joint empirical distribution of the sample. That is, (x_i^*, y_i^*) is drawn *with replacement* from the n pairs $\{(x_i, y_i) : i = 1, \ldots, n\}$ of the original sample, each with probability $1/n$. This form of the bootstrap has been widely used in applications of quantile regression.

Given the bootstrap realizations $\{\hat{\beta}_b^*(\tau) : b = 1, \ldots, B\}$, there are several options that have been considered for constructing tests and confidence intervals. Most straightforwardly, one can compute the empirical covariance matrix of the realizations and construct tests and confidence intervals directly from it. Alternatively, one can form percentile intervals as discussed, for example, by Efron and Tibshirani (1993). Many important practical aspects of the implementation of the bootstrap, including the crucial question of how to choose the number of replications, B, are treated by Andrews and Buchinsky (2000, 2001).

3.9.1   Bootstrap Refinements, Smoothing, and Subsampling

There have been several proposals for refinements of the (x, y) bootstrap based on smoothing. Horowitz (1998) considers smoothing the quantile regression objective function. Under sufficiently smooth conditional density conditions, using higher order kernels, he obtains refinements in the asymptotic accuracy of rejection probabilities based on bootstrap critical values for symmetrical t and χ^2 tests. For univariate quantiles, similar results for smoothed bootstrap procedures are developed by Janas (1993). Horowitz reports simulations showing that conventional $O(n^{-1/5})$ bandwidth rules for sparsity estimation yield too-conservative tests and confidence intervals for the unsmoothed median regression estimator, whereas his smoothed median regression approach appears somewhat less sensitive to bandwidth choice. It would be valuable to have further comparisons of performance including power and confidence interval length comparisons for competing methods. Note that this form of the bootstrap does not entirely escape the problem of estimating the sparsity and its attendant bandwidth issues; it merely advances these issues to an earlier stage of the process by inserting bandwidth choice into the objective function defining the modified median regression estimator. In this vein, it is perhaps also worth noting that other forms of smoothing, like the local L-statistic approach described in Section 5.2, might also be considered. This approach would be closer to that considered by De Angelis, Hall, and Young (1993b) in the univariate setting.

Buchinsky (1995) reports on an extensive Monte Carlo experiment comparing several variants of the bootstrap and concludes that the (x, y) pair, or design matrix version, performs well. A valuable feature of Buchinsky's experiments involves the decoupling of the size of the bootstrap samples, m, and the size of the original sample, n. The option of choosing $m \neq n$ was emphasized already by Bickel and Freedman (1981), but in much of the early bootstrap literature it is presumed that $m = n$. Buchinsky's results suggested that $m < n$ produced more accurate confidence levels than $m = n$ for the residual bootstrap, whereas performance is about the same for the (x, y) bootstrap. This is interesting for at least two reasons. Computationally, $m < n$ has very significant advantages, especially when n is very large. And from a theoretical standpoint, the observation is quite consonant with recent results of Bickel and Sakov (2000), who show that the $m < n$ bootstrap has significant advantages for approximating the behavior of the sample median. In effect, choosing $m < n$ acts as a smoothing device operating on the empirical distribution function. Bickel and Sakov (1999) suggested data-dependent rules for choosing m; theory suggests $m = kn^{2/5}$ and, rather surprisingly, numerical experiments indicate that the constant k can be chosen as small as one. For samples of size 1000, they find empirically optimal m: for the normal distribution, $m = 110$; for Cauchy, $m = 26$; and for logistic, $m = 14$. Compromising on an intermediate value, say $k = 5$, would yield $m \approx 80$ for $n = 1000$ and $m \approx 500$ for $n = 100,000$. Subsampling also appears to be an attractive option in inference based on the quantile regression process.

Another approach to refinement of inference for quantile regression is provided by the saddlepoint methods introduced by Daniels (1954). Spady (1991) has explored the saddle-point approach for the median regression estimator when the underlying conditional density of the response is bimodal. The saddle-point approximation performs extremely well in this setting closely mimicking the multi-modal behavior seen in the Monte-Carlo simulations. Recent work by de Jongh, de Wet, and van Deventer (2003) reenforces this positive impression of saddlepoint methods for quantile regression applications.

3.9.2   Resampling on the Subgradient Condition

The subgradient

$$S_n(b) = -n^{-1/2} \sum_{i=1}^{n} x_i \psi_\tau \left(y_i - x_i^\top b \right)$$

is a pivotal statistic when evaluated at $b = \beta(\tau)$ in the linear quantile regression model; that is, it has a distribution that is, independent of the parameter $\beta(\tau)$. Replacing $\beta(\tau)$ with an estimate yields an asymptotically pivotal quantity. This observation, due to Parzen, Wei, and Ying (1994), has been the source of a number of innovative resampling proposals for quantile regression. Since

$$\psi_\tau \left(y_i - x_i^\top b \right) = \tau - I \left(y_i \leq x_i^\top b \right),$$

we can generate independent Bernoulli random variables $\{\xi_i\}$, taking the value 1 with probability τ and 0 with probability $1 - \tau$, and compute

$$U_n = -n^{-1/2} \sum_{i=1}^{n} x_i(\tau - \xi_i).$$

For any realization, u_n, of U_n, we can find

$$\beta_n^* = \{b : S_n(b) = u_n\}$$

by solving the augmented quantile regression problem

$$\beta_n^* = \text{argmin}_{b \in \Re} \sum \rho_\tau(y_i - x_i b) + \rho_\tau\left(\zeta - n^{1/2} u_n^\top b / \tau\right),$$

where ζ is chosen to be sufficiently large to insure that it exceeds $n^{1/2} u_n^\top b / \tau$. This ensures that the contribution of the last term to the subgradient is

$$-n^{1/2} u_n = - \sum x_i(\tau - \xi_i)$$

and, thus, that $S_n(b) = u_n$ is satisfied.

To prove that $\sqrt{n}(\beta_n^* - \hat{\beta}_n)$ has the same asymptotic distribution as $\sqrt{n}(\hat{\beta}_n - \beta_0)$, it is first shown that, for $\| b - \beta_0 \| \leq n^{-1/3}$ and $\| b^* - \beta_0 \| < n^{-1/3}$,

$$\sup \| S_n(b^*) - S_n(b) - n^{-1/2} \sum x_i \left[\left(F_i\left(x_i^\top b^* - \beta_0\right)\right) - F_i\left(x_i^\top (b - \beta_0)\right)\right] \| \to 0$$

and then that

$$n^{-1/2} \sum x_i \left[F_i\left(x_i^\top (b^* - \beta_0)\right) - F_i\left(x_i^\top (b - \beta_0)\right)\right]$$
$$= n^{-1} \sum (f_i(0) + o(1)) x_i x_i^\top \sqrt{n}(b^* - b).$$

Now taking $b^* = \beta_n^*(\tau)$ and $b = \hat{\beta}_n(\tau)$ and noting that $S_n(\beta_n^*(\tau)) - S_n(\hat{\beta}_n(\tau)) = U_n$, we have that

$$\sqrt{n}(\beta_n^*(\tau) - \hat{\beta}_n(\tau)) \rightsquigarrow D_1^{-1} U_n,$$

from which the result follows.

The advantages of this resampling strategy have been exploited in recent work of Bilias, Chen, and Ying (2000) for the censored quantile regression model. For this model,

$$Q_{Y_i}(\tau | x_i) = \max\{0, x_i^\top \beta\}.$$

Powell (1986) suggested the estimator

$$\hat{\beta}_n(\tau) = \text{argmin}_{b \in \Re^p} \sum \rho_\tau\left(y_i - \max\left\{0, x_i^\top b\right\}\right),$$

which has very attractive statistical properties. However, as we have seen, computation of the Powell estimator is complicated by the nonconvexity of the objective function and this makes direct application of the (x, y) bootstrap problematic. This problem has been investigated in considerable detail by

Fitzenberger (1996). However, a simple modification of the (x, y) bootstrap based on computing

$$\hat{\beta}_n^*(\tau) = \text{argmin}_{b \in \Re^p} \sum \rho_\tau \left(y_i^* - x_i^\top b \right) I(x_i^* \hat{\beta}_n(\tau) > 0)$$

for (x_i^*, y_i^*) drawn with replacement from the empirical distribution of the $\{(x_i, y_i) : i = 1, \ldots, n\}$ succeeds in providing a bootstrap distribution that is correct to first order for $\sqrt{n}(\hat{\beta}_n(\tau) - \beta(\tau))$. Note that $\hat{\beta}_n(\tau)$ is fixed in the indicator function so that computing $\hat{\beta}_n^*(\tau)$ can be accomplished with conventional linear quantile regression algorithms, thus avoiding the nonconvexities introduced by the piecewise linear form of the response function.

A related approach has recently been proposed by He and Hu (2002). They consider generating a Markov chain resampler based on solutions to a marginal coefficient-by-coefficient version of the gradient condition for general M-estimation problems. This approach has been implemented for quantile regression by Kocherginsky, He, and Mu (2004) and seems especially attractive in large problems with high parametric dimension.

3.10 MONTE CARLO COMPARISON OF METHODS

I will conclude this chapter with a report on a small Monte Carlo experiment designed to compare the performance of some of the methods described earlier. I focus primarily on the computationally less demanding Wald and inverted rankscore methods and three of the resampling methods. Preliminary results indicated that the Hall and Sheather bandwidths performed considerably better than the Bofinger choice and so the reported results are restricted to this choice of bandwidth. We also focus exclusively on the problem of confidence intervals for the median regression parameters, partly because this is the most representative problem and also because it restricts the amount of computation and reporting required. Two models will be considered: one is a pure location-shift model the other involves a more complicated location–scale shift. All eight of the methods considered are implemented as options in the function `summary.rq` of the Quantreg package described in Appendix A. They include the following:

- `Riid` – rank test inversion assuming iid errors
- `Rnid` – rank test inversion assuming independent, not identically distributed (nid) errors
- `Wiid` – Wald interval assuming iid errors, with scalar sparsity estimate
- `Wker` – Wald interval assuming nid errors, with Powell's sandwich estimate
- `Wnid` – Wald interval assuming nid errors, with Siddiqui sandwich estimate
- `Bxy` – Bootstrap interval using (x, y) pair method
- `Bpwy` – Bootstrap interval using Parzen–Wei–Ying method
- `Bmcmb` – Bootstrap interval using Markov chain marginal bootstrap method

Table 3.3. *Confidence interval performance: model 1*

	Riid	Rnid	Wiid	Wker	Wnid	Bxy	Bpwy	Bmcmb
Coverage								
$n = 100$	0.889	0.897	0.871	0.981	0.860	0.919	0.936	0.909
$n = 500$	0.892	0.895	0.880	0.930	0.837	0.900	0.909	0.880
Length								
$n = 100$	0.313	0.322	0.308	0.464	0.303	0.355	0.367	0.337
$n = 500$	0.119	0.120	0.116	0.143	0.120	0.126	0.128	0.122
CPU time								
$n = 100$	0.052	0.206	0.041	0.012	0.039	0.091	0.110	0.128
$n = 500$	0.221	0.466	0.050	0.017	0.104	0.477	0.564	0.471

The Wald and bootstrap intervals are all based on estimating standard deviations; the rank inversion intervals are found by the parametric programming algorithm described in Section 3.5.5.

3.10.1 Model 1: A Location-Shift Model

As our first model, we consider a classical linear regression model in which the covariates have a pure location shift effect:

$$y_i = \beta_0 + \beta_1 x_{i1} + \cdots + \beta_p x_{ip} + u_i. \tag{3.30}$$

Quite arbitrarily, I've taken $p = 3$ and u_is to be iid Student t on three degrees of freedom, and each of the covariates is also independently generated from the $t(3)$ distribution. The coefficients are all set to zero and so the conditional median of the response given the covariates is identically zero. In Table 3.3 we report results for experiments for two different sample sizes, focusing exclusively on the conditional median. In all cases we report results for confidence intervals that are intended to have coverage 0.90. The results are based on 1000 replications of the simulation experiment. The bootstrap results are each based on 100 bootstrap replications. The reported timings are in fractions of a second for each method based on mean timings over the 1000 simulation realizations. The reported coverage and lengths are based on averaging over the 1000 realizations and over the three slope coefficients of the model. Reported confidence interval lengths are median lengths of the 3000 realizations; mean lengths are quite similar except in the case of the Rnid method, which has a small number of realizations with infinite length.

All of the methods perform quite well for this baseline model. The two Wald methods designed to adapt to non-iid error models exhibit some size distortion, but the remaining methods have quite accurate size and quite similar mean lengths. The Wald methods have a clear advantage from a computational efficiency viewpoint.

Table 3.4. *Confidence interval performance: model 2 (linear version)*

	Riid	Rnid	Wiid	Wker	Wnid	Bxy	Bpwy	Bmcmb
Coverage								
$n = 100$ b0	0.765	0.889	0.824	0.898	0.731	0.912	0.917	0.950
$n = 100$ b1	0.844	0.901	0.382	0.801	0.838	0.884	0.892	0.891
$n = 500$ b0	0.827	0.891	0.889	0.899	0.792	0.903	0.891	0.943
$n = 500$ b1	0.832	0.898	0.532	0.865	0.857	0.880	0.881	0.880
Length								
$n = 100$ b0	1.625	2.261	1.897	2.400	1.584	2.359	2.384	2.784
$n = 100$ b1	3.444	4.207	1.230	3.717	3.558	4.132	4.175	4.166
$n = 500$ b0	0.696	0.817	0.818	0.879	0.670	0.857	0.849	1.028
$n = 500$ b1	1.448	1.697	0.725	1.642	1.479	1.684	1.659	1.683
CPU time								
$n = 100$	0.039	0.118	0.041	0.012	0.035	0.056	0.073	0.085
$n = 500$	0.103	0.225	0.047	0.015	0.091	0.274	0.359	0.256

3.10.2   Model 2: A Location–Scale-Shift Model

In model 2 we consider a case in which a single covariate has an effect on both the location and scale of the conditional distribution of the response variable,

$$y_i = \beta_0 + \beta_1 x_i + (1 + x_i)^2 u_i. \tag{3.31}$$

In this model we take the u_i as iid standard normal, and the x_is are generated as $\chi_3^2/3$. As in the case of model 1, the design is drawn only once for the experiment. Again we take the coefficients $\beta_0 = \beta_1 = 0$, and so the conditional median of the response is identically zero. However, in contrast to model 1, where other conditional quantile functions of the response are parallel to the conditional median function and thus only the intercept parameter depends on the quantile specified, now quantile functions other than the median are quadratic in the covariate x. We consider two variants of this model for purposes of evaluating the confidence interval methods: one in which the quantile regression model is specified as linear in x at the median, the other in which it is specified as quadratic in x. In this phase of the experiment, it is more interesting to distinguish the performance of the various coefficients of the model, and so they are reported separately rather than averaging over them as in Table 3.3.

Table 3.4 reports the results from model 2, treating the estimated model as linear in variables. Not surprisingly, the methods based on the iid error assumption now perform rather poorly, but the rank inversion intervals based on the local density model perform quite well, as do the the bootstrap methods. Note that in this case the conditional quantile functions of the adjacent $\tau \pm h$ quantiles are assumed to be linear but are actually quadratic in x, and so the performance is better than might be expected.

Table 3.5. *Confidence interval performance: model 2 (quadratic version)*

	Riid	Rnid	Wiid	Wker	Wnid	Bxy	Bpwy	Bmcmb
Coverage								
$n = 100$ b0	0.712	0.850	0.883	0.894	0.825	0.906	0.932	0.935
$n = 100$ b1	0.696	0.852	0.478	0.727	0.824	0.875	0.907	0.820
$n = 100$ b2	0.752	0.846	0.297	0.514	0.776	0.863	0.912	0.802
$n = 500$ b0	0.747	0.878	0.891	0.874	0.840	0.905	0.913	0.923
$n = 500$ b1	0.774	0.898	0.530	0.812	0.868	0.896	0.906	0.859
$n = 500$ b2	0.804	0.895	0.289	0.661	0.853	0.881	0.900	0.842
Length								
$n = 100$ b0	1.790	2.590	2.505	2.394	2.404	2.685	2.892	3.079
$n = 100$ b1	5.872	8.352	3.742	5.824	8.241	8.939	9.775	8.280
$n = 100$ b2	3.280	4.394	1.049	1.725	4.217	4.730	5.202	4.366
$n = 500$ b0	0.852	1.153	1.168	1.087	1.145	1.212	1.234	1.337
$n = 500$ b1	2.901	3.998	1.782	3.154	3.940	4.151	4.229	3.734
$n = 500$ b2	1.702	2.178	0.526	1.379	2.195	2.291	2.353	2.107
CPU time								
$n = 100$	0.046	0.165	0.042	0.012	0.039	0.076	0.095	0.107
$n = 500$	0.178	0.392	0.049	0.016	0.100	0.402	0.493	0.363

Table 3.5 reports the results from model 2, treating the estimated model as quadratic in variables. Now it is of interest to distinguish the three separate coefficients. Again the rank-based intervals assuming nid errors perform quite well, as do the bootstrap procedures. The Wald nid intervals are somewhat overly optimistic. The computational cost of the rank-based methods is roughly comparable for the rank and bootstrap methods; however, larger sample sizes would reveal that the cost of the rank approach grows more rapidly with n than it does for the bootstrap.

3.11 PROBLEMS

Problem 3.1. Suppose $X_1, \ldots X_n$ are iid from df F with $f(x) = F'(x) > 0$ on the real line. Generalize (3.5) for a single quantile to obtain result (3.6) on the joint asymptotic distribution of several sample quantiles.

Problem 3.2. Let $X_1, \ldots, X_n$ be iid from F and denote the order statistics $X_{(1)}, \ldots, X_{(n)}$. Show that the probability that random interval $I_n(r) = [X_{(r)}, X_{(s)}]$ for $1 \le r \le s = n - r + 1$ covers the τth quantile $\xi_\tau = F^{-1}(\tau)$ is

$$P(\xi_\tau \in I_n(r)) \equiv P\left(X_{(r)} \le \xi_\tau \le X_{(s)}\right)$$
$$= P\left(X_{(r)} \le \xi_\tau\right) - P(X_{(s)} < \xi_\tau)$$
$$\ge C_n(r),$$

where

$$C_n(r) = \sum_{i=r}^{n-r} \binom{n}{i} \tau^i (1 - \tau)^{n-1}.$$

Equality holds in the last line if and only if (iff) F is continuous at ξ_τ.

Problem 3.3. An interesting extension of Problem 3.2 is provided by Guilbaud (1979), who shows that, for intervals of the form

$$I_n(r, t) = \left[\frac{X_{(r)} + X_{(r+t)}}{2}, \frac{X_{(s)} + X_{(s+t)}}{2} \right],$$

where $1 \leq r \leq s = n - r + 1$, and $0 \leq t < s - r$, we have, *for the median,*

$$P(\xi_{1/2} \in I_n(r, t)) \geq \frac{1}{2} C_n(r) + \frac{1}{2} C_n(r + t)$$

for general F, and for continuous, strictly increasing F,

$$P(\xi_{1/2} \in I_n(r, t)) \leq C_{n-t}(r)$$

with equality in the latter expression iff F is symmetric.

Problem 3.4. Show that the interval in Problem 3.1 may be interpreted as an inversion of the following sign test of the hypothesis $H_0 : \xi_\tau = \xi$: let Q_n be the number of observations $\{X_1, \ldots, X_n\}$ less than ξ. Because Q_n is Bin (n, τ), we can choose $\gamma \in (0, 1)$ and c_α such that, under H_0,

$$P(Q_n < c_\alpha)) + \gamma P(Q_n = c_\alpha) = \alpha$$

and reject H_0 when $Q_n < c_\alpha$ or with probability γ when $Q_n = c_\alpha$, for a one-sided alternative. For a two-sided alternative, we choose a corresponding upper critical value as well. Note that for n moderate to large we can approximate the binomial probabilities with their normal approximation (see e.g., Lehmann, 1959, Problem 3.28).

Problem 3.5. To explore a simple version of the asymptotics for quantile regression consider the scalar parameter (regression through the origin model)

$$y_i = x_i \beta + u_i,$$

where the u_is are iid and satisfy the F conditions of Problem 3.1. Formulate conditions on the design sequence $\{x_i\}$ which ensure that

$$\hat{\beta}_n = \text{argmin}_{b \in \mathbb{R}} \sum_{i=1}^{n} |y_i - x_i b|$$

satisfies

$$\sqrt{n}(\hat{\beta}_n - \beta) \rightsquigarrow N(0, \omega^2 Q^{-1})$$

and $Q = \lim n^{-1} \sum x_i^2$.

Problem 3.6 (Bofinger 1975). Show using standard density estimation techniques that the optimal bandwidth for minimum mean-squared error estimation of the sparsity function at τ is

$$h_n = n^{-1/5} \left(\frac{4.5 s^2(t)}{(s''(t))^2} \right)^{1/5}.$$

Of course, if we knew $s(t)$ and $s''(t)$ we wouldn't need h_n, but fortunately $s(t)/s''(t)$ is not very sensitive to F. Show that h_n is invariant to location and scale of F, for example. Compare h_n for some typical distributional shapes – say, the Gaussian, Student, and log-normal. Show

$$\frac{s(t)}{s''(t)} = \frac{f^2}{2(f'/f)^2 + [(f'/f)^2 - f''/f]}$$

and, for example, if f is Gaussian, $(f'/f)(F^{-1}(t)) = -\Phi^{-1}(t)$ so that the term in square brackets is 1, and the optimal bandwidth becomes

$$h_n = n^{-1/5} \left(\frac{4.5 \phi^4(\Phi^{-1}(t))}{(2\Phi^{-1}(t)^2 + 1)^2} \right)^{1/5}.$$

Plot this bandwidth, as a function of n for several quantiles, and compare the plots across the distributions. Sheather and Maritz (1983) discuss preliminary estimation of s and s'' as a means of estimating a plug-in h_n.

Problem 3.7. Compare the Sheather–Hall bandwidth rule given in the text with the Bofinger bandwidth of the preceding problem.

CHAPTER 4

Asymptotic Theory of Quantile Regression

Although the finite-sample distribution theory of regression quantiles can be represented explicitly as has been illustrated in Chapter 3, the practical application of this theory would entail a host of hazardous assumptions and an exhausting computational effort. It is generally conceded throughout statistics that approximation methods involving local linearization and the central limit theorem play an indispensable role in the analysis of the performance of statistical procedures and in rendering such procedures practical tools of statistical inference. The zealous pursuit of these objectives is inevitably met with accusations that we live in a cloud-cuckoo land of "asymptopia," but life is full of necessary compromises and approximations. And it is fair to say that those who try to live in the world of "exact results" in finite-sample statistical distribution theory are exiled to an even more remote and exotic territory.

Fortunately, there are many tools available to help us evaluate the adequacy of our asymptotic approximations. Higher order expansions, although particularly challenging in the present context, may offer useful assessments of the accuracy of simpler approximations and possible refinement strategies. Monte Carlo simulation can be an extremely valuable tool, and the rapid development of resampling methods for statistical inference offers many new options for inference.

The fundamental task of asymptotic theory is to impose some discipline and rigor on the process of developing statistical procedures. The natural enthusiasm that arises from the first few "successful" applications of a new technique can be effectively tempered by some precisely cast questions of the following form: suppose data arose according to the conditions A, does the procedure produce a result that converges in some appropriate sense to object B? Under what precise conditions does the procedure "work"? And, if possible, how well does it "work" relative to other competing procedures?

An important virtue of quantile regression, one that I have tried to stress throughout, is the interpretability of the conditional quantile functions as an natural objective for data analysis. The robustness literature on location estimation has introduced myriad criteria, all intended to capture the conditional central tendency of distributions. All these location functionals have the virtue that they agree in the convenient circumstance that the distributions in question are symmetric, but in the absence of symmetry they all differ. In regression the discrepancies are compounded by heteroscedasticity and other non-location-shift covariate effects. In contrast to these "obscure objects of desire," conditional quantile functions offer an easily interpretable objective for statistical analysis. This chapter will survey the existing literature on the asymptotic theory of quantile regression and describe how these results are used for inference.

4.1 CONSISTENCY

If quantile regression is to "work," a minimal asymptotic requirement should be consistency. Suppose that the τth conditional quantile function of Y given $X = x$ takes the parametric form

$$Q_Y(\tau | X = x) = g(x, \beta_0(\tau)).$$

Under what conditions does the estimator,

$$\hat{\beta}_n(\tau) = \text{argmin}_{\beta \in \mathbb{R}^p} \sum_{i=1}^{n} \rho_\tau(y_i - g(x_i, \beta)),$$

converge in probability to $\beta_0(\tau)$, that is, $\| \hat{\beta}_n(\tau) - \beta_0(\tau) \| \to 0$ as $n \to \infty$?

4.1.1 Univariate Sample Quantiles

The simplest setting is evidently the case of the ordinary univariate sample quantile,

$$\hat{\xi}_n(\tau) = \text{argmin}_{\xi \in \mathbb{R}} \sum_{i=1}^{n} \rho_\tau(y_i - \xi),$$

based on a random sample $\{y_1, \ldots, y_n\}$ from the distribution F. Suppose that F has a unique τth quantile, $\xi_0(\tau) = F^{-1}(\tau)$; does $\hat{\xi}_n(\tau) \to \xi_0(\tau)$? We have already seen that this can be easily deduced from the monotonicity of the subgradient as described in Section 2.2.2. It is also a direct consequence of the uniform convergence of the empirical distribution function, or Glivenko–Cantelli theorem, a result that Vapnik (1995) characterizes as "the most important result in the foundation of statistics."

Rates of convergence and the form of the limiting distribution of $\hat{\xi}_n(\tau)$ depend on the behavior of $\xi_0(\cdot)$ in a neighborhood of τ. As we have seen in Section 3.2, if F has a continuous density $f(F^{-1}(\tau))$ bounded away from 0 and ∞ near τ, then it is easy to show that

$$\sqrt{n}(\hat{\xi}_n(\tau) - \xi_0(\tau)) \rightsquigarrow \mathcal{N}(0, \omega^2),$$

where $\omega^2 = \tau(1 - \tau)/f^2(F^{-1}(\tau))$. When $f(F^{-1}(\cdot))$ has a singularity at τ, improvements on $O(1/\sqrt{n})$ convergence are possible, whereas slower rates may prevail in cases that $f(F^{-1}(\cdot))$ tends to 0 at τ. Smirnov (1952) provides a definitive catalog of these cases for independently and identically distributed (iid) observations. See Problems 4.1 to 4.3 for further details.

If F is actually flat in a neighborhood of $\xi_0(\tau)$, so that there exist $\xi_L(\tau) < \xi_U(\tau)$ such that

$$F(\xi_L(\tau) + 0) = F(\xi_U(\tau) + 0) = \tau,$$

then $\hat{\xi}_n(\tau)$ exhibits an inherent instability: we can say only that the sum of the probabilities that $\hat{\xi}_n(\tau)$ falls near $\xi_L(\tau)$ or $\xi_U(\tau)$ tends to 1 as $n \to \infty$. One may view this as a rather benign form of an identification problem: there is a *set* of population quantiles and all we can hope to achieve is that the sample quantile will approach *some element* of the set. Ellis (1998) has recently argued that this form of instability "casts doubt on the trustworthiness" of median-like methods. On the contrary, one could argue that such behavior is inherent in contexts where the estimand is set-valued and is not *statistically* harmful *per se*. Indeed, if the population quantile consisted of an interval, we would expect that any reasonable estimation method would yield confidence regions that contain this interval. And as long as the precision is accurately represented, the procedure cannot be faulted. Mizera (1999) offers a careful consideration of these issues grounded in formal set-valued analysis.

A necessary and sufficient condition that $\hat{\xi}_n(\tau) \to \xi_0(\tau)$ under iid sampling is simply that

$$F(\xi_0(\tau) - \varepsilon) < \tau < F(\xi_0(\tau) + \varepsilon)$$

for all $\varepsilon > 0$. Mizera and Wellner (1998) extend this to independent, but heterogeneously distributed, sampling by considering sequences $\{Y_i\}_{i=1}^n$ distributed as $\{F_{ni}\}_{i=1}^n$ with common τth quantile, $F_{ni}(\tau) = \xi_0(\tau)$ for $i = 1, 2, \ldots n$. Setting $\bar{F}_n = n^{-1} \sum_{i=1}^n F_{ni}$ and

$$a_n(\varepsilon) = \bar{F}_n(\xi_0(\tau) + \varepsilon)$$
$$b_n(\varepsilon) = \bar{F}_n(\xi_0(\tau) - \varepsilon),$$

they show that the conditions $\sqrt{n}(a_n(\varepsilon) - \tau) \to \infty$ and $\sqrt{n}(\tau - b_n(\varepsilon)) \to \infty$ are necessary and sufficient for consistency of the τth sample quantile.

4.1.2   Linear Quantile Regression

The introduction of regression covariates brings some added complications to the asymptotic theory of estimating *conditional quantile functions*, but much of this theory is already familiar from the univariate case. Suppose that the τth conditional quantile function of $Y|x$ may be written as

$$Q_y(\tau|x) = x^\top \beta(\tau),$$

and that the conditional distribution functions F_{ni} of Y_i, $i = 1, 2, \ldots$, satisfy

$$\text{Condition F} \quad \sqrt{n}(a_n(\varepsilon) - \tau) \to \infty \quad \text{and} \quad \sqrt{n}(\tau - b_n(\varepsilon)) \to \infty \quad (4.1)$$

with

$$a_n(\varepsilon) = n^{-1} \sum F_{ni} \left(x_i^\top \beta(\tau) - \varepsilon \right)$$
$$b_n(\varepsilon) = n^{-1} \sum F_{ni} \left(x_i^\top \beta(\tau) + \varepsilon \right).$$

El Bantli and Hallin (1999) show that Condition F is necessary and sufficient for consistency (i.e., $\hat{\beta}_n(\tau) \to \beta(\tau)$), provided we assume that the sequence of design matrices X satisfies the following conditions.

Condition D1. There exists $d > 0$ such that

$$\liminf_{n \to \infty} \inf_{\|u\|=1} n^{-1} \sum I \left(\left| x_i^\top u \right| < d \right) = 0.$$

Condition D2. There exists $D > 0$ such that

$$\limsup_{n \to \infty} \sup_{\|u\|=1} n^{-1} \sum \left(x_i^\top u \right)^2 \leq D.$$

The former condition ensures that the $\{x_i\}$s are not concentrated on a proper linear subspace of $\mathbb{R}^p$ and is needed for identifiability. The latter condition (D2) controls the rate of growth of the $\{x_i\}$s and is satisfied, for example, under the classical condition that $n^{-1} \sum x_i x_i^\top$ tends to a positive definite matrix.

Not surprisingly, there is some scope for rescuing consistency of $\hat{\beta}(\tau)$ by strengthening Condition F and relaxing Conditions D1 and D2. It is well known that, for the classical linear model with iid errors, $Eu_i = 0$ and $V(u_i) = \sigma^2 < \infty$, the condition

$$\lim_{n \to \infty} \left(\sum x_i x_i^\top \right)^{-1} = 0 \tag{4.2}$$

is necessary and sufficient for strong consistency of the least-squares estimator. This is equivalent to the condition that the smallest eigenvalue of $Q_n = \sum x_i x_i^\top$ tends to infinity.

The sufficiency of this condition for the weak consistency of the quantile regression estimator has been shown by Zhao, Rao, and Chen (1993) for linear models with iid errors under relatively mild conditions on the common distribution function of the errors. Necessary conditions for weak consistency of linear quantile regression involve a rather delicate interplay between $\{x_i\}$ conditions and $\{F_i\}$ conditions as is evident from the fact that sufficient mass at or near a quantile of the condition distribution of Y can salvage consistency even when the design is very uninformative. See Koenker and Bassett (1984) for some examples. Chen, Wu, and Zhao (1995) describe some quite stringent conditions on the conditional densities under which Condition H is *necessary* for consistency. Bassett and Koenker (1986) discuss some related conditions for strong consistency. Oberhofer (1982) considers consistency for median regression when the response function is nonlinear in parameters.

4.2 RATES OF CONVERGENCE

Having established the consistency of an estimator, we have answered the fundamental question: What are we estimating when we use a particular procedure in a specified sequence of circumstances? But this leaves many subsidiary questions. The first is, "How quickly does convergence occur?" In the case of ordinary sample quantiles based on iid sampling, the answer is relatively simple and again depends crucially on the behavior of the distribution function F near the quantile being estimated.

We will consider a general form of the linear quantile regression model. Let $Y_1, Y_2, \ldots$ be independent random variables with distribution functions $F_1, F_2, \ldots$ and suppose that the τth conditional quantile function,

$$Q_{Y_i}(\tau | x) = x^\top \beta(\tau),$$

is linear in the covariate vector x. The conditional distribution functions of the Y_is will be written as $P(Y_i < y | x_i) = F_{Y_i}(y | x_i) = F_i(y)$, and so

$$Q_{Y_i}(\tau | x_i) = F_{Y_i}^{-1}(\tau | x_i) \equiv \xi_i(\tau).$$

We will employ the following regularity conditions to explore the asymptotic behavior of the estimator:

$$\hat{\beta}_n(\tau) = \mathrm{argmin}_{b \in \mathbb{R}^p} \sum \rho_\tau \left(y_i - x_i^\top b \right).$$

Condition A1. The distribution functions $\{F_i\}$ are absolutely continuous, with continuous densities $f_i(\xi)$ uniformly bounded away from 0 and ∞ at the points $\xi_i(\tau)$, $i = 1, 2, \ldots$.

Condition A2. There exist positive definite matrices D_0 and $D_1(\tau)$ such that

(i) $\lim_{n \to \infty} n^{-1} \sum x_i x_i^\top = D_0$

(ii) $\lim_{n \to \infty} n^{-1} \sum f_i(\xi_i(\tau)) x_i x_i^\top = D_1(\tau)$

(iii) $\max_{i=1,\ldots,n} \| x_i \| / \sqrt{n} \to 0$.

As has already been emphasized, the behavior of the conditional density of the response in a neighborhood of the conditional quantile model is crucial to the asymptotic behavior of $\hat{\beta}_n(\tau)$. Conditions A2(i) and A2(iii) are familiar throughout the literature on M-estimators for regression models; some variant of them is necessary to ensure that a Lindeberg condition is satisfied. Condition A2(ii) is really a matter of notational convenience and could be deduced from Condition A2(i) and a slightly strengthened version of Condition A1.

Theorem 4.1. *Under Conditions A1 and A2,*

$$\sqrt{n}(\hat{\beta}_n(\tau) - \beta(\tau)) \rightsquigarrow \mathcal{N} \left(0, \tau(1-\tau) D_1^{-1} D_0 D_1^{-1} \right)$$

In the iid error model $\sqrt{n}(\hat{\beta}_n(\tau) - \beta(\tau)) \rightsquigarrow \mathcal{N}(0, \omega^2 D_0^{-1})$, where $\omega^2 = \tau(1 - \tau)/f_i^2(\xi_i(\tau))$.

Proof. The behavior of $\sqrt{n}(\hat{\beta}(\tau) - \beta(\tau))$ follows from consideration of the objective function

$$Z_n(\delta) = \sum_{i=1}^{n} \rho_\tau \left(u_i - x_i^\top \delta/\sqrt{n} \right) - \rho_\tau(u_i),$$

where $u_i = y_i - x_i^\top \beta(\tau)$. The function $Z_n(\delta)$ is obviously convex and is minimized at

$$\hat{\delta}_n = \sqrt{n}(\hat{\beta}_n(\tau) - \beta(\tau)).$$

Following Knight (1998), it can be shown that the limiting distribution of $\hat{\delta}_n$ is determined by the limiting behavior of the function $Z_n(\delta)$. Using Knight's identity,

$$\rho_\tau(u - v) - \rho_\tau(u) = -v\psi_\tau(u) + \int_0^v (I(u \le s) - I(u \le 0))ds \qquad (4.3)$$

with $\psi_\tau(u) = \tau - I(u < 0)$; we may write

$$Z_n(\delta) = Z_{1n}(\delta) + Z_{2n}(\delta),$$

where

$$Z_{1n}(\delta) = -\frac{1}{\sqrt{n}} \sum_{i=1}^{n} x_i^\top \delta \psi_\tau(u_i)$$

$$Z_{2n}(\delta) = \sum_{i=1}^{n} \int_0^{v_{ni}} (I(u_i \le s) - I(u_i \le 0))ds \equiv \sum_{i=1}^{n} Z_{2ni}(\delta)$$

and $v_{ni} = x_i^\top \delta/\sqrt{n}$. It follows from the Lindeberg–Feller central limit theorem, using Condition A2, that $Z_{1n}(\delta) \rightsquigarrow -\delta^\top W$ where $W \sim \mathcal{N}(0, \tau(1 - \tau)D_0)$.

Now, writing the second term as

$$Z_{2n}(\delta) = \sum EZ_{2ni}(\delta) + \sum(Z_{2ni}(\delta) - EZ_{2ni}(\delta)),$$

we have

$$\sum EZ_{2ni}(\delta) = \sum \int_0^{v_{ni}} (F_i(\xi_i + s) - F_i(\xi_i))ds$$

$$= \frac{1}{\sqrt{n}} \sum \int_0^{x_i^\top \delta} (F_i(\xi_i + t/\sqrt{n}) - F_i(\xi_i))dt$$

$$= n^{-1} \sum \int_0^{x_i^\top \delta} \sqrt{n}(F_i(\xi_i + t/\sqrt{n}) - F_i(\xi_i))dt$$

$$= n^{-1} \sum \int_0^{x_i^\top \delta} f_i(\xi_i)t\,dt + o(1)$$

$$
\begin{aligned}
&= (2n)^{-1} \sum f_i(\xi_i) \delta^\top x_i x_i^\top \delta + o(1) \\
&\rightarrow \frac{1}{2} \delta^\top D_1 \delta.
\end{aligned}
$$

Thus, the bound

$$
V(Z_{2n}(\delta)) \le \frac{1}{\sqrt{n}} \max \left| x_i^\top \delta \right| \sum E Z_{2ni}(\delta),
$$

and Condition A2(iii) then implies that

$$
Z_n(\delta) \rightsquigarrow Z_0(\delta) = -\delta^\top W + \frac{1}{2} \delta^\top D_1 \delta.
$$

The convexity of the limiting objective function, $Z_0(\delta)$, assures the uniqueness of the minimizer and, consequently, that

$$
\sqrt{n}(\hat{\beta}(\tau) - \beta(\tau)) = \hat{\delta}_n = \operatorname{argmin} Z_n(\delta) \rightsquigarrow \hat{\delta}_0 = \operatorname{argmin} Z_0(\delta).
$$

(See, e.g., Pollard, 1991; Hjørt and Pollard, 1993; Knight, 1998). Finally, we see that $\hat{\delta}_0 = D_1^{-1} W$ and the result follows. ∎

This form of the argument is particularly expedient and appears grounded entirely in elementary computations. It is certainly more direct than the laborious limiting argument for the finite-sample density function of Koenker and Bassett (1978) and appears considerably simpler than the stochastic equicontinuity of the gradient argument used by Ruppert and Carroll (1980). This simplicity is somewhat deceptive, however; in effect, the subtlety of the "chaining arguments" of modern empirical process theory are conveniently subsumed by the final appeal to convexity of the limiting form of the objective function. For Ruppert and Carroll (1980) and many subsequent authors, this piece of the argument was provided by the chaining argument of Bickel (1975) and an elegant monotonicity-of-the-gradient argument of Jurečková (1977) that used the convexity of $\rho_\tau(u)$, albeit in a less explicit fashion.

4.3 BAHADUR REPRESENTATION

There is an extensive literature employing these methods designed to establish some form of linear representation for the quantile regression estimator. One could mention Jurečková and Sen (1984), Portnoy (1984b), Koenker and Portnoy (1987), Portnoy and Koenker (1989), Gutenbrunner and Jurečková (1992), Hendricks and Koenker (1991), He and Shao (1996), and Arcones (1996), all of whom provide some variant of the linear representation for $\hat{\beta}_n(\tau)$:

$$
\sqrt{n}(\hat{\beta}_n(\tau) - \beta(\tau)) = D_1^{-1} \frac{1}{\sqrt{n}} \sum_{i=1}^{n} x_i \psi_\tau(Y_i - \xi_i(\tau)) + R_n. \tag{4.4}
$$

The beauty of such representations lies in expression of a rather complicated nonlinear estimator as a normalized sum of iid random variables from which asymptotically normal behavior follows easily.

The representation is a direct consequence of the preceding proof, and it is thus easy to show that $R_n = o_p(1)$, but establishing the precise stochastic order of R_n is more challenging. In the one-sample iid error model, the celebrated Bahadur (1966) and Kiefer (1967) results establish that

$$R_n = O(n^{-1/4}(\log\log n)^{3/4}).$$

A crucial aspect of linear representation (4.4) is that it can be shown to hold uniformly for $\tau \in \mathcal{T} = [\varepsilon, 1 - \varepsilon]$ for some $0 < \varepsilon < 1$. This extension of the asymptotic theory of quantile regression to the entire process $\{\hat{\beta}_n(\tau) : \tau \in \mathcal{T}\}$ greatly expands the potential scope of both estimation and inference methods based on $\hat{\beta}_n(\tau)$. Chapter 5 will consider L-estimation methods based on linear functionals of the $\hat{\beta}_n(\tau)$ process. Section 3.8 considers inference methods that rely on convergence results for the entire process.

Strengthening our prior conditions to hold uniformly for $\tau \in \mathcal{T}$ so that the conditional quantile functions of the response, Y_i, are linear on the entire interval $\mathcal{T}$, that is,

$$Q_{Y_i}(\tau | x_i) \equiv \xi_i(x_i, \tau) = x_i^\top \beta(\tau), \quad \tau \in \mathcal{T},$$

and assuming that the conditional densities $f_i(\xi_i)$ are uniformly bounded away from 0 and ∞ at the $\xi_i(x_i, \tau)$, $i = 1, \dots, n$ for $\tau \in \mathcal{T}$, and that Condition A2(ii) holds uniformly over $\mathcal{T}$, we have

$$v_n(\tau) = \sqrt{n} D_0^{-1/2} D_1(\hat{\beta}(\tau) - \beta(\tau)) \Rightarrow v_0(\tau) \quad \tau \in \mathcal{T},$$

where $v_0(\cdot)$ is a p-variate process of independent Brownian bridges. From this and related results, there flows a rich theory of specification tests for quantile regression. This theory is further developed by Koenker and Machado (1999) and Koenker and Xiao (2002).

4.4 NONLINEAR QUANTILE REGRESSION

Whereas the linear-in-parameters quantile regression model

$$Q_{Y_i}(\tau | x_i) = x_i^\top \beta(\tau)$$

offers a flexible approach in many applications, it is also of considerable interest to investigate conditional quantile models that are *nonlinear* in parameters;

$$Q_{Y_i}(\tau | x_i) = g(x_i, \beta_0(\tau)).$$

We can define the nonlinear quantile regression estimator

$$\hat{\beta}_n(\tau) = \operatorname{argmin}_{b \in \mathcal{B}} \sum \rho_\tau(y_i - g(x_i, b)),$$

where $\mathcal{B} \subset \mathbb{R}^p$ is compact. The situation is quite closely analogous to the linear case. Oberhofer (1982) treats consistency of the estimator. We can maintain

Condition A1 on the conditional densities with $\xi_i(\tau) = g(x_i, \beta_0(\tau))$. However, we need some further conditions on the quantile response function $g(\cdot, \cdot)$. We will assume the following.

Condition G1. There exist constants k_0, k_1, and n_0 such that, for $\beta_1, \beta_2 \in \mathcal{B}$ and $n > n_0$,

$$k_0 \parallel \beta_1 - \beta_2 \parallel \le \left(n^{-1} \sum_{i=1}^{n} (g(x_i, \beta_1) - g(x_i, \beta_2))^2 \right)^{1/2} \le k_1 \parallel \beta_1 - \beta_2 \parallel .$$

Condition G2. There exist positive definite matrices D_0 and $D_1(\tau)$ such that, with $\dot{g}_i = \partial g(x_i, \beta)/\partial \beta|_{\beta=\beta_0}$,

(i) $\lim\limits_{n \to \infty} n^{-1} \sum \dot{g}_i \dot{g}_i^\top = D_0$

(ii) $\lim\limits_{n \to \infty} n^{-1} \sum f_i(\xi_i) \dot{g}_i \dot{g}_i^\top = D_1(\tau)$

(iii) $\max\limits_{i=1,\dots,n} \parallel \dot{g}_i \parallel / \sqrt{n} \to 0$.

The latter condition obviously plays the role of Condition A2, whereas the former ensures that the objective function has a unique minimum at β_0 and is sufficiently smooth (see, e.g., Powell, 1991; Jurečková and Procházka, 1994; and the discussion by van de Geer, 2000, Section 12.3). Under these conditions, it can again be shown that we have the Bahadur representation,

$$\sqrt{n}(\hat{\beta}_n(\tau) - \beta_0(\tau)) = D_1^{-1} \frac{1}{\sqrt{n}} \sum_{i=1}^{n} \dot{g}_i \psi_\tau(u_i(\tau)) + o_p(1),$$

where $u_i(\tau) = y_i - g(x_i, \beta_0(\tau))$. Consequently,

$$\sqrt{n}(\hat{\beta}_n(\tau) - \beta_0(\tau)) \rightsquigarrow \mathcal{N}(0, \tau(1 - \tau)D_1^{-1} D_0 D_1^{-1}),$$

and as in the linear context we can easily extend this result to provide a uniform linear representation and weak convergence of the process on compact subintervals of $(0, 1)$. In contrast to the linear case, where computation of the entire process is quite easy, this task is considerably more challenging in the nonlinear case. This problem is addressed in Chapter 6.

4.5 THE QUANTILE REGRESSION RANKSCORE PROCESS

The regression rankscore process introduced by Gutenbrunner and Jurečková (1992) arises as the formal dual problem of the linear programming formulation of the (primal) quantile regression problem. It may be viewed as providing a natural generalization to the linear model of the familiar statistical duality of the order statistics and ranks in the one-sample model. Just as the p-element subsets of observations solving the primal quantile regression problem play the role of regression order statistics, the rankscore process may be viewed as generating rank statistics for the linear regression model. As such, the rankscore process provides a fundamental link between quantile regression and the classical theory of rank statistics as presented by Hájek and Šidák (1967).

To further explore the asymptotic behavior of the regression rankscore process, we consider the location–scale linear quantile regression model

$$Q_{Y_i}(\tau|x_i) = x_i^\top \beta + x_i^\top \gamma F_u^{-1}(\tau)$$

arising from the iid error model

$$Y_i = x_i^\top \beta + \left(x_i^\top \gamma\right) u_i$$

with $\{u_i\}$ iid from df F_u. This model will constitute the null, or restricted version, of the model and we wish to explore whether a new set of q covariates $Z = z_{ij}$ should be added to the model.

The regression rank scores under the null model are

$$\hat{a}_n(\tau) = \operatorname{argmax}\{y^\top a \,|\, X^\top a = (1-\tau)X^\top 1_n, a \in [0,1]^n\}.$$

Following Gutenbrunner and Jurečková (1992), we will denote the diagonal matrix with entries $x_i^\top \gamma$ as Γ_n.

The residuals from the *weighted* least-squares projection of the q-dimensional Z_n into the space spanned by X_n will be written as

$$\tilde{Z}_n = Z_n - X_n \left(X_n^\top \Gamma_n^{-1} X_n\right)^{-1} X_n \Gamma_n^{-1} Z_n.$$

Gutenbrunner and Jurečková (1992) require that the array $\{z_{ij}\}$ satisfies, as $n \to \infty$, (i) $\max \| z_i \| / \sqrt{n} \to 0$, (ii) that $n^{-1} \sum z_i z_i^\top$ tends to a positive definite matrix, and (iii) $n^{-1} \tilde{Z}_n^\top \tilde{Z}_n \to Q_0$, a positive definite matrix. The process

$$\hat{W}_n = \left\{ \hat{W}_n(\tau) \equiv \frac{1}{\sqrt{n}} \sum \tilde{z}_i(\hat{a}_{ni}(\tau) - (1-\tau)), \ \tau \in (0,1) \right\}$$

is asymptotically approximable by the process

$$\tilde{W}_n = \left\{ \tilde{W}_n(\tau) \equiv \frac{1}{\sqrt{n}} \sum \tilde{z}_{ni}(\tilde{a}_{ni}(\tau) - (1-\tau)), \ \tau \in (0,1) \right\}$$

in the sense that

(i) $\sup_{\tau \in \mathcal{T}} \| \hat{W}_n - \tilde{W}_n \| = o_p(1)$

(ii) $Q_0^{-1/2} \hat{W}_n \Rightarrow W_0^{(q)} \quad \tau \in \mathcal{T},$

where $W_0^{(q)}$ denotes a q, dimensional vector of independent Brownian bridges.

Remark 4.1. In the iid error case, with $x_i^\top \gamma$ constant, the primal quantile regression process $\sqrt{n}((\hat{\beta}_n(\tau) - \beta(\tau))$ and the dual quantile regression process $\hat{W}_n(\tau)$ are asymptotically independent. As noted by Gutenbrunner and Jurečková (1992, Corollary 1), this extends also to the case of contiguous heteroscedasticity of the form $\gamma = \gamma_0 + O(n^{-1/2})$, a fact that follows from the orthogonality of X_n and $\tilde{Z}_n$ and (weak) convergence of the joint process.

The convergence of the rankscore process leads immediately to an attractive approach to inference for quantile regression, as we have seen in the previous chapter. Further details are provided by Gutenbrunner and Jurečková (1992), Gutenbrunner, Jurečková, Koenker, and Portnoy (1993), and Koenker (1996).

4.6 QUANTILE REGRESSION ASYMPTOTICS UNDER DEPENDENT CONDITIONS

Relaxation of the independence condition on the observations is obviously possible and offers considerable scope for continuing research. Bloomfield and Steiger (1983) showed the asymptotic normality of a median autoregression estimator for a model in which the observations $\{(x_i, y_i) : i = 1, \ldots, n\}$ were assumed to be stationary and ergodic martingale differences. Weiss (1991) considers models under α-mixing conditions. Portnoy (1991) considers a considerably more general class of models with "m-decomposable" errors, a condition that subsumes m-dependent cases with m tending to infinity sufficiently slowly. Using large deviation results for dependent processes, he obtains a uniform Bahadur representation for $\{\sqrt{n}(\hat{\beta}_n(\tau) - \beta(\tau)) : \tau \in \mathcal{T}\}$. More recently, Koul and Mukherjee (1994) and Mukherjee (2000) have considered the asymptotic behavior of both the primal and dual quantile regression process under conditions of long-range dependence of the error process. This work relies heavily on the theory of weighted empirical processes developed by Koul (1992).

4.6.1   Autoregression

There is already quite an extensive literature on estimation and inference for linear time-series models with quantile regression methods. Bloomfield and Steiger (1983) considered the autoregressive model

$$y_t = \alpha_0 + \alpha_1 y_{t-1} + \cdots + \alpha_p y_{t-p} + u_t \tag{4.5}$$

with the usual stationarity condition that the roots of the characteristic polynomial $1 - \alpha_1 z - \cdots - \alpha_p z^p = 0$ lie outside the unit circle and with iid errors $\{u_t\}$ having nonlattice distribution, F, satisfying the following conditions: (i) $E(\log_+ |u_t|) < \infty$, (ii) median $\{u_t\} = 0$, and (iii) $E|u_t| < \infty$. They proved that the median regression estimator

$$\hat{\alpha}_n = \text{argmin}_{\alpha \in \mathbb{R}^{p+1}} \sum_{t=1}^{n} |y_t - \alpha_0 - \alpha_1 y_{t-1} - \cdots - \alpha_p y_{t-p}|$$

is strongly consistent. When F has density $f(0) > 0$, and $Eu_t^2 = \sigma^2 < \infty$, the techniques described earlier (see Pollard, 1991, Example 2) can be used to establish asymptotic normality of $\hat{\alpha}_n(\tau)$.

It is worthwhile to consider the simple AR(1) case,

$$y_t = \alpha y_{t-1} + u_t, \tag{4.6}$$

to illustrate some special features of the AR specification. Recalling that $n^{-1} \sum y_{t-1}^2 \to \sigma^2/(1 - \alpha^2)$ and using a quantity that we may denote as D_0 to emphasize the analogy with the regression case, it is easy to show that

$$\sqrt{n}(\hat{\alpha}_n - \alpha) \rightsquigarrow \mathcal{N}\left(0, \omega^2 D_0^{-1}\right),$$

where $\omega = (2f(0))^{-1}$. In contrast, the least-squares estimator of α,

$$\tilde{\alpha}_n = \frac{\sum_{t=2}^{n} y_t y_{t-1}}{\sum_{t=2}^{n} y_{t-1}^2},$$

satisfies, under these conditions,

$$\sqrt{n}(\tilde{\alpha}_n - \alpha) \rightsquigarrow \mathcal{N}(0, \sigma^2 D_0^{-1}).$$

Since $\sigma^2 D_0^{-1} = (1 - \alpha^2)$ is distribution free (i.e., independent of F), it is tempting to conclude that $\tilde{\alpha}_n$ has some form of robustness. Certainly it is remarkable that heavy-tailed innovations yield, at least asymptotically, the same precision for $\tilde{\alpha}_n$ as do lighter-tailed innovations. However, if we pause to consider the asymptotic relative efficiency of the two estimators, we see that, just as in the location model, ARE (asymptotic relative efficiency) $= \omega^2/\sigma^2$. Therefore, while it is true that the performance of the least-squares estimator $\tilde{\alpha}_n$ does not deteriorate as F becomes heavier tailed, its performance *relative to* the median regression estimator $\hat{\alpha}_n$ does deteriorate.

The explanation for this mildly paradoxical finding would be quite apparent in AR(1) scatterplots for data from several different Fs. For the least-squares estimator the price one pays for the influence of larger innovations exactly compensates the benefit derived from "more informative design observations" in the next period. This is the cancellation of σ^2 in the asymptotic variance expression for $\tilde{\alpha}_n$. In contrast, for the median regression estimation it is possible to fix the density at zero and consider Fs with increasingly heavy tails. In such cases ω^2 stays fixed, $D_0^{-1} \to 0$, and the precision of $\tilde{\alpha}_n$ improves. The relative efficiency of the two estimators tends to zero. Martin (1982) provides an elegant generalization of this example to pth-order autoregressions that include an intercept, focusing on a general class of smooth M-estimators.

It is natural to ask, in view of the preceding example, whether we can be more precise about what happens in autoregressive models with *infinite* variance innovations. Apparently, we have convergence at $\hat{\alpha}_n = o_p(n^{-1/2})$, but can we be more precise about the rate? And what about limiting distributions? These questions have spawned a surprisingly large literature. Davis, Knight, and Liu (1992) offer an exhaustive treatment of the stationary case with iid innovations in the domain of attraction of a stable law with index $a \in (0, 2)$. In this case, they show that there exist slowly varying functions $L_1(n)$ and $L_2(n)$ such that $n^{1/a} L_1(n)(\hat{\alpha}_n - \alpha)$ and $n^{1/a} L_2(n)(\tilde{\alpha}_n - \alpha)$ converge in distribution. In the special case of Pareto tails for the u_is, $L_1(n) = 1$ and $L_2(n) = (\log n)^{-1/\alpha}$, and so the median regression estimator $\hat{\alpha}_n$ exhibits a (modest) rate improvement over its least-squares rival. Monte Carlo evidence from Bloomfield and Steiger (1983) and others also suggests a rate improvement; however, this evidence needs to be interpreted cautiously in view of the heavy tails of the limiting distribution of the least-squares estimator.

In integrated, infinite variance autoregressive models, the situation is even more striking. Knight (1989) shows, for example, that in AR(1) example (4.6) with $\alpha = 1$ and Cauchy errors, the median regression estimator $\hat{\alpha}_n$ converges at order $O(n^{-3/2})$ while the least-squares estimator exhibits $\tilde{\alpha}_n = O_p(n^{-1})$ behavior. Furthermore, if the deterministic norming $n^{3/2}(\hat{\alpha} - 1)$ is replaced by random norming, we have

$$D_n^{1/2}(\hat{\alpha}_n - 1) \rightsquigarrow \mathcal{N}(0, (2f(0))^{-2}),$$

where $D_n = \sum_{t-2}^n y_{t-1}^2$. Knight (1991) extends this result to models in which the iid condition on the u_ts is replaced by weaker mixing conditions.

Tests of the unit root hypothesis $\alpha = 1$ based on quantile regression methods have been considered by Hercé (1996), Hasan and Koenker (1997), Thompson (2004), and Koenker and Xiao (2004). For stationary autoregressions, Koul and Saleh (1995) treat the asymptotics of the full quantile regression process. Hallin and Jurečková (1999) treat the dual process and associated inference problems for this model.

4.6.2   ARMA Models

Autoregressive models fit nicely into the original framework of quantile regression: computation is straightforward and much of the asymptotic theory carries forward relatively easily from the regression setting. Other linear time-series models pose more of a challenge and the literature is consequently more sparse. Davis and Dunsmuir (1997) have provided a very general treatment of the asymptotics of the median regression estimator for regression models with autoregressive moving average (ARMA) errors, obtaining an asymptotically normal theory under quite general conditions. In the general ARMA case, the situation is complicated by the nonconvexity of the objective function, a difficulty that is overcome by judicious approximation of the objective function in a neighborhood of the true parameter. This ensures a sequence of *local* minimizers that converge as specified but also entails some concern over computational methods that will lead to the appropriate minimizer. This problem is further addressed by Breidt, Davis, and Trindade (2001) in work on median regression methods for all-pass time-series models.

To date, most of the literature on time-series applications of quantile regression has focused on models with iid innovations. There seems to be considerable scope for exploring models that depart from this restrictive condition. Some first steps in this direction are described in Section 8.3.

4.6.3 ARCH-like Models

It is increasingly common, especially in financial time-series analysis, to consider models in which the dispersion of the conditional distribution of the response is modeled as a linear parametric function of prior information. The autoregressive conditional heteroscedasticity (ARCH) model of Engle (1982) was the highly influential prototype and new variants with new acronyms have proliferated. Initially, these models were formulated in terms of underlying Gaussian likelihoods, but there has been a widespread recognition that even the most careful conditioning often fails to produce a credibly Gaussian model. Student-t innovations, Hermite expansions, and other alternatives have been explored in the literature.

Koenker and Zhao (1996) considered the model

$$y_t = \alpha_0 + \alpha_1 y_{t-1} + \cdots + \alpha_p y_{t-p} + v_t$$

with

$$v_t = (\gamma_0 + \gamma_1 |v_{t-1}| + \cdots + \gamma_q |v_{t-q}|) u_t$$

and u_t iid. This model is strictly stationary and ergodic, provided $\mu_r \equiv (E|u_t|^r)^{1/r} < \infty$ for some $1 \le r \le \infty$, and the polynomial

$$\phi_\gamma(z) = z^q - \mu_r(\gamma_1 z^{q-1} + \cdots + \gamma_{q-1} z + \gamma_q)$$

has all its roots inside the unit circle and

$$\phi_\alpha(z) = 1 - \alpha_1 z - \cdots - \alpha_p z^p$$

has all its roots outside the unit circle. For symmetric innovation distributions, the median regression estimator

$$\hat{\alpha}_n = \text{argmin}_{\alpha \in \mathbb{R}^p} \sum |y_t - x_t^\top \alpha|,$$

where $x_t = (1, y_{t-1}, \ldots, y_{t-p})^\top$, is consistent, and the ARCH parameter γ may be estimated by

$$\hat{\gamma}(\tau, \hat{\alpha}_n) = \text{argmin}_\gamma \sum \rho_\tau \left(\hat{e}_t - \hat{z}_t^\top \gamma \right),$$

where $\hat{e}_t = y_t - x_t \hat{\alpha}_n$ and $\hat{z}_t = (1, |e_{t-1}|, \ldots, |e_{t-q}|)^\top$. When $\hat{\alpha}_n$ is $\sqrt{n}$-consistent, that is,

$$\hat{\alpha}_n = \alpha + n^{-1/2} \delta_n$$

for some $\| \delta_n \| = O_p(1)$, we have a reasonably simple Bahadur representation for $\hat{\gamma}(\tau, \hat{\alpha}_n)$ and a limiting normal asymptotic theory. However, with asymmetric innovations it is more difficult to find an appropriate initial estimator and it may be preferable to turn to nonlinear quantile regression methods. This is discussed very briefly by Koenker and Zhao (1996), but many details remain unexplored.

4.7   EXTREMAL QUANTILE REGRESSION

Throughout the preceding discussion, attention has been restricted to a central interval of quantiles, $\mathcal{T} = [\varepsilon, 1 - \varepsilon]$, that ensures that we stay away from the tails of the conditional distribution of the response. In some applications, however, it is of considerable interest to extend the theory further into the tails of the conditional distribution. In the context of asymptotic theory, we may consider sequences $\{\hat{\beta}_n(\tau_n)\}$ with $\tau_n \to 0$ or $\tau_n \to 1$ as *extremal*. This discussion will focus on the former case, $\tau_n \to 0$, but the same considerations evidently apply to the $\tau_n \to 1$ case. As in the classical extreme value literature, we may distinguish two situations in which $\tau_n \to 0$: those with $n\tau_n$ tending to a constant and those with $n\tau_n \to \infty$.

There have been several early efforts to treat the asymptotics of the intermediate case, $n\tau_n \to \infty$, in iid error models (Portnoy and Koenker, 1989; Gutenbrunner, Jurečková, Koenker, and Portnoy, 1993; Jurečková, 1999). The intent in these papers was to extend the Bahadur representations of the primal and dual quantile regression processes far enough into the tails to accommodate asymptotic theory of linear functionals of the processes defined on the entire unit interval.

For the most extreme regression quantiles with $n\tau_n \to o$, the literature, like the data, is somewhat more sparse. An early paper by Aigner and Chu (1968) considered the estimator that solves the linear program

$$\min_{b \in \mathbb{R}^p} \left\{ \sum_{i=1}^n x_i^\top b \,|\, x_i^\top b \geq y_i, i = 1, \ldots, n \right\}. \tag{4.7}$$

This estimator was motivated by the econometric problem of estimating a production "efficiency frontier." Firms were assumed to face a production technology under which the efficient (i.e., maximum achievable) level of output, Y, given inputs x, is given by

$$\sup\{Y|x\} = x^\top \beta_0.$$

Firms necessarily achieve lesser output than that predicted by the efficiency frontier, and so we obtain a regression model for which all the residuals are negative. Minimizing the sum of absolute regression residuals, subject to the constraint that they are all negative, yields problem 4.7. It is easy to see that this is equivalent to the limiting quantile regression problem

$$\hat{\beta}_n(0) = \lim_{\tau \to 0} \hat{\beta}_n(\tau) = \lim_{\tau \to 0} \operatorname{argmin}_{b \in \mathbb{R}^p} \sum \rho_\tau \left(y_i - x_i^\top b \right).$$

The asymptotics of this extreme quantile regression estimator is, not surprisingly, closely tied to the classical theory of extreme values. Following Smith (1994), there have been several papers dealing with the asymptotics of $\hat{\beta}_n(0)$. Portnoy and Jurečková (1999) and Knight (2001) treat the iid error model in considerable generality.

Chernozhukov (2004a, 2004b) considers the important intermediate situations with $n\tau_n \to k$, a positive integer. Here tail behavior of the response distriburion plays a crucial role, and a non-normal limiting behavior of $\hat{\beta}_n(\tau_n)$ emerges based on the theory of point processes. This theory leads to new inference methods for extreme and near extreme quantile regression that can significantly improve performance particularly when the response distribution exhibits algebraic tails.

The systematic study of regression models for *conditional* extremes is an especially welcome development. There are many potentially important applications in economics in finance, insurance, demography, ecology, and other fields.

An intriguing application of extreme quantile regression methods in time series is the work of Feigin and Resnick (1994, 1997), who use it to estimate autoregressive models with asymmetric innovations.

4.8 THE METHOD OF QUANTILES

In parametric models a common variant of the method of moments involves minimizing some measure of distance between a vector of sample quantiles and the corresponding vector of population quantiles expressed as a function of unknown parameters. Aitchison and Brown (1957) call this the "method of quantiles" and illustrate it for the case of the three-parameter log-normal.

Let Y be a scalar random variable with distribution function F indexed by the parameter $\theta \in \mathbb{R}^p$. Let $\hat{q}_n = (\hat{q}(\tau_1), \ldots, \hat{q}(\tau_M))^\top$ denote an M-vector of sample quantiles, where $\hat{q}(\tau)$ is the τth quantile. Denote the corresponding M-vector of population quantiles as $q(\theta) = (Q_r(\tau_i))_{i=1}^M$. We can consider estimating θ by minimizing the distance:

$$\| \hat{q}_n - q(\theta) \|_v = (\hat{q} - q(\theta))^\top V^{-1}(\hat{q} - q(\theta)).$$

As usual, we would like to choose V to be the covariance matrix of $\hat{q}$ (i.e., $V = \Omega = (\omega_{ij})$), with

$$\omega_{ij} = \frac{\tau_i \wedge \tau_j - \tau_i \tau_j}{\lambda(\tau_i)\lambda(\tau_j)},$$

where $\lambda(\tau) = f(F^{-1}(\tau))$ is the sparsity function of the random variable Y.

Example 4.1. If $Y = \exp(Z) + \alpha$ with $Z \sim \mathcal{N}(\mu, \sigma^2)$, then

$$Q_r(\tau) = \alpha + \exp(\mu + \sigma \Phi^{-1}(\tau)),$$

$\theta = (\alpha, \mu, \sigma) \in \mathbb{R}^2 \times \mathbb{R}_+$, and $\lambda(\tau) = \phi(\Phi^{-1}(\tau))/[\sigma \exp(\mu + \sigma \Phi^{-1}(\tau))]$. The example is particularly apt, because the maximum likelihood estimator is notoriously foolish, as is evident from the fact that the likelihood can be driven to infinity by letting $\alpha \to X_{(1)}$.

The asymptotic behavior of the estimator,

$$\hat{\theta}_n = \mathrm{argmin}_{\theta \in \mathbb{R}^p} \parallel \hat{q}_n - q(\theta) \parallel_v,$$

is a familiar exercise. Provided that $\sqrt{n}(\hat{q}_n - q(\theta_0)) \rightsquigarrow \mathcal{N}(0, \Omega(\theta_0))$ and the mappings $q(\theta_0)$ and $\Omega(\theta)$ satisfy some natural continuity and rank conditions, it can be easily shown (see, e.g., Ferguson, 1996) that

$$\sqrt{n}(\hat{\theta}_n - \theta_0) \rightsquigarrow \mathcal{N}(0, \Sigma_v),$$

where $J = \nabla q(\theta_0)$ and

$$\Sigma_v = (J^\top V^{-1} J)^{-1} J^\top V^{-1} \Omega V^{-1} J (J^\top V^{-1} J).$$

It is then evident that choosing $V = \Omega$ is optimal for given choices of τ_is. For this choice, $\Sigma_\Omega = (J^\top \Omega^{-1} J)^{-1}$.

The optimization underlying $\hat{\theta}_n$ is potentially troublesome and so it may be convenient to consider linearizations of the estimators, a tactic that leads to the L-estimators considered in Chapter 5. By careful choice of weights, these linear combinations of sample quantiles can be made to achieve the same (first-order) efficiency as $\hat{\theta}_n$.

The foregoing strategy can be successfully adapted to some important *conditional* quantile models. Consider the linear quantile regression model

$$Q_{Y_i}(\tau | x_i) = x_i^\top \beta(\tau),$$

where there are only a finite set of distinct covariate settings $\{x_i : i = 1, \ldots, K\}$, and n_i repeated measurements of the response Y_i at each x_i. In asymptotic frameworks where the n_i all tend to infinity, we can again consider computing a τth sample quantile, $\hat{q}_i(\tau)$, for each covariate configuration. The limiting normality of the $\hat{q}_i(\tau)$s provides a convenient rationalization for least-squares estimation of the model:

$$\hat{q}_i(\tau) = x_i^\top \beta(\tau) + u_i.$$

But it pays to be careful about the covariance structure.

For independent observations satisfying Conditions A1 and A2, the u_is have asymptotic variances

$$\omega_{ii} = n_i^{-1} \tau(1 - \tau)/f_i^2(F_i^{-1}(\tau)).$$

Therefore, the ordinary least-squares estimator is easily seen to be asymptotically normal with covariance matrix of the Huber–Eicker–White form:

$$\Sigma = (X^\top X)^{-1} X^\top \Omega X (X^\top X)^{-1}.$$

Clearly, we could reweight the observations by $\sqrt{n_i}$ to correct for the heterogeneity in sample size effect, but it would be preferable to weight by $1/\sqrt{\omega_{ii}}$, that is, to compute

$$\tilde{\beta}_n(\tau) = (X^\top \Omega^{-1} X)^{-1} X^\top \Omega^{-1} \hat{q}.$$

This weighted least-squares estimator achieves an asymptotic efficiency bound and has limiting covariance matrix

$$\tilde{\Sigma} = (X^{\top}\Omega^{-1}X)^{-1}.$$

It is of some interest to compare these results with what could have been obtained by simply computing the usual quantile regression estimator on the full data set using all $n = \sum n_i$ observations. We have already seen that

$$\hat{\beta}_n = \operatorname{argmin}_{b\in\mathbb{R}^p} \sum_{i=1}^{K}\sum_{j=1}^{n_i} \rho_\tau(y_{ij} - x_i b)$$

has asymptotic covariance matrix:

$$\hat{\Sigma} = (X^{\top}\Omega^{-1/2}X)^{-1}X^{\top}X(X^{\top}\Omega^{-1/2}X)^{-1}.$$

This is precisely what we would have achieved if, instead of weighting by $\omega_{ii}^{-1/2}$, we had used the weights $\omega_{ii}^{-1/4}$. It is tempting to conjecture that "half a loaf is better than none," and therefore we have the positive semidefinite ordering $\tilde{\Sigma} \leq \hat{\Sigma} \leq \Sigma$, but this need not be true (see Wiens, 2003).

Chamberlain (1994) considers the minimum-distance formulation of linear quantile regression for discrete designs and provides an interesting treatment of the consequences of misspecification of the linear model. Bassett, Tam, and Knight (2002) have recently compared several minimum distance methods in the context of an economic study of school performance.

4.9 MODEL SELECTION, PENALTIES, AND LARGE-P ASYMPTOTICS

In applications it is rare that we are so firmly convinced of a parametric specification that we would maintain it in the face of ever-increasing multitudes of data. And yet this is still a common paradigm for asymptotic theory. Gradually, however, a broader view of asymptotics has emerged that incorporates aspects of the model selection process and explicitly recognizes that the parametric dimension of appropriate model sequences may tend to infinity with the sample size. Such considerations are, of course, quite explicit in most nonparametric settings, but they are *implicit* in virtually all applied regression settings as well.

Huber (1973) introduced these issues in the robustness literature. He noted that for the least-squares estimator, $\hat{\beta}_n = (X^{\top}X)^{-1}X^{\top}y$, the behavior of the diagonal elements h_{ii} of the least-squares projection matrix $H = X(X^{\top}X)^{-1}X^{\top}$ plays a critical role. Since $HH = H$ and $\hat{y} = Hy$, we have

$$V(\hat{y}_i) = \sum_{k=1}^{n} h_{ik}^2\sigma^2 = h_{ii}\sigma^2.$$

And thus, by Chebyshev's inequality,

$$P(|\hat{y}_i - Ey_i| \geq \varepsilon) \leq h_{ii}\frac{\sigma^2}{\varepsilon^2}.$$

Therefore, least-squares fitted values are consistent if $h_{ii} \to 0$, and the converse is also true. Since $\text{trace}(H) = p$, the rank of X,

$$\bar{h}_n = \max_i h_{ii} \geq n^{-1}\sum h_{ii} = p/n,$$

a *necessary* condition for $\bar{h}_n \to 0$, is that $p/n \to 0$. Consistency of the fitted values is intimately tied to asymptotic normality of linear contrasts of the parameters. Consider $a = \alpha^\top\hat{\beta}$ for some $\|\alpha\| = 1$. For iid errors with finite variance σ^2, we can reparameterize so that $X^\top X = I_p$, and so $a = \alpha^\top X^\top y \equiv s^\top y$ and $V(a) = \sigma^2 s^\top s = \sigma^2$. The Lindeberg version of the central limit theorem then implies that a is asymptotically Gaussian if and only if $\max s_i \to 0$, but this is just the condition that $\bar{h}_n \to 0$. Bickel (1976) reformulates this nicely as follows. Estimable functions $\alpha^\top\hat{\beta}$ are asymptotically Gaussian with natural parameters if and only if fitted values are consistent. The "natural parameters" qualifier is needed to rule out pathologies that arise when the original observations are themselves Gaussian.

For other regression estimators, the conditions required for asymptotic normality when $p \to \infty$ with n are more problematic. Huber (1973) conjectured that $p^2/n \to 0$ was necessary for a uniform normal approximation for a typical (smooth ψ) M-estimator. Subsequently, Yohai and Maronna (1979) showed that $p^{3/2}\bar{h}_n \to 0$ was sufficient for a uniform normal approximation. Portnoy (1984, 1985) substantially improved these results, showing that under quite mild design conditions $p \log n/n \to 0$ suffices for $\|\hat{\beta}_n - \beta\| \to 0$ for M-estimators with smooth, monotone ψ functions, and $(p \log n)^{3/2}/n \to 0$ suffices for normality. Unfortunately, these results do not apply to the quantile regression estimator $\hat{\beta}_n(\tau)$ and its discontinuous ψ_τ function.

Welsh (1989), in an elegant synthesis of M-estimator asymptotics, has shown that $p^3(\log n)^2/n \to 0$ suffices for a normal approximation in the quantile regression setting. This is somewhat more stringent than the $p^2(\log n)^{2+\varepsilon}/n \to 0$ rates derived by Welsh for smooth M-estimators, but it is encouraging because it gives some support to the viability of observed rates of parametric growth in the applied literature. Koenker (1988) considers a sample of 733 published "wage equations" and finds that $p_n = O(n^{1/4})$ is roughly consistent with empirical practice in this (large) segment of the econometrics literature.

4.9.1   Model Selection

Sequences of models with dimension tending to infinity naturally raise questions about model selection strategies. There is a vast literature on this subject; I will touch on only a few recent developments that seem particularly germane to quantile regression applications.

Machado (1993) considers variants of the Schwarz (1978) penalty for M-estimators of regression, including the quantile regression case. He emphasizes the need for location–scale invariant procedures: for median regression this yields the criterion

$$\text{SIC}(j) = \log(\hat{\sigma}_j) + \frac{1}{2} p_j \log n,$$

where $\hat{\sigma}_j = n^{-1} \sum_{i=1}^{n} \rho_{1/2}(y_i - x_i^\top \hat{\beta}_n(1/2))$ and p_j denotes the dimension of the jth model. This yields a consistent model selection procedure in the perhaps implausible circumstance that one of the p_j-dimensional models is actually correct. Alternatively, one can consider the Akaike criterion:

$$\text{AIC}(j) = \log(\hat{\sigma}_j) + p_j.$$

With positive probability, selection based on minimizing $\text{AIC}(j)$ overestimates the model dimension but may have superior performance for prediction. The asymptotics of such penalized quantile regression estimators fits nicely within the epiconvergence framework of Knight and Fu (2000). Stochastic equi-lower-semi-continuity of the objective function is the crucial requirement.

4.9.2 Penalty Methods

Penalty methods for model selection may be viewed as a special class of more general shrinkage methods. The well-known least-squares "ridge regression" estimator,

$$\hat{\beta}_n(\lambda) = \text{argmin}_{b \in \mathbb{R}^p} \sum \left(y_i - x_i^\top b\right)^2 + \lambda \|b - \beta_0\|_2^2,$$

which shrinks the unconstrained least-squares estimator toward β_0, typically taken to be zero, can be modified to use the the the ℓ_1 penalty $\|v\|_1 = \sum |v_i|$. Tibshirani (1996) calls this penalty the "lasso." The resulting estimator,

$$\hat{\beta}_n(\lambda) = \text{argmin}_{b \in \mathbb{R}^p} \sum \left(y_i - x_i^\top b\right)^2 + \lambda \parallel b - \beta_0 \parallel_1,$$

behaves somewhat like the ridge estimator, but rather than shrinking coefficients smoothly along the "curve décolletage," in the evocative terminology of Dickey (1974), the lasso acts more like a model selection penalty, shrinking coefficients all the way to their β_0 coordinates for sufficiently large λ. The computation of the lasso-penalized, least-squares estimator may be formulated as a quadratic programming problem and solved quite efficiently. See Osborne, Presnell, and Turlach (2000) for further details.

The lasso penalty is in several respects even more natural for the quantile regression context. Consider the estimator,

$$\hat{\beta}_n(\tau, \lambda) = \text{argmin}_{b \in \mathbb{R}^p} \sum \rho_\tau \left(y_i - x_i^\top b\right) + \lambda \parallel b - \beta_0 \parallel_1.$$

For $\tau = 1/2$, this estimator can be computed with a simple data augmentation device. For $\tau \neq 1/2$, the situation is slightly more complicated because we want asymmetric weighting of the fidelity (residual) term and symmetric weighting of the penalty term. But the problem retains its linear program structure, and so this is also easy to accommodate.

Knight and Fu (2000) have investigated the asymptotic behavior of a wide variety of lasso-penalized regression estimators. Using methods similar to the proof of Theorem 4.1, they consider the objective function

$$V_n(\delta) = \sum \left[\rho_\tau \left(u_i - x_i^\top \delta / \sqrt{n} \right) - \rho_\tau(u_i) \right] + \lambda_n \sum_{j=1}^{p} [|\beta_j + \delta_j / \sqrt{n}| - |\beta_j|],$$

where for convenience we have set $\beta_0 = 0$ and $u_i = y_i - x_i^\top \beta(\tau)$. The function V_n is minimized at $\hat{\delta} = \sqrt{n}(\hat{\beta}(\tau) - \beta(\tau))$. As we have already seen, under the conditions of Theorem 4.1, for the fidelity term,

$$V_{1n}(\delta) = \sum [\rho_\tau(u_i - x_i^\top \delta / \sqrt{n}) - \rho_\tau(u_i)]$$

$$\rightsquigarrow -\delta^\top W + \frac{1}{2} \delta^\top D_1 \delta,$$

whereas, for the penalty term, with $\lambda_n / \sqrt{n} \to \lambda_0$,

$$V_{2n}(\delta) = \lambda_n \sum [|\beta_j + \delta_j / \sqrt{n}| - |\beta_j|]$$

$$\to \lambda_0 \sum \delta_j \operatorname{sgn}(\beta_j) I(\beta_j \neq 0) + |\delta_j| I(\beta_j = 0).$$

Thus, $V_n(\delta) \rightsquigarrow V_0(\delta)$; since V_n is convex and V_0 has a unique minimum, it follows that the penalized estimator satisfies

$$\sqrt{n}(\hat{\beta}_n(\tau, \lambda_n) - \beta(\tau)) \rightsquigarrow \operatorname{argmin}_\delta V_0(\delta).$$

Example 4.2. Suppose $\beta_1, \ldots, \beta_q$ are nonzero and $\beta_{q+1} \ldots, \beta_p$ equal zero. Then

$$V_0(\delta) = -\delta^\top W + 1/2\delta^\top D_1 \delta + \lambda_0 \sum_{j=1}^{q} \delta_j \operatorname{sgn}(\beta_j) + \lambda_0 \sum_{j=q+1}^{p} |\delta_j|.$$

Partitioning, as Knight and Fu (2000), so that

$$D_1 = \begin{pmatrix} D_{11} & D_{12} \\ D_{21} & D_{22} \end{pmatrix}, \quad W = \begin{pmatrix} W_1 \\ W_2 \end{pmatrix}, \quad \delta = \begin{pmatrix} \delta_1 \\ \delta_2 \end{pmatrix},$$

if $V_0(\delta)$ happens to be minimized at $\delta_2 = 0$, then

$$D_{11}\delta_1 - W_1 = -\lambda_0 s(\beta),$$

where $s(\beta) = (\operatorname{sgn}(\beta_j))_{j=1}^{q}$. And

$$-\lambda_0 e \leq D_{21}\delta_1 - W_2 \leq \lambda_0 e,$$

where e denotes a $(p - q)$-vector of 1s. Thus, solving for δ_1 and substituting, we have a solution to the limiting problem with $\delta_2 = 0$ if and only if

$$-\lambda_0 e \leq D_{21} D_{11}^{-1}(W_1 - \lambda_0 s(\beta)) - W_2 \leq \lambda_0 e.$$

This occurs with positive probability, and so there is positive probability of correctly estimating that $\delta_2 = 0$. However, the price we pay is an asymptotic bias in the nonzero coefficient estimator of $-\lambda_0 D_{11}^{-1} s(\beta)$. Obviously, λ_0 controls the tradeoff between these effects: large λ_0 implies considerable shrinkage and large bias; small λ_0 implies less shrinkage, less bias, and correspondingly less likelihood of correctly identifying zero coefficients.

Knight and Fu (2000) explore a broader class of penalties, based on ℓ_p norms, for $\gamma > 0$:

$$\| v \|_\gamma^\gamma = \sum |v_i|^\gamma .$$

The Akaike information criterion may be viewed as a limiting case because

$$\lim_{\gamma \to 0} \| v \|_\gamma^\gamma = \sum_{i=1}^p I(v_i \neq 0).$$

These "bridge" penalties were introduced by Frank and Friedman (1993). An influential application of the $\gamma = 1$ lasso penalty is developed by Donoho, Chen, and Saunders (1998), who use it to discriminate among competing families of nonparametric basis functions. A closely related development is the use of total variation (L_1-type) penalties in smoothing problems as a measure of roughness discussed in Chapter 7.

There are many other contexts in which penalized estimation may prove to be advantageous. We will briefly consider one more example to illustrate the flexibility of this approach. The penalties we have considered thus far presume that, for some affine transformation of the model parameters, departures from the origin should be treated symmetrically. Tibshirani (1996) provides a useful heuristic discussion of the interpretation of the ℓ_p "balls" in this context. From a subjectivist viewpoint one may interpret these balls as contours of prior probability. Rather than shrinking toward a central point, however, it is often desirable to shrink toward some plausible set – for example, a cone.

Consider the simplest case of estimating a regression model subject to the restriction $\hat{\beta} \in \mathbb{R}_+^p$ (i.e., that the estimator lie in the nonnegative orthant). After linear reparameterization, a variety of "qualitatively constrained" spline problems can be formulated in this way. Monotonicity, convexity, and other features can be imposed by simply constraining linear combinations of coefficients to be nonnegative (see, e.g., Ramsay, 1988; He and Ng, 1999). To adhere to the earlier formulation, we will consider procedures that shrink toward the positive orthant rather than those that simply impose the constraint.

To this end, consider the penalty

$$P(v) = \sum_{i=1}^p |v_i|^- ,$$

where $|v|^- = |v| I(v < 0)$. The piecewise linear nature of the penalty is again especially convenient in the quantile regression framework. We can consider the estimator,

$$\hat{\beta}_n(\tau, \lambda_n) = \operatorname{argmin}_{b \in \mathbb{R}^p} \left\{ \sum_{i=1}^{n} \rho_\tau(y_i - x_i^\top b) + \lambda_n P(b) \right\}.$$

Now decomposing the objective function

$$V_n(\delta) = V_{1n}(\delta) + V_{2n}(\delta)$$

as we did for the lasso, and again with $\lambda_n = \lambda_0/\sqrt{n}$,

$$\begin{aligned} V_{2n}(\delta) &= \lambda_n \sum [|\beta_j + \delta_j/\sqrt{n}|^- - |\beta_j|^-] \\ &\to \lambda_0 \sum \delta_j I(\beta_j < 0) + |\delta_j|^- I(\beta_j = 0). \end{aligned}$$

Clearly, for β in the interior of $\mathbb{R}_+^p$ we have no contribution, asymptotically, from the penalty term. For strictly negative β_j there is a bias proportional to λ_0, but the more interesting case involves some of the $\beta_j = 0$.

Example 4.3. Suppose, as in the previous example, $\beta_{q+1} = \ldots = \beta_p = 0$ and $(\beta_1 \ldots, \beta_q)^\top \in \mathbb{R}_+^q$. Then

$$V_0(\delta) = -\delta^\top W + 1/2\delta^\top D_1 \delta + \lambda_0 \sum_{j=q+1}^{p} |\delta_j|^-.$$

Again partitioning, $V_0(\delta)$ is minimized with $\delta_2 = 0$ if

$$D_{11}\delta_1 - W_1 = 0$$

and

$$-\lambda_1 q \le D_{21}\delta_1 - W_2 \le 0.$$

so that $\delta_2 = 0$ is a solution to the limiting problem if and only if

$$-\lambda_0 1 \le D_{21} D_{11}^{-1} W_1 - W_2 \le 0.$$

Again this occurs with positive probability, but now the asymptotic bias term for the δ_1 estimator has vanished, and it appears that we are getting something for nothing! Of course, the limiting distribution also places positive mass on negative values of δ_2 and these contribute to a bias effect for the δ_1 parameter unless $D_1(\tau)$ is block diagonal.

4.10 ASYMPTOTICS FOR INFERENCE

Thus far in this chapter we have focused on the asymptotic behavior of the quantile regression process, $\hat{\beta}_n(\tau)$, but application of the foregoing results to problems of inference introduce a host of subsidiary asymptotic considerations. Can nuisance parameters be consistently estimated? Does the presence of estimated nuisance parameters in test statistics alter their asymptotic behavior? If so, what recourses are available?

4.10.1 Scalar Sparsity Estimation

There is an extensive literature on the estimation of the density quantile function $\varphi(\tau) = f(F^{-1}(\tau))$ and its reciprocal $s(\tau) = 1/f(F^{-1}(\tau))$, the sparsity function. In iid error quantile regression models this parameter plays a role analogous to the standard deviation of the errors in least-squares estimation of the iid error regression model. The precision of $\hat{\beta}_n(\tau)$, because it depends entirely on the sample information *in the neighborhood* of the τth quantile, depends directly on this quantity.

Sparsity estimation is just the flip side of density estimation. Since

$$s(\tau) = dF^{-1}(\tau)/d\tau,$$

it is natural to consider estimators of $s(\tau)$ that are simple difference quotients of an empirical quantile function; that is,

$$\hat{S}_n(\tau) = [F_n^{-1}(\tau + h_n) - F_n^{-1}(\tau - h_n)]/2h_n.$$

Such estimates were originally suggested by Siddiqui (1960) for constructing confidence intervals for univariate sample quantiles. Bofinger (1975), using standard density estimation asymptotics, showed that the bandwidth sequence

$$h_n = n^{1/5}[4.5s^2(\tau)/(s''(\tau))^2]^{1/5}$$

was optimal from the standpoint of minimizing mean squared error. Obviously, if we knew $s(\tau)$ and $s''(\tau)$, we would not need h_n, but fortunately $s(\tau)/s''(\tau)$ is not very sensitive to F and so little is lost if we substitute some typical distributional shape, say, the Gaussian. Note that the ratio is invariant to location and scale shift.

In general,

$$\frac{s}{s''} = \frac{f^2}{2(f'/f)^2 + [f'/f - f''/f]}$$

and so for $f = \phi, (f'/f)(F^{-1}(t)) = \Phi^{-1}(t)$, so that

$$h_n = n^{-1/5} \left[\frac{4,5\phi^4(\Phi^{-1}(t))}{(2\Phi^{-1}(t)^2 + 1)^2} \right]^{1/5}.$$

In Figure 4.1, the bandwidth h_n is plotted as a function of sample size n for three distinct quantiles: $\tau = 0.50, 0.75$, and 0.90. For symmetric F, like the Gaussian, the h_n sequences for τ and $(1 - \tau)$ are obviously identical.

The mean-squared-error optimality of the Bofinger h_n would be a natural criterion if one were interested in estimating $s(\tau)$ as an end in itself, but usually we are not. Sparsity estimation is almost always an intermediate input to the construction of test statistics, confidence intervals, and related inference apparatus.

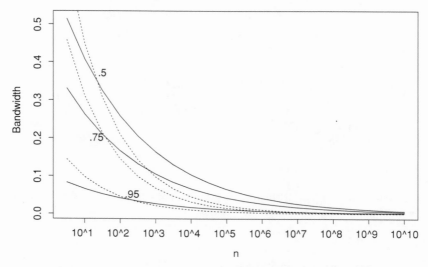

Figure 4.1. This figure illustrates the bandwidth rules suggested by Bofinger (solid lines) and Hall and Sheather (dotted lines). Note that for moderately large sample sizes the latter rule yields narrower bandwidths.

Based on Edgeworth expansions for studentized univariate sample quantiles, Hall and Sheather (1988) suggest the bandwidth sequence

$$h_n = n^{-1/3} z_\alpha^{2/3} [1.5 s(t)/s''(t)]^{1/3},$$

where z_α satisfies $\Phi(z_\alpha) = 1 - \alpha/2$, and α denotes the desired size of the test. These bandwidths are depicted in Figure 4.1 by the dotted lines and give somewhat narrower bandwidths for moderate and large n than those depicted for the corresponding Bofinger rule.

Having chosen a bandwidth, h_n, the next question is, "How should we compute F_n^{-1}?" The simplest approach is to use the residuals from the quantile regression fit:

$$\hat{u}_i = y_i - x_i^\top \hat{\beta}(\tau) \quad i = 1, \dots, n.$$

The empirical quantile function based on this "sample" is simply

$$F_n^{-1}(t) = \hat{u}_{(i)} \quad t \in [(i-1)/n, i/n).$$

A potential pitfall of residual-based estimates of F^{-1} is that we need to ensure that the bandwidth is sufficiently large to avoid the p zero residuals that inevitably arise as a consequence of the fitting. Obviously, this is only a problem if p/n is large relative to h_n, but careful implementation should account for the possibility. One approach, analogous to the usual degrees-of-freedom correction in estimating σ^2 in least-squares regression, would be to drop the p

zero residuals from the "sample" of $\hat{u}_i$s and to treat the effective sample size, for purposes of sparsity estimation, as $n - p$.

As noted in Section 3.4, an alternative to estimating F^{-1} by the empirical quantile function of the residuals is to use

$$F_n^{-1}(\tau) = \bar{x}^\top \hat{\beta}_n(\tau),$$

where $\bar{x} = n^{-1} \sum x_i$. This is advantageous in small-to-moderate sample sizes where computing the whole process $\hat{\beta}_n(\tau)$ is tractable; in large problems, the residual-based approach is usually preferable.

4.10.2 Covariance Matrix Estimation

The iid error model that underlies the limiting result

$$\sqrt{n}(\hat{\beta}_n(\tau) - \beta(\tau)) \rightsquigarrow \mathcal{N}(0, \omega^2(\tau)D_0^{-1}),$$

with $\omega^2(\tau) = \tau(1 - \tau)/f^2(F^{-1}(\tau))$ and $D_n = \lim n^{-1} \sum x_i x_i^\top$, is very restrictive. We have seen that in more general settings, like those of Theorem 4.1, estimation of the limiting covariance matrix involves estimating

$$D_1(\tau) = \lim_{n \to \infty} n^{-1} \sum_{i=1}^{n} f_i(x_i^\top \beta(\tau)) x_i x_i^\top.$$

We have already described consistent methods of estimating $D_1(\tau)$ in Section 3.4 as well as some associated caveats.

4.11 RESAMPLING SCHEMES AND THE BOOTSTRAP

Following the approach of Knight (2002), consider the behavior of the bootstrapped objective function

$$Z_n^*(u) = \sum_{i=1}^{n} \rho_\tau \left(Y_i^* - x_i^\top \beta(\tau) - u^\top x_i^*/\sqrt{n}\right) - \rho_\tau \left(Y_i^* - x_i^\top \beta(\tau)\right),$$

where $\{(Y_i^*, x_i^*) : i = 1, \ldots, n\}$ constitute a random sample from the empirical distribution function

$$\hat{F}_n(y, x) = n^{-1} \sum I(Y_i < y, x_i < x).$$

Clearly $Z_n^*(u)$ is convex and is minimized at $\sqrt{n}(\hat{\beta}^*(\tau) - \beta(\tau))$. The argument of Section 4.3 shows that

$$Z_n^*(u) = -u^\top W_n^* + u^\top D_1 u + R_n^*(u),$$

where

$$W_n^* = \frac{1}{\sqrt{n}} \sum_{i=1}^{n} x_i^* \psi_\tau(Y_i^* - \xi_i)$$

and, for any compact set K,

$$\hat{P}_n(\sup_{u \in K} |R_n^*(u)| > \varepsilon) \to 0.$$

Here $\hat{P}_n$ is the random probability measure associated with iid sampling from $\hat{F}_n$. It follows that W_n^* has a limiting Gaussian distribution with mean zero and covariance matrix $\tau(1 - \tau)D_0$ and we have the representation

$$\sqrt{n}(\hat{\beta}_n^*(\tau) - \beta(\tau)) = D_1^{-1} W_n^* + \xi_n^*,$$

which thus, has the same limiting distribution as $\sqrt{n}(\hat{\beta}_n(\tau) - \beta(\tau))$. To explore the adequacy of the bootstrap approximation of the limiting distribution, one would need to examine ξ_n^* more closely. For the residual bootstrap, Knight (2002) gives the limiting distribution of ξ_n^* under iid errors. The following result for the (x, y)-pair bootstrap extends this to our non-iid setting.

Theorem 4.2. *Under Conditions A1 and A2, for each $s \in \mathbb{R}^P$ and x,*

$$\hat{P}_n(n^{1/4} s^\top \xi_n^* < x) \rightsquigarrow \hat{P}_n(s^\top D_1^{-1}(G_1^*(U) + G_1(U)) \leq x),$$

where G_1^* and G_1 are independent mean zero Gaussian processes with covariance function $B(u, v)$ and $U \sim \mathcal{N}(0, \tau(1 - \tau)D_1^{-1} D_0 D_1^{-1})$ and independent of G_1^* and G_1.

4.12   ASYMPTOTICS FOR THE QUANTILE REGRESSION PROCESS

We have seen that tests based on the quantile regression process can be built on all three of the classical testing principles: Wald, score, and likelihood ratio tests are all available when the null hypothesis is free of nuisance parameters. New challenges arise when nuisance parameters are present and these challenges are taken up in this final section of the chapter.

4.12.1   The Durbin Problem

To illustrate the fundamental difficulties, we may begin with the most elementary testing problem, the one-sample goodness-of-fit problem. Given a random sample $\{Y_1, \ldots, Y_n\}$ on a real-valued random variable Y, suppose that we want to test the hypothesis that Y comes from distribution F_0. Tests based on the empirical distribution function

$$F_n(y) = n^{-1} \sum_{i=1}^{n} I(Y_i \leq y)$$

can be based on the Kolmogorov–Smirnov statistic,

$$K_n = \sup_{y \in \mathbb{R}} \sqrt{n} |F_n(y) - F_0(y)|.$$

Such tests are especially attractive because they are asymptotically distribution free; that is, the limiting distribution of the statistic K_n is the same for every continuous distribution function F_0. This remarkable property is a simple consequence of the fact that we can transform the test to a test of uniformity via the change of variable $y \to F_0^{-1}(y)$, so that K_n becomes

$$K_n = \sup_{t \in (0,1)} \sqrt{n} |F_n(F_0^{-1}(t)) - t|.$$

Because the process

$$v_n = \sqrt{n} |F_n(F_0^{-1}(t)) - t|$$

converges weakly to the Brownian bridge process, v_0, the behavior of K_n is asymptotically independent of F_0.

It is rare, however, that we are able to specify F_0 so completely. Usually our hypothesis places F in some parametric family $\mathcal{F}_\theta$, and we would like to test that Y has a distribution $F \in \mathcal{F}_\theta$ for some $\theta \in \Theta \subset \mathbb{R}^p$. It is natural to ask what would happen if we simply replace F_0 in K_n by $F_{\hat{\theta}_n}$, where $\hat{\theta}_n$ denotes an estimator of θ. If we consider $\sqrt{n}(F_n(y) - F_{\hat{\theta}_n}(y))$, and again change variables, we have the parametric empirical process

$$\hat{v}_n(t) = \sqrt{n}(G_n(t) - G_{\hat{\theta}_n}^{-1}(t)),$$

where $G_n(t) = F_n(F_{\theta_0}^{-1}(t))$ and $G_{\hat{\theta}_n}(t) = F_{\hat{\theta}_n}(F_{\theta_0}^{-1}(t))$. Under mild conditions on the estimator $\hat{\theta}_n$ we have the linear representation

$$\sqrt{n}(\hat{\theta}_n - \theta_0) = \int_0^1 h_0(s) dv_n(s) + o_p(1).$$

Then, under regularity conditions given by Koenker and Xiao (2002), we may write

$$G_{\hat{\theta}_n}(t) = t + (\hat{\theta}_n - \theta_0)^\top g(t) + o_p(\|\hat{\theta}_n - \theta_0\|)$$

for some function g representing the Fréchet derivative of the mapping $\theta \to G_\theta$. We can thus approximate the parametric empirical process by the conventional empirical process minus a correction term due the estimation of the parameter θ:

$$\hat{v}_n(t) = v_n(t) + g(t)^\top \int_0^1 h_0(s) dv_n(s) + o_p(1),$$

and it can be shown that

$$\hat{v}_n(t) \Rightarrow v_0(t) + g(t)^\top \int_0^1 h_0(s) dv_0(s),$$

where v_0 denotes the standard Brownian bridge process.

This is all well and good, but the second term introduces a drift in the process that is F dependent and, consequently, it disrupts the attractive distribution-free character of the limiting behavior of the proposed test statistic.

4.12.2   Khmaladization of the Parametric Empirical Process

The literature dealing with consequences of this drift effect is elegantly surveyed by Durbin (1973). A general approach to dealing with this so-called Durbin problem was proposed by Khmaladze (1981) based on an extension of the classical Doob–Meyer decomposition of the empirical process. In finite-dimensional inference problems involving nuisance parameters, a familiar strategy involves projecting a proposed test statistic into the space orthogonal to that spanned by the nuisance parameters. Khmaladze's proposal accomplishes the same objective for tests based on the infinite-dimensional parametric empirical process.

The Doob–Meyer decomposition asserts that for any nonnegative submartingale, say x, there exists an increasing right-continuous predictable process a such that $a(t) < \infty$ and a right-continuous martingale component m such that

$$x(t) = a(t) + m(t) \qquad a.s.$$

Suppose $X_1, \ldots, X_n$ are iid from F_0 so that $Y_i = F_0(X_i)$, $i = 1, \ldots, n$, are iid uniform. Then

$$G_n(t) = F_n(F_0^{-1}(t)) = n^{-1} \sum_{i=1}^{n} I(Y_i < t)$$

is a submartingale, and increments are binomial; that is,

$$n\Delta G_n(t) = n(G_n(t + \Delta t) - G_n(t)) = Bin(n(1 - G_n(t)), \Delta t/(1 - t))$$

with $G_n(0) = 0$. Thus, we have

$$E(\Delta G_n(t)|\mathcal{F}_t) = \frac{1 - G_n(t)}{1 - t} \Delta t, \tag{4.8}$$

where $\mathcal{F}_t$ denotes the natural filtration associated with G_n. This suggests writing

$$G_n(t) = \int_0^t \frac{1 - G_n(s)}{1 - s} ds + m_n(t).$$

That $m_n(t)$ is a martingale follows from the fact that

$$E(m_n(t)|\mathcal{F}_s) = m_n(s),$$

using (4.8), and we can write the classical Doob–Meyer decomposition of v_n as

$$v_n(t) = w_n(t) + \int_0^t \frac{v_n(s)}{1 - s} ds,$$

where $w_n(t) = \sqrt{n} m_n(t)$ converges to a standard Brownian motion, w_0.

Conditioning only on t gives us the Doob–Meyer decomposition, but it does not help with our real problem, which is how to deal with the effect of the parametric drift component of the parametric empirical process. Khmaladze's insight was to extend the conditioning to include not only t but also the components of a vector of other real-valued functions: $g(t) = (t, g_1(t), \ldots, g_m(t))^\top$. We assume that the functions $\dot{g}(t) = dg(t)/dt$ are linearly independent in a neighborhood of 1, and so

$$C(t) = \int_t^1 \dot{g}(s)\dot{g}(s)^\top ds$$

is nonsingular for all $t < 1$. Now consider the prediction of an arbitrary function $\eta : (0, 1) \to \mathbb{R}$ at s based on a recursive least-squares regression on the function $\dot{g}$ and using the information from s to 1; that is,

$$\hat{\eta}(t) = \int_0^t \dot{g}(s)C^{-1}(s)\int_s^1 \dot{g}(r)d\eta(r)ds.$$

Let Q_g denote the operator defining the corresponding residual process,

$$Q_g\eta(t) = \eta(t) - \hat{\eta}(t).$$

Khmaladze (1981) shows that the residual parametric empirical process constructed in this way,

$$\tilde{v}_n(t) = Q_g\hat{v}_n(t),$$

converges asymptotically to a standard Brownian motion. Thus, the transformation Q_g successfully annihilates the parametric drift component of $\hat{v}_n$ and in so doing restores the asymptotically distribution-free character of tests. Employing the test statistic,

$$\tilde{K}_n = \sup \|\tilde{v}_n\|,$$

circumvents the Durbin problem by removing the effect of the estimated parameters.

4.12.3   The Parametric Quantile Process

Khmaladze's martingalization method may be also applied to the parametric quantile process. I will briefly sketch the univariate version of this approach as a convenient way to introduce the general case of handling the parametric quantile regression process.

Suppose as in the previous section we wish to test that $F_Y(y) = F_0((y - \mu_0)/\sigma_0)$ for some unspecified μ_0 and σ_0 and specified F_0. Rather than using the empirical distribution function, we may employ the empirical quantile function

$$\hat{\alpha}(\tau)) = \inf\{a \in \mathbb{R} | \sum \rho_\tau(y_i - a) = \min!\}.$$

Under the null, we have $\alpha(t) = F_Y^{-1}(t) = \mu_0 + \sigma_0 F_0^{-1}(t)$. For known μ_0 and

σ_0, tests may be based on

$$v_n(t) = \sqrt{n}\varphi_0(t)(\hat{\alpha}(t) - \alpha(t))/\sigma_0.$$

With $\varphi_0(t) = f_0(F_0^{-1}(t))$, it can be shown that v_n converges to the Brownian bridge process v_0. When $\theta_0 = (\mu_0, \sigma_0)$ is not known, we can usually find an estimator $\hat{\theta}_n$ satisfying, for some h_0,

$$\sqrt{n}(\hat{\theta}_n - \theta_0) = \int_0^1 h_0(s)dv_n(s) + o_p(1).$$

Set

$$\tilde{\alpha}_n(t) = \hat{\mu}_0 + \hat{\sigma}_0 F_0^{-1}(t) = \hat{\theta}_n^\top \xi(t),$$

where $\xi(t) = (1, F_0^{-1})^\top$. Then

$$\begin{aligned}
\hat{v}_n(t) &= \sqrt{n}\varphi_0(t)(\hat{\alpha}(t) - \tilde{\alpha}(t))/\sigma_0 \\
&= v_n(t) - \sqrt{n}\varphi_0(t)(\hat{\theta}_n - \theta_0)^\top \xi(t)/\sigma_0 \\
&= v_n(t) - \sigma_0^{-1}\varphi_0(t)\xi(t)^\top \int_0^1 h_0(s)dv_n(s) + o_p(1).
\end{aligned}$$

Again we have a parametric drift component that requires treatment. Now we take $g(t) = (t, \varphi_0(t)\xi(t)^\top)^\top$ so that $\dot{g}(t) = (1, \dot{f}/f, 1 + F_0^{-1}(t)\dot{f}/f)^\top$, where $\dot{f}/f = d\log f/dt$ is evaluated at $F_0^{-1}(t)$. Applying Q_g yields

$$\tilde{v}_n(t) = Q_g\hat{v}_n(t)$$

and, since $Q_g\xi = 0$, we have, for the empirical distribution function,

$$\tilde{v}_n(t) = Q_g v_n(t) + o_p(t) \Rightarrow w_0(t).$$

Thus, asymptotically distribution-free tests may again be based on Kolmogorov–Smirnov statistics of the form,

$$K_n = \sup_{\tau \in T} \|\tilde{v}_n(\tau)\|,$$

or on Cramér –von Mises statistics of the form

$$K_n = \int_T \tilde{v}_n(\tau)^\top W(\tau)\tilde{v}_n(\tau)d\tau,$$

where $W(t)$ denotes a conformable weight matrix.

4.12.4   The Parametric Quantile Regression Process

In the regression setting, the location–scale model asserts that

$$Q_{y_i}(\tau|x_i) = x_i^\top \alpha + x_i^\top \gamma F_0^{-1}(\tau). \tag{4.9}$$

Covariates are allowed to affect both the location and scale of the conditional distribution of y_i given x_i in this model, but the covariates have no effect on the *shape* of the conditional distribution. Typically, the vectors $\{x_i\}$ "contain an intercept"; for example, $x_i = (1, z_i^\top)^\top$ and (4.9) may be seen as arising from the linear model

$$y_i = x_i^\top \alpha + \left(x_i^\top \gamma \right) u_i,$$

where the "errors" $\{u_i\}$ are iid with distribution function F_0. Further specializing the model, we may write

$$x_i^\top \gamma = \gamma_0 + z_i^\top \gamma_1,$$

and the restriction $\gamma_1 = 0$ then implies that the covariates affect only the *location* of the y_is. We will call this model the *location-shift model*:

$$Q_{y_i}(\tau | x_i) = x_i^\top \alpha + \gamma_0 F_0^{-1}(\tau). \tag{4.10}$$

Although this model underlies much of classical econometric inference, it obviously posits a very narrowly circumscribed role for x_i. The problem of testing the location- and location–scale-shift hypotheses against a general linear quantile regression alternative raises essentially the same difficulties we have already characterized as the "Durbin problem." Rather than testing for the plausibility of some fixed reference distribution like the Gaussian, we are interested instead in testing that two or more conditional distributions are identical up to a location–scale or, more simply, a location shift. In the two-sample model described in Section 2.1, we might wish to test that the treatment and control distributions differ only by an affine transformation. We will consider a linear hypothesis of the general form

$$R\beta(\tau) - r = \Psi(\tau), \quad \tau \in \mathcal{T}, \tag{4.11}$$

where R denotes a $q \times p$ matrix, $q \le p$, $r \in \mathbb{R}^q$, and $\Psi(\tau)$ denotes a known function $\Psi : \mathcal{T} \to \mathbb{R}^q$. Tests will be based on the quantile regression process,

$$\hat{\beta}(\tau) = \operatorname{argmin}_{b \in \mathbb{R}^p} \sum_{i=1}^n \rho_\tau \left(y_i - x_i^\top b \right).$$

Under the location–scale-shift form of quantile regression model (4.9), we will have, under mild regularity conditions,

$$\sqrt{n}\varphi_0(\tau)\Omega^{-1/2}(\hat{\beta}(\tau) - \beta(\tau)) \Rightarrow v_0(\tau), \tag{4.12}$$

where $v_0(\tau)$ now denotes a p-dimensional independent Brownian bridge process. Here $\beta(\tau) = \alpha + \gamma F^{-1}(\tau)$, and $\Omega = H_0^{-1} J_0 H_0^{-1}$ with $J_0 = \lim n^{-1} \sum x_i x_i^\top$, and $H_0 = \lim n^{-1} \sum x_i x_i^\top / (\gamma^\top x_i)$. It then follows quite easily under null hypothesis (4.11) that

$$v_n(\tau) = \sqrt{n}\varphi_0(\tau)(R\Omega R^\top)^{-1/2}(R\hat{\beta}(\tau) - r - \Psi(\tau)) \Rightarrow v_0(\tau),$$

and so tests that are asymptotically distribution free can be readily constructed. Indeed, Koenker and Machado (1999) consider tests of this type and show that the nuisance parameters $\varphi_0(\tau)$ and Ω can be replaced by consistent estimates without jeopardizing the distribution-free character of the tests. Under local sequences of alternatives,

$$R\beta_n(\tau) - r - \Psi(\tau) = \zeta(\tau)/\sqrt{n}.$$

It can be shown (Koenker and Xiao, 2002) that

$$v_n(\tau) \Rightarrow v_0(\tau) + \eta(\tau) \text{ for } \tau \in \mathcal{T},$$

where $\mathcal{T} = [\varepsilon, 1 - \varepsilon]$ for some $\varepsilon \in (0, 1/2)$, $v_0(\tau)$ denotes a q-variate standard Brownian bridge process, and

$$\eta(\tau) = \varphi_0(\tau)(R\Omega R^\top)^{-1/2}\zeta(\tau).$$

Under the null hypothesis, so that $\zeta(\tau) = 0$, the test statistic

$$\sup_{\tau \in \mathcal{T}} \| v_n(\tau) \| \Rightarrow \sup_{\tau \in \mathcal{T}} \| v_0(\tau) \| .$$

Typically, even if the hypothesis is fully specified, it is necessary to estimate the matrix Ω and the function $\varphi_0(t) \equiv f_0(F_0^{-1}(t))$. Fortunately, these quantities can be replaced by consistent estimates under quite mild conditions without affecting the limiting behavior of the tests.

An important class of applications of these results involves partial orderings of conditional distributions under stochastic dominance. In the   simplest case of the two-sample treatment control model, this would involve testing the hypothesis that the treatment distribution stochastically dominates the control distribution, or that the quantile treatment effect $\delta(\tau) > 0$ for $\tau \in \mathcal{T}$. Such tests can be implemented using the one-sided, positive-part Kolmogorov–Smirnov statistic. Similarly, tests of second order stochastic dominance can be based on the indefinite integral process of $\delta(\tau)$. These two-sample tests extend nicely to general quantile regression settings and thus complement the important work of McFadden (1989) on testing for stochastic dominance and that of Abadie (2002) on related tests for treatment effects.

When the null hypothesis involves unknown (nuisance) parameters, we are led back to the approach of Khmaladze (1981). Suppose that we have replaced R and r by the estimates R_n and r_n and wish to consider the behavior of the parametric quantile regression process:

$$\hat{v}_n(\tau) = \sqrt{n}\varphi_0(\tau)\left[R_n\Omega R_n^\top \right]^{-1/2} (R_n\hat{\beta}(\tau) - r_n - \Psi(\tau)).$$

Assuming that $\sqrt{n}(R_n - R) = \mathcal{O}_p(1)$ and $\sqrt{n}(r_n - r) = \mathcal{O}_p(1)$, it can be shown that

$$\hat{v}_n(\tau) - Z_n^\top \xi(\tau) \Rightarrow v_0(\tau) + \eta(\tau),$$

where $\xi(\tau) = \varphi_0(\tau)(1, F_0^{-1}(\tau))^\top$, and $Z_n = \mathcal{O}_p(1)$, with $v_0(\tau)$ and $\eta(\tau)$ as specified in the previous subsection. As in the univariate case this conclusion retains its validity when $\varphi_0(\tau)$ and Ω are replaced by consistent estimates.

The presence of the Z_n term disrupts the nice asymptotically distribution-free Bessel process behavior of the v_n process and makes the parametric process $\hat{v}_n$ somewhat more challenging. As in the univariate case, let $g(t) = (t, \xi(t)^\top)^\top$ so that $\dot{g}(t) = (1, \psi(t), \psi(t)F^{-1}(t))^\top$ with $\psi(t) = (\dot{f}/f)(F^{-1}(t))$. We will assume that $g(t)$ satisfies the following conditions:

(i) $\int \| \dot{g}(t) \|^2 \, dt < \infty$,
(ii) $\{\dot{g}_i(t) : i = 1, \ldots, m\}$ are linearly independent in a neighborhood of 1.

The latter condition assures that the inverse of the matrix,

$$C(t) \equiv \int_t^1 \dot{g}(s)\dot{g}(s)^\top ds,$$

exists for all $\tau < 1$. The transformed process,

$$\tilde{v}_n(\tau)^\top \equiv Q_g \hat{v}_n(\tau)^\top = \hat{v}_n(\tau)^\top - \int_0^\tau \dot{g}(s)^\top C^{-1}(s) \int_s^1 \dot{g}(r) d\hat{v}_n(r)^\top ds,$$

(4.13)

yields the martingale component of the parametric process. (The recursive least squares transformation should now be interpreted as operating coordinate by coordinate on the $\hat{v}_n$ process.) Under conditions specified in more detail by Koenker and Xiao (2002), we have

$$\tilde{v}_n(\tau) \Rightarrow w_0(\tau) + \tilde{\eta}(\tau),$$

where $w_0(\tau)$ denotes a q-variate standard Brownian motion, and $\tilde{\eta}(\tau)^\top = Q_g \eta(\tau)^\top$. Under the null hypothesis $- \zeta(\tau) = 0 -$

$$\sup_{\tau \in T} \| \tilde{v}_n(\tau) \| \Rightarrow \sup_{\tau \in T} \| w_0(\tau) \|,$$

thereby restoring the asymptotically distribution-free character of the testing procedure.

Unless we are willing to make distributional assumptions about the underlying model, the function $g(t)$ will *not* be specified under the null hypothesis and, thus, will need to be estimated. Fortunately, a mild consistency condition enables us to replace g by an estimate. This and other issues of implementation of these tests are discussed by Koenker and Xiao (2002).

4.13 PROBLEMS

In the spirit of the famous three-types theorem of Fisher and Tippett (1928) and Gnedenko (1943) in extreme value theory, Smirnov (1952) undertook a similar catalog of the possible limiting forms of the asymptotic distribution of the central sample quantiles. Four limiting forms were found, with the behavior of the parent distributions near the quantile of interest determining the form of the limiting distribution. The next three problems illustrate some of the nonnormal limiting forms that arise when the density of the parent distribution is zero at the quantile of interest. Extensions of these results to the quantile regression setting have been explored recently by Knight (1998) and Rogers (2001).

Problem 4.1. To explore the role of the condition $f(0) > 0$, reconsider Problem 3.1 assuming instead that $F(0) = 1/2$, $f(0) = 0$, and $f'(0\pm) = \pm 1$. How does this alter (a) the rate of convergence of $\hat{\mu}$ and (b) the form of the limiting distribution?

Problem 4.2. Suppose $X_1, \ldots, X_n$ constitutes a random sample from a distribution with median zero and continuous distribution function F at zero. If, for some $\alpha > 0$,

$$F(x) - F(0) = \lambda \operatorname{sgn}(x)|x|^\alpha$$

for x in a neighborhood of zero, show using the machinery of Section 3.2 that the sample median $\hat{\xi}_n(1/2)$ satisfies, for a sequence $a_n = n^{1/2\alpha}$,

$$P(a_n \hat{\xi}_n > \delta) \to 1 - \Phi(\sqrt{2}\lambda\delta^\alpha)$$

for $\delta > 0$, and thus $\hat{\xi}_n$ has limiting density

$$f(x) = \sqrt{\frac{2}{\pi}} \lambda\alpha|x|^{\alpha-1} \exp\{-2\lambda^2|x|^{2\alpha}\}.$$

Note that when $\alpha > 1$, then this density is bimodal, whereas for $\alpha < 1$ the density has a singularity at zero.

Problem 4.3. For an even more extreme example, consider the median from a population with distribution function:

$$F(x) = \begin{cases} 1 & x > \alpha \\ 1/2 + \exp\{-x^{-2}\} & x \in (0, \alpha] \\ 1/2 & x = 0 \\ 1/2 - \exp\{-x^{-2}\} & x \in [-\alpha, 0) \\ 0 & x < -\alpha \end{cases}$$

so that not only F has density $f(0) = 0$, but all the higher order derivatives of F are also zero at zero. Show that, after normalizing by $\sqrt{\log n}$, the limiting distribution of the sample median is a discrete distribution with only two points of support. (This is Smirnov's type 4 limit.)

CHAPTER 5

L-Statistics and Weighted Quantile Regression

As in the theory of least-squares regression, reweighting plays an important role in quantile regression theory and applications. Reweighting arises in many different guises. Weighted averages of quantile regression estimates at a few distinct quantiles were suggested already by Koenker and Bassett (1978) as analogs of univariate L-statistics. This approach provides a simple way to estimate location, scale, and tail behavior functionals tailored to particular applications. It can also be adapted to do local smoothing of the quantile regression process. Reweighting the summands of the underlying optimization problem also provides an important strategy for improving the efficiency of quantile regression estimates.

5.1 L-STATISTICS FOR THE LINEAR MODEL

Linear combinations of functions of a few sample quantiles often provide a surprisingly efficient, yet extremely simple, means of estimating salient characteristics of a random variable. Weighted averages of the quantiles as an estimator of location, interquantile ranges for scale, and Hill's (1975) estimator of the tail exponent of a distribution function are all of this form. In special cases, such estimators can even be optimal: the median as an estimator of location for the Laplace, or double exponential, distribution, or the midrange for the location of the uniform distribution, for example. But generally, L-statistics with smoother weight functions are preferred for reasons of both efficiency and robustness.

The leading example of a "smooth" L-estimator is undoubtedly the trimmed mean. Denoting the τth quantile by

$$\hat{\xi}(\tau) = \operatorname{argmin}_{\xi} \sum \rho_\tau(y_i - \xi),$$

we may express the α-trimmed mean as

$$\hat{\mu}_\alpha = \int_0^1 \varphi_\alpha(t)\hat{\xi}(t)dt,$$

where $\varphi_\alpha(\tau) = I(\alpha \leq \tau \leq 1 - \alpha)/(1 - 2\alpha)$, which is simply the sample average of the central $[(1 - 2\alpha)n]$-order statistics. This estimator has a long history of applications in astronomy and other fields, and has been singled out by several prominent authors as the quintessential robust estimator of location (see, e.g., Bickel and Lehmann, 1975; Stigler, 1977).

L-statistics were initially regarded by Mosteller (1946) as "quick and dirty" substitutes when maximum likelihood estimation was either infeasible, due to lack of confidence in the parametric form of the model, or intractable due to computational difficulties. But it was quickly recognized that asymptotically fully efficient L-statistics could be constructed to compete with maximum likelihood estimators on an equal footing.

An important example of the contrast between M- and L-estimators is the well-known "least-favorable" density of Huber (1964), which takes the form

$$f_\varepsilon(x) = \begin{cases} c \ \exp(-x^2/2) & \text{if } |x| \leq k \\ c \ \exp(k^2/2 - k|x|) & \text{otherwise,} \end{cases}$$

where $c = (1 - \varepsilon)/\sqrt{2\pi}$ and k satisfies $2\phi(k)/k - 2\Phi(k) = \varepsilon(1 - \varepsilon)$, with ϕ and Φ denoting the standard normal density and distribution function, respectively. This density, which is Gaussian in the center with exponential tails, has minimal Fisher information in the class

$$\mathcal{F} = \{F = (1 - \varepsilon)\Phi + \varepsilon H | H \in \mathcal{H}\},$$

where $\mathcal{H}$ denotes the set of distribution functions symmetric about zero, and ε is a fixed number between zero and one. Given ε, an M-estimator of location for this "minimax" family of densities may be constructed by solving

$$\hat{\mu}_\varepsilon = \text{argmin}_\xi \sum \rho_{H_k}(y_i - \xi),$$

where $\rho_{H_k}(x) = [x^2 I(|x| \leq k) + k^2 I(|x| > k)]$. Because scale is generally unknown, and $\hat{\mu}_\varepsilon$ as just formulated is not scale equivariant, in practice we need to replace it by something of the form

$$\hat{\mu}_\varepsilon = \text{argmin}_\xi \sum \rho_{H_k}((y_i - \xi)/\hat{\sigma})$$

for some scale equivariant estimator $\hat{\sigma}$. Alternatively, we could jointly minimize with respect to location and scale parameters.

A dramatically simpler, yet asymptotically fully efficient, alternative to such M-estimators for this least-favorable model is the α-trimmed mean. The latter has the advantage of being automatically scale equivariant as well as avoiding the necessity of computing the Huber constant $k(\varepsilon)$. The form of the α-trimmed mean weight function $\varphi_\alpha(\cdot)$ reflects clearly the form of the Huber least-favorable density with the central, Gaussian portion of the sample receiving constant weight $(1 - 2\alpha)^{-1}$ and the exponential tail portion receiving weight zero. Because the density was designed to minimize the information provided by the tails, it seems hardly surprising that the tail observations are uninformative about location and therefore receive zero weight in the efficient form of the L-statistic.

5.1.1 Optimal L-Estimators of Location and Scale

Tukey (1965) posed the intriguing question, "Which part of the sample contains the information?" The answer crucially depends on what is being estimated as well as the form of the underlying distribution of observations. For the location parameter of the Huber density, the question is clearly answered at least in an asymptotic sense by "the central $[(1 - 2\alpha)n]$-order statistics." The tail observations contribute nothing asymptotically to the design of an efficient estimator of location for this density. Other models are even more extreme in this respect. We have already mentioned the Laplace density, for which the sample median contains, asymptotically, *all* the available sample information about location. This is obviously a limiting form of the Huber model.

In general, the optimal L-estimator weight function provides a concise, asymptotic answer to Tukey's question. As shown, for example, by Serfling (1980), the optimal weight function for the L-estimator of location takes the form

$$\varphi_0(t) = -(\log f)''(F^{-1}(t)).$$

For scale, the optimal weight function is

$$\varphi_1(t) = [(\log f)' + x(\log f)''](F^{-1}(t)).$$

Under some regularity conditions, these optimal L-estimators have the same asymptotic efficiency as the corresponding maximum likelihood estimator. Figure 5.1 illustrates these weight functions for a variety of familiar densities. In addition, for purpose of comparison, we include a sketch of the influence function of these estimators that can also be interpreted as the ψ-function, which serves to determine the optimal M-estimator in each case.

We note first that the Gaussian density is unique in its treatment of each observation as equally informative about location. Thus, the apparently natural, highly democratic principle embodied in the sample mean is seen to be quite specifically tailored to the peculiar features of the Gaussian model. For the logistic, Student-t, and Huber densities, the location weights fall off sharply in the tails. The Student densities illustrate a curious phenomenon. When, as in the Student cases, the tail behavior of the density is heavier than exponential, then the optimal weight function can be negative in the tails. This has the apparently paradoxical effect that, given a sample, if we move observations, say, in the right tail further to the right, we may actually move our estimate to the left. Accentuating the outliers in the Student-t model increases our willingness to discount them. This paradox is only a thinly disguised variant of the familiar tendency for an enthusiastic movie review by a dubious reviewer to send us running in the opposite direction looking for another film.

Not surprisingly, virtually all the sample information *about location* in our asymmetric densities is contained in the first few order statistics. In the even more extreme case of the uniform model, it is well known that the extreme order statistics are sufficient and carry all the information about the unknown

M-IF   M-IF   L-score   L-score

location   scale   location   scale

ψ_0 ψ_1 φ_0 φ_1

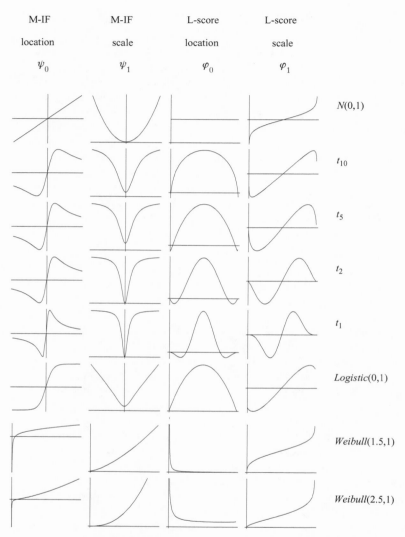

Figure 5.1. Comparative zoology of score functions. This figure illustrates the shapes of the optimal score functions for L-estimators of location and scale for some representative distributions as well as the shapes of the ψ-functions for optimal M-estimators of location and scale. The horizontal axis for the M-estimator plots is the real (half) line; for the L-estimators it is the interval [0, 1].

parameters characterizing the support of the distribution. Note that, for the last Weibull example, all of the order statistics receive positive weight. The L-estimators of scale exhibit rather different behavior than their corresponding location estimators. For symmetric densities, the weight functions for the optimal scale L-estimators are odd functions, thus assuring location invariance. In the Gaussian case we have $\varphi_1(t) = \Phi^{-1}(t)$ and so our estimator is

$$\hat{\sigma} = \int_0^1 \Phi^{-1}(t)\hat{\xi}(t)dt,$$

where the empirical quantile function $\hat{\xi}(t)$ satisfies $\hat{\xi}(t) \to \mu + \sigma\Phi^{-1}(t)$; and so we have, changing variables,

$$\hat{\sigma} \to \sigma \int_0^1 (\Phi^{-1}(t))^2 dt = \sigma \int_{-\infty}^{\infty} x^2 d\Phi(t) = \sigma.$$

As in the case of location estimation, heavy tails in the model density induce a downweighting of tail observations for scale L-estimators. The χ^2 densities yield a constant weighting for scale estimation, whereas for the Weibull model the corresponding weight functions are sharply increasing in the tails, reflecting their "light" highly informative tails.

5.1.2 L-Estimation for the Linear Model

Most aspects of the theory of L-estimation in the univariate case can be carried forward to the linear model directly via quantile regression. For example, consider the linear location–scale model

$$y_i = x_i^\top \beta + \left(x_i^\top \gamma\right) u_i \tag{5.1}$$

with u_i iid from F. Asymptotically efficient estimators of β and γ are available as

$$\hat{\beta} = \int_0^1 \varphi_o(t)\hat{\beta}(t)dt$$

$$\hat{\gamma} = \int_0^1 \varphi_1(t)\hat{\beta}(t)dt,$$

where φ_0 and φ_1 are as defined earlier, and $\hat{\beta}(t)$ denotes the p-dimensional quantile regression process. Obviously, the integrals should be interpreted as computed coordinatewise in each case.

In some cases, such "efficient" L-statistics are a bit surprising in their departure from more-familiar M-estimators. For example, in the Gaussian case, the estimator

$$\hat{\beta} = \int_0^1 \hat{\beta}(t)dt,$$

which simply averages each coordinate of the quantile regression process, appears quite different from the familiar least-squares estimator. However, under Gaussian conditions, it performs quite well in Monte Carlo comparison with least squares (see Portnoy and Koenker, 1989). In the case of the Gaussian scale estimator, we now have, for F Gaussian,

$$\hat{\beta}(t) \rightarrow \beta + \gamma \Phi^{-1}(t)$$

and so

$$\hat{\gamma} = \int_0^1 \Phi^{-1}(t)\hat{\beta}(t)dt \rightarrow \gamma.$$

Indeed, for general F we obtain

$$\hat{\gamma} = \int_0^1 \Phi^{-1}(t)\hat{\beta}(t)dt \rightarrow \gamma \int_0^1 \Phi^{-1}(t)F^{-1}(t)dt,$$

and so we estimate γ "consistently up to scale"; that is, ratios of the coordinates of $\hat{\gamma}$ are consistent for corresponding ratios of the vector γ.

It is a significant advantage of the L-statistic approach to the estimation of linear models that, in cases in which there are both heteroscedasticity and asymmetric innovations, it is possible to distinguish the location and scale effects of the covariates, whereas with conventional least-squares-based methods this proves to be much more difficult. Consider, for example, the simple version of (5.1):

$$y_i = \alpha + \beta x_i + \gamma x_i^2 u_i$$

with u_i iid from F, and F asymmetric so that $E u_1 = \mu \neq 0$. Least-squares estimation of the quadratic model would estimate the parameters of the conditional mean function

$$E(y_i|x_i) = \alpha + \beta x_i + \mu \gamma x_i^2.$$

Now, if we proceed conventionally, we would regress absolute residuals on the available covariates, assuming

$$E|y_i - \hat{y}_i| = c_0 + c_1 x_i + c_2 x_i^2.$$

It is easy to see that least-squares estimation of this model would yield $\hat{c}_0 \rightarrow 0$, $\hat{c}_1 \rightarrow 0$, and $\hat{c}_2 \rightarrow \gamma E|u_i - \mu|$. However, if in the first step we estimated the simpler linear model and then tried to introduce the quadratic effect only in the second step, we introduce a bias resulting from the approximation of a quadratic function by something linear and this misspecification is then transmitted to the next step as well. In contrast, the quantile regression estimation of the quadratic model yields, via the L-statistic approach, a family of estimators of γ that are all "consistent up to scale." In addition, as we saw in Chapter 3, rank-based tests for the heteroscedasticity parameter γ may be based on preliminary quantile regression estimation of the simpler linear model.

L-estimation also provides a convenient approach to adaptive estimation linear models. Suppose that we wish to estimate the median of an unknown, symmetric distribution, $F(x - \theta_0)$, with finite Fisher information, $\mathcal{I}(F)$, based on a random sample $\{X_1, \ldots, X_n\}$. Drawing on earlier work of Hájek and Stein, a remarkable confluence of papers in the early 1970's, including van Eeden (1970), Sacks (1975), Beran (1974), and Stone (1975) showed that the center of symmetry was *adaptively eastimable*, that is that estimators $\hat{\theta}_n$ existed that achieved the optimal parametric asymptotic variance bound,

$$\sqrt{n}(\hat{\theta}_n - \theta_0) \rightsquigarrow \mathcal{N}(0, \mathcal{I}(F)^{-1}).$$

Our ignorance of the shape of F imposes no asymptotic penalty on the estimation of the median in these symmetric settings. How is it possible to achieve this bound? Sacks (1975) proposed an L-estimator approach in which the empirical distribution function of the X_i's is first symmetrized around the median, then smoothed to produce an estimate of the optimal score function, $\hat{\varphi}_0$, which is then employed to compute an approximately optimal L-estimator. This approach was adapted to the linear model by Portnoy and Koenker (1989).

Having seen that under symmetry there is no impediment to a fully efficient parametric estimator of location, it is natural to ask: "Can we improve upon the the asymptotic performance of the median in asymmetric models, or more generally, can we improve upon the asymptotic performance of any sample quantile as an estimator of the corresponding population quantile. In the strict sense of Pfanzagl (1982), the answer is no:

> If nothing is known about the true p-measure (except that it has a positive Lebesgue density), one cannot do better asymptotically than use the sample quantile of the true p-measure." (p. 239)

As we will see in the next section, local smoothing can be quite effective in reducing the variability of the sample quantiles, but at the price of a bias that ultimately must dominate the variance effect. Newey and Powell (1990), as noted following Theorem 5.1, generalize the Pfanzagl result to the weighted quantile regression setting.

Finally, we should add that the integrals that appear in the foregoing L-statistics are usually quite simple to compute due to the piecewise constant form of the quantile regression process. We can illustrate this for the case of scale estimation with the Gaussian weight function, $\Phi^{-1}(t)$:

$$\hat{\gamma} = \int_0^1 \Phi^{-1}(t)\hat{\beta}(t)dt$$

$$= \sum_{j=1}^{J} \hat{\beta}(t_{j+1}) \int_{t_j}^{t_{j+1}} \Phi^{-1}(t)dt$$

$$= \sum_{j=1}^{J} \beta(t_{j+1})[\phi(\Phi^{-1}(t_{j+1})) - \phi(\Phi^{-1}(t_j))].$$

Note that, by the left-continuity convention for quantile functions, $\hat{\beta}(t) = \hat{\beta}(t_{j+1})$ for $t \in (t_j, t_{j+1}]$. A robustified version of this Gaussian scale estimator is easily adapted by restricting the domain of the integration to avoid the tails and, possibly, the center of the unit interval. Welsh and Morrison (1990) discuss such estimators in considerable further detail for the univariate setting.

5.2 KERNEL SMOOTHING FOR QUANTILE REGRESSION

Kernel smoothing may be used to improve the performance of univariate quantile estimators. The idea is quite simple and may be extended in a straightforward manner to regression using the L-estimation approach of the previous section.

Let $k(x)$ be a kernel function of some conventional form; for purposes of illustration we may take the Epanechnikov kernel:

$$k(t) = \frac{3}{4}\left(1 - \frac{1}{5}t^2\right) I(|t| < \sqrt{5})/\sqrt{5}.$$

We wish to consider replacing $\hat{\beta}_n(\tau)$ by the smoothed local average of the quantile regression process,

$$\tilde{\beta}_n(\tau) = \int_0^1 \hat{\beta}_n(\tau)k((\tau - t)/h_n(\tau))/h_n(\tau)dt. \tag{5.2}$$

The degree of smoothing is determined by the bandwidth function $h_n(\tau)$. Because the function $\hat{\beta}_n(\tau)$ is piecewise constant, we can simplify the computation by an integration by parts:

$$\tilde{\beta}_n(\tau) = \int_0^1 K((\tau - t)/h_n(\tau))d\hat{\beta}(t) - \hat{\beta}(t)K((\tau - t)/h_n) \mid_0^1$$

$$= \sum_{i=1}^J K((\tau - t_i)/h_n(\tau))\Delta\hat{\beta}(t_i) + \hat{\beta}(0),$$

where $K(t) = \int_{-\infty}^t k(s)ds$, and the summation is over the jump points of the $\hat{\beta}_n(\tau)$ process. Because most of the popular kernel functions take the form of familiar densities, direct methods to evaluate the corresponding distribution functions are easily available, and the computation can be carried out quite efficiently.

Table 5.1 reports the results of a small Monte Carlo experiment in which data were generated from several independently and identically distributed (iid) linear models and the performance of several smoothed quantile regression estimators were compared. Data for the linear model

$$y_i = \beta_1 + \beta_2\Phi^{-1}(i/(n + 1)) + \beta_3|\Phi^{-1}(i/(n + 1))| + u_i \quad i = 1, \ldots, n$$

$$\tag{5.3}$$

Table 5.1. *Monte Carlo mean squared errors for*
kernel-smoothed quantile regression estimators

Quantile	Bandwidth	β_1	β_2	β_3
0.75	0.200	0.026	0.004	0.014
0.75	0.100	0.024	0.007	0.022
0.75	0.050	0.025	0.008	0.024
0.75	0.020	0.027	0.009	0.026
0.75	0.000	0.029	0.009	0.028
0.90	0.080	0.049	0.008	0.026
0.90	0.050	0.040	0.011	0.037
0.90	0.020	0.041	0.013	0.041
0.90	0.010	0.043	0.014	0.043
0.90	0.000	0.045	0.015	0.045
0.95	0.040	0.078	0.012	0.041
0.95	0.020	0.061	0.018	0.059
0.95	0.010	0.062	0.019	0.061
0.95	0.005	0.065	0.020	0.064
0.95	0.000	0.069	0.021	0.069

The table reports Monte Carlo mean squared errors for several
kernel-smoothed quantile regression estimators. The data for the
experiment were generated from model (5.3) with $\{u_i\}$ iid standard normal, and $n = 200$ and 1000 replications per cell of the
experiment. In each cell we compute five different degrees of
smoothing, represented by the bandwidth parameter h_n. It can
be seen that more smoothing is advantageous for the slope parameters, because the kernel averages estimates of a common
quantity. However, for the intercept, kernel smoothing introduces a bias, which is reflected in the poor performance of the
largest bandwidth in each panel of the table.

were generated with y_i iid Gaussian. This Gaussian iid error setting is particularly favorable for kernel smoothing of the slope parameters and we see
considerable improvement due to smoothing for these parameters. For the intercept parameter there is an obvious bias effect due to smoothing, but the
smoothing still has generally favorable consequences for experimental mean
square errors. This bias would extend to the estimation of slope parameters as
well as the intercept parameter in heteroscedastic models. We have observed
earlier that the estimated quantile regression surfaces may intersect near the
boundary of the observed design space. Some smoothing of the estimates offers a simple approach to ameliorating this effect. This lunch, of course, is not
free. Even in the iid error model there is inevitably some bias introduced in
the intercept estimation due to the smoothing, and in non-iid models there may
be bias in slope parameter estimation as well. Replacing the "locally constant"
model of smoothing implicit in the usual kernel approach by a locally polynomial model, as described, for example, by Hastie and Loader (1993), may offer
further improvements.

5.2.1   Kernel Smoothing of the ρ_τ-Function

A third form of local averaging for quantile regression that has received some attention in the literature involves smoothing the function ρ_τ itself. Several motivations have been offered. Amemiya (1982) used such a smoothing device to simplify the analysis of the asymptotic behavior of his two-stage median regression estimator.

We have already noted that the Huber M-estimator can be viewed as an alternative to the trimmed quantile regression L-estimator:

$$\hat{\beta}_\alpha = (1 - 2\alpha)^{-1} \int_\alpha^{1-\alpha} \hat{\beta}(\tau) d\tau.$$

By replacing the V-shaped absolute values of the median regression estimator by a function that is nicely quadratic near its minimum, we achieve a local averaging much like the kernel averaging described in Section 5.2. One could easily extend this Huberization to quantiles other than the median. A disadvantage of the Huber approach is its lack of scale equivariance.

Horowitz (1998) has recently considered smoothing methods of this type in work on bootstrapping the median regression estimator. In this context, the degree of smoothing can be made to vanish in such a way that the resulting estimator has more conventional smooth M-estimator asymptotics, yielding improved asymptotic performance for the bootstrap. Whether these gains are sufficient to justify the use of this approach in applications remains an open question.

It is also sometimes claimed that such smoothing strategies are desirable on the grounds of computational efficiency; however, this remains as yet unsubstantiated.

5.3   WEIGHTED QUANTILE REGRESSION

When the conditional densities of the response are heterogeneous, it is natural to consider whether weighted quantile regression might lead to efficiency improvements. Rather than weighting by the reciprocals of the standard deviations of the observations, quantile regression weights should be proportional to the local density evaluated at the quantile of interest.

5.3.1   Weighted Linear Quantile Regression

We will consider the weighted estimator

$$\check{\beta}_n(\tau) = \mathrm{argmin}_{b \in \mathbb{R}^p} \sum_{i=1}^n f_i(\xi_i) \rho_\tau(y_i - x_i^\top b).$$

Theorem 5.1. *Under Conditions A1 and A2 of Theorem 4.1,*

$$\sqrt{n}(\check{\beta}(\tau) - \beta(\tau)) \rightsquigarrow \mathcal{N}(0, \tau(1 - \tau)D_2^{-1}(\tau))$$

provided $D_2(\tau) = \lim_{n \to \infty} n^{-1} \sum f_i^2(\xi_i) x_i x_i^\top$ *is positive definite.*

Proof. Modifying the argument for Theorem 4.1 to incorporate the weights, we obtain

$$Z_n(\delta) \rightsquigarrow Z_0(\delta) = -\delta \breve{W} + \frac{1}{2}\delta^\top D_2 \delta,$$

where $\breve{W} \sim \mathcal{N}(0, \tau(1-\tau)D_2)$ and the result follows. $\blacksquare$

It is easy to see that $\breve{\beta}_n(\tau)$ is unambiguously more efficient than $\hat{\beta}_n(\tau)$. Let

$$D = \begin{pmatrix} D_2 & D_1 \\ D_1 & D_0 \end{pmatrix} = \lim_{n \to \infty} \sum_{i=1}^{n} \begin{pmatrix} f_i^2 & f_i \\ f_i & 1 \end{pmatrix} \otimes x_i x_i^\top,$$

where $\otimes$ denotes the usual Kronecker product. That D is nonnegative definite follows from the fact that the constituent matrices of the Kronecker product are. Because D_2 is positive definite, there exists an orthogonal matrix P such that

$$P^\top D P = \begin{pmatrix} D_2 & 0 \\ 0 & D_0 - D_1 D_2^{-1} D_1 \end{pmatrix}$$

and so $D_0 - D_1 D_2^{-1} D_1$ is nonnegative definite and consequently $D_1^{-1} D_0 D_1^{-1} - D_2^{-1}$ is nonnegative definite because D_1 is nonsingular. Newey and Powell (1990) study a related weighted quantile regression estimator in the censored case and show that the estimator attains a semiparametric efficiency bound. Clearly, this is a local notion of efficiency because we are restricting attention to a model that only specifies structure at the τth quantile.

Naturally, we would like to know, in view of the foregoing result, whether it is possible to *estimate* the weights, $w_i = f_i(\xi_i)$, to achieve full efficiency for a *feasible* version of $\breve{\beta}_n(\tau)$. This is a difficult question to resolve in its full generality. Koenker and Zhao (1994) treat the linear location–scale model, providing a uniform Bahadur representation for the empirically weighted quantile regression process. L-estimators based on the weighted process are then investigated. Some related results in the context of autoregressive conditional heteroscedasticity–type models are developed by Koenker and Zhao (1996). Zhao (1999) considers a more general form of the model in which the weights are estimated by nearest-neighbor nonparametric methods.

5.3.2 Estimating Weights

The asymptotics of weighted quantile regression may appear somewhat quixotic until reasonable methods of estimating the desired weights are specified. Analysis of such estimation schemes requires some assumptions on the variability of the conditional density. Essentially, it must be possible to "borrow" strength from neighboring observations to estimate the conditional density at specific points. Several possible models may be suggested.

One approach is to assume that only the scale of the density depends on x. That is, let $u_i = \sigma(x_i)v_i$, where $\{v_i\}$ are iid. Equivalently, we may write

$f_i(u) = g(u/\sigma(x_i))/\sigma(x_i)$, where $g(u)$ is the common density of the $\{v_i\}$. One major problem with this assumption is that the conditional quantile functions may no longer be linear in x. The easiest way to avoid this problem is to assume that $\sigma(x)$ is linear in x; that is, let $\sigma(x_i) = x_i^\top \gamma$ subject to the condition that γ is such that $\sigma(x_i)$ is positive on the support of x. Linearity of the conditional quantile functions follows directly from this assumption. We should stress that by linearity in this context we mean linearity in parameters. It is quite reasonable to consider models for scale that are nonlinear in covariates while maintaining the linearity-in-parameters assumption.

An alternative approach is to assume $\sigma(x)$ is a smooth function of x and to use some form of nonparametric regression methods to estimate $\sigma(x_i)$. Even more generally, one may use nonparametric density estimation to estimate f_i directly. Although nonparametric estimators converge more slowly, generally at a rate $n^{-2/5}$ instead of the parametric rate $n^{-1/2}$, we will see that this is not critical for adaptive estimation of the weights.

Rather than present the previous results in a formal manner, I will try to indicate informally what is needed to estimate the weights $\{w_i\}$ with sufficient accuracy so that the resulting estimator is efficient. Consider the estimator

$$\hat{\beta}_{\hat{w}}(\tau) = \arg\min \sum_{i=1}^n \hat{w}_i \rho_\tau (y_i - x_i^\top b)$$

with estimates $\{\hat{w}_i\}$ replacing the optimal weights $\{w_i\}$. It is generally not difficult to show that a Bahadur representation still holds for fixed τ:

$$n^{1/2}(\hat{\beta}_{\hat{w}} - \beta) = n^{-1/2} \sum_{i=1}^n \hat{w}_i R_i + o_p(1),$$

where $R_i = x_i(\tau - I(U_i \leq 0))$. This essentially requires showing that the representation for fixed weights is in fact uniform in the weights; to make this rigorous would obviously require some restrictions on the weights.

Now, consider estimating the weights as a smooth function of the residuals from a $\sqrt{n}$ consistent preliminary estimator of $\beta(\tau)$. Since the preliminary estimate yields $\sqrt{n}$ consistent of the population quantiles, the residuals are $\sqrt{n}$-consistent estimates of the errors. This suggests an expansion for the weights of the form

$$\hat{w}_i = w_i + m_n^{-1} \sum_{j \neq i}^n W_i(u_j) + o_p (m_n^{-1}),$$

where W_i is a bounded function and where the contribution of the error $W_i(u_i)$ to $\hat{w}_i$ is absorbed into the error term. When $\sigma(x)$ is linear in x, we can expect to get parametric rates of convergence so that $m_n = n$. In nonparametric cases, we may expect to be able to take $m_n = n^{4/5}$ for both kernel and spline estimators.

In either case, we have

$$\frac{1}{m_n} = o(n^{-1/2}) \quad \text{and} \quad \frac{n}{m_n^2} = o(n^{-1/2}),$$

which we will assume throughout the remainder of this subsection. Then we may write

$$n^{-1/2} \sum_{i=1}^{n} \hat{w}_i R_i = n^{-1/2} \sum_{i=1}^{n} w_i R_i + n^{-1/2} \sum_{i=1}^{n} S_i R_i + o_p(1),$$

where $S_i = m_n^{-1} \sum_{j \neq i}^{n} W_i(u_j)$. The first term yields the efficient covariance matrix. Therefore, it remains for us to show that the second term is negligible. Consider the variance:

$$Q \equiv Var\left(n^{-1/2} \sum_{i=1}^{n} S_i R_i\right) = n^{-1} \sum_{i=1}^{n} \sum_{j=1}^{n} E S_i S_j R_i R_j.$$

Note that we may write $S_i = T_{ij} + W_i(u_j)/m_n$, where we define

$$T_{ij} = m_n^{-1} \sum_{k \notin \{i,j\}} W_i(u_k).$$

Because $W_i(u)$ is uniformly bounded, the last terms in T_{ij} are, $\mathcal{O}(m_n^{-1})$; and, furthermore, $E S_i^2 = E T_{ij}^2 = \mathcal{O}(1/m_n)$, using independence of $\{u_i\}$. Thus, we have

$$Q = n^{-1} \sum\sum E T_{ij} T_{ji} R_i R_j$$
$$+ (nm_n)^{-1} \sum\sum E S_i T_{ji} R_i R_j W_j(u_i)$$
$$+ (nm_n)^{-1} \sum\sum E S_j T_{ij} R_i R_j W_i(u_j)$$
$$+ (nm_n^2)^{-1} \sum\sum E W_j(u_i) W_i(u_j) R_i R_j.$$

In the first term of the preceding equation, all summands with $i \neq j$ vanish because $\{T_{ij}, T_{ji}\}$ are independent of $\{R_i, R_j\}$, and $E R_i R_j = 0$ if $i \neq j$. The second and third terms are each $(nm_n)^{-1}$ times a double sum of n^2 summands, each of which is bounded by a term of the form

$$\mathcal{O}\left(\left(E S_i^2 E T_{ij}^2\right)^{1/2}\right) = \mathcal{O}(1/m_n)$$

because $\{R_i\}$ and $\{W_i\}$ are bounded. Thus, both terms are of order $\mathcal{O}\left(n/m_n^2\right)$. Finally, bounding each of the summands in the last term gives this same order. Thus,

$$Q = \mathcal{O}(1/m_n) + \mathcal{O}\left(n/m_n^2\right) = o(n^{-1/2}),$$

and we conclude that

$$n^{-1/2} \sum_{i=1}^{n} \hat{w}_i R_i = n^{-1/2} \sum_{i=1}^{n} w_i R_i + o_p(1)$$

and, consequently, the weights are adaptively estimable.

5.4 QUANTILE REGRESSION FOR LOCATION–SCALE MODELS

The location–scale model of regression takes the form

$$Y_i = \mu(x_i) + \sigma(x_i)u_i \tag{5.4}$$

with $\{u_i\}$ iid as F. If the location and scale functions could be parameterized by $\theta \in \Theta \subset \mathbb{R}^p$, then the conventional maximum-likelihood M-estimation approach would suggest solving

$$\min_{\theta \in \Theta} \sum_{i=1}^{n} [\rho((Y_i - \mu(x_i, \theta))/\sigma(x_i, \theta)) + \log \sigma(x_i, \theta)], \tag{5.5}$$

for some appropriate choice of ρ. Ideally, we would like to choose $\rho = -\log f$ when f is the density of the u_is, but robustness considerations might suggest other choices if f were unknown. Carroll and Ruppert (1988) offer an excellent treatment of the state of the art based on M-estimation in this parametric setting.

If we are only willing to assume some smoothness in $\mu(x)$, $\sigma(x)$, not an explicit parametric form, the situation is less clear. Various kernel and nearest-neighbor approaches have been suggested, but penalized likelihood also seems very attractive. We might begin by ignoring the scale heterogeneity and minimize

$$\sum \rho(Y_i - \mu(x_i)) + \lambda_\mu \int (\mu''(x))^2 dx$$

over μ in a (Sobolev) space of functions with absolutely continuous first derivative and square integrable second derivative. Having estimated $\mu(x)$ in this manner, we could proceed to estimate the scale function by minimizing

$$\sum \rho(\hat{u}_i/\sigma(x_i)) + \log \sigma(x_i) + \lambda_\sigma \int (\sigma''(x))^2 dx,$$

where $\hat{u}_i = Y_i - \hat{\mu}(x_i)$ and, again ideally, $\rho = -\log f$. Iteration of this scheme would yield a penalized maximum likelihood estimator for the location–scale regression model.

An alternative approach based on L-estimation seems somewhat more flexible. Since the conditional quantile functions of Y_i in the location–scale regression model are simply

$$Q_Y(\tau|x) = \mu(x) + \sigma(x)Q_u(\tau),$$

we may estimate these functions by minimizing

$$\sum \rho_\tau(Y_i - \xi(x_i)) + \lambda_\tau \int (\xi''(x))^2 dx,$$

where $\rho_\tau(u) = u(\tau - I(u < 0))$, as usual, and λ_τ denotes a penalty parameter that governs the smoothness of the resulting estimate. However, as we will emphasize in Chapter 7, the L_2 roughness penalty may be more conveniently chosen to be the L_1 or L_∞ norm of ξ''. Denoting the minimizer as $\hat{Q}_Y(\tau|x)$, standard L-estimation ideas may be employed to average over τ, thereby obtaining estimates of μ and σ. Again, optimality at a known f would suggest

$$\hat{\mu}(x) = \int_0^1 \varphi_0(t)\hat{Q}_Y(t|x)dt$$

$$\hat{\sigma}(x) = \int_0^1 \varphi_1(t)\hat{Q}_Y(t|x)dt,$$

where $\varphi_0(t) \equiv (\log f)''(Q(t)) = (f'/f)'(Q(t))$ and $\varphi_1(t) \equiv (xf'/f)'(Q(t))$.

A particularly simple example of the foregoing approach is offered by the case where the functions $\mu(x)$ and $\sigma(x)$ are assumed to be linear in parameters, and so we may rewrite (5.4) as

$$Y_i = x_i^\top \beta + \left(x_i^\top \gamma\right) u_i. \tag{5.6}$$

It should be emphasized that linearity in the covariates is not essential, and so this formulation includes various "series-expansion" models in which the x_is may be interpreted as basis functions evaluated at the observed values of the original covariates.

In model (5.6) the conditional quantile functions are simply

$$Q_Y(\tau|x) = x^\top(\beta + \gamma Q_u(\tau))$$

and the linear quantile regression estimator,

$$\hat{\beta}(\tau) = \text{argmin}_{b \in \mathbb{R}^p} \sum \rho_\tau(Y_i - x^\top b),$$

converges under rather mild conditions to $\beta(\tau) = \beta + \gamma F^{-1}(\tau)$. Nevertheless, there is something inherently unsatisfactory about $\beta(\tau)$ in this context; this is reflected clearly in the sandwich form of the asymptotic covariance of $\hat{\beta}(\tau)$.

As in the more familiar context of least-squares estimation, the presence of heteroscedasticity resulting from the dependence of $x'\gamma$ on x in (5.6) introduces no asymptotic bias in $\hat{\beta}(\tau)$, but it does introduce a source of asymptotic inefficiency. We have seen that the asymptotic covariance matrix of $\sqrt{n}(\hat{\beta}(\tau) - \beta(\tau))$ is $\omega(\tau, F)D_1^{-1}D_0D_1^{-1}$, an expression analogous to the Eicker–White least-squares sandwich formula, where $D_r = \lim X'\Gamma^{-r}X$ and Γ is the diagonal matrix with typical element $x^\top \gamma$ and $\omega(\tau, F) = \tau(1 - \tau)/f^2(F^{-1}(\tau))$. Reweighting the quantile regression minimization problem, we may define a weighted quantile regression estimator as

$$\hat{\beta}(\tau, \gamma) = \text{argmin}_{b \in \mathbb{R}^p} \sum_{i=1}^n \rho_\tau \left(Y_i - x_i^\top b\right) / \left(x_i^\top \gamma\right)$$

and show that $\sqrt{n}(\hat{\beta}(\tau, \gamma) - \beta(\tau))$ is asymptotically Gaussian with mean zero and covariance matrix $\tau(1 - \tau)D_2^{-1}$. As we have already noted, $D_1^{-1}D_0D_1^{-1} - D_2^{-1}$ is nonnegative definite. Again, as in the least-squares case, we may estimate γ, and $\hat{\beta}(\tau, \hat{\gamma})$ will have the same asymptotic behavior as $\hat{\beta}(\tau, \gamma)$ for any

$\sqrt{n}$-consistent estimator $\hat{\gamma}$. Simple $\sqrt{n}$-consistent estimators of γ may be easily constructed as interquantile ranges:

$$\hat{\gamma}_n = \hat{\beta}_n(\tau_1) - \hat{\beta}_n(\tau_0).$$

It is evident that such estimators need only be consistent "up to scale"; that is, we require only that

$$\hat{\gamma}_n = \kappa\gamma + O_p(n^{-1/2})$$

for some scalar κ, because κ plays no role in the minimization problem defining $\hat{\beta}(\tau, \gamma)$. For the interquantile range estimator we would have, for example,

$$\kappa^{-1} = Q_u(\tau_1) - Q_u(\tau_0).$$

Improved estimators of γ may be constructed as L-estimators with smooth weight functions along the lines described in Section 5.1. In practice there may be cases in which $x_i^\top \hat{\gamma}_n$ is negative for some indices i, and it may be reasonable to modify these cases. Because we must assume that $\sigma(x) = x'\gamma$ is strictly positive over the entire design space, this must occur with probability tending to zero.

Since $\rho_\tau(\cdot)$ is piecewise linear, and $\hat{\sigma}(x) = x'\hat{\gamma}_n > 0$, at least eventually, we may rewrite the weighted quantile regression model as

$$\tilde{Y}_i = \tilde{x}_i^\top \beta + u_i,$$

where $\tilde{Y}_i = Y_i/\hat{\sigma}(x_i)$ and $\tilde{x}_i = x_i/\hat{\sigma}(x_i)$. In these transformed variables we have

$$Q_{\tilde{Y}_i}(\tau|x_i) = \hat{\sigma}_i^{-1}(x_i)x_i(\beta + \gamma Q^{-1}(\tau)) = \tilde{x}_i^\top \beta + \hat{\sigma}^{-1}(x_i)x_i^\top \gamma Q^{-1}(\tau),$$

and because $\hat{\sigma}(x_i) \to x_i^\top \gamma$, in probability, it follows that the weighted quantile regression estimator $\hat{\beta}(\tau, \hat{\gamma})$ converges to $\beta + \gamma Q^{-1}(\tau)$ like its unweighted counterpart, but because the weighted model now has iid errors it achieves full efficiency. This is the basic message from the work of Koenker and Zhao (1994), who provide a detailed analysis of this approach.

Within the general class of linear quantile regression models – that is, the class of models with conditional quantile functions that are linear in parameters, location–scale models (5.6) are quite special. Before plunging ahead with reweighting as just described, one may wish to test whether the location–scale hypothesis is plausible. A simple test of this form could be based on the p-vector of ratios:

$$T_n = (T_{ni}) = \left(\frac{\hat{\beta}_{ni}(\tau_1) - \hat{\beta}_{ni}(\tau_0)}{\hat{\beta}_{ni}(\tau_1') - \hat{\beta}_{ni}(\tau_0')}\right).$$

Under the location–scale hypothesis, the components of T_n would all converge to

$$\frac{Q_u(\tau_1) - Q_u(\tau_0)}{Q_u(\tau_1') - Q_u(\tau_0')}$$

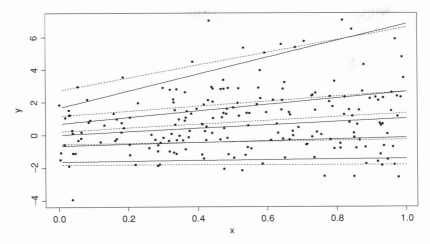

Figure 5.2. Non-location–scale linear quantile regression. The 200 plotted points are generated from a model with linear conditional quantile functions illustrated by the solid lines in the figure. Corresponding unweighted quantile regression estimates appear as dotted lines. Note that, although all the conditional quantile functions are linear, the model is not of the location–scale form: the conditional distribution of the response is symmetric at $x = 0$ but quite asymmetric at $x = 1$.

and, consequently, one could base a test on some measure of the maximal discrepancy between the observed components. More sophisticated strategies for carrying out tests of this type based on the approach of Khmaladze are described in Section 3.8.

Example 5.1. A simple example of a non-location–scale linear conditional quantile function model is given in Figure 5.2. Here 200 observations have been generated from a model with conditional quantile functions

$$Q_Y(\tau|x) = \Phi^{-1}(\tau) + \exp(\Phi^{-1}(\tau))x$$

with the xs generated as uniform on the interval $[0, 1]$. It is immediately apparent that the *shape* of the conditional density of Y is very different at $x = 0$ than it is at $x = 1$. At 0, Y is conditionally standard normal and the solid lines that indicate the true conditional quantile functions are symmetric, whereas at $x = 1$ the conditional density is quite asymmetric, reflecting the effect of the log-normal component proportional to x. The corresponding fitted quantile regression lines appear as dotted lines in the figure. It is easy to show that the coefficients of these unweighted estimates are consistent for their corresponding population parameters but, as in the location–scale model, the question arises: Can we improve upon the unweighted estimators?

This question has a straightforward answer. The appropriate weights for the τth quantile regression are the vector of conditional densities evaluated at the τth quantile, $w_i = f_Y(Q_Y(\tau|x_i)) = (x'\dot{\beta}(\tau))^{-1}$, where $\dot{\beta}(\tau) = d\beta(\tau)/d\tau$. Estimating these weights is quite straightforward, given estimates of the entire unweighted quantile regression process, using any of the sparsity estimation methods discussed in Section 3.4.1. In the location–scale case the situation is somewhat simplified because $(x'\dot{\beta}(\tau))^{-1} = (x^\top \gamma)\dot{Q}_u(\tau)$ for some p-vector γ and, consequently, we can ignore the sparsity estimation problem because it would contribute the same factor to each weight. In general, this is not the case and we are required to estimate $\dot{\beta}$.

5.5   WEIGHTED SUMS OF FUNCTIONS

Having considered weighted averages of the argmins, $\hat{\beta}(\tau)$, as analogs of L-statistics for the regression model, it worthwhile to also consider argmins of weighted averages of quantile regression objective functions. Suppose we have the classical iid error location-shift regression model, and consider the estimator,

$$(\hat{\alpha}_H, \hat{\gamma}_H) = \operatorname{argmin}_{(\alpha,\gamma)} \sum_{j=1}^{m} \sum_{i=1}^{n} w_j \rho_{\tau_j} \left(y_i - \alpha_j - z_i^\top \gamma \right).$$

Here we are estimating m distinct intercepts corresponding to the specified quantiles and one vector of slope parameters constrained to be identical at all of the specified quantiles. The subscript H identifies this as the "Hogg estimator" because it was proposed by Hogg (1979).

The asymptotic behavior of the Hogg estimator was analyzed by Koenker (1984) and bears an interesting relationship with discrete L-statistics formed as weighted averages of argmins. To focus the comparison of the two approaches, consider the classical iid error model:

$$y_i = \alpha_0 + z_i^\top \gamma_0 + u_i.$$

Suppose that the u_i have distribution function F with density f, such that $0 < f(F^{-1}(\tau)) < \infty$ for $\tau \in \{\tau_1, \ldots, \tau_m\}$, and suppose that $\lim n^{-1} \sum z_i z_i^\top = D$ is positive definite and that $\sum z_i = 0$. The last condition can be viewed as an innocuous normalization because the design can always be reparameterized to satisfy it, provided there is an intercept in the model. Under these conditions the usual quantile regression estimator of the slope parameters, $\hat{\gamma}(\tau)$, is consistent for γ_0 for any fixed $\tau \in (0, 1)$. Thus, it is natural to compare the discrete average of argmins,

$$\hat{\gamma}_M = \sum_{j=1}^{m} w_j \hat{\gamma}(\tau_j),$$

with $\hat{\gamma}_H$. Here we employ the subscript M for Mosteller (1946), who pioneered the consideration of these discrete weighted averages of the sample quantiles in the one-sample model.

Theorem 5.2. (Koenker, 1984). *Under the foregoing conditions,*

$$\sqrt{n}(\hat{\gamma}_M - \gamma_0) \rightsquigarrow \mathcal{N}\left(0, \sigma_M^2(w, F)D^{-1}\right)$$
$$\sqrt{n}(\hat{\gamma}_H - \gamma_0) \rightsquigarrow \mathcal{N}(0, \sigma_H^2(w, F)D^{-1}),$$

where

$$\sigma_H^2(w, F) = \sum\sum \frac{w_i w_j (\tau_i \wedge \tau_j - \tau_i \tau_j)}{f(F^{-1}(\tau_i))f(F^{-1}(\tau_j))}$$
$$\sigma_M^2(w, F) = \frac{\sum\sum w_i w_j (\tau_i \wedge \tau_j - \tau_i \tau_j)}{\sum\sum w_i w_j f(F^{-1}(\tau_i))f(F^{-1}(\tau_j))}.$$

This leads to a simple characterization of optimal weights. Let B denote the $m \times m$ matrix with typical entry $(\tau_i \wedge \tau_j - \tau_i \tau_j)$, let v denote the m-vector with typical element $f(F^{-1}(\tau_j))$, and let $V = \text{diag}(v)$. The following result characterizes the efficiency bounds achievable with the two classes of estimators.

Corollary 5.1. *We have the following bounds:*

$$\sigma_M^2(w, F) = w^\top V^{-1} B V^{-1} w \geq (v^\top B v)^{-1}$$

and

$$\sigma_H^2(w, F) = \frac{w^\top B w}{(w^\top v)^2} \geq (v^\top B v)^{-1}.$$

The former is achieved with $w_M = (v^\top B v)^{-1} V B^{-1} v$, and the latter with $w_H = B^{-1} v$.

Proof. The proof follows immediately from the bounds of Rao (1973, Section 1f). ∎

Thus, we see that what can be achieved by the more expedient L-statistic estimators can also be achieved by minimizing weighted sums of quantile objective functions. However, the choice of the weights is different in the two cases and obviously depends on the distribution F. This should not detract from the important observation of Mosteller (1946) that remarkably efficient and robust estimators can be constructed in this fashion with only a few summands. The bounds, of course, are dependent on the choice of the τs and this imposes another layer of optimization, one that would typically entail numerical techniques.

An obvious advantage of averaging argmins over argminning averages is that the former problems can be solved efficiently by parametric programming for the whole process, and thus even smoothly weighted L-statistics can be easily computed from the resulting piecewise linear process, $\hat{\beta}(\tau)$. On the other hand, averages of quantile regression objective functions lead eventually to rather large and unwieldy optimization problems. Fortunately, it is rarely necessary to consider problems with very large m, and the sparsity of the resulting problems offers some assistance. Some further details are described in Section 6.8, and an application to portfolio choice is discussed in Section 8.9.

5.6 PROBLEMS

Problem 5.1. Let $X_1, \ldots, X_n$ be a random sample from a df $F(x - \theta_0)$. Consider L-estimators of location of the form

$$\hat{\theta}_0 = \int_0^1 J(u) F_n^{-1}(u) du,$$

where $F_n(\cdot)$ denotes the empirical distribution function constructed from the X_is. If F has finite Fisher information $I(F)$ and a twice continuously differentiable log density, then the optimal L-estimator has weight function of the form

$$J^*(F(x)) = -\frac{(\log f(x))''}{I(F)}.$$

1. Explain the observation that $\hat{\theta}_n$ is location equivariant, since

$$\int_{-\infty}^{\infty} J^*(F(y)) dF(y) = \int_0^1 J^*(u) du = 1.$$

2. The optimality of $\hat{\theta}_n$ may be seen by computing the influence function of the general L-estimator as follows:

   I. The IF of the uth sample quantile is

   $$IF(x, F^{-1}(u), F) = \frac{d}{d\varepsilon} F_\varepsilon^{-1}(u) = \frac{u - \delta_x(F^{-1}(u))}{f(F^{-1}(u))},$$

   which may be shown by differentiating the identity
   $$F_\varepsilon\left(F_\varepsilon^{-1}(u)\right) = u,$$
   where $F_\varepsilon(y) = (1 - \varepsilon) F(y) + \varepsilon \delta_x(y)$, to obtain

   $$0 = -F\left(F_\varepsilon^{-1}(u)\right) + \delta_x\left(F_\varepsilon^{-1}(y)\right) + f_\varepsilon\left(F_\varepsilon^{-1}(u)\right) \frac{d}{d\varepsilon} F_\varepsilon^{-1}(u)$$

   and evaluating at $\varepsilon = 0$.

   II. Thus,

   $$\begin{aligned} IF(x, \hat{\theta}_n, F) &= \int_0^1 (J^*(u)(u - \delta_x(F^{-1}(u)))/f(F^{-1}(u)) du \\ &= \int_{-\infty}^{\infty} J^*(F(y))(F(y) - \delta_x(y)) dy \\ &= \int_{-\infty}^{x} J^*(F(y)) dy - \int_{-\infty}^{\infty} (1 - F(y)) J^*(F(y)) dy \\ &= -I(F)^{-1} \int_{-\infty}^{x} (\log f)''(y) dy \\ &= -I(F)^{-1} (\log f)'(x). \end{aligned}$$

III. Setting $\psi(x) = -(\log f)'(x) = -f'(x)/f(x)$, we conclude that $\sqrt{n}(\hat\theta_n - \theta_0) \rightsquigarrow \mathcal{N}(0, EIF^2)$, where

$$EIF^2 = \int (\psi^2(x)/I(F)^2)dF(x) = I(F)^{-1}.$$

Explain briefly the foregoing result. Focus on the following aspects:

(i) How do we compute $\hat\theta_n$?
(ii) How does $\hat\theta_n$ differ from the mle?
(iii) What does the IF tell us about $\hat\theta_n$?

Problem 5.2. Consider the mean squared error of the kernel-smoothed quantile estimator, $\tilde\beta_n(\tau)$, of (5.2). Show that the bias may be expressed as

$$\text{bias}(\tilde\beta_n(\tau)) = \frac{1}{2}h_n^2\sigma_k^2 + o(h^2) + O(n^{-1}),$$

and the variance as

$$V(\tilde\beta_n(\tau)) = n^{-1}\tau(1-\tau)s^2(\tau) - n^{-1}h_n s^2(\tau)\eta_k + o(h/n),$$

where $\sigma_k^2 = \int t^2 k(t)dt$ and $\eta_k = \int tk(t)K(t)dt$. Conclude from this that the optimal (mean-squared-error-minimizing) bandwidth is of the form

$$h^* = (\kappa/n)^{1/3}[s(\tau)/s'(\tau)]^{2/3},$$

where $\kappa = 2\eta_k/(\sigma_k^2)^2$. For the Epanechnikov kernel, show that $\kappa = 0.287494$, and illustrate them for few representative ns for the standard normal distribution. Even for quite large sample sizes, these bandwidths are quite wide and one might be reluctant to recommend such aggressive smoothing.

Problem 5.3. Any sample quantile can be considered a candidate location estimator, since it is location equivariant. But in regular settings, that is when Fisher information is finite, any sample quantile must have larger asymptotic variance than the maximum likelihood estimator of location. Thus for all $r \in \mathbf{R}$,

$$I(F) = \int (f'(x)/f(x))^2 f(x)dx \geq \frac{f(r)^2}{F(r)(1-F(r))}. \tag{5.7}$$

To see this, take $r \in \mathbf{R}$, and let

$$g(x) = \begin{cases} 1 - F(r) & x \leq r \\ -F(r) & x > r. \end{cases} \tag{5.8}$$

Cauchy-Schwartz gives us,

$$\left(\int g(x)f'(x)dx\right)^2 \leq \int g(x)^2 f(x)dx \int \frac{f'(x)^2}{f(x)}dx. \tag{5.9}$$

Fill in the remaining details and note that the result also shows that finite Fisher information implies a bounded density for the distribution F. See Pfanzagl (1976).

Problem 5.4. Pfanzagl (1982) shows that the asymptotic variance bound for estimating the $\tau \le 1/2$ quantile of a symmetric distribution, F, with finite Fisher information, $\mathcal{I}(F)$ is,

$$\sigma_\tau^2(F) = \mathcal{I}(F)^{-1} + a(\tau)/f^2(F^{-1}(\tau)),$$

where $a(\tau) = (1/2 - \tau)\tau$. Interpret the bound and suggest an estimator that would achieve it.

Problem 5.5. There have been several other proposals for analogs of the trimmed mean for the linear regression model. Koenker and Bassett (1978) conjectured that in the iid error linear model,

$$y_i = x_i^\top \beta + u_i$$

the "trimmed least squares estimator"

$$\hat\beta_\alpha = (X^\top W X)^{-1} X^\top W y,$$

where $W = \mathrm{diag}(w)$ with $w_i = I(x_i^\top \hat\beta(\alpha) \le y_i \le x_i^\top \hat\beta(1 - \alpha))$ would satisfy,

$$\sqrt{n}(\hat\beta_\alpha - \beta_\alpha) \rightsquigarrow \mathcal{N}(0, \sigma^2(\alpha, F)D_0^{-1}),$$

where $\beta_\alpha = \beta + \int_\alpha^{1-\alpha} F^{-1}(u)du e_1$ and $\sigma^2(\alpha, F) = \int_\alpha^{1-\alpha}(F^{-1}(u))^2 du + \alpha(F^{-1}(a)^2 + F^{-1}(1 - \alpha)^2)$. Confirm. (Ruppert and Carroll (1980) first proved this result and showed that similar schemes based on trimming least squares residuals failed to achieve this form of limiting behavior. Subsequently, Welsh (1987b) showed that Winsorizing rather than trimming least squares residuals was also capable of achieving the same limit.)

CHAPTER 6

Computational Aspects of Quantile Regression

Although early advocates of absolute error methods like Boscovitch, Laplace, and Edgeworth all suggested ingenious methods for minimizing sums of absolute errors for bivariate regression problems, it was not until the introduction of the simplex algorithm in the late 1940s, and the formulation of the ℓ_1 regression problem as a linear program somewhat later, that a practical, general method for computing absolute error regression estimates was made available.

We have already seen that the linear programming formulation of quantile regression is an indispensable tool for understanding its statistical behavior. Like the Euclidean geometry of the least-squares estimator, the polyhedral geometry of minimizing weighted sums of absolute errors plays a crucial role in understanding these methods. This chapter begins with a brief account of the classical theory of linear programming, stressing its geometrical nature and introducing the simplex method. The simplex approach to computing quantile regression estimates is then described and the special role of simplex-based methods for "sensitivity analysis" is emphasized.

Parametric programming in a variety of quantile regression contexts is treated in Section 6.3. Section 6.4 describes some recent developments in computation that rely on "interior point" methods for solving linear programs. These new techniques are especially valuable in large quantile regression applications, where the simplex approach becomes impractical. Further gains in computational efficiency are possible by preprocessing of the linear programming problems as described in Section 6.5. Interior point methods are also highly relevant for nonlinear quantile regression problems, a topic addressed in Section 6.6. The introduction of inequality constraints on the parameters is considered in Section 6.7. Exploitation of sparse linear algebra is taken up in Section 6.9.

6.1 INTRODUCTION TO LINEAR PROGRAMMING

Problems that seek to optimize a linear function subject to linear constraints are called *linear programs*. Such problems play an important role throughout applied mathematics. One of the earliest explicit examples is the so-called diet problem: an individual has a choice of n foods that may be consumed in quantities $x = (x_1, \ldots, x_n)$. The foods provide nutrients in varying degrees, and we may represent the requirements for such nutrients by the m linear constraints,

$$
\begin{aligned}
a_{11}x_1 + \cdots + a_{1n}x_n &\geq b_1 \\
\vdots \qquad\qquad \vdots \quad\; &\; \vdots \\
a_{m1}x_1 + \cdots + a_{mn}x_n &\geq b_m,
\end{aligned}
\tag{6.1}
$$

where a_{ij} denotes the amount of nutrient i provided by food j, and $b_1, \ldots, b_m$ denote the annual requirements of each of the m nutrients. The cost of the diet x may be represented as

$$
c(x) = c_1 x_1 + \cdots + c_n x_n,
$$

and so we may concisely formulate the problem of finding the least-expensive diet achieving our nutritional requirements as

$$
\min\{c^\top x \,|\, Ax \geq b, \; x \geq 0\}.
\tag{6.2}
$$

The first formulation of this problem to be solved by formal linear programming methods was that of Stigler (1945). The simplex method applied to Stigler's problem produced a rather appalling diet consisting of flour, corn meal, evaporated milk, peanut butter, lard, beef liver, cabbage, potatoes, and spinach and achieved the staggering annual cost of \$39.47, a saving of almost 50 cents per year over a diet found earlier by Stigler by somewhat less systematic methods. According to Dantzig (1951), computing this simplex solution by hand in 1947 required 120 man hours.

Why were so few foods represented in the "optimal diet" when the original problem offered an enticing menu of 77 different foods? The answer to this question is fundamental to the basic understanding of linear programming, and so it is worth considering in some detail. Stigler's formulation of the diet problem involved nine different nutritional requirements. It is no coincidence that the optimal diet consisted of exactly nine distinct foods.

6.1.1   Vertices

To see this we must delve a bit deeper into the geometry of the constraint set $S = \{x \,|\, Ax \geq b, x \geq 0\}$. Because S is polyhedral and convex, being the intersection of a finite number of half-spaces, vertices of S have a special status. The vertices of S are extreme points, or "corners" – isolated points that do not lie on a line connecting distinct points in S. To further characterize such vertices, consider the augmented $n + m \times n$ system of linear inequalities:

$$
\tilde{A}x \equiv \begin{pmatrix} A \\ I_n \end{pmatrix} x \geq \begin{pmatrix} b \\ 0 \end{pmatrix}.
$$

Associated with any point $x \in S$, the *active constraints* will refer to the constraint rows that hold with equality. Nonbinding constraints, which hold with strict inequality, will be called *inactive*. A vertex of S is a point $x \in S$ whose submatrix of active constraints contains at least one subset of n linearly independent rows of $\tilde{A}$. It is this linear independence that prohibits vertices from being expressed as proper linear combinations of two or more distinct points in S. The crucial role of vertices in the theory of linear programming is revealed by the following proposition.

Proposition 6.1. *If linear program (6.2) has a bounded solution, then it has a vertex solution.*

This proposition has a rather self-evident geometric interpretation. We may regard the constraint set S as an n-dimensional object like a cut diamond with flat facets, with linear edges connecting a finite number of distinct vertices. Level surfaces of the "cost," or objective, function $c(x)$ are simply a family of parallel hyperplanes and so the solution may be envisioned as gradually "lowering" the cost planes until they just touch the set S. This "tangency" may occur at a vertex, in which case the solution is unique, or it may occur along an entire edge, or facet in higher dimensions, in which case the solution consists of an entire convex set delimited by vertices. In either case, the crucial role of vertex solutions is apparent. If the objective function can be reduced without bound while maintaining feasibility, the notional solution "at infinity" does not occur at a vertex. A formal proof of this proposition, which is somewhat more arduous than this geometric intuition, may be found, for example, in Gill, Murray, and Wright (1991, Theorem 7.7.4)

Presuming that the m constraint rows defined by the matrix A are linearly independent, we can form vertices of S by replacing m rows of I_n by the rows of A, and setting the remaining $n - m$ coordinates of x to zero. Let h denote the indices of the active constraints thus selected and partition the constraints, writing them as

$$\begin{pmatrix} A(h) & A(\bar{h}) \\ 0 & I_{n-m} \end{pmatrix} \begin{pmatrix} x(h) \\ x(\bar{h}) \end{pmatrix} = \begin{pmatrix} b \\ 0 \end{pmatrix},$$

where $\bar{h} = \{1, \ldots, n\} \setminus h$ and $A(h)$ denotes a submatrix of A consisting of the columns corresponding to the active indices h. Solving, we have, presuming that $A(h)^{-1}$ exists,

$$x(h) = A(h)^{-1}b \tag{6.3}$$
$$x(\bar{h}) = 0. \tag{6.4}$$

Provided $x(h) \geq 0$, this point is a vertex of S. Whether this vertex is optimal remains to be seen, but the proposition assures us that we need only check the finite number of such vertices and pick the one that achieves the lowest cost. This comment may not have come as a great solace to early pioneers of linear programming computation, because there are $\binom{n}{m}$ such vertices, each requiring the solution of an $m \times m$ linear system of equations. Even for Stigler's original problem, the number of such solutions $\binom{77}{9}$ that exceeds 1.6×10^{11} appears prohibitively large. Fortunately, we need not visit every vertex. We need only to find an intelligent way of passing from one vertex to the next; the convexity of the constraint set and the linearity of the objective function assure us that, starting at any vertex, there is a path through adjacent vertices along which the objective function decreases on each edge. To explore such strategies, we need a criterion for deciding that a vertex is optimal and a rule for choosing an adjacent vertex if the optimality condition is not satisfied.

6.1.2   Directions of Descent

Let x_0 be an initial, not necessarily feasible, point and consider the feasibility of a step of length σ in the direction p with respect to the ith constraint, $a_i^\top x \geq b_i$. Since

$$a_i^\top (x_0 + \sigma p) = a_i^\top x_0 + \sigma a_i^\top p,$$

we may write the step length to constraint i from x_0 in direction p as

$$\sigma_i = \frac{a_i^\top x_0 - b_i}{-a_i^\top p} \quad \text{if} \quad a_i^\top p \neq 0.$$

If $a_i^\top p = 0$, the step moves x_0 parallel to the constraint and we regard the step length to the constraint as infinite with sign determined by the sign of the initial "residual" associated with the constraint.

Given that x_0 is feasible, we need to know what directions are feasible in the sense that the point $x_0 + \sigma p$ remains feasible for some sufficiently small σ. Suppose first that constraint i is inactive at x_0, so that $a_i^\top x_0 > b_i$. In this case, any direction p is feasible: if $a_i^\top p \geq 0$, $x_0 + \sigma p$ remains feasible for any $\sigma > 0$. If $a_i^\top p < 0$, both numerator and denominator of the step length to the ith constraint are positive and there is a strictly positive σ at which the constraint becomes active. We conclude that inactive constraints do not restrict the set of feasible directions; only the length of the feasible step is constrained.

For active constraints the situation is reversed. If $a_i^\top x_0 = b_i$ and $a_i^\top p < 0$, even the smallest step $\sigma > 0$ violates the feasibility condition. On the other hand, if $a_i^\top p \geq 0$, feasibility is maintained for all $\sigma > 0$. Thus, for active constraints, the feasible directions are constrained, but once a direction is determined to be feasible, active constraints impose no further restriction on step length.

Feasible directions with respect to several constraints may be derived immediately from this analysis of a single constraint. If p is feasible at x_0 for the system of constraints $Ax \geq b$, then, for some $\sigma > 0$, $A(x_0 + \sigma p) \geq b$ and this in turn requires that, for the active constraints (i.e., the rows h such that $A(h)x_0 = b$), we have $A(h)p \geq 0$.

Note that because equality constraints of the form $Ax = b$ must be active, and because they require both $Ax \geq b$ and $Ax \leq b$, so that $-Ax \geq -b$, the preceding argument implies that any feasible direction p must satisfy both $Ap \geq 0$ and $-Ap \geq 0$; therefore, for equality constraints the only feasible directions are those that lie in the null space of A (i.e., such that $Ap = 0$).

This brings us to the existence of feasible directions of descent. Since

$$c^\top(x_0 + \sigma p) = c^\top x_0 + \sigma c^\top p,$$

a direction p is a direction of descent at x_0 if and only if $c^\top p < 0$. Given an initial point x_0, how do we determine whether we have a feasible direction of descent? Let $\mathcal{S}(A^\top)$ denote the space spanned by the column vectors of $A^\top$:

$$\mathcal{S}(A^\top) = \{y \mid y = A^\top v \text{ for some } v\};$$

then, if $y \in \mathcal{S}(A^\top)$ and $Ap = 0$, there exists v such that $y^\top p = v^\top Ap = 0$, and so p is not a descent direction. On the other hand, if $y \notin \mathcal{S}(A^\top)$, then there exists $p \in \mathbb{R}^n$ such that $Ap = 0$ and $y^\top p < 0$, and p is a direction of descent at x_0.

6.1.3 Conditions for Optimality

In the special case of linear programs with only equality constraints, the conditions for optimality of a solution are quite simple. Since this simple case illustrates certain aspects of the more general problem, we may begin by considering the problem

$$\min\{c^\top x \mid Ax = b\}.$$

There are three possible situations:

1. The constraints $Ax = b$ are inconsistent, and so the feasible set is empty and no optimal point exists.
2. The constraints $Ax = b$ are consistent, and so the feasible set is nonempty, and either
   a. $c \in \mathcal{S}(A^\top)$, so that there exists v such that $c = A^\top v$, and for any feasible point x,

   $$c(x) = c^\top x = v^\top Ax = v^\top b,$$

   so that any feasible point achieves the same value of the objective function. Thus, all feasible points are optimal, or
   b. $c \notin \mathcal{S}(A^\top)$, so that there exists a direction p such that $Ap = 0$, and $c^\top p < 0$. This direction is feasible and thus, starting from any feasible point x, the objective function can be driven to $-\infty$ by taking a step $x + \sigma p$ for σ arbitrarily large.

None of these options seems particularly attractive and together they illustrate the crucial role of inequality constraints in determining vertex solutions in linear programming.

The situation for problems with inequality constraints is somewhat more challenging. In this case we must carefully distinguish between active and inactive constraints in determining feasible directions, and obviously sets of active and inactive constraints may depend on the initial feasible point. Let h denote the index set of active constraints and $\bar{h}$ denote the index set of inactive constraints at an initial (feasible) point x_0. A feasible direction of descent, p, exists if

$$A(h)p \geq 0 \quad \text{and} \quad c^\top p < 0.$$

The feasible point x_0 is optimal if and only if no direction of descent exists.

For equality-constrained linear programs (LPs) it was possible to provide a simple test for the optimality of an initial feasible point based on whether c was contained in the span of $A^\top$. For inequality constrained LPs the situation is somewhat more complicated and relies on the following classical result.

Lemma 6.1 (Farkas). *Let A be an $m \times n$ matrix and let c be a vector in $\mathbb{R}^n$; then*

$$c^\top p \geq 0 \quad \text{for all } p \text{ such that } Ap \geq 0$$

if and only if

$$c = A^\top v \quad \text{for some } v \geq 0.$$

Either c can be expressed as a linear combination of the columns of A with nonnegative weights, or there is a direction p such that $c^\top p \leq 0$ and $Ap \geq 0$. Applying the lemma to obtain optimality conditions for the purely inequality-constrained LP, we have the following result.

Theorem 6.1 (Gill, Murray, and Wright, 1991, Theorem 7.7.2). *For the problem*

$$\min\{c^\top x \,|\, Ax \geq b\},$$

either

1. *The constraints $Ax \geq b$ are inconsistent and therefore the problem has no solution, or*
2. *There is a feasible point $\hat{x}$ and a vector $\hat{v}$ such that*
   $$c = A(h)^\top \hat{v} \text{ with } \hat{v} \geq 0, \tag{6.5}$$
   where $A(h)$ denotes the submatrix of A corresponding to the active constraints at $\hat{x}$. In this case, $c(\hat{x})$ is the unique minimum value of $c^\top x$ for $\{x \,|\, Ax \geq b\}$ and $\hat{x}$ is an optimizer, or,
3. *The constraints $Ax \geq b$ are consistent, but condition (6.5) is not satisfied for any feasible point x. In this case, the solution is unbounded from below.*

6.1.4   Complementary Slackness

Optimality conditions (6.5) require that a weighted sum of the m possible columns of the matrix $A^\top$ equals the cost vector c. In Theorem 6.1 we have not specified the dimension of the vector $\hat{v}$, but we have seen that if $\hat{x}$ is a vertex then $A(h)^\top$ must consist of at least n linearly independent columns from the full set of m columns of $A^\top$. It is perhaps more convenient, and obviously equivalent, to take $u \in \mathbb{R}^m$ and let $v = u(h)$, and to set $u(\bar{h}) = 0$. We may then express (6.5) as

$$c = A^\top u \quad \text{and} \quad u \ge 0$$

with the added "complementary slackness" condition that

$$r_i u_i = 0 \qquad i = 1, \ldots, m,$$

where $r_i = a_i^\top \hat{x} - b_i$. For $i \in h$ we are assured that $r_i u_i = 0$, because $r_i = 0$, by definition for active constraints, whereas, for $i \in \bar{h}$, $u_i = 0$. The vector $u \in \mathbb{R}^m$ may be regarded as a vector of Lagrange multipliers corresponding to the constraints $Ax \ge b$. For binding constraints we expect these multipliers, which may be interpreted as the "marginal costs" of their respective constraints, to be strictly positive. For nonbinding (inactive) constraints, tightening the constraint infinitesimally imposes no cost and so the multiplier is zero.

Combining the conclusions for equality and inequality constraints, we have the following result.

Theorem 6.2. *Consider the* LP

$$\min\{c^\top x | Ax = b, \quad x \ge 0\}$$

and suppose $\hat{x}$ is a feasible point. The point $\hat{x}$ is optimal if and only if there exists $\hat{u} \in \mathbb{R}^n$ and $\hat{v} \in \mathbb{R}^m$ such that

$$c = A^\top \hat{v} + \hat{u} \quad \hat{u} \ge 0$$

with $\hat{x}_i \hat{u}_i = 0, \qquad i = 1, \ldots, n.$

The canonical form of the LP given in Theorem 6.2 appears somewhat restrictive, but more general forms may be transformed into this canonical form by the introduction of new variables. For example, consider the problem

$$\min\{c^\top x | Ax = b, Dx \ge d\}.$$

Rewriting this as

$$\min\{\tilde{c}^\top z | \tilde{A}z = \tilde{b}, \quad z \ge 0\},$$

where $\tilde{c} = (c^\top, 0^\top)^\top, \tilde{b} = (b^\top, d^\top)^\top, z = (x^\top, y^\top)^\top$, and

$$\tilde{A} = \begin{pmatrix} A & 0 \\ D & -I \end{pmatrix},$$

we are back to canonical form. The variables appearing in the new vector y are usually called "slack" variables, connoting that they take the value zero when the original constraints are active and "take up the slack" associated with inactive constraints.

6.1.5   Duality

The Lagrange multiplier interpretation of the vector u in Theorem 6.2 is our first hint of the elegant theory of duality rising in linear programming and related contexts. Corresponding to any primal LP, we may formulate a *dual* LP, a reflection of the original problem "through the looking glass," in which minimizing with respect to the original variables turns into maximizing with respect to the Lagrange multipliers of the dual formulation.

In the dual formulation of the diet problem, for example, we have seen from Theorem 6.2 that at a solution $\hat{x}$ there exists a vector of Lagrange multipliers, say, $(\hat{v}^\top, \hat{u}^\top)^\top$, such that

$$c = A^\top \hat{v} + \hat{u}$$

and such that $(a_i \hat{x}_i - b_i)\hat{v}_i = 0, \ i = 1, \ldots, m$ and $\hat{x}_i \hat{u}_i = 0, \ i = 1, \ldots, n$. At such a point, note that

$$c^\top \hat{x} = \hat{v}^\top A \hat{x} + \hat{u}^\top \hat{x} = \hat{v}^\top b.$$

This suggests that we might consider reformulating the original problem of finding the optimal diet $\hat{x}$ as a problem of finding the vector of Lagrange multipliers solving the LP

$$\max\{b^\top v \,|\, A^\top v + u = c, (v, u) \geq 0\}.$$

Because the slack vector u is simply a "residual" immediately obtained from the constraint

$$A^\top v + u = c,$$

once we have specified v, we can view this dual problem as asking us to find a vector of "shadow prices," v, corresponding to the m nutritional requirements. These prices may be interpreted at a solution as the prices that consumers would be willing to pay for dietary supplements corresponding to each of the m nutritional requirements. One way to interpret the duality of the diet problem is as a search for a revenue-maximizing vector of these "diet supplement" shadow prices that would be sustainable given the current prices of the available foods of the primal problem. Obviously, these prices are constrained by the current levels of food prices and the quantities of each nutritional requirement provided by the foods. Finding the optimal shadow prices is equivalent to finding the optimal diet for the original problem, because in effect it identifies a subset of active constraints: ones for which the dual constraints are binding. These active constraints define a basis h which, in turn, can be used to find the explicit primal solution as in (6.3). Note also that the requirement that, at a solution, all the nutrients have positive shadow prices ensures that all of the rows of A appear in the active set of the primal solution; this is the essential requirement that ensures that there will be precisely m foods in the optimal diet.

To examine this duality more generally, it is useful, following Berman (1973), to formulate the primal problem as

$$\min_{x}\{c^{\top}x|Ax - b \in T, \ x \in S\}, \tag{6.6}$$

where the sets S and T are arbitrary closed convex cones. A set $K \subseteq \mathbb{R}^n$ is a convex cone if it is closed under (i) nonnegative scalar multiplication, $\alpha K \subseteq K$, $\alpha \geq 0$, and (ii) convex combinations, $\alpha K + (1 - \alpha)K \subseteq K$, $\alpha \in (0, 1)$. The corresponding dual problem is

$$\max_{y}\{b^{\top}y|c - A^{\top}y \in S^*, \ y \in T^*\}, \tag{6.7}$$

where S^* and T^* are the respective dual cones of S and T. The dual of a cone K is the set

$$K^* = \{y \in \mathbb{R}^n|x^{\top}y \geq 0, \text{ if } \ x \in K\}.$$

In what follows it suffices to consider only two simple examples: $K = \mathbb{R}^n$, where $K^* = 0_n$, and $K = \mathbb{R}^n_+$, where $K^* = \mathbb{R}^n_+$, and their Cartesian products.

Note that for any feasible point (x, y) we have

$$b^{\top}y \leq y^{\top}Ax \leq c^{\top}x,$$

and so

$$c^{\top}x - b^{\top}y \geq 0.$$

The left-hand side is usually called the "duality gap" – the discrepancy between the primal and dual objective functions. Reduction in the duality gap can be taken as an indication of progress toward the optimal solution. This relationship plays a central role in the theory of interior point algorithms for solving LPs.

In the next section we explore the application of the foregoing ideas in the specific context of the quantile regression optimization problem.

6.2 SIMPLEX METHODS FOR QUANTILE REGRESSION

The primal formulation of the basic linear quantile regression problem,

$$\min_{b \in \mathbb{R}^p} \sum_{i=1}^{n} \rho_{\tau}\left(y_i - x_i^{\top}b\right),$$

may be written as

$$\min \left\{\tau e_n^{\top}u + (1 - \tau)e_n^{\top}v|y - Xb = u - v, \ b \in \mathbb{R}^p, \ (u, v) \in \mathbb{R}^{2n}_+\right\},$$

which may be seen to be in canonical form (6.6) by making the following identifications: $c = (0_p^{\top}, \tau e_n^{\top}, (1 - \tau)e_n^{\top})^{\top}, x = (b^{\top}, u^{\top}, v^{\top})^{\top}, A = [X \vdots I \vdots - I], b = y, T = 0_n$, and $S = \mathbb{R}^p \times \mathbb{R}^{2n}_+$. As we have already noted, the polyhedral nature of the constraint set and the linear objective function imply that we may focus attention on the vertices of the constraint set. These vertices, as we observed in Chapter 2, may be indexed by the $\binom{n}{p}$ elements $h \in \mathcal{H}$ and take the form

$$b(h) = X(h)^{-1} y(h),$$

$$u(h) = v(h) = 0,$$

$$u(\bar{h}) = (y - Xb(h))^+,$$

$$v(\bar{h}) = (y - Xb(h))^-.$$

Clearly, at any such vertex, the complementary slackness conditions, $u_i v_i = 0$, hold, and there are at least p indices, $i \in h$, with $u_i = v_i = 0$. Such points provide an exact fit to the p observations in the subset h and set the corresponding u and v vectors of the solution equal to the positive and negative parts of the resulting residual vector.

The primal quantile regression problem has the corresponding dual problem

$$\max\{y^\top d | X^\top d = 0, \ d \in [\tau - 1, \tau]^n\}.$$

To see this, note that the constraint $c - A^\top y \in S^*$ becomes

$$\begin{pmatrix} 0_p \\ \tau e_n \\ (1-\tau)e_n \end{pmatrix} - \begin{pmatrix} X^\top \\ I_n \\ -I_n \end{pmatrix} d \in 0_p \times \mathbb{R}_+^{2n},$$

while the condition that $y \in T^*$ becomes the innocuous $d \in \mathbb{R}^n$. Equivalently, we may reparameterize the dual problem to solve for

$$a = d + (1 - \tau)e_n,$$

yielding the new problem,

$$\max\{y^\top a | X^\top a = (1 - \tau)X^\top e_n, \ a \in [0, 1]^n\}.$$

In dual form, the problem may be seen to be one of optimizing with respect to a vector that lies in a unit cube. Such "bounded variables" problems have received considerable special attention in the linear programming literature.

Since, at any solution, $\{(\hat{b}, \hat{u}, \hat{v}), \hat{d}\}$, we must have

$$\tau e_n^\top \hat{u} + (1 - \tau)e_n^\top \hat{v} = y^\top \hat{d},$$

we see that, for $i \in \bar{h}$,

$$\hat{d}_i = \begin{cases} \tau & \text{if } \hat{u}_i > 0 \\ (\tau - 1) & \text{if } \hat{v}_i > 0. \end{cases}$$

whereas for observations $i \in h$ with $\hat{u}_i = \hat{v}_i = 0$, $\hat{d}(h)$ is determined from the equality constraint $X^\top d = 0$ as

$$\hat{d}(h) = -[X(h)^\top]^{-1} X(\bar{h})^\top \hat{d}(\bar{h}).$$

The dual vector $\hat{d}(h)$ at a solution corresponding to the basic observations h is thus the same as the vector $-\xi_h$ of Theorem 2.1. The fact that $\hat{d}(h) \in [\tau - 1, \tau]^p$ at a solution is precisely the optimality requirement that appears in that result.

It is conventional in describing implementations of simplex-type algorithms for solving LPs to speak of phase I of the algorithm, in which an initial feasible vertex of the problem is found, and then phase II, in which we proceed from one such vertex to another until optimality is achieved. In some LPs, just determining whether a feasible vertex *exists* can be quite difficult. However, in quantile regression problems we can choose any subset h and define a basic feasible point to the problem, thereby completing phase I, provided that the matrix $X(h)$ is of full rank. Thus, we can focus later attention on phase II of the computation, describing an approach implemented in the path-breaking median regression algorithm of Barrodale and Roberts (1974). In the remainder of this section I will describe a modified version of the Barrodale and Roberts algorithm designed to solve the general quantile regression problem. Further details may be found in Koenker and d'Orey (1987).

Let $h_0 \in \mathcal{H}$ denote the index set corresponding to an initial feasible vertex of the constraint set. Consider the directional derivative of the objective function,

$$R(b) = \sum_{i=1}^{n} \rho_\tau \left(y_i - x_i^\top b \right),$$

evaluated at $b(h_0) = X(h_0)^{-1} y(h_0)$ in direction δ, which we may write, as in Section 2.2.2, as

$$\nabla R(b(h_0), \delta) = - \sum_{i=1}^{n} \psi_\tau^* \left(y_i - x_i^\top b(h_0), -x_i^\top \delta \right) x_i^\top \delta,$$

where $\psi_\tau^*(u, w) = \tau - I(u < 0)$ if $u \neq 0$ and $\psi_\tau^*(u, w) = \tau - I(w < 0)$ if $u = 0$. Because we are already at a vertex, and the constraint set is convex, we can restrict attention to certain extreme directions δ that correspond to moving away from the vertex along the edges of the constraint set that intersect at the current vertex. These edges may be represented algebraically as

$$\eta(\alpha, h_0, \delta_j) = b(h_0) + \alpha \delta_j. \tag{6.8}$$

where δ_j is the jth column of the matrix $X(h)^{-1}$ and α is a scalar that controls where we are along the edge. This representation of the edge is just the usual parametric representation of a line through the point $b(h_0)$ in direction δ_j. Here δ_j is the vector orthogonal to the constraints formed by the remaining basic observations with the jth removed. Note that α can be either positive or negative in (6.8) and the directional derivative will be different for δ_j and $-\delta_j$.

Let

$$d(h) = -X(h)^{-1} \sum_{i \in \bar{h}} \psi_\tau^* \left(y_i - x_i^\top b(h) \right) x_i^\top$$

and note that, if δ_j is the jth column of $X(h)^{-1}$, then for $i \in h$, $x_i^\top \delta_j = 0$ for $j \neq i$ and 1 for $i = j$; and so, for such δ_j,

$$\nabla R(b(h_0), \delta_j) = d_j(h) + 1 - \tau$$

and

$$\nabla R(b(h_0), -\delta_j) = -d_j(h) + \tau.$$

If these directional derivatives are all nonnegative for $j = 1, \ldots, p$, then the optimality condition of Theorem 2.1 – $d(h) \in [\tau - 1, \tau]^p$ – is satisfied. Otherwise there is an edge that is a direction of descent leading away from the point $b(h_0)$, and we can reduce $R(b)$ by moving in this direction away from $b(h_0)$.

Which edge should be chosen? The natural choice adopted by the simplex algorithm is the direction of "steepest descent." This is the one for which the directional derivative $\nabla R(b(h), \pm \delta_j)$ is most negative. Having selected a direction $\delta^* = \sigma \delta_j$ for some j and $\sigma \in \{-1, 1\}$, we face the question: how far should we travel in this direction?

Barrodale and Roberts (1974) provided a quite innovative answer to this question. Rather than simply adopting the conventional simplex strategy of traveling only as far as the next vertex – that is, only as far as needed to drive one of the nonbasic observation's residuals to zero – they proposed to continue in the original direction as long as doing so continued to reduce the value of the objective function. Thus, as we travel in the direction δ^*, we encounter points at which observations not in the original basis have residuals that are eventually driven to zero. Conventional simplex strategies, when encountering such a situation, would introduce the new observation into to the basis, recompute a descent direction, and continue. Instead, Barrodale and Roberts elect to continue in the originally determined direction as long as it remains a viable direction of descent. In this way, they dramatically reduce the number of simplex pivot operations required when the basis changes. At the intermediate points, all that is required is a change of sign in the contribution to the gradient of the observation whose residual is passing through zero. This strategy constitutes what is sometimes called a Cauchy algorithm in general nonlinear optimization theory (see, e.g., Nazareth, 1994) A direction of steepest descent is selected at each iteration and then a one-dimensional line search is used to minimize the chosen direction.

The resulting line search has a simple interpretation that takes us back to the discussion of the regression-through-the-origin example of Chapter 1. At each step, we solve a problem of the form

$$\min_{\alpha \in \mathbb{R}} \sum_{i=1}^n \rho_\tau \left(y_i - x_i^\top b(h) - \alpha x_i^\top \delta^* \right),$$

which is just a quantile regression-through-the-origin problem in α with the response $y_i - x_i^\top b(h)$ and a design consisting of the single variable $x_i^\top \delta^*$. This subproblem is easily solved by finding a weighted quantile. We simply need to generalize slightly the weighted median characterization already described in Chapter 1.

Consider the through-the-origin quantile regression problem,

$$\min_{b\in\mathbb{R}} \sum \rho_\tau(y_i - x_i b).$$

Basic solutions $b(h)$ are of the simple form $b_i = y_i/x_i$. Directional derivatives take the form

$$\nabla R(b, \delta) = -\sum \psi_\tau^*(y_i - x_i b, -x_i \delta) x_i \delta$$

and at a solution must be nonnegative for $\delta \in \{-1, 1\}$. Adopting the temporary convention that $\mathrm{sgn}(0) = 1$, we may write

$$\sum (\tau - I(y_i < x_i b) x_i = \sum \left[\tau - \frac{1}{2} + \frac{1}{2}\mathrm{sgn}(y_i - x_i b)\right] x_i$$

$$= \sum \left[\tau - \frac{1}{2} + \frac{1}{2}\mathrm{sgn}(y_i/x_i - b)\,\mathrm{sgn}\,(x_i)\right] x_i$$

$$= \left(\tau - \frac{1}{2}\right)\sum x_i - \frac{1}{2}\sum |x_i| + \frac{1}{2} I(y_i/x_i \geq b)|x_i|.$$

Thus, as with the somewhat simpler case of the median that was discussed in Chapter 1, we may order the candidate slopes $b_i = y_i/x_i$ as $b_{(i)}$ and look for the smallest index j such that the corresponding sum of $\frac{1}{2}|x_i|$s exceeds the quantity

$$-\left(\tau - \frac{1}{2}\right)\sum x_i + \frac{1}{2}\sum |x_i|.$$

The algorithm continues in this manner until there is no longer a direction of descent, at which point optimality has been achieved and the algorithm terminates. This algorithm provides an extremely efficient approach to quantile regression computations for problems of modest size. For problems with sample size up to several hundred observations, the algorithm is comparable in speed to least-squares estimation of the conditional mean regression as implemented in current software packages. In very large problems, however, the simplex approach, and exterior point methods more generally, becomes painfully slow relative to least squares. Section 6.4.2 describes some recent developments that significantly improve upon the performance of the Barrodale and Roberts algorithm in large problems. But, before introducing these new methods, I will describe some applications of parametric programming ideas, which offer extremely effective exterior point computational strategies for important families of quantile regression problems.

6.3 PARAMETRIC PROGRAMMING FOR QUANTILE REGRESSION

One aspect of quantile regression computation that seems puzzling to many newcomers to the subject is the idea that we can solve

$$\min_{b\in\mathbb{R}^p} \sum_{i=1}^n \rho_\tau\left(y_i - x_i^\top b\right)$$

efficiently for *all* $\tau \in [0, 1]$. One solution to a linear programming problem for fixed τ seems bad enough. How is it possible to find a solution for a continuum of τs? The answer to this question again lies in the elementary geometry of linear programming.

Consider the primal version of the quantile regression LP and imagine that we are at a vertex solution for some initial $\tau = \tau_0$. What happens when we decide that we would also like to know the solution for some $\tau_1 > \tau_0$? Geometrically, changing τ tilts the orientation of the (hyper)planes representing the level surfaces of the objective function but has no effect on the constraint set of the primal problem. Thus, if we are at a unique vertex solution corresponding to τ_0, there is a neighborhood of τ_0 within which the solution remains unperturbed. Eventually, of course, the plane tilts enough so that not only the original solution at τ_0, but an entire edge of the constraint set, solves the perturbed problem. There will be a whole line segment of solutions in $\mathbb{R}^p$ corresponding to the "tangency" of the plane representing the minimal attainable level of the objective function on an edge of the constraint set.

Tilting the plane a bit beyond this τ_1 restores the uniqueness of the solution at the opposite end of the line segment defining the edge. What has happened algebraically is quite simple. The edge may be represented as in the previous subsection as

$$\eta(\alpha, h, \delta_j) = b(h) + \alpha\delta_j,$$

where $b(h)$ is the initial vertex solution at τ_0 and δ_j is the jth column of $X(h)^{-1}$. As in our description of the Barrodale and Roberts algorithm, we travel along this edge until we come to the next adjacent vertex. At this new vertex we have driven a new residual, say, the kth, to zero, and at this value τ_1 any point between $b(h)$ and $b(h')$ with $h' = k \cup h \setminus j$ solves the problem. For $\tau > \tau_1$, the plane representing the objective function again tilts away from the edge and we have a unique solution at $b(h')$.

Proceeding in this manner, we identify breakpoints $\tau_j \in \{0 = \tau_0, \tau_1, \ldots, \tau_J = 1\}$ at which the primal solution flips from one basis to another. (At these points we have an interval of solutions; elsewhere the solution is unique.) Of course, in the simplest one-sample setting where $x_i \equiv 1$, we have exactly n of these breakpoints at $\tau_j = j/n$. However, in general the number and location of the τ_js depend in a complicated way on the design configuration as well as the observed response. Under mild regularity conditions that can be expected to hold in most quantile regression applications, Portnoy (1989) has shown that the number of breakpoints J is $\mathcal{O}_p(n \log n)$. There is an extensive LP literature on related problems of this sort, which are usually called parametric programming problems or sensitivity analysis. See Gál (1995) for a detailed treatment of this literature.

An explicit formulation of the aforementioned computations returns us to the dual form of the problem. At the initial solution $b(h)$, at $\tau = \tau_0$ we have the dual constraint

$$X^\top \hat{a}(\tau) = (1 - \tau)X^\top e$$

for some $\hat{a}(\tau) \in [0, 1]^n$, and, for the nonbasic observations, $\hat{a}_i(\tau) = I(u_i > 0)$ for $i \in \bar{h}$. Define

$$\mu = (X(h)^\top)^{-1} \left[X^\top e - \sum_{i \in \bar{h}} x_i \hat{a}_i(\tau) \right]$$

and

$$\lambda = (X(h)^\top)^{-1} X^\top e$$

so that, for τ sufficiently close to τ_0,

$$\hat{a}_i(\tau) = \mu_i - \lambda_i \tau \quad i \in h.$$

To find the *next* τ we need to find, among all the τs that solve either

$$\mu_i - \lambda_i \tau = 0$$

or

$$\mu_i - \lambda_i \tau = 1,$$

the one that changes least. To accomplish this we simply examine the set of $2p$ numbers:

$$\mathcal{T} = \{\mu_i/\lambda_i, (\mu_i - 1)/\lambda_i, \ i \in h\}.$$

Presuming that we are looking for the next *largest* τ, we select

$$\tau_1 = min\{\tau \in \mathcal{T} | \tau > \tau_0\}.$$

This selection determines not only the length of the interval for which the point $b(h)$ remains optimal but also identifies which edge is optimal at the new breakpoint τ_1. The direction of movement along this edge is given by

$$\sigma = \begin{cases} 1 & \text{if } \tau_1 = \mu_i/\lambda_i \ i \in h \\ -1 & \text{if } \tau_1 = (\mu_i - 1)/\lambda_i \ i \in h \end{cases}.$$

Let the index of the minimizing edge be $i_0 \in h$; then the parametric representation of the edge is $b(h) + \sigma \delta_{i_0}$, where δ_{i_0} is the i_0 column of $X(h)^{-1}$. Finally, to determine how far we can go in this direction, we define the ratios

$$\mathcal{S} = \left\{ s_j = r_j / \left(\sigma x_j^\top \delta_{i_0} \right), \ j \in \bar{h} \right\}.$$

The smallest positive element of $\mathcal{S}$ identifies the distance we may travel along our selected edge before forcing one of the nonbasic residuals to become zero. The j so selected now replaces the deleted basic observation i_0 in h, and we proceed as from the beginning. In this way we find the entire quantile regression process $\{\hat{\beta}(t) : t \in [0, 1]\}$ and the corresponding dual process, $\{\hat{a}(t) : t \in [0, 1]\}$, in roughly $n \log n$ simplex pivots. For modest n this is extremely quick; for large n, alternative computational strategies that can significantly reduce the computational effort without sacrificing the informational content of the estimated processes would be desirable.

6.3.1   Parametric Programming for Regression Rank Tests

Another important parametric family of quantile regression problems arises in the computation of the inverted rank test confidence intervals described in Chapter 3. In this case, we begin with the solution to a $(p + 1)$-dimensional quantile regression problem. And we would like to construct a confidence interval for the jth parameter of the model by inverting a particular form of the Gutenbrunner, Jurečková, Koenker, and Portnoy (1993) rank test of the hypothesis

$$H_0 : \beta_j = \xi;$$

that is, we would like to find an interval $(\hat{\beta}_j^L, \hat{\beta}_j^U)$ with asymptotic coverage $1 - \alpha$. Statistical aspects of this confidence interval are described in Chapter 3. Here we focus on computational details of the procedure.

Let $\tilde{X}$ denote the full $(p + 1)$-column design matrix of the problem and let X denote the reduced design matrix with the jth column deleted. Let $\hat{h}$ denote the index set of the basic observations corresponding to the solution of the full problem, and let u denote the jth row of the matrix $\tilde{X}(\hat{h})^{-1}$. Denote the jth column of $\tilde{X}$ by X_j. Our first task is to reduce the basis $\hat{h}$ by one element, in effect finding a new basis $\tilde{h}$, for the dual problem

$$\max\{y - X_j\xi)^\top a | X^\top a = (1 - \tau)X^\top e, a \in [0, 1]^n\}$$

for ξ near $\hat{\beta}_j$. Clearly, this reduced solution has $\tilde{a}_i = \hat{a}_i$ for $i \notin \hat{h}$, but we must identify the observation to be removed from the basic set. Consider the ratios, for $i \in \hat{h}$ and $u_i = y_i - x_{ij}\xi \neq 0$,

$$s_i = \begin{cases} (\hat{a}_i - 1)/u_i & \text{if } u_i < 0 \\ \hat{a}_i/u_i & \text{if } u_i \geq 0 \end{cases},$$

and let $k \in \hat{h}$ denote the index of the minimal s_i:

$$w^* = s_k = min_{i \in \hat{h}}\{s_i : i \in \hat{h}\}.$$

The new dual solution is thus

$$\tilde{a}_i = \hat{a}_i - w^* u_i \qquad i \in \tilde{h} = \hat{h} \setminus k.$$

Note that this modification of the dual solution does not alter the primal solution; we have simply reduced the rank of the problem by one and incorporated the effect of the jth covariate into the response variable.

Now we are ready to begin the parametric programming exercise. But in this case we must focus attention on the dual form of the quantile regression problem. As we change ξ in the dual problem, we again may view this as tilting the plane of the objective function, this time in the dual formulation while the dual constraint set remains fixed. Again we are looking for a sequence of steps around the exterior of the constraint set; this time the path terminates at the value of ξ for which we first reject H_0.

Each step begins by identifying the nonbasic observation that will next enter the basis. This is the observation whose residual is first driven to zero by the process of increasing ξ. This is fundamentally different than the primal parametric problem over τ. In that case, the primal solution $\hat{\beta}(\tau)$ was piecewise constant in τ and the dual solution $\hat{a}(\tau)$ was piecewise linear in τ. Now the situation is reversed, viewed as a function of ξ; $\hat{a}(\xi)$ is piecewise constant and the primal solution $\hat{\beta}(\xi)$ is piecewise linear in ξ. If $b(h)$ is the unique vertex solution to the reduced problem at $\xi = \hat{\beta}_j$, then there is a neighborhood around this value for which the basic observations h remain optimal and we can write the residual vector of the perturbed problem as

$$r(\xi) = y - X_j\xi - XX(h)^{-1}(y(h) - X_j(h)\xi)$$
$$= y - XX(h)^{-1}y(h) - (X_j - XX(h)^{-1}X_j(h))\xi.$$

The incoming observation i is the minimal element corresponding to

$$\delta^* = \min_i \left\{ y_i - x_i^\top X(h)^{-1}y(h)/\left(x_{ij} - x_i^\top X(h)^{-1}X_j(h)\right)\right\},$$

where the minimum is over the *positive* candidates, presuming, of course, that we are interested in *increasing* ξ. Finally, we must find the observation leaving the basis. Let

$$v = X(h)^{-1}x_i(h).$$

If the incoming residual

$$r_{i*} = y_{i*} - x_{i*}^\top X(h)^{-1}(y(h) - X_j(h)\hat{\beta}_j)$$

is greater than zero, we set

$$g_i = \begin{cases} -\hat{a}_i/v_i & \text{if } v_i < 0 \\ (1 - \hat{a}_i)/v_i & \text{otherwise} \end{cases}$$

or, if $r_i* < 0$, we set

$$g_i = \begin{cases} \hat{a}_i/v_i & \text{if } v_i < 0 \\ (\hat{a}_i - 1)/v_i & \text{otherwise}. \end{cases}$$

The outgoing observation is the one corresponding to the minimal value of the g_is. We can now update the basis and continue the process, until we we reject H_0. The process may be repeated to find the other endpoint of the confidence interval and continued to determine the confidence intervals for each parameter appearing in the model. As can be seen, for example, in Table 1.3, these confidence intervals are asymmetric and so they cannot be represented in the form of the usual "point estimate $\pm k_\alpha$ standard deviation." In this respect they resemble the confidence intervals one obtains from the bootstrap percentile method.

When sample sizes are large, there are typically a large number of vertices that must be traversed to find solutions using the simplex approach just described. Indeed, there are infamous examples, notably that of Klee and Minty

(1972), which have shown that, in problems of dimension n, simplex methods can take as many as 2^n pivots, each requiring $\mathcal{O}(n)$ effort. Such worst-case examples are admittedly pathological, and one of the great research challenges of recent decades in numerical analysis has been to explain why simplex is so quick in more typical problems (see Shamir, 1993), Nonetheless, we will see that, for quantile regression problems with p fixed and $n \to \infty$, the modified algorithm of Barrodale and Roberts exhibits $\mathcal{O}(n)$ behavior in the number of pivots and therefore has $\mathcal{O}(n^2)$ growth in CPU time. The next section introduces interior point methods for solving LPs that have been shown to dramatically improve the computational efficiency of simplex for large quantile regression problems.

6.4 INTERIOR POINT METHODS FOR CANONICAL LPS

Although prior work in Soviet literature offered theoretical support for the idea that LPs could be solved in polynomial time, thus avoiding the pathological exponential growth of the worst-case Klee–Minty examples, the paper of Karmarker (1984) constituted a watershed in the numerical analysis of linear programming. It offered not only a cogent argument for the polynomiality of interior point methods of solving LPs but also provided direct evidence for the first time that interior point methods were demonstrably faster than simplex in specific, large, practical problems.

The close connection between the interior point approach of Karmarker (1984) and earlier work on barrier methods for constrained optimization, notably that of Fiacco and McCormick (1968), was observed by Gill, Murray, Saunders, Tomlin, and Wright (1986) and others and has led to, what may be called without much fear of exaggeration, a paradigm shift in the theory and practice of linear and nonlinear programming. Remarkably, some of the fundamental ideas required for this shift appeared already in the 1950s in a sequence of Oslo working papers by the economist Ragnar Frisch. This work is summarized in Frisch (1956). I will sketch the main outlines of the approach, with the understanding that further details may be found in the excellent expository papers of Wright (1992), Lustig, Marsden, and Shanno (1994), and the references cited therein.

Consider the canonical LP,

$$\min \ \{c^\top x \mid Ax = b, \ x \geq 0\}, \tag{6.9}$$

and associate with this problem the following logarithmic barrier (potential-function) reformulation:

$$\min \ \{B(x, \mu) \mid Ax = b\}, \tag{6.10}$$

where

$$B(x, \mu) = c^\top x - \mu \sum \log x_k.$$

In effect, (6.10) replaces the inequality constraints in (6.9) by the penalty term of the log barrier. Solving (6.10) with a sequence of parameters μ such that $\mu \to 0$, we obtain in the limit a solution to original problem (6.9). This approach was elaborated by Fiacco and McCormick (1968) for general constrained optimization but was revived as a linear programming tool only after its close connection to the approach of Karmarkar was pointed out by Gill, Murray, Saunders, Tomlin, and Wright (1986). The use of the logarithmic potential function seems to have been introduced by Frisch (1956), who described it in the following vivid terms:

> My method is altogether different than simplex. In this method we work systematically from the interior of the admissible region and employ a logarithmic potential as a guide – a sort of radar – to avoid crossing the boundary.

Suppose that we have an initial feasible point x_0 for (6.9), and consider solving (6.10) by the classical Newton method. Writing the gradient and Hessian of B with respect to x as

$$\nabla B = c - \mu X^{-1} e$$
$$\nabla^2 B = \mu X^{-2},$$

where $X = \text{diag}(x)$ and e denotes an n-vector of ones, we have, at each step the Newton problem,

$$\min_{p} \left\{ c^\top p - \mu p^\top X^{-1} e + \frac{1}{2} \mu p^\top X^{-2} p \mid Ap = 0 \right\}. \tag{6.11}$$

Solving this problem and moving from x_0 in the resulting direction p toward the boundary of the constraint set maintains feasibility and is easily seen to improve the objective function. The first-order conditions for this problem may be written as

$$\mu X^{-2} p + c - \mu X^{-1} e = A^\top y \tag{6.12}$$
$$Ap = 0, \tag{6.13}$$

where y denotes an m-vector of Lagrange multipliers. Solving for y explicitly, by multiplying through in the first equation by $A X^2$ and using the constraint to eliminate p, we have

$$A X^2 A^\top y = A X^2 c - \mu A X e. \tag{6.14}$$

These normal equations may be recognized as being generated from the linear least-squares problem:

$$\min_{y} \| X A^\top y - X c - \mu e \|_2^2 . \tag{6.15}$$

Solving for y, computing the Newton direction p from (6.12), and taking a step in the Newton direction toward the boundary constitute the essential features of the primal log barrier method. A special case of this approach is the affine scaling algorithm in which we take $\mu = 0$ at each step in (6.14), an approach anticipated by Dikin (1967) and studied by Vanderbei and Freedman (1986) and numerous subsequent authors.

Recognizing that similar methods may be applied to the primal and dual formulations, recent theory and implementation of interior point methods for linear programming have focused on attacking both formulations simultaneously. The dual problem corresponding to (6.9) may be written as

$$\max\{b^\top y \mid A^\top y + z = c, \ z \geq 0\}. \tag{6.16}$$

Optimality in the primal implies

$$c - \mu X^{-1} e = A^\top y, \tag{6.17}$$

and so setting $z = \mu X^{-1} e$ we have the system

$$
\begin{aligned}
Ax &= b & x &> 0 \\
A^\top y + z &= c & z &> 0 \\
Xz &= \mu e.
\end{aligned}
\tag{6.18}
$$

Solutions $(x(\mu), y(\mu), z(\mu))$ of these equations constitute the central path of solutions to the logarithmic barrier problem, which approach the classical complementary slackness condition $x^\top z = 0$, as $\mu \to 0$, while maintaining primal and dual feasibility along the path.

If we now apply Newton's method to this system of equations, we obtain

$$
\begin{pmatrix} Z & 0 & X \\ A & 0 & 0 \\ 0 & A^\top & I \end{pmatrix}
\begin{pmatrix} p_x \\ p_y \\ p_z \end{pmatrix}
=
\begin{pmatrix} \mu e - Xz \\ b - Ax \\ c - A^\top y - z \end{pmatrix},
\tag{6.19}
$$

which can be solved explicitly as

$$
\begin{aligned}
p_y &= (A Z^{-1} X A^\top)^{-1} [A Z^{-1} X (c - \mu X^{-1} e - A^\top y) + b - Ax] \\
p_x &= X Z^{-1} [A^\top p_y + \mu X^{-1} e - c + A^\top y] \\
p_z &= -A^\top p_y + c - A^\top y - z.
\end{aligned}
\tag{6.20}
$$

Like the primal method, the real computational effort of computing this step is the Cholesky factorization of the diagonally weighted matrix $A Z^{-1} X A^\top$. Note that the consequence of moving from a purely primal view of the problem to one that encompasses both the primal and dual is that $A X^{-2} A^\top$ has been replaced by $A Z^{-1} X A^\top$ and the right-hand side of the equation for the y-Newton step has altered somewhat. But the computational effort is essentially identical. To complete the description of the primal–dual algorithm we would need to specify how far to go in the Newton direction p, how to adjust μ as the iterations proceed, and how to stop. In fact, the most prominent examples of implementations of the primal–dual log barrier approach now employ a procedure due to Mehrotra (1992), which resolves all of these issues. I will briefly

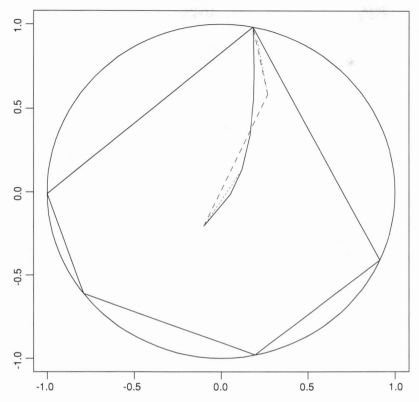

Figure 6.1. A simple example of interior point methods for linear programming. The figure illustrates a random pentagon of which we would like to find the northeast-most vertex. The central path beginning with an equal weighting of the five extreme points of the polygon is shown as the solid curved line. The dotted line emanating from this center is the first affine scaling step. The dashed line is the modified Newton direction computed according to the proposal of Mehrotra. Subsequent iterations are unfortunately obscured by the scale of the figure.

describe this procedure in the next section in the context of a slightly more general class of linear programs. But before doing so, I will illustrate the ideas by describing a simple example of the foregoing theory.

6.4.1   Newton to the Max: An Elementary Example

To illustrate the shortcomings of the simplex method, or indeed of any strategy for solving linear programs that relies on an iterative path along the *exterior* of the constraint set, consider the problem depicted in Figure 6.1. We have a random polygon whose vertices lie on the unit circle and our objective is to find a point in the polygon that maximizes the sum of its coordinates – that is, the point furthest northeast in the figure.

Because any point in the polygon can be represented as a convex weighting of the extreme points, the problem may be formulated as

$$\max\{e^\top u | X^\top d = u, \ e^\top d = 1, \ d \in \mathbb{R}_+^n\}, \tag{6.21}$$

where e denotes a (conformable) vector of ones, X is an $n \times 2$ matrix with rows representing the n vertices of the polygon, and d is the vector of convex weights to be determined. By eliminating u we may rewrite (6.21) somewhat more simply as

$$\max\{s^\top d | e^\top d = 1, \ d \in \mathbb{R}_+^n\}, \tag{6.22}$$

where $s = Xe$. This is an extremely simple LP that serves as a convenient geometric laboratory animal for studying various approaches to solving such problems. Simplex is particularly simple in this context, because the constraint set *is* literally a simplex. If we begin at a random vertex and move around the polygon until optimality is achieved, we pass through $O(n)$ vertices in the process. Of course, a random initial vertex is rather naive, and one could do much better with an intelligent "Phase 1" approach that found a *good* initial vertex. In effect we can think of the "interior point" approach as a class of methods to accomplish this, rendering further travel around the outside of the polygon unnecessary.

The log barrier formulation of Frisch is

$$\max \left\{ s^\top d + \mu \sum_{i=1}^n \log d_i | e^\top d = 1 \right\}, \tag{6.23}$$

where the barrier term $\mu \sum \log d_i$ serves as a penalty that keeps us away from the boundary of the positive orthant in the space of the dual vector d. By judicious choice of a sequence $\mu \to 0$, we might hope to converge to a solution of the original problem.

Restricting attention, for the moment, to primal log-barrier formulation (6.23) and defining

$$B(d, u) = s^\top d + \mu \sum \log d_i, \tag{6.24}$$

we have $\nabla B = s + \mu D^{-1} e$ and $\nabla^2 B = -\mu D^{-2}$, where $D = \mathrm{diag}(d)$. Thus, at any initial feasible d, we have the associated Newton subproblem,

$$\max_p \left\{ (s + \mu D^{-1} e)^\top p - \frac{\mu}{2} p^\top D^{-2} p | e^\top p = 0 \right\}.$$

This problem has first-order conditions

$$s + \mu D^{-1} e - \mu D^{-2} p = ae$$
$$e^\top p = 0,$$

where a denotes a Lagrange multiplier associated with the equality constraint, $e^\top p = 0$. Multiplying through by $e^\top D^2$, and using the constraint, we have

$$e^\top D^2 s + \mu e^\top D e = a e^\top D^2 e.$$

Thus, solving for the Lagrange multiplier $\hat{a}$, we obtain the Newton direction

$$p = \mu^{-1} D^2 s + D e - \hat{a} \mu^{-1} D^2 e, \tag{6.25}$$

where $\hat{a} = (e^\top D^2 e)^{-1} (e^\top D^2 s + \mu e^\top D e)$. Pursuing the iteration $d \leftarrow d + \lambda p$, thus defined, *with μ fixed*, yields the central path $d(\mu)$ that describes the solution d^* of the original problem, (6.21). We must be careful of course to keep the step lengths λ small enough to maintain the interior feasibility of d. Note that the initial feasible point $d = e/n$ represents $d(\infty)$.

As emphasized by Gonzaga (1992) and others, this central path is a crucial construct for the interior point approach. Competing algorithms may be usefully evaluated on the basis of how well they are able to follow this path. Clearly, there is some tradeoff between staying close to the path and moving along the path, thus trying to reduce μ, iteration by iteration. Improving upon existing techniques for balancing these objectives is the subject of a vast outpouring of recent research.

Thus far, we have considered only the primal version of our simple polygonal problem, but it is also advantageous to consider the primal and dual forms together. The dual of (6.21) is very simple:

$$\min\{a | ea - z = s, \quad z \geq 0\}. \tag{6.26}$$

The scalar a is the Lagrange multiplier on the equality constraint of the primal introduced earlier, while z is a vector of "residuals" – slack variables in the terminology of linear programming. This formulation of the dual exposes the real triviality of the problem: we are simply looking for the maximal element of the vector $s = Xe$. This is a very special case of the linear programming formulation of finding any ordinary quantile. But the latter would require us to split z into its positive and negative parts and would also introduce upper bounds on the variables d in the primal problem.

Another way to express the central path, one that nicely illuminates the symmetric roles of the primal and dual formulations of the original problem, is to solve the following equations:

$$\begin{aligned} e^\top d &= 1 \\ ea - z &= s \\ Dz &= \mu e. \end{aligned} \tag{6.27}$$

Solving these equations is equivalent to solving (6.23), which may be immediately seen by writing the first-order conditions for (6.23) as

$$\begin{aligned} e^\top d &= 1 \\ ea - \mu D^{-1} e &= s \end{aligned}$$

and then appending the definition $z = \mu D^{-1} e$. The equivalence then follows from the negative definiteness of the Hessian $\nabla^2 B$. This formulation is also useful in highlighting a crucial interpretation of the log-barrier penalty parameter μ. For any feasible pair (z, d) we have

$$s^\top d = a - z^\top d,$$

and so $z^\top d$ is equal to the duality gap: the discrepancy between the primal and dual objective functions at the point (z, d). At a solution, we have the complementary slackness condition $z^\top d = 0$, thus implying a duality gap of zero. Multiplying through by $e^\top$ in the last equation of (6.27), we may take $\mu = z^\top d / n$ as a direct measure of progress toward a solution.

Applying Newton's method to these equations yields

$$\begin{pmatrix} Z & 0 & D \\ e^\top & 0 & 0 \\ 0 & e & -I \end{pmatrix} \begin{pmatrix} p_d \\ p_a \\ p_z \end{pmatrix} = \begin{pmatrix} \mu e - Dz \\ 0 \\ 0 \end{pmatrix}, \tag{6.28}$$

where we have again presumed initial, feasible choices of d and z. Solving for p_a we have

$$\hat{p}_a = (e^\top Z^{-1} De)^{-1} e^\top Z^{-1} (Dz - \mu e),$$

which yields the primal–dual Newton direction:

$$\hat{p}_d = Z^{-1}(\mu e - Dz - De \hat{p}_a) \tag{6.29}$$

$$\hat{p}_z = e \hat{p}_a. \tag{6.30}$$

It is of obvious interest to compare this primal-dual direction with the purely primal step derived earlier. To do so, however, we need to specify an adjustment mechanism for μ.

To this end I will now describe an approach suggested by Mehrotra (1992) that has been widely implemented by developers of interior point algorithms, including the interior point algorithm for quantile regression described by Portnoy and Koenker (1997). Given an initial feasible triple (d, a, z), consider the affine-scaling Newton direction obtained by evaluating the first equation of (6.28) at $\mu = 0$. Now compute the step lengths for the primal and dual variables, respectively, using

$$\lambda_d = \mathrm{argmax}\{\lambda \in [0, 1] | d + \lambda p_d \geq 0\}$$

$$\lambda_z = \mathrm{argmax}\{\lambda \in [0, 1] | z + \lambda p_z \geq 0\}.$$

But, rather than precipitously taking this step, Mehrotra suggests adapting the direction somewhat to account for both the "recentering effect" introduced by the μe term in (6.28) and the nonlinearity introduced by the last of the first-order conditions.

Consider first the recentering effect. If we contemplate taking a full step in the affine scaling direction, we would have

$$\hat{\mu} = (d + \lambda_d p_d)^\top (z + \lambda_z p_z)/n,$$

whereas at the current point we have

$$\mu = d^\top z/n.$$

Now, if $\hat{\mu}$ is considerably smaller than μ, it means that the affine scaling direction has brought us considerably closer to the optimality condition of complementary slackness: $z^\top d = 0$. This suggests that the affine scaling direction is favorable – that we should reduce μ, in effect downplaying the contribution of the recentering term in the gradient. If, on the other hand, $\hat{\mu}$ is not much different than μ, it suggests that the affine scaling direction is unfavorable and that we should leave μ alone, taking a step that attempts to bring us back closer to the central path. Repeated Newton steps with μ fixed put us exactly on this path. These heuristics are embodied in Mehrotra's proposal to update μ by

$$\mu \leftarrow \mu(\hat{\mu}/\mu)^3.$$

To deal with the nonlinearity, Mehrotra (1992) proposed the following "predictor-corrector" approach. A full affine scaling step would entail

$$(d + p_d)^\top (z + p_z) = d^\top z + d^\top p_z + p_d^\top z + p_d^\top p_z.$$

The linearization implicit in the Newton step ignores the last term, in effect predicting that because it is of $\mathcal{O}(\mu^2)$ it can be neglected. But since we have already computed a preliminary direction, we might as well reintroduce this term to correct for the nonlinearity as well to accomplish the recentering. Thus, we compute the modified direction by solving

$$\begin{pmatrix} Z & 0 & D \\ e^\top & 0 & 0 \\ 0 & e & I \end{pmatrix} \begin{pmatrix} \delta_d \\ \delta_a \\ \delta_z \end{pmatrix} = \begin{pmatrix} \mu e - Dz - P_d p_z \\ 0 \\ 0 \end{pmatrix},$$

where $P_d = \text{diag}\,(p_d)$. This modified Newton direction is then subjected to the same step-length computation and a step is finally taken. It is important in more realistic problem settings that the linear algebra required to compute the solution to the modified step has already been done for the affine scaling step. This usually entails a Cholesky factorization of a matrix which happens to be scalar here, and so the modified step can be computed by simply backsolving the same system of linear equations already factored to compute the affine scaling step.

Figure 6.1 provides an example intended to illustrate the advantage of the Mehrotra modified step. The solid line indicates the central path. Starting from the same initial point $d = e/n$, the dotted line represents the first affine scaling step. It is successful in the limited sense that it stays very close to the central path, but it only takes a short step toward our final destination. In contrast, the

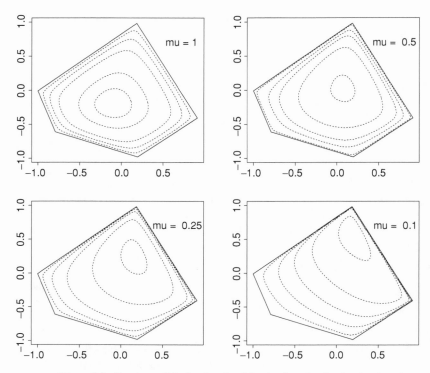

Figure 6.2. Contours of the log-barrier objective function for the simple polygonal linear program. The figure illustrates four different contour plots of log-barrier objective function (6.23) corresponding to four different choices of μ. In the first panel, $\mu = 1$ and the contours are centered in the polygon. As μ is reduced, the penalized objective function is less influenced by the penalty term and is more strongly influenced by the linear component of the original LP formulation of the problem. Thus, for $\mu = 0.1$, we find that the unconstrained maximum of the log-barrier function occurs quite close to the optimal vertex of the original LP. The locus of solutions to the log-barrier problems for various μs is called the central path and is illustrated in Figure 6.1 by the solid curved line.

first modified step, which is indicated by the dashed line, takes us much further. By anticipating the curvature of the central path, it takes a step more than twice the length of the unmodified, affine scaling step. On the second step, the initial affine scaling step is almost on target but again somewhat short of the mark. The modified step is more accurately pointed at the desired vertex and is thus, again, able to take a longer step.

Figure 6.2 illustrates the log-barrier approach by plotting four versions of the contours corresponding to the penalized objective function for four distinct values of the penalty parameter μ. In the first panel, with $\mu = 1$ we are strongly repelled from the boundary of the constraint set and the unconstrained maximum of the barrier function occurs near the center of the polygon. In the next panel, with μ reduced to $1/2$, the barrier penalty exerts a somewhat weaker effect and the contours indicate that the unconstrained maximum occurs somewhat closer to the upper vertex of the polygon. This effect is further accentuated in the $\mu = 1/4$ panel, and in the last panel with $\mu = 1/10$ we find that the maximum occurs quite close to the vertex. The path connecting the maximum of the family of fixed-μ problems is generally called the central path.

It is difficult in a single example like this to convey a sense of the overall performance of these methods. After viewing a large number of realizations of these examples, one comes away convinced that the Mehrotra modified step consistently improves upon the affine scaling step, a finding that is completely consistent with the theory.

6.4.2 Interior Point Methods for Quantile Regression

We have seen that the problem of solving

$$\min_{b \in \mathbb{R}^p} \sum_{i=1}^{n} \rho_\tau \left(y_i - x_i^\top b \right),$$ (6.31)

where $\rho_\tau(r) = r(\tau - I(r < 0))$ for $\tau \in (0, 1)$, may be formulated as the linear program

$$\min\{\tau e^\top u + (1 - \tau)e^\top v \mid y = Xb + u - v, (u, v) \in \mathbb{R}_+^{2n}\}$$ (6.32)

and has dual formulation

$$\max\{y^\top d \mid X^\top d = 0, \ d \in [\tau - 1, \tau]^n\};$$ (6.33)

or, setting $a = d + 1 - \tau$,

$$\max\{y^\top a \mid X^\top a = (1 - \tau)X^\top e, \ a \in [0, 1]^n\}.$$ (6.34)

The dual formulation of the quantile regression problem fits nicely into the standard formulations of interior point methods for linear programs with bounded variables. The algorithm described in this section is the Frisch–Newton method proposed by Portnoy and Koenker (1997) and implemented in the quantreg package for R described in Appendix A. Adding slack variables s, and the constraint $a + s = e$, we obtain the barrier function

$$B(a, s, \mu) = y^\top a + \mu \sum_{i=1}^{n} (\log a_i + \log s_i),$$ (6.35)

which should be maximized subject to the constraints $X^\top a = (1 - \tau)X^\top e$ and $a + s = e$. The Newton step, δ_a, solving

$$\max y^\top \delta_a + \mu \delta_a^\top (A^{-1} + S^{-1})e - \frac{1}{2}\mu \delta_a^\top (A^{-2} + S^{-2})\delta_a$$ (6.36)

subject to $X^\top \delta_a = 0$, satisfies

$$y + \mu(A^{-1} + S^{-1})e - \mu(A^{-2} + S^{-2})\delta_a = Xb$$ (6.37)

for some $b \in \mathbb{R}^p$ and δ_a such that $X^\top \delta_a = 0$. As before, multiplying through by $X^\top (A^{-2} + S^{-2})^{-1}$ and using the constraint, we can solve explicitly for the vector b:

$$b = (X^\top W X)^{-1} X^\top W (y + \mu(A^{-1} + S^{-1})e), \tag{6.38}$$

where $W = (A^{-2} + S^{-2})^{-1}$. This is a form of the primal log-barrier algorithm described earlier. Setting $\mu = 0$ in each step yields an affine scaling variant of the algorithm. It should be stressed that the basic linear algebra of each iteration is essentially unchanged; only the form of the diagonal weighting matrix W has changed. It should also be emphasized that there is nothing especially sacred about the explicit form of the barrier function used in (6.35). Indeed, one of the earliest proposed modifications of Karmarkar's original work was the affine scaling algorithm of Vanderbei and Freedman (1986), which used $\mu \sum_{i=1}^{n} \log(\min(a_i, s_i))$ implicitly instead of the additive specification.

Again, it is natural to ask if a primal–dual form of the algorithm could improve performance. In the bounded variables formulation we have the Lagrangian

$$\begin{aligned} L(a, s, b, u, \mu) &= B(a, s, \mu) - b^\top (X^\top a - (1-\tau)X^\top e) \\ &\quad - u^\top (a + s - e). \end{aligned} \tag{6.39}$$

Setting $v = \mu A^{-1}$ we have the first-order conditions describing the central path:

$$\begin{aligned} X^\top a &= (1-\tau)X^\top e \\ a + s &= e \\ Xb + u - v &= y \\ USe &= \mu e \\ AVe &= \mu e. \end{aligned} \tag{6.40}$$

Solving the system,

$$\begin{pmatrix} X^\top & 0 & 0 & 0 & 0 \\ I & I & 0 & 0 & 0 \\ 0 & 0 & I & -I & X \\ 0 & U & S & 0 & 0 \\ V & 0 & 0 & A & 0 \end{pmatrix} \begin{pmatrix} \delta_a \\ \delta_s \\ \delta_u \\ \delta_v \\ \delta_b \end{pmatrix} = \begin{pmatrix} (1-\tau)X^\top e - X^\top a \\ e - a - s \\ y - Xb - u + v \\ \mu e - USe \\ \mu e - AVe, \end{pmatrix} \tag{6.41}$$

yields the Newton step,

$$\begin{aligned} \delta_b &= (X^\top W X)^{-1}((1-\tau)X^\top e - X^\top a - X^\top W \xi(\mu)) \\ \delta_a &= W(X\delta_b + \xi(\mu)) \\ \delta_s &= -\delta_a \\ \delta_u &= \mu S^{-1} e - Ue + S^{-1} U \delta_a \\ \delta_v &= \mu A^{-1} e - Ve + A^{-1} V \delta_s, \end{aligned} \tag{6.42}$$

where $\xi(\mu) = y - Xb + \mu(A^{-1} - S^{-1})e$ and $W = (S^{-1}U + A^{-1}V)^{-1}$. We have also used the fact that the constraint $a + s = e$ is satisfied by construction at each iteration. Rather than solving for Newton step (6.42) directly, following Mehrotra (1992) we substitute the step directly into (6.40) to obtain

$$X^\top(a + \delta_a) = (1 - \tau)X^\top e$$

$$(a + \delta_a) + (s + \delta_s) = e$$

$$X(b + \delta_b) + (u + \delta_u) - (v + \delta_v) = y \qquad (6.43)$$

$$(U + \Delta_u)(S + \Delta_s) = \mu e$$

$$(A + \Delta_a)(V + \Delta_v) = \mu e,$$

where $\Delta_a, \Delta_v, \Delta_u, \Delta_s$ denote the diagonal matrices with diagonals, $\delta_a, \delta_v, \delta_u, \delta_s$, respectively. The primary difference between solving this system and the prior Newton step is the presence of the nonlinear terms $\Delta_u\Delta_s$, $\Delta_a\Delta_v$ in the last two equations. To approximate a solution to these equations, we find affine primal–dual direction by setting $\mu = 0$ in (6.42). Given this preliminary direction, we may then compute the step length using the following ratio test:

$$\hat{\gamma}_P = \sigma \min\{\min_j\{-a_j/\delta_{a_j}, \delta_{a_j} < 0\}, \min_j\{-s_j/\delta_{s_j}, \delta_{s_j} < 0\}\} \quad (6.44)$$

$$\hat{\gamma}_D = \sigma \min\{\min_j\{-u_j/\delta_{u_j}, \delta_{u_j} < 0\}, \min_j\{-v_j/\delta_{v_j}, \delta_{v_j} < 0\}\} \quad (6.45)$$

using scaling factor $\sigma = 0.99995$, as did Lustig, Marsden, and Shanno (1994). Then defining the function

$$\hat{g}(\hat{\gamma}_P, \hat{\gamma}_D) = (s + \hat{\gamma}_P\delta_s)^\top(u + \hat{\gamma}_D\delta_u) + (a + \hat{\gamma}_P\delta_a)^\top(v + \hat{\gamma}_D\delta_v),$$

$$(6.46)$$

the new μ is taken as

$$\mu = \left(\frac{\hat{g}(\hat{\gamma}_P, \hat{\gamma}_D)}{\hat{g}(0, 0)}\right)^3 \frac{\hat{g}(0, 0)}{2n}. \qquad (6.47)$$

To interpret (6.46) we may use the first three equations of (6.40) to write, for any primal–dual feasible point (u, v, s, a),

$$\tau e^\top u + (1 - \tau)e^\top v - (a - (1 - \tau)e)^\top y = u^\top s + a^\top v. \qquad (6.48)$$

Therefore, the quantity $u^\top s + a^\top v$ is equal to the duality gap – that is, the difference between the primal and dual objective function values at (u, v, s, a) – and $\hat{g}(\hat{\gamma}_P, \hat{\gamma}_D)$ is the duality gap after the tentative affine scaling step. Note that the quantity $a - (1 - \tau)e$ is simply the vector d appearing in dual formulation (6.33). At a solution, classical duality theory implies that the duality gap vanishes; that is, the values of the primal and dual objective functions are equal and the complementary slackness condition, $u^\top s + a^\top v = 0$, holds. If, in addition to feasibility, (u, v, s, a) happened to lie on the central path, the last two equations of (6.40) would imply that

$$u^\top s + a^\top v = 2\mu n.$$

Thus, the function $\hat{g}$ in (6.46) may be seen as an attempt to adapt μ to the current iterate in such a way that, for any given value of the duality gap, μ is chosen to correspond to the point on the central path with that gap. By definition, $\hat{g}(\hat{\gamma}_P, \hat{\gamma}_D)/\hat{g}(0, 0)$ is the ratio of the duality gap after the tentative affine scaling step to the gap at the current iterate. If this ratio is small, the proposed step is favorable and we should reduce μ further, anticipating that the recentering and nonlinearity adjustment of the modified step will yield further progress. If, on the other hand, $\hat{g}(\hat{\gamma}_P, \hat{\gamma}_D)$ is not much different from $\hat{g}(0, 0)$, the affine scaling direction is unfavorable, and further reduction in μ is ill advised. Because leaving μ fixed in the iteration brings us back to the central path, such unfavorable steps are intended to enable better progress in subsequent steps by bringing the current iterate back to the vicinity of the central path. The rationale for the cubic adjustment in (6.47) that implements these heuristics is based on the fact that the recentering of the Newton direction embodied in the terms $\mu A^{-1} e$ and $\mu S^{-1} e$ of (6.42) and (6.49) accommodates the $\mathcal{O}(\mu)$ term in the expansion of the duality gap function $\hat{g}$ while the nonlinearity adjustment described in the following accommodates the $\mathcal{O}(\mu^2)$ effect of the $\delta_s \delta_u$ and $\delta_a \delta_v$ terms.

We compute the following approximation to the solution of system (6.43) with this μ and the nonlinear terms $\Delta_s \Delta_u$ and $\Delta_a \Delta_v$ taken from the preliminary primal–dual affine direction:

$$
\begin{aligned}
\delta_b &= (X^\top W X)^{-1}((1 - \tau) X^\top e - X^\top a + X^\top W \xi(\mu)) \\
\delta_a &= W(X \delta_b + \xi(\mu)) \\
\delta_s &= -\delta_a \\
\delta_u &= \mu S^{-1} e - U e + S^{-1} U \delta_a + S^{-1} \Delta_s \Delta_u e \\
\delta_v &= \mu A^{-1} e - V e + A^{-1} V \delta_s + A^{-1} \Delta_a \Delta_v e.
\end{aligned}
\tag{6.49}
$$

The iteration proceeds until the algorithm terminates when the duality gap becomes smaller than a specified ϵ. Recall that the duality gap is zero at a solution; thus, this criterion offers a more direct indication of convergence than is usually available in iterative algorithms.

6.4.3   Interior vs. Exterior: A Computational Comparison

Our expectations about satisfactory computational speed of regression estimators are inevitably strongly conditioned by our experience with least squares. This section reports the results of a small experiment designed to compare

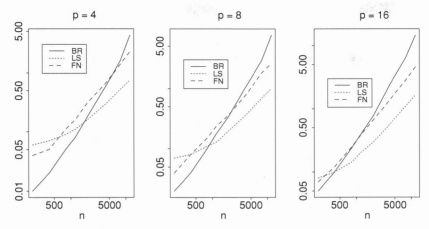

Figure 6.3. Timing comparison of two algorithms for median regression. Times are in seconds for the median of five replications for iid Gaussian data. The parametric dimension of the models is $p + 1$ with p indicated above each plot; p columns are generated randomly and an intercept parameter is appended to the resulting design. Timings were made at 8 design points in n: 200, 400, 800, 1200, 2000, 4000, 8000, and 12,000. The solid line represents the results for the simplex-based Barrodale and Roberts algorithm implemented in Splus as BR, the FN dashed line represents a Frisch–Newton interior point algorithm, and the dotted line represents least-squares timings based on $\text{lm}(y \sim x)$.

the computational speed of two quantile regression algorithms with a standard implementation of least squares. Figure 6.3 compares the performance of the Barrodale and Roberts (1974) variant of the simplex algorithm described in Section 6.2 with the Frisch–Newton algorithm described in Section 6.4.2. The former is indicated in the figure as BR and the latter as FN; timings for the corresponding least-squares fitting is indicated as LS. Both quantile regression algorithms are coded in Fortran and incorporated as functions into Splus. Timings are based on the Splus function $\text{unix-time}()$. The Barrodale and Roberts timings are based on the Splus implementation $\text{l1fit}(x,y)$. The least-squares timings are based on the Splus function $\text{lm}(y \sim x)$.

The test problems used in the comparison were all generated with Gaussian response y and independent Gaussian designs with the indicated sample sizes and parametric dimensions.

The main message of the timings is that, for problems of modest size, both quantile regression algorithms are competitive with least squares in terms of computational speed. However, as sample size increases, such comparisons are inevitably fraught with qualifications about programming style, system overhead, and other factors. It is worth noting that the code underlying the least-squares computations is the product of decades of refinement, whereas the interior point routines are still in their infancy. There is still considerable scope for improvement in the latter.

Several features of the figures are immediately striking. For small problems, both median regression algorithms perform impressively. Both are faster than the Splus implementation of least squares. For small problems, the simplex implementation of Barrodale and Roberts is the clear winner, but its roughly quadratic (in sample size) growth over the illustrated range quickly dissipates its initial advantage. The Frisch–Newton algorithm does considerably better than simplex at larger sample sizes, exhibiting roughly linear growth, as does least squares.

Beyond the range of problem sizes illustrated here, the advantage of the interior point method over simplex grows exorbitant, fully justifying the initial enthusiasm with which Karmarkar was received. Nevertheless, there is still a significant gap between ℓ_1 and ℓ_2 performance in large samples. We explore this gap from the probabilistic viewpoint of computational complexity in the next two sections.

6.4.4   Computational Complexity

This section investigates the computational complexity of the interior point algorithms for quantile regression described earlier. It should be stressed at the outset, however, that the probabilistic approach to complexity analysis adopted here is rather different than that employed in some of the interior-point literature, where the focus on worst-case analysis has led to striking discrepancies between theoretical rates and observed computational experience. The probabilistic approach has the virtue that the derived rates are much sharper and consequently more consonant with observed performance. A similar gap between worst-case theory and average practice can be seen in the analysis of parametric linear programming via the simplex algorithm, where it is known that in certain problems with an $n \times p$ constraint matrix there can be as many as n^p distinct solutions. However, exploiting some special aspects of the quantile regression problem and employing a probabilistic approach, Portnoy (1989) was able to show that the number of distinct vertex solutions (in τ) is $\mathcal{O}_p(n \log n)$, a rate that provides excellent agreement with empirical experience.

For interior point methods the crux of the complexity argument rests on showing that at each iteration the algorithm reduces the duality gap by a proportion, say $\theta_n < 1$. Thus, after K iterations, an initial duality gap of Δ_0 has been reduced to $\theta_n^K \Delta_0$. Once the gap is sufficiently small, say, less than ε, there is only one vertex of the constraint set at which the duality gap can be smaller. This follows obviously from the fact that the vertices are discrete. Thus, the vertex with the smaller duality gap must be the optimal one, and this vertex may be identified by taking p simplex-type steps. This process, called purification by Gonzaga (1992, Lemma 4.7), requires, in our notation, p steps involving

$\mathcal{O}(np^2)$ operations, or $\mathcal{O}(np^3)$ operations. Hence, the number of iterations, K, required to make $\theta_n^K \Delta_0 < \epsilon$ is

$$K < \log(\Delta_0/\epsilon)/(-\log\theta_n).$$

In the worst-case analysis of the interior point literature, ε is taken to be 2^{-L}, where L is the total number of binary bits required to encode all the data of the problem. Thus, in our notation ε would be $\mathcal{O}(np)$. Furthermore, the conventional worst-case analysis employs the bound $\theta_n < (1 - cn^{-1/2})$ and takes Δ_0 independent of n so that the number of required iterations is $\mathcal{O}(\sqrt{n}L)$. Since each iteration requires a weighted least-squares solution of $\mathcal{O}(np^2)$ operations, the complexity of the algorithm as a whole would be $\mathcal{O}(n^{5/2}p^3)$, apparently hopelessly disadvantageous relative to least squares. Fortunately, however, in the random problems for which quantile regression methods are designed, the ε bound on the duality gap at the second-best vertex can be shown to be considerably larger, at least with probability tending to 1, than this worst-case value of 2^{-L}. Lemma A.1 of the appendix to Portnoy and Koenker (1997) provides the bound $\log \epsilon = \mathcal{O}_p(p \log n)$ under mild conditions on the underlying regression model. This leads to a considerably more optimistic view of these methods for large problems.

Renegar (1988) and numerous subsequent authors have established the existence of a large class of interior point algorithms for solving linear programs that, starting from an initially feasible primal–dual point with duality gap Δ_0, can achieve convergence to a prescribed accuracy ϵ in $\mathcal{O}(\sqrt{n}\log(\Delta_0/\epsilon))$ iterations *in the worst case*. Sonnevend, Stoer, and Zhao (1991) have shown under somewhat stronger nondegeneracy conditions that this rate can be improved to $\mathcal{O}(n^a \log(\Delta_0/\epsilon))$ with $a < 1/2$. We will call an algorithm that achieves this rate an n^a-algorithm. Explicit conditions are given, which hold with probability one if the ys have a continuous density, for the case $a = 1/4$. The following result then follows immediately from the previously cited lemma.

Theorem 6.3. *In the linear model* $Y_i = x_i^\top \beta + u_i, \quad i = 1, \ldots, n,$ *assume*

(i) $\{(x_i, Y_i), i = 1, \ldots, n\}$ *are iid with a bounded continuous density, and*
(ii) $E|x_{ij}|^p < \infty$ *and* $E|Y_i|^a < \infty,$ *for some* $a > 0.$

An n^a-*algorithm for median regression converges in* $\mathcal{O}_p(n^a p \log n)$ *iterations. And with* $\mathcal{O}(np^2)$ *operations required per iteration and* $\mathcal{O}(np^3)$ *operations required for the final "purification" process, such an algorithm has complexity* $\mathcal{O}_p(n^{1+a}p^3 \log n).$

Mizuno, Todd, and Ye (1993) provide an alternative probabilistic approach to the existence of an n^a-algorithm with $a < 1/2$ and provide a heuristic argument for $a = 1/4$. They also conjecture that n^a might be improvable to $\log n$ by a more refined probabilistic approach. This would improve the overall complexity in Theorem 6.3 to $\mathcal{O}_p(np^3 \log^2 n)$ and seems quite plausible in light of the empirical evidence reported later in this chapter and elsewhere in the interior point literature. In either case we are still faced with a theoretical gap between ℓ_1 and ℓ_2 performance that substantiates the empirical experience reported in the previous section. We now introduce a new form of preprocessing for ℓ_1 problems that has been successful in further narrowing this gap.

6.5   PREPROCESSING FOR QUANTILE REGRESSION

Many modern linear programming algorithms include an initial phase of preprocessing that seeks to reduce problem dimensions by identifying redundant variables and dominated constraints. See, for example, the discussion in Section 8.2 of Lustig, Marsden, and Shanno (1994) and the   remarks of the discussants. Bixby, in this discussion, reports reductions of 20–30% in the row and column dimensions of a sample of standard commercial test problems due to "aggressive implementation" of preprocessing. Standard preprocessing strategies for LPs are not, however, particularly well suited to the statistical applications of quantile regression. This section describes some preprocessing ideas designed explicitly for quantile regression that can be used to reduce dramatically the effective sample sizes for these problems. These methods are particularly useful in extremely large problems with exchangeable observations.

The basic idea underlying the preprocessing step rests on the following elementary observation. Consider the directional derivative of the median regression problem,

$$\min_b \sum_{i=1}^n |y_i - x_i^\top b|,$$

which may be written in direction w as

$$g(b, w) = \sum_{i=1}^n x_i^\top w \, \mathrm{sgn}^*(y_i - x_i^\top b, x_i^\top w),$$

where

$$\mathrm{sgn}\,^*(u, v) = \begin{cases} \mathrm{sgn}(u) & \text{if } u \neq 0 \\ \mathrm{sgn}(v) & \text{if } u = 0. \end{cases}$$

Optimality may be characterized as a b^* such that $g(b^*, w) \geq 0$ for all $w \in \mathbb{R}^p$. Suppose for the moment that we "knew" that a certain subset J_H of the observations $N = \{1, \ldots n\}$ would fall above the optimal median plane and another subset J_L would fall below. Then in the revised problem,

$$\min_{b \in \mathbb{R}^p} \sum_{i \in N \setminus (J_L \cup J_H)} |y_i - x_i^\top b| + |y_L - x_L^\top b| + |y_H - x_H^\top b|,$$

where $x_K = \sum_{i \in J_K} x_i$, for $K \in \{H, L\}$ and y_L, y_H could be chosen as arbitrarily small and large enough, respectively, to ensure that the corresponding residuals remain negative and positive. We will refer in what follows to these combined pseudo-observations as "globs." The new problem, under our provisional hypothesis, has exactly the same gradient condition as the original one, and therefore has exactly the same solutions. But the revision has reduced effective sample size by $\{J_L, J_H\} - 2$ – that is, by the number of observations in the globs.

How might we *know* J_L, J_H? Consider computing a preliminary estimate $\hat{\beta}$ based on a subsample of m observations. Compute a simultaneous confidence band for $x_i^\top \beta$ based on this estimate for each $i \in N$. Under plausible sampling assumptions for independent data, we will see that the length of each interval is proportional to $p/\sqrt{m}$, and so if M denotes the number of y_i falling inside the band, $M = \mathcal{O}_p(np/\sqrt{m})$. Take J_H, J_L to be composed of the indices of the observations falling above and below the band. The "globbed" observations (y_K, x_K), $K \in \{L, H\}$, can now be chosen and the model reestimated based on $M + 2$ observations. Finally, we must check to verify that all the observations in J_H, J_L have the anticipated residual signs: if so, we are done, if not, we must repeat the process. If the coverage probability of the bands is P, presumably near 1, then the expected number of repetitions of this process is the expectation of a geometric random variable Z with expectation P^{-1}. We will call each repetition a cycle.

6.5.1 "Selecting" Univariate Quantiles

There is a vast literature on efficient computation of the median and other order statistics. Knuth (1998, Section 5.3.3) offers an authoritative review. Suppose that we would like to find the kth smallest element from a sample of n observations. While it clearly suffices to sort the entire sample and select the kth smallest element, it is highly inefficient to do so. Floyd and Rivest (1975) proposed an algorithm that requires only $n + k + \mathcal{O}(n^{2/3}(\log n)^{1/3})$ comparisons (see Kiwiel, 2004). In large samples this represents a very significant gain over naive methods based on complete sorting.

The "select" algorithm of Floyd and Rivest (1975) relies on a form of preprocessing. Given an initial sample of n observations, it selects two values intended to bracket the quantile of interest from a random subsample of n^α observations. Proceeding recursively, one can apply the algorithm to the subset of observations lying between the bracketing values, thereby refining the bounds. Resulting implementations come very close to achieving the theoretical lower bound of $1.5n$ comparisons for the median. Again see Kiwiel (2004) for details on computational experience.

6.5.2 Implementation

This subsection sketches further details of the preprocessing strategy. It should be emphasized that there are many aspects of the approach that deserve further research and refinement. I will refer in what follows to the Frisch–Newton quantile regression algorithm *with preprocessing* as PFN.

The basic structure of the PFN algorithm looks like this:

$$k \leftarrow 0$$
$$l \leftarrow 0$$
$$m \leftarrow [2n^{2/3}]$$
while(k is small){
    $k = k + 1$
    solve for initial rq using first m observations
    compute confidence interval for this solution
    reorder globbed sample as first M observations
    while(l is small){
        $l = l + 1$
        solve for new rq using the globbed sample
        check residual signs of globbed observations
        if no bad signs: return optimal solution
        if only few bad: adjust globs, reorder, update M, continue
        if too many bad: increase m and break to outer loop
        }
    }

The algorithm presumes that the data have undergone some initial randomization and so the first m observations may be considered representative of the sample as a whole. The experiments reported in the following use the Frisch–Newton primal–dual algorithm to compute the subsample solutions.

6.5.3   Confidence Bands

The confidence bands used in the reported computational experiments are of the standard Scheffé type. Under iid error assumptions, the covariance matrix of the initial solution is given by

$$V = \omega^2 (X^\top X)^{-1},$$

where $\omega^2 = \tau(1 - \tau)/f^2(F^{-1}(\tau))$; the reciprocal of the error density at the τth quantile is estimated using the Hall–Sheather (1986) bandwidth for Siddiqui's (1960) estimator.   Quantiles of the residuals from the initial fit are computed using the Floyd and Rivest (1975) algorithm. We then pass through the entire sample, computing the intervals

$$B_i = \left(x_i^\top \hat{\beta} - \zeta \left\| \hat{V}^{1/2} x_i \right\|, \; x_i^\top \hat{\beta} + \zeta \left\| \hat{V}^{1/2} x_i \right\| \right).$$

The parameter ζ is currently set naively at 2, but could, more generally, be set as $\zeta = (\Phi^{-1}(1 - \alpha) + \sqrt{2p - 1})/\sqrt{2} = \mathcal{O}(\sqrt{p})$ to achieve $(1 - \alpha)$ coverage for the band and, thus, ensures that the number of cycles is geometric. Under the moment condition of the previous theorem, if $p \to \infty$, the quantity $\| \hat{V}^{1/2} x_i \|$

also behaves like the square root of a χ^2 random variable, the width of the confidence band is of $\mathcal{O}_p(p/\sqrt{m})$.

Unfortunately, using the Scheffé bands requires $\mathcal{O}(np^2)$ operations: a computation of the same order as that required by least-squares estimation of the model. It seems reasonable, therefore, to consider alternatives. One possibility, suggested by the Studentized range, is to base intervals on the inequality

$$|x_i'\hat{\beta}| \leq \max_j \left\{ |\hat{\beta}_j| / s_j \right\} \times \sum_{j=1}^{p} |x_{ij}| s_j , \tag{6.50}$$

where s_j is $\hat{\omega}$ times the jth diagonal element of the $(X'X)^{-1}$ matrix and $\hat{\omega}$ is computed as for the Scheffé intervals. This approach provides conservative (though not "exact") confidence bands with width $c_q \sum_{j=1}^{p} |x_j| s_j$. Note that this requires only $\mathcal{O}(np)$ operations, thus providing an improved rate. Choice of the constant c_q is somewhat problematic, but some experimentation with simulated data showed that c_q could be taken conservatively to be approximately one and that the algorithm was remarkably independent of the precise value of c_q. For these bands the width is again $\mathcal{O}_p(p/\sqrt{m})$, as for the Scheffé bands. Although these $\mathcal{O}(np)$ confidence bands worked well in simulation experiments, and thus merit further study, the computational experience reported here is based entirely on the more traditional Scheffé bands.

After creating the globbed sample, we again solve the quantile regression problem, this time with the M observations of the globbed sample. Finally we check the signs of the globbed observations. If they all agree with the signs predicted by the confidence band, we may declare victory and return the optimal solution. If there are only a few incorrect signs, we have found it expedient to adjust the globs, reintroduce these observations into the new globbed sample, and resolve. If there are too many incorrect signs, we return to the initial phase, increasing the initial sample size somewhat, and repeat the process. One or two repetitions of the inner (fixup) loop are not unusual; more than two cycles of the outer loop are highly unusual given current settings of the confidence band parameters.

6.5.4 Choosing m

The choice of the initial subsample size m and its implications for the complexity of an interior point algorithm for quantile regression *with preprocessing* is resolved by the next result.

Theorem 6.4. *Under the conditions of Theorem 6.3, for any nonrecursive quantile regression algorithm with complexity $\mathcal{O}_p(n^\alpha p^\beta \log n)$, for problems with dimension (n, p), there exists a confidence band construction based on an initial subsample of size m with expected width $\mathcal{O}_p(p/\sqrt{m})$, and, consequently, the optimal initial subsample size is $m^* = \mathcal{O}((np)^{2/3})$. With this choice of m^*, M is also $\mathcal{O}((np)^{2/3})$. Then, with $\alpha = 1 + a$ and $\beta = 3$, from Theorem 6.3, the* *overall complexity of the algorithm with preprocessing is, for any n^a underlying interior point algorithm,*

$$\mathcal{O}_p((np)^{2(1+a)/3} p^3 \log n) + \mathcal{O}_p(np).$$

For $a < 1/2$, n sufficiently large, and p fixed, this complexity is dominated by the complexity of the confidence band computation and is strictly smaller than the $\mathcal{O}(np^2)$ complexity of least squares.

Proof. Formally, only the case of p fixed is treated, but the role of p in the determination of the constants is indicated where possible. Thus, for example, for $p \to \infty$, as suggested earlier, the width of both the Scheffé bands and the Studentized range bands are $\mathcal{O}_p(p/\sqrt{m})$. For p fixed, this condition is trivially satisfied. By independence we may conclude that the number of observations inside such a confidence band will be

$$M = \mathcal{O}_p(np/\sqrt{m}),$$

and minimizing, for any constant c,

$$m^\alpha p^\beta \log m + (cnp/\sqrt{m})^\alpha p^\beta \log(cnp/\sqrt{m}) \qquad (6.51)$$

yields

$$m^* = \mathcal{O}((np)^{2/3}).$$

Substituting this m^* back into (6.51), Theorem 6.3 implies that we have complexity

$$\mathcal{O}((np)^{2(1+a)/3} p^3 \log n)$$

for each cycle of the preprocessing. The required number of cycles is bounded in probability because it is a realization of a geometrically distributed random variable with a finite expectation. The complexity computation for the algorithm as a whole is completed by observing that the required residual checking is $\mathcal{O}(np)$ for each cycle, and employing the Studentized range confidence bands also requires $\mathcal{O}(np)$ operations per cycle. Thus, the contribution of the confidence band construction and residual checking is precisely $\mathcal{O}_p(np)$, and for any $a < 1/2$ the complexity of the ℓ_1 algorithm is therefore dominated by this term for any fixed p and n sufficiently large. ∎

If the explicit rates in p of the theorem hold for $p \to \infty$, and if the Mizuno–Todd–Ye conjecture that n^a can be improved to $\log n$ holds, then the complexity of the algorithm becomes

$$\mathcal{O}(n^{2/3} p^3 \log^2 n) + \mathcal{O}_p(np).$$

The contribution of the first term in this expression would then ensure an improvement over least squares for n sufficiently large, provided $p = o(n^{1/5})$, a rate approaching the domain of nonparametric regression applications. It is tempting to consider the recursive application of the preprocessing approach described earlier, as implemented in the Floyd and Rivest (1975) algorithm. This could be effective in reducing the complexity of the solution of the initial subsample m problem, but it does not appear possible to make it effective in dealing with the globbed sample. This accounts for the qualifier "nonrecursive" in the statement of the theorem. Further computational experience with algorithms that combine the interior point approach and preprocessing is reported by Portnoy and Koenker (1997).

6.6 NONLINEAR QUANTILE REGRESSION

Although there has been extensive computational experience with quantile regression computation for models that are linear in parameters, nonlinear quantile regression experience is much more limited. The asymptotic behavior of the nonlinear quantile regression estimator, as we have seen, closely parallels the well-established theory for nonlinear least squares, and so the inference apparatus for nonlinear quantile regression can be adapted directly from existing methods. This section briefly considers an interior point algorithm for nonlinear quantile regression proposed by Koenker and Park (1996), and some extensions required for inference will be discussed. The methods described are implemented in the function `nlrq` in the `quantreg` package. Section 8.4 considers a general strategy for deriving families of nonlinear-in-parameters conditional quantile functions from parametric copula models.

Consider the problem

$$\min_{\theta \in \mathbb{R}^p} \sum_{i=1}^{n} \rho_\tau(g_i(\theta)), \tag{6.52}$$

where, for example, we might have $g_i(\theta) = y_i - g_0(x_i, \theta)$. Provided that the functions g_i are continuously differentiable in θ, a necessary condition (see El-Attar, Vidyasagar, and Dutta, 1979) for θ^* to solve (6.52) is that there exists a vector $a \in [0, 1]^n$ such that

$$J(\theta^*)^\top a = (1 - \tau) J(\theta^*)^\top e$$

and

$$g(\theta^*)^\top a = \sum_{i=1}^{n} \rho_\tau(g_i(\theta^*)),$$

where $g(\theta) = (g_i(\theta))$, $J(\theta) = (\partial g_i / \partial \theta_j)$, and e is an n-vector of ones. Thus, one approach considered by Osborne and Watson (1971) to solving (6.52) is to solve a sequence of linear-in-parameters problems

$$\min_{\delta_\theta \in \mathbb{R}^p} \sum_{i=1}^{n} \rho_\tau(g_i(\theta) - J_i(\theta)\delta_\theta) \tag{6.53}$$

and iterating with $\theta \leftarrow \theta + \delta_\theta$ until the steps δ_θ decrease below some specified norm tolerance. However, there are several disadvantages to this approach.

Obtaining a full solution to (6.53) may be costly; moreover, it may be counterproductive, because the directions determined at each iteration may not be as good as those determined by the initial steps of the solution process for the linearized problems. Applying log-barrier methods to the locally linearized formulation,

$$g(\theta) = J(\theta)\delta_\theta + u,$$

we have the dual problem

$$\max\{g^\top a | a \in [0, 1]^n, J^\top a = (1 - \tau)J^\top e\}.$$

Suppressing the dependence of g and J on θ and writing this in log barrier form, we have

$$\max\left\{g^\top a + \mu \sum(\log a_i + \log(1 - a_i)) | a \in [0, 1]^n, J^\top a = (1 - \tau)J^\top e\right\}.$$

Expanding the maximand gives the quadratic approximation

$$G(\delta) = g^\top a + \mu\delta_a^\top(A^{-1} + S^{-1}) + \frac{1}{2}\mu\delta_a^\top(A^{-2} + S^{-2})\delta_a, \qquad (6.54)$$

where, as before, $A = \text{diag}(a_i)$ and $S = \text{diag}(1 - a_i)$. Maximizing (6.54) subject to the constraint $J^\top\delta_a = 0$ requires $\delta_\theta \in \mathbb{R}^p$ such that

$$g + \mu(A^{-1} + S^{-1})e + \mu(A^{-2} + S^{-2})\delta_a = J^\top\delta_\theta.$$

Multiplying through by $J^\top(A^{-2} + S^{-2})^{-1}$, using the constraint, and solving for δ_θ, we have

$$\delta_\theta = (J^\top W^{-1}J)^{-1}J^\top W^{-1}(g + \mu(A^{-1} + S^{-1})e),$$

where $W = (R^{-2} + S^{-2})$. Setting $\mu = 0$ in the last term yields the affine scaling step. In its simplest form, the algorithm of Koenker and Park (1996) takes this affine scaling direction and chooses a step length by one-dimensional line search – that is, by choosing λ to solve

$$\min_{\theta \in \mathbb{R}^p} \sum_{i=1}^n \rho_\tau(g_i(\theta_0 + \lambda\delta_\theta)).$$

At this point we update g and J and proceed to the next iteration. Rather than restarting the iterations with $a = (1 - \tau)e$ at each step, it was proposed to update a by projecting the current a onto the null space of the current J (i.e., $a \leftarrow (I - J(J^\top J)^{-1}J^\top)a$) and shrinking the result until it satisfies the feasibility requirement that $a \in [0, 1]$.

A variant of the foregoing approach was implemented by Koenker and Park (1996) with the log-barrier penalty taking the Meketon (1986) form $\log(\min\{a_i, 1 - a_i\})$, rather than the additive form suggested earlier. This illustrates that there really is a large variety of implementation decisions that might be explored to improve performance. Figure 6.4 illustrates the different behavior of the two log-barrier forms. Clearly they have very similar behavior near the boundary – and it should be stressed that near a solution most of the

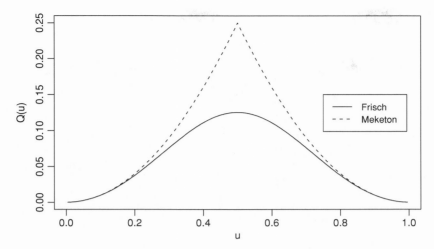

Figure 6.4. Comparison of two log-barrier functions. The Hessian contribution of the additive Frisch form of the log-barrier is $Q(u) = 1/(u^{-2} + (1-u)^{-2})$ and is somewhat smoother than the Meketon form, $Q(u) = \min\{u, 1-u\}^2$.

elements of a will be near the boundary – but the behavior of the two barrier functions in the first few iterations may be quite different.

Another choice, one that seems more critical to performance, is the decision of when to update g and J. Koenker and Park (1996) explored this in a variety of test problems, and a procedure in which two interior point steps were taken for each linearization seemed preferable to the one-step procedure described earlier. This deserves further study, as do variants of the approach that incorporate both primal and dual information and the Mehrotra predictor-corrector updating procedure for μ.

6.7 INEQUALITY CONSTRAINTS

An early example of the use of median regression in econometrics appears in the work of Arrow and Hoffenberg (1959) on estimating input–output coefficients. In the linear regression setting they wished to impose the condition that their estimated coefficients were nonnegative. Rather than venture into the morass of quadratic programming, they opted instead for the briar patch of linear programming, minimizing absolute errors subject to the inequality constraints.

Consider the problem of solving the standard quantile regression problem

$$\min_{b \in \mathbb{R}^p} \sum_{i=1}^n \rho_\tau \left(y_i - x_i^\top b \right) \tag{6.55}$$

subject to the constraints

$$Rb \geq r.$$

In the formulation of primal problem (6.6), the constraint $Ax - b \in T$ may be written as

$$\begin{bmatrix} I & -I & X \\ 0 & 0 & R \end{bmatrix} \begin{bmatrix} u \\ v \\ b \end{bmatrix} - \begin{bmatrix} y \\ r \end{bmatrix} \in \{0_n\} \times \mathbb{R}_+^q, \qquad (6.56)$$

where q denotes the row dimension of the matrix R. In the associated dual formulation, the constraint $c - Ay \in S^*$ becomes

$$\begin{pmatrix} \tau e \\ (1 - \tau)e \\ O_p \end{pmatrix} - \begin{bmatrix} I & 0 \\ -I & 0 \\ X^\top & R^\top \end{bmatrix} \begin{bmatrix} d_1 \\ d_2 \end{bmatrix} \in \{\mathbb{R}_+^{2n} \times O_p\}. \qquad (6.57)$$

As before, the vector of dual variables associated with the equality constraints, d_1, introduces no additional constraints in the dual, but the new dual variables associated with the inequality constraints, d_2, are required to be nonnegative. (The cone $T = 0_n \times \mathbb{R}_+^q$ has dual $T^* = \mathbb{R}^n \times \mathbb{R}_+^q$.) Therefore, we have the dual problem

$$\max_d \{y^\top d_1 + r^\top d_2 | X^\top d_1 + R^\top d_2 = 0, \quad d_1 \in [\tau - 1, \tau]^n, d_2 \in \mathbb{R}_+^q\}.$$

Again, transforming variables $a_1 = 1 - \tau + d_1$, and $a_2 = d_2$, we have

$$\max_a \{y^\top a_1 + r^\top a_2 | X^\top a_1 + R^\top a_2 = (1 - \tau)X^\top e, a_1 \in [0, 1]^n, a_2 \in \mathbb{R}_+^q\}.$$
$$(6.58)$$

This problem can be solved with essentially the same Frisch–Newton approach described in Section 6.4.2. Full details are provided by Koenker and Ng (2004). See Appendix A for further details about the implementation of these methods in the R package `quantreg`.

An important class of applications of inequality-constrained quantile regression involves nonparametric smoothing problems subject to qualitative constraints such as monotonicity or convexity. This is considered in more detail in the next chapter.

6.8 WEIGHTED SUMS OF ρ_τ-FUNCTIONS

In Section 5.5 we considered estimators suggested by Hogg minimizing a weighted sum of quantile regression objective functions:

$$(\hat{\alpha}_H, \hat{\gamma}_H) = \mathrm{argmin}_{(\alpha, \gamma)} \sum_{j=1}^m \sum_{i=1}^n w_j \rho_{\tau_j} \left(y_i - \alpha_j - z_i^\top \gamma \right).$$

In primal form the problem can be easily expressed as the LP

$$\min \sum_{j=1}^{m} w_j (\tau_j e^\top u_j + (1 - \tau_j) e^\top v_j)$$

subject to

$$\begin{bmatrix} Z & e & 0 & \cdots & 0 & I_n & 0 & \cdots & -I_n & 0 \\ Z & 0 & e & 0 & \cdots & 0 & I_n & & & -I_n \\ \vdots & \vdots & & \ddots & & \vdots & & & \\ Z & 0 & & & e & & I_n & & & -I_n \end{bmatrix} \begin{bmatrix} \gamma \\ \alpha \\ u \\ v \end{bmatrix} = \begin{bmatrix} y \\ y \\ \vdots \\ y \end{bmatrix},$$

where $e = e_n$ denotes an n-vector of ones, $u = (u_1^\top, \cdots, u_m^\top)^\top$, and $v = (v_1^\top, \cdots, v_m^\top)^\top$. In an abuse of our usual notational conventions, u_j and v_j denote the postitive and negative parts of the residual *vector* corresponding to τ_jth fit.

This primal formulation of the problem is somewhat inconvenient and the dual proves to be more tractable. In the notation of (6.6) we have $T = O_{mn}$ and $S = \mathbb{R}^{p+m} \times \mathbb{R}_+^{2mn}$, consequently, $T^* = \mathbb{R}^{mn}$ and $S^* = O_{p+m} \times \mathbb{R}_+^{2mn}$ and so the dual becomes

$$\max \sum_{j=1}^{M} y^\top d_j$$

subject to

$$\begin{bmatrix} O_p \\ O_m \\ w_1 \tau_1 e \\ \vdots \\ w_m \tau_m e \\ w_1(1 - \tau_1)e \\ \vdots \\ w_m(1 - \tau_m)e \end{bmatrix} - \begin{bmatrix} Z^\top & Z^\top & \cdots & Z^\top \\ e^\top & & & \\ & e^\top & & \\ & & & e^\top \\ \cdots & \cdots & \cdots & \cdots \\ & & I_{mn} & \\ & & -I_{mn} & \end{bmatrix} \begin{bmatrix} d_1 \\ \vdots \\ \vdots \\ d_m \end{bmatrix} \in S^*.$$

Transforming variables so that $a_j = d_j / w_j + (1 - \tau_j)e$, for $j - 1, \ldots, m$, we have

$$\max\{(e_m \otimes y)^\top a | B^\top a = b, a \in [0, 1]^{mn}\},$$

where

$$B = \begin{bmatrix} w \otimes Z^\top \\ w \otimes e^\top \end{bmatrix} \qquad b = \begin{bmatrix} \sum_{j=1}^{m} w_j (1 - \tau_j) Z^\top e \\ w_1(1 - \tau_1)n \\ \vdots \\ w_m(1 - \tau_m)n \end{bmatrix}.$$

This is not quite a garden-variety quantile regression problem, but the only difference appears in the slighly unusual form of the "right-hand-side" vector, b. This is easily accomodated in the Frisch–Newton formulation. Applications to models for longitudinal data and portfolio optimization are discussed in Chapter 8.

6.9 SPARSITY

The original implementations of the Frisch–Newton algorithm described by Portnoy and Koenker (1997) were quite explicitly designed for what might be called tall, thin problems: problems with large sample size n but small parametric dimension p. Such problems were efficiently handled because the algorithm requires only a modest number of iterations consisting of a single Cholesky factorization. Even when p is quite small, most of the effort of the algorithm is absorbed in these factorizations.

As sample size grows, there is an almost irresistible tendency to explore larger, more elaborate models. This tendency has been explored empirically in the econometric literature on wage equations by Koenker (1988). When the sample size is large, it is tempting to consider inclusion of industry and occupation indicator variables, pushing the dimension of the model into the mildly obese range of a few hundred parameters. For least-squares estimation of such models there are well-established computational strategies. For example, in models with a one-way layout of fixed effects, it is possible to transform to deviations from group means – in effect decomposing the computation into two successive projects. Such tricks are not available in the quantile regression setting, and so alternative strategies are required.

A common feature of most large-p quantile regression problems is the extreme sparsity of their design. The matrix X may have a few hundred, or even a few thousand, columns, but most of the entries in these matrices are *zero*. Modern developments in sparse linear algebra provide an extremely effective approach to these problems. For matrices with a very specific sparse structure, like the tridiagonal matrices of cubic spline smoothing, there have long been routines specially designed for efficient performance. More recently, however, efficient methods of solving large systems of sparse linear equations with arbitrary sparse structure have become available. As we have emphasized, the crucial step in the Frisch–Newton algorithm for quantile regression is the Cholesky decomposition of the matrix required to find the Newton steps. This is just a diagonally weighted least-squares problem; but when the parametric dimension is large, ignoring the sparse structure can be fatal.

The R package SparseM described by Koenker and Ng (2003) constitutes an exploratory effort to exploit sparse linear algebra in the general context of statistical computing. It provides several storage modes for arbitrary sparse matrices; most operations are conducted with compressed sparse row format that stores the column and row indices of the nonzero elements of the matrix in two integer vectors, and the elements themselves in another real vector. The package offers a reasonably full panoply of basic linear algebra functionality. Linear equation solving is handled by the sparse Cholesky algorithm of Ng and Peyton (1993). Algorithmic options to the basic function rq to use the sparse versions of the Frisch–Newton interior point algorithm are provided by the quantreg package. Sparse linear algebra offers two important advantages in large problems. The first is the significant reduction in memory required. Problems that would be unthinkably large with dense methods are often surprisingly manageable with sparse methods. The second advantage is computational effort. Cholesky factorization of sparse matrices is roughly proportional to the number of nonzero elements in the matrix. Because the Newton subproblems of the quantile regression algorithm generally preserve the sparse structure of the design quite well, each factorization is quite efficient.

To illustrate these general observations, we can describe a typical smoothing problem exploiting sparsity and employing the penalized triogram methods described in the next chapter. We generate data from the model

$$z_i = f_0(x_i, y_i) + u_i \quad i = 1, \cdots, n, \tag{6.59}$$

where the u_i are taken as iid Gaussian and

$$f_0(x, y) = \frac{40 \exp\left(8\left((x - .5)^2 + (y - .5)^2\right)\right)}{\exp\left(8\left((x - .2)^2 + (y - .7)^2\right)\right) + \exp\left(8\left((x - .7)^2 + (y - .2)^2\right)\right)}.$$

This is a standard test function for bivariate smoothing problems used by Koenker and Mizera (2004); fitting is carried out with the total variation penalized triogram methods introduced there. The sparsity structure of the design matrix is illustrated in Figures 6.5. Dots in this image indicate the presence of a nonzero element; white space indicates zero elements. The upper diagonal in the figure represents the fidelity component of the objective function which is an $n \times n$ identity matrix. The lower rectangle represents the penalty component of the problem. In this instance, the sample size $n = 200$, and the X matrix is 200 by 777. Of the total 155,400 elements of this matrix, only 1.61% are nonzero. Forming $X^\top X$ yields the matrix represented in Figure 6.6. It is somewhat less sparse, but still only 6.09% of its entries are nonzero. As the number of observations increases, the number of entries in the dense form of these design matrices increases quadratically, whereas the number of entries in their sparse form increases only linearly. Because computational effort is proportional to the number of nonzero entries for the sparse form of the Cholesky factorization, this greatly facilitates the feasibility of the approach.

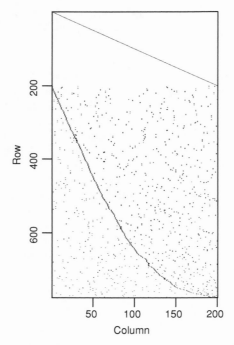

Figure 6.5. Sparsity of a typical pseudodesign matrix for the penalized tri-ogram problem. Dark pixels indicate the presence of nonzero elements of the matrix.

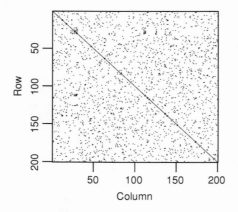

Figure 6.6. A typical $X^\top Q^{-1} X$ matrix of the penalized triogram problem.

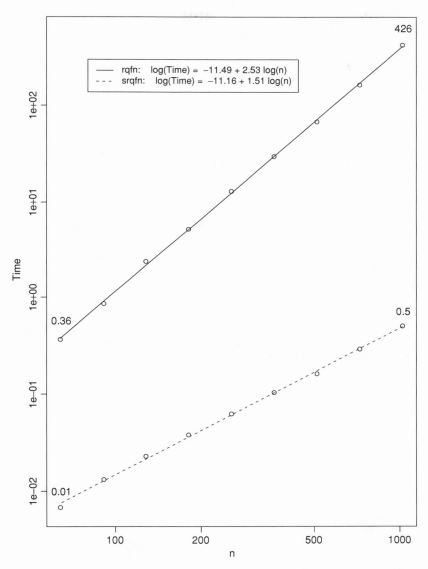

Figure 6.7. Median execution time to obtain the penalized triogram solution to model (6.59) for rqfn and srqfn.

A comparison of the computational effort required by the sparse Cholesky factorization versus the standard dense algorithm is shown in Figure 6.7 for samples sizes in the range 50 to 1000. Both algorithms exhibit roughly log-linear growth, but the efficiency gain of the sparse method is quite striking, particularly for the larger sample sizes. Continued development of algorithms capable of exploiting the sparse structure of large problems should significantly expand the applicability of quantile regression methods in many application settings.

6.10 CONCLUSION

In 1887, six years after publishing his path-breaking work in economics, *Mathematical Psychics*, F.Y. Edgeworth began a series of papers "on a new method of reducing observations relating to several quantities." Edgeworth's new method, which he called the "plural median," was intended to revive the Boscovich/Laplace *methode de situation* as a direct competitor to the least-squares approach to regression championed by Galton and others. Edgeworth (1888) proposed dropping the zero-mean constraint on residuals employed by his predecessors, arguing that it conflicted with the median intent of the absolute error approach. Appealing to the univariate results of Laplace, he conjectured that the plural median should be more accurate than the least-squares estimator when the observations were more "discordant" than those from the Gaussian probability law. Finally, he proposed an arcane geometric algorithm for computing the plural median and remarked, rather cryptically,

> the probable error is increased by about 20 percent when we substitute the Median for the Mean. On the other hand, the labour of extracting the former is rather less: especially, I should think in the case of many unknown variables. At the same time, that labour is more "skilled." There may be needed the attention of a mathematician; and, in the case of many unknowns, some power of hypergeometrical conception.

Edgeworth's "20 percent" is slightly optimistic. At the normal model, for example, we know that the median would have confidence intervals that are about 25% wider than those based on the mean. But many of the details of Edgeworth's conjectures concerning the improvements achievable by the plural median over comparable least-squares methods of inference in discordant situations have been filled in over the past 20 years. We are now on the verge of fully vindicating Edgeworth's other claim that the "plural median" is less laborious – as well as more robust – than its least-squares competitor. In the metaphor of Portnoy and Koenker (1997), the common presumption that Laplace's old median tortoise was forever doomed to lag behind the quicker Gaussian hare representing least squares may finally be overturned.

6.11 PROBLEMS

Problem 6.1. To compare variants of the interior point method for quantile regression, it is useful to consider the simplest case of computing the sample median. The dual problem is

$$\max\{y^\top a | e^\top a = .5n, a \in [0, 1]^n\}.$$

For the barrier function,

$$B(a) = y^\top a + \mu \sum_{i=1}^{n} (\log(a_i) + \log(1 - a_i)),$$

compare the affine scaling and primal–dual algorithms. Note that in this case each least-squares iteration is just a weighted mean.

Problem 6.2. Another iteratively reweighted least-squares approach to computing quantile regression estimators is based on the elementary observation that

$$\sum_{i=1}^{n} |u_i| = \sum_{i=1}^{n} u_i^2 / |u_i|,$$

provided that none of the u_i are equal to 0. And so it appears that one could try to minimize the right-hand side by solving a sequence of weighted least-squares problems with weights $w_i = 1/|u_i|$. Of course, one should be cautious about the right-hand side because we know that minimizers may have several u_i equal to 0. Nevertheless, the appealing simplicity of the weighting has led many researchers down this path. An algorithm of this type using weights $w_i = (|u_i| + \epsilon)^{-1}$ has been recently proposed by Hunter and Lange (2000). Implement an algorithm like this for the sample median and compare its performance with those of the previous problem. (Limited experience suggests that the affine scaling algorithm requires roughly twice the number of least-squares iterations as the primal–dual method, and the Hunter–Lange algorithm requires roughly twice as many iterations as affine scaling to achieve the same accuracy.)

CHAPTER 7

Nonparametric Quantile Regression

Parametric models play a critical role throughout the realm of scientific data analysis; whether they are interpreted as natural law or only as convenient approximations, they offer important advantages. Nevertheless, there are inevitable occasions when parametric specifications fail, and data analysis must turn to more flexible, nonparametric methods. Most of the vast literature on nonparametric regression deals with the estimation of conditional mean models; however, as in the parametric context, these methods are usefully complemented by nonparametric estimation of families of conditional quantile functions. Such families may reveal systematic differences in dispersion, tail behavior, and other features with respect to the covariates.

There is an extensive literature dealing with nonparametric estimation of conditional quantile functions. Stone's seminal paper (1977) considers nearest-neighbor methods and establishes consistency and rates of convergence for locally constant nonparametric estimators. Chaudhuri (1991) introduced locally polynomial quantile regression. In this chapter I will begin by briefly describing the locally polynomial approach and then describe some recent work on regularization methods using the total variation roughness penalty.

7.1 LOCALLY POLYNOMIAL QUANTILE REGRESSION

Suppose we have bivariate observations $\{(x_i, y_i)\ i = 1, \ldots, n\}$ and would like to estimate the τth conditional quantile function of the response y, given $X = x$:

$$g(x) = Q_Y(\tau | x).$$

Let K be a positive, symmetric, unimodal (kernel) function and consider the weighted quantile regression problem

$$\min_{\beta \in \mathbb{R}^2} \sum_{i=1}^{n} w_i(x) \rho_\tau (y_i - \beta_0 - \beta_1(x_i - x)), \tag{7.1}$$

where $w_i(x) = K((x_i - x)/h)/h$. Having centered the covariate observations at the point x, our estimate of $g(x)$ is simply $\hat{\beta}_0$, the first component of the minimizer of (7.1). If we require an estimate of the slope of the function g at the point x, this is delivered by $\hat{\beta}_1$. Extending the procedure to higher order polynomials, we can define

$$\min_{\beta \in \mathbb{R}^{p+1}} \sum_{i=1}^{n} w_i(x)\rho_\tau(y_i - \beta_0 - \beta_1(x_i - x) - \cdots - \beta_p(x_i - x)^p), \qquad (7.2)$$

enabling us to estimate higher derivatives, provided the function g is sufficiently smooth. Inevitably, of course, there is some loss in precision as we consider estimating higher order derivatives.

A critical question that arises in all nonparametric estimation is the choice of the bandwidth parameter h that controls the degree of smoothness of the estimated function. Too large an h and we obscure too much local structure by too much smoothing; too small an h and we introduce too much variability by relying on too few observations in our local polynomial fitting.

Example 7.1. Figure 7.1 illustrates several estimates of the conditional median function for the well-known "motorcycle data." The data come from experimental measurements of the acceleration of the head of a test dummy in motorcycle crash tests: see Härdle (1990) and Silverman (1986) for further details and discussion of comparable estimates of conditional mean functions. This figure is based on a Gaussian kernel, with four bandwidths as specified in the legend of the figure; evaluation of the estimate is made at 50 equally spaced points. Figure 7.2 illustrates the corresponding estimated first-derivative functions. And Figure 7.3 illustrates several different conditional quantile curves, all estimated with the bandwidth set at $h = 2$. Note the crossing of the estimated quantile curves beyond about 55 milliseconds; this is embarrassing, but not surprising, given that there is only one observation in this region.

The example clearly illustrates that the conventional assumption of nonparametric regression theory – that there is additive, independently and identically distributed (iid) error around a smooth underlying conditional mean function – is extremely implausible. For the first few milliseconds, variability is almost negligible and gradually increases thereafter. It is worth emphasizing that the family of nonparametric conditional quantile curves provides a natural complement to the mean analysis, allowing us to construct nonparametric prediction intervals for problems of this type. The example also illustrates the need for more smoothing (i.e., larger bandwidth) in estimating derivatives. We will return to this point in the discussion of the asymptotic behavior of the estimates.

Chaudhuri (1991) considers the asymptotic behavior of locally polynomial quantile regression estimators in a general multivariate setting, establishing conditions under which the estimators attain optimal rates of convergence and,

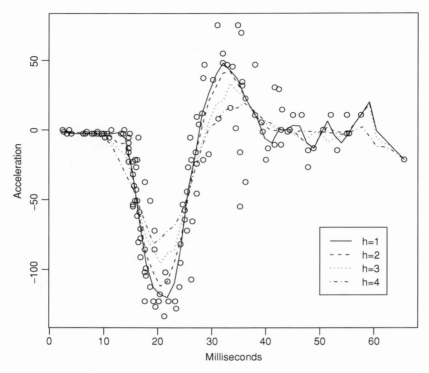

Figure 7.1. Locally linear median regression. Four estimated median regression curves for the motorcycle data for differing choices of the bandwidth parameter.

thus, resolving a question raised by Stone (1982). Chaudhuri considers the standard model

$$Y_i = g(X_i) + u_i.$$

The X_i are assumed to be drawn randomly from a distribution that has absolutely continuous density in a fixed, open neighborhood, $V \subset \mathbb{R}^d$, that contains the point $0 \in \mathbb{R}^d$. The errors, u_i, are assumed to be iid, independent of X_i, and possessing a strictly positive Holder continuous density in a neighborhood of their τth quantile, which is assumed to be zero. Interest focuses on the estimation of g and its derivatives at the point 0.

Let D^u denote the differential operator $\partial^{[u]}/\partial x_1^{u_1} \cdots \partial x_d^{u_d}$, where $[u] = u_1 + \cdots + u_d$. The function g is assumed to be smooth in the sense that, for all $x \in V$ and some fixed integer $k > 0$,

$$\|D^u g(x) - D^u g(0)\| \le c\|x\|^{\gamma}$$

for some $c > 0$, $[u] < k$, and $\gamma \in (0, 1)$. The order of smoothness of g, $p = k + \gamma$, plays a fundamental role in determining the rate of convergence of the estimator. Chaudhuri considers a variant of the kernel weighting just described

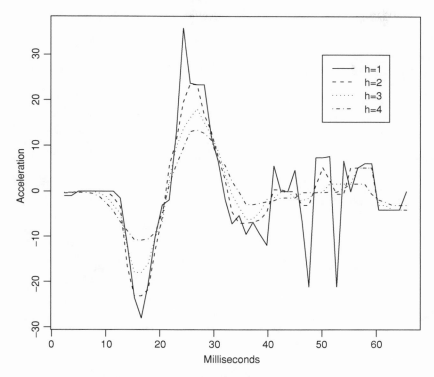

Figure 7.2. Locally linear median regression. Four estimates of the derivative of the acceleration curves for differing choices of the bandwidth parameter.

in which points get weight 1 if X_i lies in the set $C_n = [-\delta_n, \delta_n]^d$ and weight 0 otherwise. The bandwidth is taken as $\delta_n = \delta_0 n^{-1/(2p+d)}$, and so for n sufficiently large, C_n is necessarily inside the set V. One may, of course question the choice of *cubes*, because cubes implicitly assume the same degree of smoothing in all d coordinates. Some form of rescaling of the covariates may be desirable prior to estimation to justify this choice.

The estimator is based on the following polynomial model:

$$g(x) = P_n(\beta, x) + R_n$$
$$= \sum_u \beta_u \delta_n^{-[u]} x^u + R_n,$$

where the sum runs over all the multi-indices, u is such that $[u] < k$, and $x^u = \prod_{i=1}^d x_i^{u_i}$. Now let

$$\hat{\beta}_n = \text{argmin} \sum \rho_\tau(Y_i - P_n(\beta, x))$$

and denote the estimator of $T(g) = D^u g(0)$ by

$$\hat{T}_n = D^u P_n(\hat{\beta}_n, 0) = u! \delta_n^{[u]} \hat{\beta}_n,$$

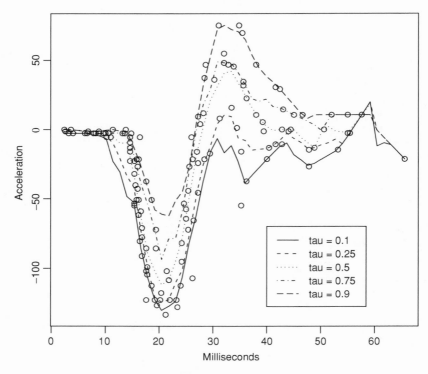

Figure 7.3. Locally linear quantile regression. Five estimated quantile curves of acceleration for the motorcycle data.

where $u! = \prod_{i=1}^{d} u_i!$. This is a somewhat arcane, but on reflection natural, multivariate generalization of the univariate situation described earlier. Chaudhuri shows that, almost surely, for $r = (p - [u])/(2p + d)$, we have

$$\|\hat{T}_n - T(g)\| = \mathcal{O}(n^r \sqrt{\log n}),$$

and he provides a local Bahadur representation for the estimator $\hat{\beta}_n$. In the simplest univariate case, with $d = 1$ and assuming $p = 2$, we have $\delta_n = \mathcal{O}(n^{-1/5})$, and so we have convergence of function estimates at (essentially) the rate $\mathcal{O}(n^{-2/5})$ and convergence of first derivatives at $\mathcal{O}(n^{-1/5})$. In higher dimensions, convergence is necessarily slower: for $d = 2$ and $p = 2$, we get pointwise convergence of function values at rate $n^{-1/3}$ and convergence of the gradient vector at rate $n^{-1/6}$.

7.1.1   Average Derivative Estimation

The inherent difficulty of estimating covariate effects nonparametrically in higher dimensions has led to a variety of proposals designed to reduce the effective dimension of the nonparametric estimation problem. One approach that has received considerable attention, particularly within econometrics, has been the estimation of "average derivatives." This entails averaging nonparametric estimates of the gradient function over some appropriate set in design space. Average derivative estimation was proposed for mean regression by Härdle and Stoker (1989) and has been developed by Chaudhuri, Doksum, and Samarov (1997) for quantile regression.

Given a locally polynomial estimator $\hat{g}$, defined at each of the observed X_i points, one can define the obvious plug-in estimator of the average derivative as

$$\hat{\gamma} = n^{-1} \sum \nabla \hat{g}(X_i) w(X_i),$$

where $w(\cdot)$ is chosen to control the weight attached to estimates of ∇g in the outlying regions of design space. Under appropriate conditions on the weight function, we can integrate by parts:

$$\gamma = \int \nabla g(x) w(x) f(x) dx = - \int g(x) \nabla(w(x) f(x)) dx$$

and this suggests the alternative estimator,

$$\tilde{\gamma} = -n^{-1} \sum g(X_i)[\nabla w(X_i) \tilde{f}(X_i) + \nabla w(X_i) \tilde{f}(X_i) / \tilde{f}(X_i)].$$

Under rather technical conditions, Chaudhuri, Doksum, and Samarov (1997) show that $\hat{\gamma}$ and $\tilde{\gamma}$ both converge to γ at the parametric rate $n^{-1/2}$, and they have identical Bahadur representations and, consequently, the same first-order asymptotic behavior. Minimum regularity conditions required for this Bahadur representation to hold, however, differ somewhat for $\hat{\gamma}$ and $\tilde{\gamma}$.

An important feature of the average derivative method involves estimation of semiparametric single index, or transformation models. Suppose, for example, we have the model

$$Q_Y(\tau | X = x) = g(x^\top \alpha). \tag{7.3}$$

If we knew the link function g, and it were monotone, we might simply transform the model to obtain

$$Q_{g^{-1}(Y)}(\tau | X = x) = x^\top \alpha, \tag{7.4}$$

but what if g is unknown? Can we jointly estimate g and α?

The average derivative in model (7.3) is given by

$$\beta = \int g'(x^\top \alpha) w(x) f(x) dx \cdot \alpha \equiv \kappa \alpha,$$

and so α can be estimated up to the scalar factor κ by the Chaudhuri–Doksum–Samarov estimator. Once this is accomplished, we have reduced the nonparametric aspect of the estimation problem to a univariate quantile regression problem of estimating the model:

$$Q_Y(\tau|z) = g(z), \tag{7.5}$$

where $z = x^\top \hat{\alpha}$, a task that can be done at the conventional univariate nonparametric $n^{-2/5}$ rate. There is an extensive literature on this approach focusing on variants of the mean regression version.

The single index model vividly illustrates the advantages of reducing highly multivariate nonparametric regression problems to lower dimensional ones based on parametric projections. Multi-index models of the form

$$Q_Y(\tau|x) = g(x^\top \alpha_1, \ldots, x^\top \alpha_m), \tag{7.6}$$

where m is considerably smaller than the dimension of the covariate space d, provide a challenging laboratory for semiparametric methods.

7.1.2   Additive Models

An alternative, and in some respects simpler, strategy for dimension reduction in multivariate nonparametric models involves additive models of the form

$$Q_Y(\tau|x) = \alpha_0 + \sum_{j=1}^{d} g_j(x_j). \tag{7.7}$$

This is a special case of the more general multi-index (projection pursuit) model

$$Q_Y(\tau|x) = \alpha_0 + \sum_{j=1}^{m} g_j(x^\top \alpha_j). \tag{7.8}$$

In either case, the objective is to reduce d-dimensional nonparametric regression problems to a series of univariate problems. It is also worth emphasizing that additive forms of this sort offer considerable advantages at the model interpretation and visualization stage compared to their more general counterparts. They do not, however, as is often claimed, repeal the "curse of dimensionality." They simply alter the question being asked by imposing very stringent new restrictions on the form of the multivariate dependence.

An important special instance of additive models is the partially linear model with a nonparametric component and an additive linear parametric component. Lee (2003) has considered such models using the locally polynomial approach. He and Liang (2000) consider an errors-in-variable setting.

A variety of ingenious methods have been introduced for estimating additive models using locally polynomial methods, again focusing predominantly on the mean regression case. An iterative approach designed to fit one g_j at a time, the backfitting algorithm of Friedman and Stuetzle (1981), has received considerable attention. Unfortunately, such methods are not very well suited to quantile regression applications. The next section considers penalty methods that are better adapted to this task.

7.2 PENALTY METHODS FOR UNIVARIATE SMOOTHING

Smoothing traditionally has been divided into two opposing camps: kernel people and spline people. Unquestionably, the competitive tension between the two camps has strengthened both approaches. Fortunately, some multicultural tendencies have emerged recently to weaken these tribal enmities and there are now quite prominent contributors with a foot in both camps. Having briefly introduced nonparametric quantile regression from a kernel viewpoint, we will now turn to penalty methods.

7.2.1 Univariate Roughness Penalties

The statistical approach to penalty methods for univariate smoothing goes back at least to Whittaker (1923), who introduced such methods for smoothing or, as it is known in actuarial science, graduation of mortality tables. For equally spaced time-series data, one variant of this approach involves solving

$$\min_{\hat{y} \in \mathbb{R}^n} \sum_{i=1}^{n} (y_i - \hat{y}_i)^2 - \lambda \sum_{i=3}^{n} (\Delta^2 \hat{y}_i)^2. \tag{7.9}$$

We can regard this as a form of (Bayesian) shrinkage: we want to choose the constants $\{\hat{y}_i : 1, \ldots, n\}$ so that they bear some reasonable degree of fidelity to the observed points, while at the same time not diverging too much from the idealized smoothness epitomized by the linear function. The parameter λ, to be chosen by the analyst, controls the degree of shrinkage or, if one prefers, the degree of belief in the smoothness of the target function. Note that if the $\hat{y}_i$s *are* linear, that is, if for some choice of constants a and b,

$$\hat{y}_i = a + bi,$$

then $\Delta^2 \hat{y}_i = 0$ and the contribution of the penalty term vanishes. Choice of λ balances the two objectives: for large λ the penalty dominates and the fitted $\hat{y}_i$s must adhere closely to the ideal of the linear fit. When λ is small the penalty only weakly influences the fit, and so the $\hat{y}_i$s can be chosen so that the fitted values (nearly) interpolate the observed points. Turning the λ knob gives us a family of curves that takes us from one extreme to the other.

Data need not arrive in this convenient equally spaced format. Unequally spaced observations can be accommodated with only slightly more complicated computations and notation. Reinsch (1967) posed the following problem, generalizing the formulation of (7.9):

$$\min_{g \in \mathcal{G}} \sum_{i=1}^{n} (y_i - g(x_i))^2 - \lambda \int (g''(x))^2 dx.$$

The natural choice of the space over which to minimize, $\mathcal{G}$, is the Sobolev space of C^2 functions with square integrable second derivatives. This variational problem has a first-order (Euler) condition that requires that the fourth derivative of g is zero almost everywhere. This condition characterizes a piecewise cubic polynomial whose third derivative jumps at the finite set of observed x_is, making its fourth derivative a sum of Dirac functions at these points. Continuity of the estimated function $\hat{g}$ and its first two derivatives reduces the problem to a finite-dimensional one of finding the values taken by $\hat{g}$ at the distinct x_is. Given the quadratic form of the objective function, solutions can be represented by a linear function of the observed y_is; that is,

$$\hat{y} = (\hat{g}(x_i)) = A(\lambda)y,$$

where $A(\lambda)$ is a matrix depending on the configuration of the x_is. As in the equally spaced case, the parameter λ controls the smoothness of the fitted function $\hat{g}$.

For quantile regression we can adopt the same penalty and consider the estimator that minimizes

$$\min_{g \in \mathcal{G}} \sum_{i=1}^{n} \rho_\tau(y_i - g(x_i)) - \lambda \int (g''(x))^2 dx.$$

Bosch, Ye, and Woodworth (1995) describe an interior point algorithm for solving the quadratic programming formulation of this problem. Solutions are still cubic splines, but they now estimate conditional quantile functions specified by the choice of τ.

Koenker, Ng, and Portnoy (1994) consider other L_p penalties, focusing on the cases $p = 1$ and $p = \infty$:

$$J(g) = \|g''\|_p = (\int (g''(x))^p)^{1/p}.$$

The latter choice effectively imposes an upper bound on the value of $|g''|$ and yields a piecewise quadratic fit that can be easily computed using linear programming methods. For $p = 1$, the situation is somewhat more delicate. One may consider minimizing

$$\min \sum_{i=1}^{n} \rho_\tau(y_i - g(x_i)) - \lambda \int |g''(x)| dx$$

over, say, the space of quadratic splines. The problem is well posed, but further consideration suggests that the resulting quadratics can be improved by sharpening the elbows at the x_i observations where the proposed solution bends. This leads us to the reformulation of the L_1 form of the penalty in terms of the total variation of the function g'.

7.2.2   Total Variation Roughness Penalties

To see why total variation plays such a crucial role, recall the total variation of the function $f : [a, b] \to \mathbb{R}$, defined by

$$V(f) = \sup \sum_{i=1}^{n} |f(x_{i+1}) - f(x_i)|,$$

where the sup is taken over all partitions $a \leq x_1 < \cdots < x_n < b$. For absolutely continuous f, $V(f)$ can be written as (see, e.g., Natanson, 1974, p. 259):

$$V(f) = \int_a^b |f'(x)|dx,$$

It follows that, for functions g whose first derivative g' is absolutely continuous, we have

$$V(g') = \int_a^b |g''(x)|dx.$$

At this point it might seem that the distinction between $V(g')$ and the L_1 norm of g'' is merely semantic, but the fact that the former quantity is well defined for a larger set of functions proves to be critical.

Consider the problem of finding a continuous function g that minimizes $V(g')$ while interpolating a specified set of points $\{(x_i, y_i) : i = 1, \ldots, n\}$. Suppose our points are ordered so that $a \leq x_1 < \cdots < x_n < b$. By the mean value theorem we can find points $u_i \in (x_i, x_{i+1})$ such that

$$g'(u_i) = (y_{i+1} - y_i)/(x_{i+1} - x_i) \qquad i = 1, \ldots, n - 1.$$

Then, for any function $g : [a, b] \to \mathbb{R}$ with absolutely continuous first derivative, we have

$$V(g') \geq \sum_{i=1}^{n-1} |\int_{u_i}^{u_{i+1}} g''(x)| \geq \sum_{i=1}^{n-1} |g'(u_{i+1}) - g'(u_i)| \equiv V(\hat{g}'), \qquad (7.10)$$

where $\hat{g}$ is the piecewise linear interpolant with knots at the x_i. Thus, $\hat{g}$ solves the variational problem and is the optimal interpolant. Does this imply that the more general variational problem,

$$\min \sum_{i=1}^{n} \rho_\tau(y_i - g(x_i)) - \lambda V(g'), \qquad (7.11)$$

has solutions that are piecewise linear functions with knots at the x_i? As can be easily argued by contradiction, the answer is "yes." Suppose there was a solution, say $\tilde{g}$, to (7.11) that was not of the piecewise linear form; then, given the function values of $\tilde{g}$ at the x_is, (7.10) implies that there exists a $\hat{g}$ with the same function values (i.e., the same fidelity) but smaller $V(g')$ that is piecewise linear on the specified mesh, and so we have reached a contradiction.

Once we have established the form of the solutions, it is straightforward to develop an algorithm for computing them. Writing the solution as

$$\hat{g}(x) = \alpha_i + \beta_i(x - x_i) \qquad x \in [x_i, x_{i+1}),$$

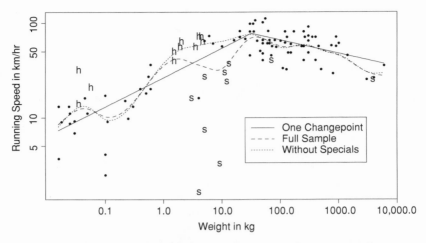

Figure 7.4. Running speed of terrestrial mammals. Three mean estimates.

for $i = 0, \ldots, n$, by continuity of $\hat{g}$ we have that $\beta_i = (\alpha_{i+1} - \alpha_i)/h_i$, where $h_i = x_{i+1} - x_i$, and so

$$V(\hat{g}') = \sum_{i=1}^{n-1} |\beta_{i+1} - \beta_i| = \sum_{i=1}^{n-1} |(\alpha_{i+2} - \alpha_{i+1})/h_{i+1} - (\alpha_{i+1} - \alpha_i)/h_i|.$$

Thus, we can parameterize $\hat{g}$ by the values it takes at the points x_i and write (7.11) as the finite-dimensional optimization problem

$$\min \sum_{i=1}^{n} \rho_\tau(y_i - \alpha_i) - \lambda \sum_{i=1}^{n-2} |d_j^\top \alpha|, \tag{7.12}$$

where d_j is an n-dimensional vector with elements $(h_j^{-1}, -(h_{j+1}^{-1} + h_j^{-1}), h_{j+1}^{-1})$ in the j, $j + 1$, and $j + 2$ positions and zeros elsewhere. If there are repeated x_i values, then we need only estimate α_is at the distinct x_is, and we have a slightly more complicated fidelity contribution.

Example 7.2. Figure 7.4 illustrates three estimates of a mean regression model expressing maximum recorded running speed as a function of body weight for a sample of 107 terrestrial mammals. In the prior analysis of Chappell (1989), two groups of animals were distinguished for special treatment: "hoppers," indicated by the plotting symbol h, are animals like the kangaroo that ambulate by hopping and are generally faster than mammals of comparable weight; "specials," indicated by letter s, are animals like the sloths, the porcupine, and the hippopotamus, which were judged "unsuitable for inclusion in the analyses on account of lifestyles in which speed does not figure as an important factor." The dashed and dotted lines in the figure indicated Reinsch's cubic smoothing

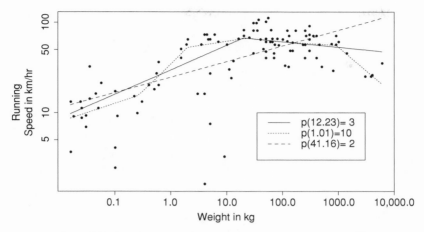

Figure 7.5. Running speed of terrestrial mammals. Three median estimates.

spline estimates with and without the "special" observations. It is immediately apparent from comparing these curves how sensitive the least-squares fitting procedure is to the outlying "specials." This is characteristic of conditional mean estimation in general, but it is sometimes overlooked in the context of nonparametric estimation. The solid piecewise linear fit is Chappell's preferred model and was obtained by omitting the specials, introducing an additive shift effect for the hoppers, and optimizing over the selection of the breakpoint using a least-squares fitting criterion.

Figure 7.5 illustrates three alternative conditional median fits employing the total variation smoothness penalty as in (7.11) with three choices of λ. For sufficiently large λ, the roughness penalty dominates the fidelity objective and we get the linear fit indicated by the dashed line. As λ is decreased, the penalty receives less weight and we get more kinks in the fitted function. The number of linear segments in the fitted function gives a useful measure of the dimensionality of the fit. We define p_λ to be the number of points interpolated by the fitted function, and so $p_\lambda - 1$ is the number of distinct linear segments of the fit. We will consider using p_λ as a device for selecting λ in the following. Note that the intermediate choice of λ, with $p_\lambda = 3$, yields a fit very close to Chappell's preferred single changepoint mean fit. No special treatment is made, or required, for the hoppers or the specials because the median fitting is inherently insensitive to these outlying observations.

Figure 7.6 illustrates quantile smoothing splines for several choices of τ. From a bioengineering or an evolutionary biology viewpoint, the upper envelope or upper conditional quantile functions of the scatter, are of particular relevance because they represent the maximum achieved running speed for a given body weight. In this sense, the $\tau = 0.9$ fit that increases up to about 60 kilograms and decreases thereafter is of particular interest.

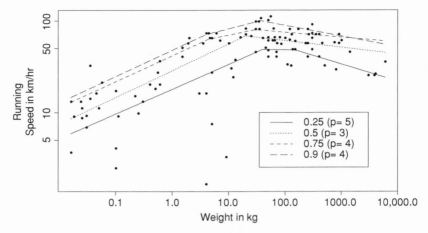

Figure 7.6. Running speed of terrestrial mammals. Four conditional quantile estimates.

The foregoing example illustrates that the quantile smoothing splines obtained by total variation regularization offer a simple, direct approach to estimating univariate changepoint models for piecewise linear continuous functions. Choice of λ in these models is effectively a choice of the number of distinct linear regimes.

Koenker, Ng, and Portnoy (1994) suggested a variant of the Schwarz (1978) criteria as a simple expedient for choosing λ. Interpreting the logarithm of the fidelity term as a quasi-likelihood, the Schwarz criterion becomes

$$SIC(\lambda) = \log(n^{-1} \sum \rho_\tau(y_i - \hat{g}_\lambda(x_i)) + .5n^{-1} p_\lambda \log n$$

and can be quite easily minimized with respect to λ. Machado (1993) considers this criterion for parametric quantile regression model selection.

An important advantage of quantile regression smoothing splines and the total variation approach is that it is relatively easy to introduce further qualitative constraints on the fitting process. For example, to impose monotonicity we need only require that the estimated α_is satisfy some additional linear inequality constraints. Likewise, imposing convexity or concavity is simply a matter of adding linear inequalities to a problem that is already in linear programming form. Boundary constraints or other constraints can also be added in this way. These options have been incorporated into the fitting function rqss in the quantreg package.

Asymptotics for univariate quantile smoothing splines have been considered by Portnoy (1997), Shen (1998), and Mammen and van de Geer (1997). For target functions that are twice continuously differentiable, the optimal sup-norm convergence rate of $\mathcal{O}(n^{-2/5}(\log n)^{2/5})$ can be achieved by appropriate choice of the λ_n sequence.

7.3 PENALTY METHODS FOR BIVARIATE SMOOTHING

The extension of penalty methods for univariate nonparametric regression to bivariate and multivariate settings raises some fundamentally new issues. One approach has been to build multivariate spline bases from tensor products of univariate bases. A disadvantage of this approach is that it privileges the initial choice of coordinate axes and consequently is unable to achieve orthogonal equivariance, a desirable objective in some applications. It is usually desirable, particularly in geographic applications, to be able to rotate the coordinate axes and not perturb the features of the fit.

For bivariate smoothing, the natural generalization of the univariate cubic smoothing spline is the thin-plate smoothing spline that minimizes

$$\sum_{i=1}^{n} (z_i - g(x_i, y_i))^2 + \lambda J\big(g, \Omega, \| \cdot \|_2^2\big),$$

where the univariate roughness penalty, $\int (g''(x))^2 dx$, is replaced by

$$J\big(g, \Omega, \| \cdot \|_2^2\big) = \int \int_\Omega \|\nabla^2 g\|_2^2 dx dy = \int \int_\Omega \big(g_{xx}^2 + 2g_{xy}^2 + g_{yy}^2\big) dx dy.$$

A considerable computational simplification is achieved by taking $\Omega = \mathbb{R}^2$ and thereby implicitly extending the fitted surface to the entire real plane. However, as noted by Green and Silverman (1994), there can be significant disparities between the solution on this expanded domain and the one constructed by solving the variational problem on a restricted domain like the convex hull of the observed (x, y) points.

7.3.1 Bivariate Total Variation Roughness Penalties

Given the pivotal role that the total variation roughness penalty plays for univariate quantile regression smoothing, it is natural to ask whether there is a total variation roughness penalty for bivariate functions. This question is considered by Koenker and Mizera (2004).

There is a variety of proposals for defining total variation in higher dimensions. For smooth functions, $f : \mathbb{R} \to \mathbb{R}$, the observation that

$$V(f) = \int |f'(x)| dx$$

suggests that for $f : \mathbb{R}^k \to \mathbb{R}^m$ we may consider, for any norm $\| \cdot \|$,

$$V(f, \Omega, \| \cdot \|) = \int \|\nabla f\| dx.$$

As in the univariate case, this definition can be extended to continuous, piecewise linear functions by computing

$$V(f) = \lim \inf V(f^\nu),$$

where $f^\nu \to f$ in the sense of (Schwartz) distributions. For a function $g : \mathbb{R}^2 \to \mathbb{R}$, we can then define a roughness penalty as

$$J(g, \Omega, \| \cdot \|) = V(\nabla g, \Omega, \| \cdot \|) = \int \int_\Omega \|\nabla^2 g\| dx dy. \qquad (7.13)$$

This penalty assigns a finite value to every continuous, piecewise linear function on bounded domains having a finite number of linear pieces. This is in sharp contrast to the thin-plate penalty, which views such functions as infinitely rough. But what norm do we choose?

Some candidate norms can be ruled out if we require some invariance of the estimator. Orthogonal invariance of a matrix norm requires that

$$\|U^\top H U\| = \|H\|$$

for any symmetric matrix H and orthogonal matrix U. Apparently, any norm that is a symmetric function of the eigenvalues satisfies this condition; there are still many viable candidates. The leading candidate seems to be the Hilbert–Schmidt (Frobenius) norm

$$J(g, \Omega, \| \cdot \|_2) = \int \int_\Omega \sqrt{g_{xx}^2 + 2g_{xy}^2 + g_{yy}^2} dx dy, \qquad (7.14)$$

but other examples include the maximal absolute eigenvalue and the absolute value of the trace of the Hessian.

7.3.2   Total Variation Penalties for Triograms

Solving the general variational problems posed by total variation roughness penalties such as these appears to be a quite challenging task. We are thus led to the consideration of restricted classes of functions whose total variation might prove more tractable. Hansen, Kooperberg, and Sardy (1998) introduced a class of continuous, piecewise linear functions defined over adaptively selected triangulations of the plane. These *triograms* enjoy a natural orthogonal invariance that competing tensor product smoothing methods lack. For triograms, the troublesome choice of norm in the total variation roughness penalty conveniently vanishes as we will now see.

Let Ω be a convex, compact region of the plane, and let Δ denote a collection of sets $\{\delta_i : i = 1, \dots, N\}$ with disjoint interiors such that $\Omega = \cup_{\delta \in \Delta} \delta$. In general the collection Δ is called a tessellation of Ω. When the $\delta \in \Delta$ are planar triangles, Δ is called a triangulation. The continuous functions g on Ω that are linear when restricted to $\delta \in \Delta$ are called triograms. Their collection $\mathcal{G}$ associated with the triangulation Δ is a finite-dimensional linear space, parameterized by the values taken by the function at the vertices of the triangulation.

Any penalty $J(g, \Omega, \| \cdot \|)$ can be considered a valid generalization of the univariate total variation penalty introduced earlier, regardless of the choice of the norm.

Theorem 7.1. *Suppose that $g : \Omega \to \mathbb{R}$ is a piecewise linear function on the triangulation Δ. For any orthogonally invariant penalty of the form (7.13), there is a constant c dependent only on the choice of the norm such that*

$$J(g, \Omega, \| \cdot \|) = c \sum_e \| \nabla g_e^+ - \nabla g_e^- \| \, \| e \|, \tag{7.15}$$

where e runs over all the interior edges of the triangulation, $\| e \|$ is the Euclidean length of the edge e, and $\| \nabla g_e^+ - \nabla g_e^- \|$ is the Euclidean length of the difference between gradients of g on the triangles adjacent to e.

Proof. Evaluating J, we split the integration domain Ω into disjoint pieces whose contribution to J is determined separately. First, the contribution of interiors of the triangles is 0, because the Hessian vanishes. The contribution of any edge e is given by the corresponding term in (7.15). Consider the trapezoidal region consisting of the two triangles adjacent to the edge. Extend the functions on the triangles linearly to produce a rectangular domain – this does not alter the penalty. Orthogonal invariance then allows us to rotate the rectangle so that the edge of interest is parallel to the y axes; this gives us a function of the form $g(x, y) = h(x) + ky$ on a rectangular domain, for a piecewise linear function h and a real constant k.

For any such function there is a constant c depending only the the matrix norm $\| \cdot \|$, such that, for any $\Omega = \Omega_x \times \Omega_y$, we have

$$J(g, \Omega, \| \cdot \|) = c J(h, \Omega_x, \| \cdot \|) |\Omega_y|,$$

where $J(h, \Omega_x, \| \cdot \|) = \int_{\Omega_x} |h''(x)| dx$ and $|\Omega_y|$ denotes the Lebesgue measure of Ω_y. To see this, let H be a 2×2 matrix with upper-left element 1 and other elements 0. Suppose $\| H \| = c$, so that $\| u H \| = c |u|$ for any real u; then

$$J(g, \Omega, \| \cdot \|_2^2) = c \int \int_\Omega |h''(x)| dx dy = c \int_{\Omega_x} |h''(x)| \, dx \cdot |\Omega_y|.$$

The result then follows by the Fubini theorem for all smooth g and, hence, by extension for all g under consideration. Note that any smooth approximation to $h(x)$ that maintains its monotonicity has the same total variation: simply the magnitude of the jump at the discontinuity.

The final and only technical part of the proof is to show that the contribution of the vertices of the triangulation is zero. For this the reader is referred to Koenker and Mizera (2004). ∎

Given this characterization of the penalty term, it is a relatively simple matter to reformulate the problem

$$\min_{g \in \mathcal{G}} \sum_{i=1}^n (z_i - g(x_i, y_i))^2 + \lambda J(g, \Omega, \| \cdot \|),$$

restricting the solution to triograms on a specified triangulation, as a linear programming problem for which log-barrier methods provide an efficient solution technique. For any choice of the norm, the penalty delivers the same roughness evaluation up to a constant so that its role can be entirely absorbed by the λ parameter. Sparsity of the resulting linear algebra plays a crucial role and can be exploited to considerable advantage.

A basis for the linear space $\mathcal{G}$ of triograms on a triangulation Δ may be constructed from the linear "tent" functions $\{B_i(u)\}$ that express the barycentric coordinates of any point u lying in a triangle $\delta \in \Delta$. Denote the (x, y) coordinates of the vertices by $v_i = (v_{i1}, v_{i2})$; then

$$u_j = \sum_{i=1}^{3} B_i(u) v_{ij} \quad j = 1, 2,$$

where the functions B_i satisfy the conditions that $0 \leq B_i(u) \leq 1$ with $\sum_{i=1}^{3} B_i(u) = 1$. Solving, we have

$$B_1(u) = \frac{A(u, v_2, v_3)}{A(v_1, v_2, v_3)},$$

where

$$A(v_1, v_2, v_3) = \frac{1}{2} \begin{vmatrix} v_{11} & v_{21} & v_{31} \\ v_{12} & v_{22} & v_{32} \\ 1 & 1 & 1 \end{vmatrix}$$

is the signed area of the triangle, δ. The remaining $B_i(u)$ are defined analogously by replacing the vertices v_2 and v_3 by u. Clearly, the $\{B_i(u)\}$ are linear in u on δ and satisfy the interpolation conditions that $B_i(v_j) = 1$ for $i = j$ and zero otherwise; thus, they are linearly independent. They are also affine equivariant; that is, for any nonsingular 2×2 matrix A and vector $b \in \mathbb{R}^2$,

$$B_i(u) = B_i^*(Au + b) \quad u \in \mathcal{U},$$

where $\{B_i(u)\}$ are formed from the vertices $\{v_i\}_{i=1}^{p}$ and $\{B_i^*\}$ are formed from the vertices $\{Av_i + b\}_{i=1}^{n}$. In particular, the basis is equivariant to rotations of the coordinate axes, a property notably missing in many other bivariate smoothing methods.

Thus, any function $g \in \mathcal{G}$ may be expressed in terms of the barycentric basis functions and the values β_i that the function takes at the vertices of the triangulation:

$$g(x, y) = \sum_{i=1}^{p} \beta_i B_i((x, y)).$$

Thus, we can express the fidelity of the function $\hat{g}(x, y)$ fitted to the observed sample $\{(x_i, y_i, z_i), i = 1, \ldots, n\}$ in ℓ_1 terms as

$$\sum_{i=1}^{n} |z_i - \hat{g}(x_i, y_i)| = \sum_{i=1}^{n} |z_i - a_i^\top \hat{\beta}|,$$

where the p-vectors a_i denote the "design" vectors with elements $a_{ij} = (B_j((x_i, y_i)))$. In the simplest case there is a vertex at every point (x_i, y_i) and the matrix $A = (a_{ij})$ is just the n-dimensional identity. However, one may wish to choose $p < n$; there would then be a need to compute some nontrivial barycentric coordinates for some elements of the matrix A. In cases where there is more than one observation at a given design point, p is obviously less than n and columns of the fidelity contribution of the design matrix will contain more than one nonzero element.

Suppose that we fix the triangulation Δ, and consider the triogram $g \in \mathcal{G}$ on a specified triangle $\delta \in \Delta$. Let $\{(x_i, y_i, \hat{z}_i), i = 1, 2, 3\}$ denote the points at the three vertices of δ. We have

$$\hat{z}_i = \theta_0 + \theta_1 x_i + \theta_2 y_i \quad i = 1, 2, 3,$$

where θ denotes a vector normal to the plane representing the triogram restricted to δ. Solving the linear system, we obtain the gradient vector

$$\nabla g_\delta = \begin{pmatrix} \theta_1 \\ \theta_2 \end{pmatrix} = [\det(D)]^{-1} \begin{pmatrix} (y_2 - y_3) & (y_3 - y_1) & (y_1 - y_2) \\ (x_3 - x_2) & (x_1 - x_3) & (x_2 - x_1) \end{pmatrix} \begin{pmatrix} \hat{z}_1 \\ \hat{z}_2 \\ \hat{z}_3 \end{pmatrix},$$

where D is the 3×3 matrix with columns $[1, x, y]$.

This gradient vector is obviously constant on δ and linear in the values of the function at the vertices. Thus, for any pair of triangles δ_i, δ_j with common edge $e_{k(i,j)}$, we have the constant gradients $\nabla g_{\delta_i}, \nabla g_{\delta_j}$ and we can define the contribution of the edge to the total roughness of the function as

$$|c_k| = \left| \eta_{ij}^\top (\nabla g_{\delta_i} - \nabla g_{\delta_j}) \right| \cdot \|e_{k(i,j)}\| = \|(\nabla g_{\delta_i} - \nabla g_{\delta_j})\| \cdot \|e_{k(i,j)}\|,$$

where η_{ij} denotes the unit vector orthogonal to the edge. The second formulation follows from the fact that η_{ij} is just the gradient gap renormalized to have unit length; this can be easily seen by considering a canonical orientation in which the edge runs from $(0, 0)$ to $(1, 0)$. The penalty is then computed by summing these contributions over all interior edges.

Since the gradient terms are linear in the parameters β_i determining the function at the vertices, the penalty may also be expressed as a piecewise linear function of these values:

$$\sum_k |c_k| = \sum_k |h_k^\top \hat{\beta}|,$$

where the index k runs over all of the edges formed by the triangulation Δ. The h_k vectors are determined solely as a function of the configuration of the triangulation – that is, as a function of the (x, y) observations. Each h_k vector has only four non-zero elements representing the contributions of the four vertices defining the quadrilateral for each edge.

7.3.3   Penalized Triogram Estimation as a Linear Program

The problem of optimizing the fidelity of the fitted function subject to a constraint on the roughness of the function may thus be formulated as the augmented linear ℓ_1 problem

$$\min_{\beta \in \mathbb{R}^p} \sum_{i=1}^{n} |z_i - a_i^\top \beta| + \lambda \sum_{k=1}^{M} |h_k^\top \beta| . \tag{7.16}$$

Problem (7.16) is piecewise linear in β, and so it is straightforward to reformulate it as a linear program. Let

$$X = \begin{bmatrix} A \\ \lambda H \end{bmatrix},$$

where A denotes the matrix with rows $(a_i^\top)_{i=1}^n$ and $H = (h_i^\top)_{i=1}^M$, and denote the augmented response vector as $\hat{z} = (z^\top, 0^\top)^\top$. Problem (7.16) of minimizing the ℓ_1 norm of the vector $\hat{z} - X\beta$ may be expressed as

$$\min_{(\beta, u, v)} \{1^\top u + 1^\top v | \hat{z} = X\beta + u - v, \ \beta \in \mathbb{R}^p, u \geq 0, v \geq 0\}.$$

Therefore, we are minimizing a linear function subject to linear equality and inequality constraints and, as usual, solutions can be characterized by a set of "basic variables." In the present case, this basic set h consists of p elements of the first $n + M$ integers. Solutions may be written as

$$\hat{\beta}(h) = X(h)^{-1} \zeta(h),$$

where $X(h)$ denotes the $p \times p$ submatrix of X with rows indexed by h, and $\zeta(h)$ denotes the p corresponding elements of ζ. (When multiple solutions exist, they constitute a convex polyhedral set with solutions of the form $\hat{\beta}(h)$ as extreme points.) Some of the rows of $X(h)$ will be drawn from the upper A part of the X matrix, and some will come from the lower λH part. If we now evaluate the fit at the n observed points, we have

$$\hat{\gamma} = (\hat{g}(x_i))_{i=1}^{n} = AX(h)^{-1} \zeta(h).$$

For any element $i \in h$, the product $x_i^\top X(h)^{-1}$ is a unit basis vector e_j such that $x_i^\top X(h)^{-1} \zeta(h) = e_j^\top \zeta(h) = \zeta_i$. When i comes from the first n integers, so that x_i is a row of A, this implies that the ith point is interpolated, because for these points $\zeta_i = z_i$. When i comes from the set $\{n + 1, \ldots, n + M\}$, the ith fitted value is determined by the contribution of the penalty part of the X matrix, in conjunction with the interpolated points. Thus, only a subset of the n observations – say p_λ of them – is needed to describe the fit. Of course *all* of the observations are needed to determine *which* observations are interpolated, but once the fit is found it can be described completely if one knows the p_λ points that are interpolated and the triangulation. As λ increases, p_λ decreases; near $\lambda = 0$ all of the observed points are interpolated, and for sufficiently large

λ only the three points necessary to determine the best "median plane" need to be interpolated.

7.3.4 On Triangulation

Up to this point we have taken the form of the triangulation Δ as fixed; we now consider how to determine Δ given the observations $\{(x_i, y_i, z_i), \ i = 1, \ldots, n\}$. In full generality, this is an extremely challenging problem that involves a delicate consideration of the function being estimated and draws us into vertex insertion/deletion schemes like those described by Hansen, Kooperberg, and Sardy. Our intention from the outset was to circumvent these aspects of the problem, replacing such model-selection strategies by shrinkage governed by the proposed roughness penalty. We restrict attention to the classical triangulation method of Delaunay, which provides an efficient, numerically stable method depending only on the configuration of the (x_i, y_i) observations.

A simple, direct characterization of the Delaunay triangulation may be stated for points in general position in the plane. We will say that points in $\mathbb{R}^2$ are in general position if no three points lie on a line and no four points lie on a circle. The Delaunay triangulation of a set of points $\mathcal{V} = \{v_i \in \mathbb{R}^2 : i = 1, \ldots n\}$ in general position consists of all triangles whose circumscribing circle contains no $\mathcal{V}$-points in their interior. There is a vast literature on Delaunay triangulation and its computation (see Okabe, Boots, Sugihara, and Chiu, 2000, for further details).

Another way to characterize the Delaunay triangulation is that it maximizes the minimum angle occurring in the triangulation. This maxmin property has been long considered a major virtue of the Delaunay method for reasons of numerical stability. Relatively recently, however, it has been noted by Rippa (1992) that the benefits of this prejudice against long, thin triangles depends on the eventual application of the triangulation. If, for example, the objective is to find a good interpolant for a function whose curvature happens to be very large in one direction and small in the other, then long thin triangles can be very advantageous.

The sensitivity of the approximation quality to the choice of the triangulations suggests the need for careful selection, especially if a small number of vertices is employed. An advantage of penalty methods in this respect is that their reliance on a considerably larger set of vertices can compensate to some degree for deficiencies in the triangulation. We may restrict attention to Delaunay triangulations based on all the observed (x, y) points, but it is straightforward to incorporate additional "dummy vertices" at other points in the plane, vertices that contribute to the penalty term, but not to the fidelity. By so doing, one can substantially ameliorate the restrictive effect of the initial triangulation and refine the fit to achieve more flexibility. Such mesh-refinement strategies have produced an extensive literature in finite element applied mathematics. Locally adaptive mesh refinement and multiresolution methods have natural applicability in statistical applications as well.

7.3.5   On Sparsity

A crucial feature of penalized triogram estimators, like their univariate total variation penalty counterparts, is the sparsity of the resulting design matrices. In the fidelity component A, rows typically have only one nonzero element. At worst, three nonzero elements are needed to represent the barycentric coordinates of the (x_i, y_i) points not included as vertices of the triangulation. In the penalty matrix H, each row has four nonzero entries, corresponding to the contribution of the four vertices of the quadrilateral corresponding to each edge.

To appreciate the consequences of this it may help to consider an example. Suppose we have $n = 1600$ observations and we introduce vertices at each of the points: $\{(x_i, y_i) : i = 1, \ldots, n\}$. The resulting matrix A is just the $n = 1600$ identity matrix. The number of interior edges of the Delaunay triangulation is given by $e = 3n - 2c - 3$, where c denotes the number of exterior edges (see Okabe, Boots, Sugihara, and Chiu, 2000). Therefore, the matrix H is 4753×1600 in a typical example, and the augmented ℓ_1 regression problem is, thus, 6353×1600. At first sight, this may appear computationally intractable and would be intractable on many machines using conventional statistical software. But recognizing the sparsity of the problem – that is, noting that only 0.2% of the more than 10 million elements of the design matrix are nonzero – drastically reduces the memory requirement from about 80 megabytes for the dense form of the matrix, to only 160 kilobytes for the sparse form. Computational complexity of the problem is reduced accordingly. Recently developed Cholesky factorization methods for sparse matrices require computational effort roughly proportional to the number of nonzero elements. By exploiting these techniques, specialized versions of the Frisch–Newton algorithms described by Koenker and Ng (2003) enable one to efficiently handle problems with otherwise prohibitive parametric dimension.

7.3.6   Automatic λ Selection

As has been suggested it is possible to automate the choice of smoothing parameter λ based on the dimension of the fitted function p_λ to minimize

$$\log\left(n^{-1} \sum \rho_\tau(z_i - \hat{g}_\lambda(x_i, y_i))\right) + \frac{1}{2}n^{-1}p_\lambda \log n.$$

It should be emphasized that this is essentially an *ad hoc* expedient at this stage and needs considerable further investigation.

Some additional support for treating the number of interpolated points as the effective dimension of the fitted function is provided by the recent work of Meyer and Woodroofe (2000), who consider the divergence,

$$\operatorname{div}(\hat{g}) = \sum \frac{\partial}{\partial y_i} \hat{g}(x_i),$$

as a general measure of effective dimension for nonparametric regression. For linear estimators, this measure yields the trace of the corresponding linear operator, which has been suggested for classical smoothing splines by several other authors. For monotone regression estimation, Meyer and Woodroofe (2000) show that the pool adjacent violators algorithm yields a piecewise constant estimate $\hat{g}$, with div$(\hat{g})$ equal to the number of distinct values taken by $\hat{g}$. For our total variation penalized quantile triograms, div$(\hat{g}) = p_\lambda$ – the number of points interpolated by $\hat{g}$ – a fact that follows from the concluding comments of Section 7.3.3.

7.3.7 Boundary and Qualitative Constraints

A triogram is convex if and only if it is convex on all pairs of adjacent triangles. This condition is easily checked for each quadrilateral because it reduces to checking a linear inequality on the values taken by the function at the four vertices of the quadrilateral. Imposing convexity on penalized triogram fitting thus amounts to adding M linear inequality constraints to the problems already introduced, where M denotes the number of interior edges of the triangulation. This is particularly straightforward in the case of the quantile fidelity given the linear programming formulation of the optimization problem. Similarly, it is straightforward to impose constraints on the boundary of the fitted surface if prior information about how to treat these edges is available. In the absence of such information, no penalty is assessed for the edges constituting the convex hull of the (x, y) observations.

7.3.8 A Model of Chicago Land Values

To illustrate the penalized triogram method we briefly describe an application to modeling Chicago land values from Koenker and Mizera (2004). The data consist of 1194 vacant land sales occurring at 758 distinct sites in the Chicago metropolitan area during the period 1995–97. We take the sale price of the land in dollars per square foot as z_i and spatial coordinates of the parcels as (x_i, y_i). In Figure 7.7 we illustrate three contour plots corresponding to fitted surfaces estimated by solving problem (7.16) for the three quartiles $\tau \in \{0.25, 0.50, 0.75\}$ of the land value distribution. In these plots, Lake Michigan appears in the upper right corner and the interstate highways are indicated in gray to provide landmarks for the metropolitan area. The central business district appears in each of the plots as a closed contour of high land value near the lake. The scattered points in the plots indicate the locations of the observed land sales used to fit the land value surfaces. In each case the smoothing parameter λ is chosen, somewhat arbitrarily, to be 0.25. This value is intermediate between the value selected by the Schwarz and the analogous Akaike criteria. Contours are labeled in dollars per square foot. It is evident that the contour maps are quite dissimilar at the quartiles-indicating that the surfaces are quite far from the simple vertical displacements we would obtain from the iid error model. As has been emphasized throughout, estimating a family of conditional quantile curves, or surfaces, reveals additional structure. For land values or annual temperatures

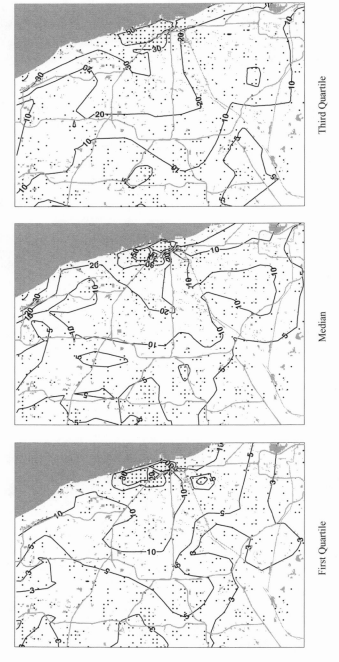

First Quartile   Median   Third Quartile

Figure 7.7. Contours of quartile surfaces of Chicago land values.

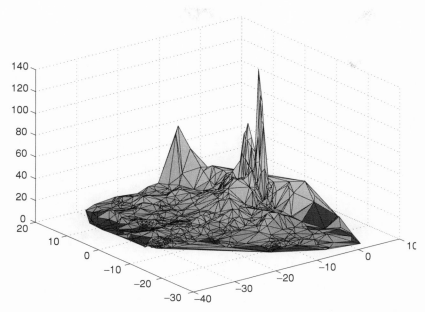

Figure 7.8. Perspective plot of median Chicago land value.

or snowfalls, this technique offers a way to explore how variability varies over the domain.

It is difficult to gauge from the contour plots the ability of the proposed methods to capture the sharp features of the land value surface. Figure 7.8 shows a perspective plot of the median fit of the Chicago land value data, again with $\lambda = 0.25$. It is possible to recognize the peak corresponding to the central business district and another mode further north along the lake. The perspective plot is somewhat difficult to interpret without further geographical reference points like those of the contour plots, but it does vividly illustrate the ability of the penalized triogram to capture the sharp peaks of the land value distribution. Attempts to fit this data with thin-plate smoothing splines gives an impression of much more gently rolling hills.

To further illustrate the flexibility of the fitting strategy, we illustrate a second perspective plot in Figure 7.9. This time we have introduced roughly 8000 new "dummy vertices" in addition to the vertices corresponding to the original observations. These new vertices are generated at random; that is, from a uniform density on the convex hull of the original (x, y) points. They contribute to the penalty term of the fitting criterion but obviously not to the fidelity. By introducing some additional flexibility in the way that the surface is permitted to bend, they contribute to the perceived smoothness of the fitted surface. The problem is now considerably larger, with a design matrix that is almost a factor of 100 larger than without the dummy vertices, but still the sparsity

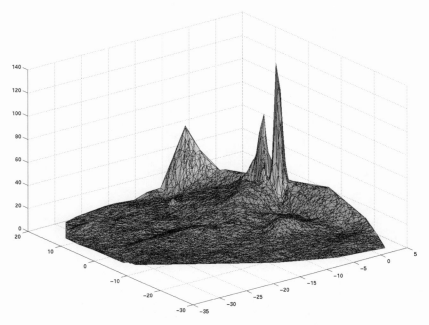

Figure 7.9. Perspective plot of median Chicago land value with 8000 dummy vertices.

of the underlying design matrix allows very efficient fitting. Clearly the random introduction of new vertices might be complemented by more systematic mesh-refinement strategies based on preliminary estimation of the surface.

7.3.9 Taut Strings and Edge Detection

Total variation penalty methods have played an important role in recent developments in image analysis and processing. Penalizing the function itself, rather than its gradient, yields methods that are advantageous for estimating sharp edges where color or grayscale values change abruptly. In univariate settings, this approach has been recently investigated by Davies and Kovac (2001), who relate it to earlier work of Hartigan and Hartigan (1985) on majorization methods motivated by physical models of the taut string. I will briefly describe this univariate version of the approach and then discuss a bivariate variant.

Davies and Kovac consider the following problem. Given observations $\{(x_i, y_i)\ i = 1, \ldots, n\}$ on the model

$$y_i = g(x_i) + u_i,$$

with $a \le x_1 < \cdots < x_n \le b$, find $\hat{g}$ to solve

$$\min \sum_{i=1}^{n} (y_i - g(x_i))^2 + \lambda V(g),$$

where $V(g)$ denotes the total variation of the function g on $[a, b]$. They offer a nice physical interpretation of the estimator. Consider a plot of the partial sums, and draw a band of width 2δ around the interpolated line connecting the integrated points. Imagine attaching a string to the extreme points, (x_1, y_1) and (x_n, y_n), running through the band and pulling the string until it is taut. The choice of the bandwidth δ obviously controls the smoothness of the resulting curve. Differentiating the resulting piecewise linear curve yields the piecewise constant fit to the original observations expressed by the preceding optimization problem. There are many variants of such problems. For robustness reasons one may wish to consider replacing the least-squares fidelity criterion with ℓ_1 fidelity and one could consider the use of total variation on the gradient rather than the function itself.

The following question also naturally arises: Can we extend the idea of total variation penalties on the fitted function to bivariate settings? One response to this question can be formulated in terms of the Voronograms introduced by Koenker and Mizera (2005). As we have seen, total variation penalties on g rather than ∇g imply a piecewise constant fit rather than a continuous, piecewise linear fit. Delaunay triangles are not well suited to play the role of the regions of constancy because they share vertices, but the (dual) Voronoi tessellation does seem to offer a reasonable approach. Given the Delaunay triangulation, the Voronoi tessellation is constructed by finding the center of all the circumscribing circles of the Delaunay triangles and connecting the adjacent centers. This yields polygons, each of which contain exactly one of the original observed points. A Voronogram is a piecewise constant function on this Voronoi tessellation.

Total variation of a piecewise constant function on a polyhedral tessellation of the plane is easy to compute using the same arguments employed in the proof of Theorem 7.1. Summing over edges of the tessellation, we simply compute the jump in the function value across the edge and multiply by the edge length. The function is obviously parameterized, as before the value that it takes at the observed points. There is one and only one such point in each Voronoi region. Therefore, the computation again reduces to a linear programming problem and thus can be efficiently solved by interior point methods.

A potentially interesting application of Voronograms is in image segmentation. The influential paper of Mumford and Shah (1989) proposed minimizing

$$\int_{\Omega} (\hat{g}(x) - g(x))^2 dx + \mathcal{H}^1(K) + \int_{\Omega} |\nabla \hat{g}(x)|^2 dx, \qquad (7.17)$$

where $g \in \mathcal{L}^{\infty}(\Omega); \Omega \subset \mathbb{R}^2$ denotes the original image; K is a closed set of one-dimensional Hausdorff measure, $\mathcal{H}^1(K)$; and $\hat{g} \in C^1(\Omega \setminus K)$ is the estimated image. The image g is assumed to be well behaved except on the exceptional set K, where it may jump, reflecting an abrupt change in color; or grayscale intensity.

Minimization of (7.17) is an extremely challenging problem that has generated a large literature (see, e.g., Meyer, 2001, Bourdin and Chambolle, 2000).

The convexity of the Voronogram objective function and the sparsity of the resulting linear algebra suggests that it might eventually prove to be useful as a component of this inquiry.

7.4   ADDITIVE MODELS AND THE ROLE OF SPARSITY

Having introduced univariate and bivariate quantile smoothing methods using total variation regularization, the following question naturally arises: What can be done in higher dimensions? This is a question that places severe strains on smoothing methods in general, and total variation regularization is certainly no exception. We can easily compute the Delaunay "triangulation" for points in $\mathbb{R}^3$ but the elementary objects are no longer planar triangles – they are tetrahedra. Adjacent tetrahedra meet on a face, and we could compute gradients as in the bivariate case and proceed as before, but the situation is considerably more complicated. In particular, visualization of such surfaces poses some serious difficulties.

Rather than venture into these deeper regions of function space, I will briefly describe some work on additive models composed of pieces assembled from the univariate and bivariate forms already introduced. This simplification should not be considered a fully satisfactory substitute for general smoothing methods for $d \geq 3$, but both theoretical and practical concerns suggest that the more restrictive assumptions underlying additivity may be prudent, leading to more reliable, more interpretable results.

As an example, suppose we wanted to extend the Chicago land value model by introducing a multiplicative effect due to the size of the parcel of land being sold. We might consider a multiplicative model of the form

$$Q_{\log(z)}(\tau | x, y, s) = g_0(x, y) + g_1(s). \tag{7.18}$$

In a parametric specification, we could take $g_1(s)$ to be quadratic in logarithms and posit, as an alternative,

$$Q_{\log(z)}(\tau | x, y, s) = g_0(x, y) + \alpha_1 \log(s) + \alpha_2 (\log(s))^2. \tag{7.19}$$

Either version of the model, or more complicated forms with additional components, can be easily incorporated in the framework we have already introduced.

Considering the "partially linear" version of model (7.18), we need only formulate the estimation problem as follows:

$$\min_{g \in \mathcal{G}, \alpha \in \mathbb{R}^2} \sum_{i=1}^n \rho_\tau (\log(z_i) - g(x_i, y_i) - \alpha_1 \log(s_i) - \alpha_2 (\log(s_i))^2 + \lambda J(g).$$

This can be implemented by simply appending the parametric block of the design matrix onto the monparametric pieces already described. Instead of

$$X = \begin{bmatrix} A \\ \lambda H \end{bmatrix},$$

we now have

$$X = \begin{bmatrix} S & A \\ 0 & \lambda H \end{bmatrix},$$

where S denotes an $n \times 2$ matrix with rows $(\log(s_i), (\log(s_i))^2)$. If the quadratic specification of the parcel size effect seems too restrictive, we can revert to an additive univariate nonparametric specification of this effect as in (7.18) and we obtain estimates by solving the following problem:

$$\min_{g_0 \in \mathcal{G}_0, g_1 \in \mathcal{G}_1} \sum_{i=1}^{n} \rho_\tau (\log(z_i) - g_0(x_i, y_i) - g_1(\log(s_i)) + \lambda_0 J_2(g_0) + \lambda_1 J_1(g_1).$$

Further terms can be introduced in an obvious way; the formula conventions of linear modeling in R make this quite straightforward using the rqss function in the quantreg package. Clearly, expanding the number of nonparametric components compounds the number of smoothing parameters and thereby increases the difficulty of that aspect of the problem. The crucial advantage of the formulation proposed here over similar proposals involving thin-plate methods as described, for example, by Gu (2002) and Wood (2003) is that we retain an extremely sparse structure for the matrix X and, consequently, the optimization can be carried out quite efficiently.

CHAPTER 8

Twilight Zone of Quantile Regression

In this penumbral chapter I would like to briefly discuss some problems that fall into the twilight of quantile regression research. In some cases there is already a solid basis for future developments, and the dawn is surely coming. For others, the way forward is more hazy, and it may be evening that is approaching. In any case, the range of these topics is quite broad and will, I hope, convey some sense of some of the opportunities that lie ahead.

8.1 QUANTILE REGRESSION FOR SURVIVAL DATA

As noted by Doksum and Gasko (1990), a wide variety of survival analysis models may be expressed as transformation models:

$$h(T_i) = x_i^\top \beta + u_i,$$

where T_i is an observed survival time – that is, a positive random variable indicating a duration – h is a monotone transformation, x_i is a p-vector of covariates, β is an unknown parameter, and the u_i are assumed to be independently and identically distributed (iid) with distribution function F.

The celebrated Cox (1972) proportional hazard model, usually written as

$$\lambda(t|x) = \lambda_0(t) \exp\left(x_i^\top \beta\right),$$

presumes that the conditional hazard of the event being modeled is the product of a baseline hazard, $\lambda_0(t)$, common to all subjects and a multiplicative effect due to the covariates. Equivalently, we may write it as

$$\log(-\log S(t|x)) = \log \Lambda_0(t) - x^\top \beta,$$

where $\Lambda_0(t) = \int_0^t \lambda_0(s)ds$ denotes the integrated baseline hazard and $S(t|x)$ denotes the conditional survival function. Now evaluating both sides at the random event time T, we have

$$\log \Lambda_0(T_i) = x_i^\top \beta + u_i,$$

where $u_i = \log(-\log S(T_i|x_i))$. Because $S(T_i|x_i))$ is a uniformly distributed random variable, it follows that the u_i are iid with distribution function $F(u) = 1 - e^{e^u}$.

Similarly, the Bennett (1983) proportional odds model is

$$\log \Gamma(t|x) = \log \Gamma_0(t) - x^\top \beta,$$

where the odds of an event occurring prior to time t, $\Gamma(t|x) = F(t|x)/(1 - F(t|x))$, can be written as

$$\log \Gamma_0(T_i) = x_i^\top \beta + u_i,$$

where the u_i are iid logistic. The accelerated failure time (AFT) model,

$$\log(T_i) = x_i^\top \beta + u_i,$$

is also of this form, but we are permitted to be somewhat more agnostic about the distribution of the u_i in this case. For the AFT model, we have

$$P(T_i > t) = P(e^{u_i} > te^{-x_i^\top \beta}) = 1 - F(te^{-x_i^\top \beta})$$

and so

$$\lambda(t|x) = \lambda_0(te^{-x_i^\top \beta})e^{-x_i^\top \beta},$$

and in contrast to the Cox specification the covariates now act to rescale time *inside* the baseline hazard function.

The quantile regression formulation of the transformation model,

$$Q_{h(T)|X}(\tau|x) = x^\top \beta(\tau), \tag{8.1}$$

abandons the iid error, location-shift viewpoint underlying the foregoing models. By allowing the slope coefficients associated with the covariates to depend on τ, a variety of forms of heterogeneity can be introduced in the conditional distribution of $h(T)$ over the space of the covariates. This formulation is illustrated in Chapter 2 for a model of unemployment durations. Koenker and Geling (2001) address related issues in a study of lifespans of the Mediterranean fruit fly *Ceratitis capitata*.

Given estimates of the conditional quantile model, it is straightforward to derive estimates of the hazard function and related objects. Given model (8.1), or, equivalently,

$$Q_{T|X}(\tau|x) = h(x^\top \beta(\tau)), \tag{8.2}$$

we may express the hazard function as

$$\lambda(Q_{T|X}(\tau|x)) = \lim_{\Delta\tau \to 0} \frac{\Delta\tau/\Delta Q_{T|X}(\tau|x)}{1 - \tau}.$$

For estimated versions of $Q_{T|X}(\tau|x)$ that are piecewise constant, it is usually convenient to evaluate at the midpoints of the steps.

It is also useful for purposes of comparison to reverse the process and explore the form of the conditional quantile functions implied by the Cox model or other forms of the survival model. For the Cox model we may write

$$S(t|x) = S_0(t)^{\gamma(x)},$$

where $S_0(t) = -\log \Lambda_0(t)$ is the baseline survival function and $\gamma(x) = e^{-x^\top \beta}$. Thus,

$$Q_{T|X}(\tau|x) = S_0^{-1}((1 - \tau)^{1/\gamma(x)}),$$

and we see that the conditional quantile functions are restricted to a rather special form determined by the baseline survival function S_0. In particular, they are all determined by a rescaling of the argument of S_0. This implies, among other things, that the estimated conditional quantile curves corresponding to different settings of the covariates cannot cross. For example, in the two-sample treatment response model, the treatment must be either always better or always worse than the control regime. Surgery cannot, for example, be risky and therefore diminish life chances in the lower tail of the outcome distribution, yet, if successful, greatly enhance them. This restriction is usually dealt with in applications of the Cox model by stratifying on such covariates and estimating a separate baseline hazard function for each stratum. But, particularly for continuously measured covariates, such effects are more difficult to handle and the quantile regression approach offers a flexible alternative.

8.1.1   Quantile Functions or Hazard Functions?

Instead of estimating models for conditional quantile functions, we could estimate models of the conditional distribution function, from which we could derive the conditional quantile functions. In survival models this is particularly natural and frequently encountered in applications, although perhaps not always recognized in this way. We may identify some critical duration values $t_1, t_2, \ldots, t_J$ and we consider a family of binary response models for the conditional probabilities:

$$P(T_i < t_j|x_i) = F_{T|X}(t_j|x_i).$$

This viewpoint is emphasized by Doksum and Gasko (1990), who stress the parametric interrelationships between conventional survival models and their binary response relatives. For the Bennett model, for example, these probabilities take the logistic form, and so we would have

$$\text{logit}(P(T_i < t_j|x_i)) = \alpha(t_j) + x_i^\top \beta$$

with an intercept effect determined by the value of the critical value t_j and the covariates relegated to a location-shift effect. Of course there is no necessity to enforce this restriction in applications, and one can certainly proceed to estimate a more general version of this model in which the vector β is permitted to depend on t_j as well. Similarly, the Cox proportional hazard model gives rise to a family of complementary log-log binary response models. An explicit comparison of the statistical performance of this conditional distribution function approach with conditional quantile methods would be a worthwhile exercise.

8.1.2 Censoring

Survival data are almost inevitably complicated by some form of censoring or nonresponse. In the simplest instances, we observe a censoring time for each subject and the observed response is the minimum of the actual event time and the censoring time. Thus, conditioning on the censoring times, if we have the linear quantile regression model for event times,

$$Q_{T|X}(\tau|x) = x^\top \beta(\tau),$$

and we observe $Y_i = \min\{T_i, C_i\}$, then we may estimate $\beta(\tau)$ by

$$\hat{\beta}(\tau) = \text{argmin}_\beta \sum_{i=1}^n \rho_\tau \left(Y_i - \min\left\{x_i^\top \beta, C_i\right\}\right).$$

This formulation was introduced by Powell (1986) and has been explored by a number of subsequent authors including Fitzenberger (1997), Buchinsky and Hahn (1998), and Chernozhukov and Hong (2002). Bilias, Chen, and Ying (2000) have suggested an attractive resampling strategy for inference in this model.

In many applications, the presumption that we observe censoring times for *all* observations is unrealistic. Often we see only the random variable, $Y_i = \min\{T_i, C_i\}$, and the indicator variable, $\delta = I(Y_i < C_i)$, identifying whether the ith observation is censored or not. Because C_i is not observed when $\delta_i = 1$, the Powell estimator is unavailable, and we require something new.

Recently, Portnoy (2003) has suggested an approach that may be regarded as a quantile regression version of the Kaplan–Meier estimator. It relies strongly on a globally linear parametric specification of the conditional quantile functions but makes relatively weak assumptions on the nature of the censoring mechanism. In particular, the censoring times C_i and the event times T_i are assumed conditionally independent given the covariates, but the distribution of the censoring times may depend on the covariates. To grasp the essential idea, it is helpful to review some basic properties of the Kaplan–Meier (product limit) estimator.

Imagine a typical Kaplan–Meier plot, like the one in Figure 8.1, based on a few observations, some of which are censored. Starting at the left of the plot, the estimate behaves exactly according to the empirical distribution function: $\hat{F}_n$ jumps up by n^{-1} at each order statistic, and so the empirical survival function, $\hat{S}_n(t) = (1 - \hat{F}_n(t))$, jumps down by n^{-1} at each order statistic until we encounter the first censored observation, indicated in the figure by "+". All we know about the response for this observation is that it occurs later than its indicated censoring time. This suggests that we should redistribute some of the

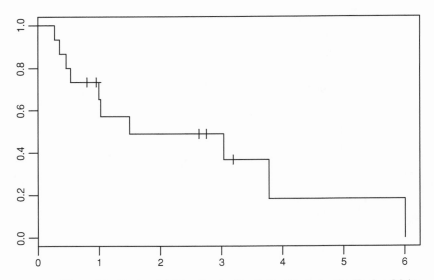

Figure 8.1. Kaplan–Meier estimate. The figure illustrates the Kaplan–Meier estimate of the survival distribution based on 15 observations from a standard log-normal model. Censored observations are indicated by the + marks. Jumps are all $1/n$ until a censored point is encountered, then jumps become larger to account for the reduced number of observations "at risk." The mass associated with the censored points is redistributed to the right according to the realized event times.

mass of such observations to the right. If we view this as a problem of designing an estimator of the quantile function of T rather than its distribution function, we can construct a modified, or reweighted, version of the usual one-sample problem:

$$\hat{\xi}(\tau) = \operatorname{argmin} \sum \rho_\tau(y_i - \xi).$$

Suppose that we have estimated the quantiles up to τ_j without encountering a censored point. Now suppose we encounter a censored point y_j and we would like to redistribute mass to the right. To accomplish this, we split the censored point into two parts: one part stays put in its current position, the other is relocated to $+\infty$. The mass is redistributed uniformly over the upper $1 - \tau_j$ tail of the distribution, and so for any $\tau > \tau_j$ we define the weights

$$w_j(\tau) = \frac{\tau - \tau_j}{1 - \tau_j}$$

as the weight of the fixed part and place the remaining weight $1 - w_j(\tau)$ on the part at infinity. This reweighted problem may be written as

$$\hat{\xi}(\tau) = \operatorname{argmin} \sum \delta_i \rho_\tau(y_i - \xi) + (1 - \delta_i)[w_i(\tau)\rho_\tau(y_i - \xi) \\ + (1 - w_i(\tau))\rho_\tau(y_\infty - \xi)].$$

The value y_∞ need not be literally infinite – this would be likely to cause computational difficulties. It needs only to be sufficiently large to ensure that it is larger than any potential value of $\hat{\xi}(\tau)$. The insensitivity of the procedure to the particular value chosen here is an obvious consequence of the fact that the gradient of the problem, and therefore the estimator, depends only on the signs of the residuals. The weights are recursively updated as the estimated process $\hat{\xi}(\tau)$ crosses successive censored observations. This procedure produces the Kaplan–Meier estimate. Efron (1967) seems to have been the first to interpret the Kaplan–Meier estimator as redistributing mass of the censored observations to the right.

The virtue of this algorithmic description based on reweighted optimization is that it has an (almost) straightforward generalization to the regression setting. As we have seen in Chapter 6, classical methods of parametric linear programming may be used to compute the entire quantile regression process, $\{\hat{\beta}(\tau) : \ \tau \in (0, 1)\}$. In the one-sample case this reduces to determining at each step the next point of increase, j/n, of the empirical quantile function and then finding the next-largest order statistic as the estimated function value. When there is censoring the procedure is the same except that there is additional book-keeping required to update the weights. In the regression case the situation is again similar. Given a solution at any τ we can compute the next τ by looking at $2p$ linear inequalities; then a simplex pivot occurs to remove one observation from the current basis and to introduce another one. When the new basis observation is a censored point, then the new point is split and reweighted; the other active censored points have their weights updated and the iteration proceeds. Further details are spelled out by Portnoy (2003).

The procedure clearly depends crucially on the validity of the parametric specification of the quantile regression process. It is not sufficient to simply specify, for example, a conditional median function and expect to estimate it under general forms of random censoring without further conditions on the nature of the process away from the median. This point is also made by Robins and Ritov (1997), but it is perhaps made even more explicitly by the parametric programming formulation of Portnoy.

8.2 DISCRETE RESPONSE MODELS

It may at first appear anomalous to consider estimating quantile regression models for discrete data. However, if we begin with a latent variable model in continuous form, as is common for such models, the situation seems less anomalous and a quite fascinating story emerges.

8.2.1 Binary Response

Consider the now-familiar model

$$Q_{Y|X}(\tau|x) = x^\top \beta(\tau),$$

but suppose that instead of observing the nice continuously distributed response that we usually associate with this model, Y, we observe realizations of the transformed variable $Z = I(Y > 0)$. As has been repeatedly emphasized, the quantile functions for this transformed random variable, because the transformation is monotone, are simply the transformed quantile functions of the original response; that is,

$$Q_{h(Y)|X}(\tau|x) = h(x^\top \beta(\tau)),$$

and so for $h(Y) = I(Y > 0)$,

$$Q_{Z|X}(\tau|x) = I(x^\top \beta(\tau) > 0). \tag{8.3}$$

This suggests that we might estimate $\beta(\tau)$ by solving the problem

$$\min_\beta \sum_{i=1}^n \rho_\tau(z_i - I(x^\top \beta(\tau) > 0)), \tag{8.4}$$

in effect trying to choose β so that we maximize the number of correct matches, or predictions, of z_is by the quantity $I(x^\top \beta(\tau) > 0)$. The median version of this problem has a long history, beginning with Rosenblatt's (1958) seminal perceptron paper. The perceptron was originally proposed as an elementary mathematical model of the neuron and has served as an important conceptual and algorithmic building block of the subsequent literature on neural networks, see, for example, Ripley (1996), Vapnik (1995) for further discussion. Manski (1975) introduced the model into the econometric literature, terming solutions to the median version of (8.4) as the maximum score estimator. Manski (1985) noted that the approach could be extended to other quantiles.

It is evident that the parameter β in model (8.3) is identified only up to scale, because $I(\sigma x^\top \beta(\tau) > 0) = I(x^\top \beta(\tau) > 0)$ for all $\sigma > 0$. It is conventional, therefore, to impose the condition $\|\beta\| = 1$ or to set one coordinate of β to unity. The latter option presumes a stronger form of *a priori* information but, as we will see, is sometimes plausible and convenient.

Like the Powell (1986) censored quantile regression estimator – one may view binary response model (8.3) as imposing an extreme form of censoring from both above and from below – computation poses a problem requiring global optimization. The nonconvexity of the objective function in (8.4) is clear, but its rather pathological piecewise constant behavior is only fully appreciated after some extensive plotting experience. This has led the neural network literature to a variety of proposals for replacing the indicator function by a smooth "sigmoidal" function. Taking K to be an integrated density kernel (i.e., smooth with $\lim_{v \to -\infty} K(v) = 0$ and $\lim_{v \to \infty} K(v) = 1$), we may consider modifying (8.4) to obtain

$$\min_\beta \sum_{i=1}^n \rho_\tau(z_i - K(x^\top \beta(\tau)/\sigma_n)). \tag{8.5}$$

Horowitz (1992) has investigated the asymptotic behavior of estimators of this type. Whether such smoothing actually improves matters in applications depends crucially on selecting σ_n well. Asymptotically, however, Horowitz shows that a qualitative improvement in performance is possible: improving rates of convergence from $\mathcal{O}(n^{-1/3})$ for the estimator solving (8.4) to $\mathcal{O}(n^{-2/5})$ for the estimator solving (8.5) with a conventional kernel, and to $\mathcal{O}(n^{-s/(2s+1)})$ for (higher) order kernels, of order s.

Most of the literature has focused on estimating model (8.3) for a single value of τ, typically the median. Kordas (2004) has recently explored extending the approach to the estimation of a family of conditional quantile models for binary response. Following the approach of Horowitz, he develops asymptotics for the finite-dimensional distributions of this binary quantile regression process. A crucial advantage of extending the approach to *families* of conditional quantile functions is that it permits the investigator to recover conditional probability estimates from the model. To see this, note that

$$P(Z = 1|x) = \int_0^1 I(x^\top \beta(u) > 0)du.$$

For $U \sim U[0, 1]$, we have

$$P(Z = 1|x) = P(x^\top \beta(U) > 0|x) = \int_0^1 I(x^\top \beta(u) > 0)du.$$

It is evident that conditional response probabilities are *not* estimable from a single binary quantile regression; however, estimating a family of such models and integrating over the full range of $\tau \in (0, 1)$ can deliver useful estimates of the conditional probabilities. Monotonicity of the function $Q_Y(u|x) = x^\top \beta(u)$ in u means that we are really just interested in finding a root – the value of u at which $x^\top \beta(u) = 0$. This simplifies the task somewhat because for not too extreme x this crossing should occur well away from $u = 0$ or $u = 1$ and once the crossing is identified there is no need to know $\beta(u)$ for more extreme u.

Of course, conventional likelihood-based models of binary response like probit, logit, or cauchit also deliver such probability estimates. What makes the binary form of quantile regression worth all the computational trouble? The answer to this question, like its counterpart for quantile regression for continuously observed response, is crucially tied to the heterogeneity of the covariate effects. If the mechanism governing the binary response is well approximated by a latent variable model in which covariates act as a pure location shift, then conventional likelihood methods are quite appropriate and estimation reduces to choice of a satisfactory link function. Generalizing somewhat, if the latent response is determined by a location–scale shift so that, for example,

$$Y_i = x_i^\top \beta + x_i^\top \gamma u_i$$

for some iid u_is independent of x, then one can adapt the likelihood framework to account for the scale effect as discussed, for example, by Stukel (1988). However, if one prefers to remain somewhat agnostic about these options, believing that covariate effects can be even more complex than the location–scale model permits, then it seems prudent to explore a less restrictive family of binary response models.

Kordas (2004) illustrates the advantages of this more flexible approach with an application to women's labor supply in the United States. He considers a sample of 20,871 households from the 1999 March supplement of the U.S. population survey. He models the labor force participation of wives based on years of education, potential labor force experience, number of children less than age 6, children between the ages of 6 and 18, family income in the preceding year excluding the wife's earned income, an indicator of whether the wife is covered under her husband's health insurance, and several other indicator variables.

Unconditionally, 73% of the sample women work. What can these covariates tell us about the determinants of the decision to go to work? It is important to keep in mind that we cannot estimate the scale of the parameter vectors, $\beta(\tau)$; only the relative magnitudes of the coefficients are identifiable from the binary response data. Suppose, for example, we consider the ratio of the coefficient on women's educational attainment to the coefficient on other family income. Education has a positive impact, making it more likely that more highly educated women will work, whereas increasing other family income reduces the likelihood. The *ratio* of these effects decreases, and so, as one moves up through the quantiles toward women with a greater propensity to work, larger amounts of other family income are required to compensate for an additional year of education and keep women indifferent to the decision to work. This reflects a form of heterogeneity in the latent variable form of the model that could not arise in a standard logit specification, for example.

As in other applications of quantile regression, one faces the important question: Over what range of τ is it practicable to estimate the model? Kordas suggests a nice heuristic to evaluate this for binary response. At each τ one can evaluate the predicted proportion of the sample with $Z = 1$, assuming that everyone in the sample at the estimated coefficients of the τth quantile:

$$\hat{G}_n(\tau) = n^{-1} \sum_{i=1}^{n} I\left(x_i^{\top} \hat{\beta}(\tau) > 0\right).$$

In Kordas' labor supply application, this quantity ranges from $\hat{G}_n(0.10) = 0.143$ to $\hat{G}_n(0.65) = 0.940$. Therefore, given the estimated coefficients at $\tau = 0.10$ and supposing, contrary to the model, that *everyone* in the sample behaved according to these coefficients, only 14% of women would work, whereas evaluating at $\tau = 0.65$ yields the prediction that 94% of women would work. Clearly, as we push against the boundaries of zero and one in these predictions, it becomes increasingly difficult to accurately estimate the corresponding parameters because the model cannot improve a fit that is already nearly unanimous in its predictions over the range of observed covariates.

In cost-benefit studies of public investment projects, it is common to rely on survey responses to questions of the form, "Would you be willing to pay

$X per year for the specified project?" The analysis of these contingent valuation surveys has focused primarily on conventional likelihood methods for binary response data, but there is an increasing awareness that further exploration of the heterogeneous nature of preferences may be valuable. An important feature of such applications in the context of the binary response models discussed here is that the problem of normalizing the estimated parameter vector is considerably simplified. In these studies it is natural to take the coefficient on the hypothetical "price" of the project as unity, and the remaining effects can be interpreted in monetary units as a consequence of this normalization. Belluzzo (2004) describes an application of this approach used to evaluate the benefits of water projects in the Amazon Basin.

8.2.2   Count Data

As with binary response, the application of quantile regression methods for count data initially appears anomalous, and yet Poisson regression models and their close relatives are often criticized for being insufficiently flexible to accommodate various forms of overdispersion, excess zero response, and other phenomena. Again, the essential difficulty is the granularity of the response. Our usual requirement that the response has a conditional density with respect to Lebesgue measure is obviously not satisfied for discrete response.

Machado and Santos Silva (2002) have recently suggested a simple smoothing device that offers a way forward for quantile regression on count data. Imagine replacing, at each possible configuration of the covariates, the discrete distribution of the response by its piecewise linear interpolant. This amounts to replacing the discrete distributions with piecewise constant (histogram-type) densities. If we now specify a model for the conditional quantiles of the smoothed densities, we can proceed as usual. For integer-valued data the transition from the discrete to the smoothed densities may be made by "jittering." For integer-valued $\{y_i : i = 1, \ldots, n\}$, we may consider

$$\tilde{y}_i = y_i + u_i$$

with the $\{u_i\}$ taken as iid $U[0, 1]$. The convolution has the simple consequence of replacing the discrete response with a smoothed (randomized) response whose distribution function now linearly interpolates the original discrete distribution:

$$P(\tilde{y}_i < y | x_i) = P(\tilde{y}_i < \lfloor y \rfloor | x_i) + P(\tilde{y}_i = \lfloor y \rfloor | x_i) P(u_i < y - \lfloor y \rfloor)$$
$$= P(\tilde{y}_i < \lfloor y \rfloor | x_i) + P(\tilde{y}_i = \lfloor y \rfloor | x_i)(y - \lfloor y \rfloor).$$

Here $\lfloor y \rfloor$ denotes the greatest integer contained in y.

Machado and Santos Silva (2002) study the asymptotic behavior of the estimator based on the jittered data and show in a small simulation experiment that the size of conventional tests for excluded covariates remains quite reliable despite the jittering. Stevens (1950), in discussing a similar approach for constructing binomial confidence intervals, remarks that

> We suppose that most people will find repugnant the idea of adding yet another random element to a result which is already subject to the errors of random sampling. But what one is really doing is to eliminate one uncertainty by introducing a new one.

In the present context, the advantages of jittering seem to outweigh an initial reluctance to consider such randomized responses, but this deserves considerable further investigation.

A frequent problem encountered with count data is the violation of the Poisson dispersion assumption that the variance of the response is equal to its mean. Counts are commonly overdispersed, exhibiting larger variance than predicted by the Poisson hypothesis. Usually this condition is treated with a mild analgesic and the introduction of a free scale parameter. It seems plausible in many instances that scale, or even other aspects of the distributional shape, may depend on covariates; in these cases, quantile regression may have a useful role to play.

8.3   QUANTILE AUTOREGRESSION

There is a substantial theoretical literature, including Weiss (1991), Knight (1989), Koul and Saleh (1995), Koul and Mukherjee (1994), Hercé (1996), Hasan and Koenker (1997), and Hallin and Jurečková (1999), that deals with the linear quantile autoregression (QAR) model. In this model, the τth conditional quantile function of the response y_t is expressed as a linear function of lagged values of the response. But a striking feature of this literature is that it has focused almost exclusively on the case of iid innovations in which the conditioning variables play their classical role of shifting the *location* of the conditional density of y_t, but they have no effect on conditional scale or shape. In this section we wish to explore estimation and inference in a more general class of QAR models in which all of the autoregressive coefficients are allowed to be τ-dependent and, therefore, are capable of altering the location, scale, and shape of the conditional densities. We will write the general form of the model as

$$Q_{y_t}(\tau|y_{t-1}, \ldots, y_{t-p}) = \alpha_0(\tau) + \alpha_1(\tau)y_{t-1} + \cdots + \alpha_p(\tau)y_{t-p},$$

or, somewhat more compactly, as

$$Q_{y_t}(\tau|\mathcal{F}_{t-1}) = x_t^\top \alpha(\tau), \tag{8.6}$$

where $\mathcal{F}_t$ denotes the σ-field generated by $\{y_s, s \leq t\}$, and the vector of lagged responses is denoted by $x_t = (1, y_{t-1}, \ldots, y_{t-p})^\top$.

To motivate the model we will emphasize the simplest, first-order version of it:

$$Q_{y_t}(\tau|\mathcal{F}_{t-1}) = \alpha_0(\tau) + \alpha_1(\tau)y_{t-1}. \tag{8.7}$$

Recall that since $Q_{y_t}(\tau|\mathcal{F}_{t-1})$ is a proper conditional quantile function, the model may also be expressed as

$$y_t = \alpha_0(U_t) + \alpha_1(U_t)y_{t-1}, \qquad (8.8)$$

where U_t are taken to be uniformly distributed on the unit interval and iid. Simulating the model is conveniently conducted employing this form. The classical Gaussian AR(1) model is obtained by setting $\alpha_0(u) = \sigma\Phi^{-1}(u)$ and $\alpha_1(u) = \alpha_1$, a constant. The formulation in (8.8) reveals that the model may be interpreted as a rather unusual form of random coefficient autoregressive model. In contrast to most of the literature on random coefficient models – see, for example, Nicholls and Quinn (1982), Tjøstheim (1986) – in which the coefficients are assumed to be stochastically independent of one another, the QAR model has coefficients that are functionally dependent. Because monotonicity is required of the quantile functions, we will see that this imposes some discipline on the forms taken by the α-functions. This discipline essentially requires that the vector $\alpha(\tau)$, or some affine transformation of it, be monotonic in each coordinate. This condition insures that the random vector $\alpha_t = \alpha(U_t)$ is comonotonic, as was elaborated in Section 2.6.

Estimation of the linear QAR model involves solving the problem

$$\min_{\alpha \in \mathbb{R}^{p+1}} \sum_{t=1}^{n} \rho_\tau\left(y_t - x_t^\top\alpha\right). \qquad (8.9)$$

Solutions $\hat{\alpha}(\tau)$ may be called autoregression quantiles. Given $\hat{\alpha}(\tau)$, the τth conditional quantile function of y_t, conditional on past information, can be estimated by

$$\hat{Q}_{y_t}(\tau|x_{t-1}) = x_t^\top\hat{\alpha}(\tau),$$

and the conditional density of y_t can be estimated by the difference quotients,

$$\hat{f}_{y_t}(\tau|x_{t-1} = (\tau_i - \tau_{i-1})/(\hat{Q}_{y_t}(\tau_i|x_{t-1}) - \hat{Q}_{y_t}(\tau_{i-1}|x_{t-1})),$$

for some appropriately chosen sequence of τs.

8.3.1 Quantile Autoregression and Comonotonicity

As in other linear quantile regression applications, linear QAR models should be cautiously interpreted as useful local approximations to more complex nonlinear global models. If we take the linear form of the model too literally then obviously, at some point or points, there will be "crossings" of the conditional quantile functions – unless these functions are precisely parallel, in which case we are back to the pure location-shift form of the model. This crossing problem appears more acute in the autoregressive case than in ordinary regression applications because the support of the design space (i.e., the set of x_ts that occur with positive probability) is determined within the model. Nevertheless, we may still regard the linear models specified earlier as valid local

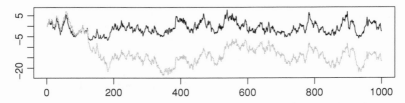

Figure 8.2. QAR and unit root time series. The figure contrasts two time series generated by the same sequence of innovations. The gray sample path is a random walk with standard Gaussian innovations; the black sample path illustrates a QAR series generated by the same innovations with random AR(1) coefficient $0.85 + 0.25\Phi(u_t)$. The latter series, although exhibiting explosive behavior in the upper tail, is stationary as described in the text.

approximations over a region of interest. The interpretation of linear conditional quantile functions as approximations to the local behavior in the central range of the covariate space should always be regarded as provisional; richer data sources can be expected to yield more elaborate nonlinear specifications that would have validity over larger regions. For an example of a more global approximation in AR(1) modeling, see the discussion of the Melbourne daily temperature data in Section 2.4.1.

Figure 8.2 illustrates a realization of the simple QAR(1) model just described. The black sample path shows 1000 observations generated from model (8.8) with AR(1) coefficient $\theta_1(u) = 0.85 + 0.25u$ and $\theta_0(u) = \Phi^{-1}(u)$. The gray sample path depicts a random walk generated from the same innovation sequence (i.e., the same $\theta_0(U_t)$s but with constant θ_1 equal to one). It is easy to verify that the QAR(1) form of the model satisfies the stationarity conditions given in the following; despite the explosive character of its upper tail behavior we observe that the series appears quite stationary, at least by comparison to the random walk series. Estimating the QAR(1) model at 19 equally spaced quantiles yields the intercept and slope estimates depicted in Figure 8.3.

Figure 8.4 depicts estimated linear conditional quantile functions for short-term (three-month) U.S. interest rates using the QAR(1) model superimposed on the AR(1) scatterplot. In this example, the scatterplot shows clearly that there is more dispersion at higher interest rates, with nearly degenerate behavior at very low rates. The fitted linear quantile regression lines in the left panel show little evidence of crossing, but at rates below 0.04 there are some violations of the monotonicity requirement in the fitted quantile functions. Fitting the data using a somewhat more complex nonlinear (in variables) model by introducing another additive component in our example, $\theta_2(\tau)(y_{t-1} - \delta)^2 I(y_{t-1} < \delta)$ with $\delta = 8$, we can eliminate the problem of the crossing of the fitted quantile functions. In Figure 8.5, which depicts the fitted coefficients of the QAR(1) model and their confidence region, we see that the estimated slope coefficient of the QAR(1) model has somewhat similar appearance to the simulated example.

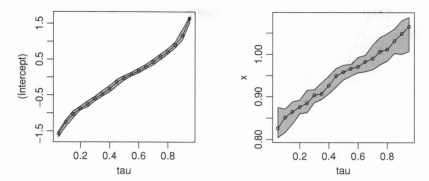

Figure 8.3. Estimating the QAR model. The figure illustrates estimates of the QAR(1) model based on the black time series of the previous figure. The left panel represents the intercept estimate at 19 equally spaced quantiles; the right panel represents the AR(1) slope estimate at the same quantiles. The shaded region is a 0.90 confidence band. Note that the slope estimate quite accurately reproduces the linear form of the QAR(1) coefficient used to generate the data.

It should be stressed again that the *estimated* conditional quantile functions,

$$\hat{Q}_y(\tau|x) = x^\top \widehat{\theta}(\tau),$$

are guaranteed to be monotone at the mean design point, $x = \bar{x}$, as they are for linear quantile regression models. Crossing, when it occurs, is generally confined to outlying regions of the design space. In our random coefficient

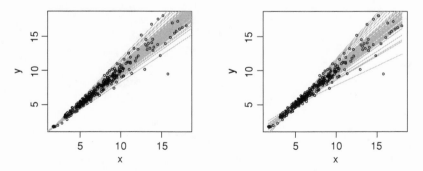

Figure 8.4. QAR(1) model of U.S. short-term interest rate. The AR(1) scatterplot of the U.S. three-month rate is superimposed in the left panel with 49 equally spaced estimates of linear conditional quantile functions. In the right panel, the model is augmented with a nonlinear (quadratic) component. The introduction of the quadratic component alleviates some nonmonotonicity in the estimated quantiles at low interest rates.

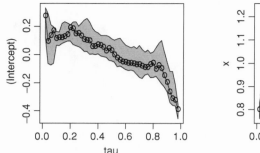
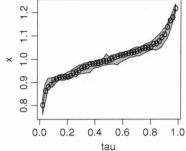

Figure 8.5. QAR(1) model of U.S. short-term interest rate. The QAR(1) estimates of the intercept and slope parameters for 19 equally spaced quantile functions are illustrated in the two plots. Note that the slope parameter is, like the prior simulated example, explosive in the upper tail but mean reverting in the lower tail.

view of the QAR model,

$$y_t = x_t^\top \theta(U_t),$$

we express the observable random variable y_t as a linear function conditioning covariates. But, rather than assuming that the coordinates of the vector θ are independent random variables, we adopt a diametrically opposite viewpoint: that they are perfectly functionally dependent, all driven by a single random uniform variable. If the functions $(\theta_0, \ldots, \theta_p)$ are all monotonically increasing, then the coordinates of the random vector α_t are comonotonic in the sense of Schmeidler (1986). This is often the case, but there are important cases for which this monotonicity fails. What then?

What really matters is that we can find a linear reparameterization of the model that does exhibit comonotonicity over some relevant region of covariate space. Because we can write, for any nonsingular matrix A,

$$Q_y(\tau|x) = x^\top A^{-1} A\theta(\tau),$$

we can choose $p + 1$ linearly independent design points $\{x_s : s = 1, \ldots, p + 1\}$, where $Q_y(\tau|x_s)$ is monotone in τ. Then, choosing the matrix A so that Ax_s is the sth unit basis vector for $\mathbb{R}^{p+1}$, we have

$$Q_y(\tau|x_s) = \gamma_s(\tau),$$

where $\gamma = A\theta$. And now inside the convex hull of our selected points we have a comonotonic random coefficient representation of the model. In effect, we have simply reparameterized the design so that the $p + 1$ coefficients are the conditional quantile functions of y_t at the selected points. The fact that quantile functions of sums of nonnegative comonotonic random variables are sums of their marginal quantile functions (see, Section 2.6) allows us to interpolate inside the convex hull. Of course, linear extrapolation is also possible but we must be cautious about possible violations of the monotonicity requirement in this region.

The QAR model offers some potential to expand the conceptual territory between classical stationary linear time-series models and their autoregressive integrated moving average (ARIMA) alternatives. Models can exhibit forms of asymmetric persistence that appear consistent with unit root behavior, whereas occasional negative realizations induce mean reversion and thus serve to undermine the persistence of the process. In model (8.8), for example, the crucial condition for (covariance) stationarity is that $E\alpha_t^2 < 1$, and so, as we have seen, we can have explosive behavior in the upper tail with occasional episodes of mean reversion. Such models may be of interest in modeling speculative bubbles in financial applications.

8.4 COPULA FUNCTIONS AND NONLINEAR QUANTILE REGRESSION

It is a well-known characterization property of the multivariate Gaussian distribution that conditional mean functions are linear in the conditioning variables and, even more powerfully, that conditional distributions are Gaussian with constant covariance structure. Thus, in a multivariate Gaussian world, families of conditional quantile functions are parallel and there is consequently little need for quantile regression. For staunch adherents of the Gaussian faith this probably comes as a relief – one less messy topic to cover in the survey of statistical methods. But for others, the ubiquitous evidence against such pure location-shift models casts some serious doubt on the Gaussian model.

Until now we have relied on linear-in-parameters models of the conditional quantile functions and argued that they often provide adequate approximations for many applications. In this section I will briefly address the possibility of deriving nonlinear parametric models for families of conditional quantile functions.

8.4.1 Copula Functions

A multivariate distribution function with uniform univariate marginal distributions is called a copula function. Thus, for example, if we have a bivariate distribution function $F_{X,Y}$, we can define a corresponding copula function, $C : [0, 1]^2 \to [0, 1]$, as

$$C(u, v) = F_{X,Y}\left(F_X^{-1}(u), F_Y^{-1}(v)\right),$$

where F_X^{-1} and F_Y^{-1} denote the univariate quantile functions of the marginal distributions of X and Y. Equivalently, we have

$$F_{X,Y}(x, y) = C(F_X(x), F_Y(y)).$$

Copula functions are a convenient class of objects for the study of general forms of stochastic dependence. They allow us to abstract from the complications introduced by marginal behavior and permit us to focus exclusively on the form of the dependence. For independent random variables X and Y, we obviously have

$$C(u, v) = uv.$$

For comonotone X and Y – that is, for X and Y with rank correlation one – $C(u, v)$ degenerates to a measure placing mass only on a one-dimensional curve connecting the points $(0, 0)$ and $(1, 1)$ in the unit square. In the latter case we may view both X and Y as "generated" by a common random variable, say Z, such that $X = f(Z)$ and $Y = g(Z)$ with functions f and g monotone increasing. Between these extremes of independence and dependence, we have many carefully investigated parametric examples and much unexplored territory.

The link between copula functions and conditional quantile functions is provided by the following important observation.

Lemma 8.1 (Bouyé and Salmon, 2002). $\partial C(u, v)/\partial u = F_{Y|X}(F_Y^{-1}(v)| F_X^{-1}(u))$.

Proof. From

$$P(Y < y, X = x) = \partial F_{X,Y}(x, y)/\partial x$$

it follows that

$$\begin{aligned}
P(Y < y | X = x) &= (f_X(x))^{-1} \partial F_{X,Y}(x, y)/\partial x \\
&= (f_X(x))^{-1} \partial C(F_X(x), F_Y(y))/\partial x \\
&= (f_X(x))^{-1} \partial C(u, v)/\partial u \, \partial F_X(x)/\partial x,
\end{aligned}$$

where the middle term is evaluated at $u = F_X(x)$ and $v = F_Y(y)$, and the last term cancels the first. ∎

This observation enables us to easily derive parametric families of conditional quantile functions from parametric copula functions. Fix the conditional probability of Y given $X = x$ at some τ, so that $\partial C(u, v)/\partial u = \tau$. Solving for v, we have

$$v = Q_{V|U}(\tau | u)$$

and, consequently,

$$y = F_Y^{-1}(Q_{V|F(X)}(\tau | F(x)).$$

We may interpret this as a fully specified stochastic model. Given observations on X, we can generate observations on Y simply by evaluating this expression for y and replacing τ by independent, uniformly distributed random draws.

To illustrate the approach, consider the Frank copula given by Bouyé and Salmon (2002):

$$C(u, v, \delta) = -\delta^{-1} \log(1 + (e^{-\delta u} - 1)(e^{-\delta v} - 1)/(e^{-\delta} - 1)).$$

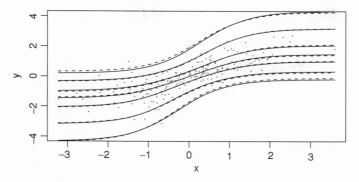

Figure 8.6. Frank copula model. The figure illustrates 200 observations from a bivariate version of the Frank copula model. Seven true conditional quantile curves for $\tau \in \{0.01, 0.05, 0.25, 0.50, 0.75, 0.95, 0.99\}$ appear as solid lines, and the seven dotted curves represent the corresponding nonlinear quantile regression estimates.

Differentiating with respect to u and solving for v yields

$$v = -\delta^{-1} \log(1 + (e^{-\delta} - 1)(1 + e^{-\delta u}(\tau^{-1} - 1))).$$

Finally, taking the marginals to be F_X and F_Y, we have the model

$$Q_{Y|X}(\tau|x) = F_Y^{-1}(-\delta^{-1} \log(1 + (e^{-\delta} - 1)(1 + e^{-\delta F_X(x)}(\tau^{-1} - 1)))).$$

This model can be estimated; that is, δ and any free parameters in F_Y can be estimated at any specified quantile τ using the methods discussed in Section 4.4. Obviously, we can produce a whole family of such estimates depending on τ, and this suggests inference strategies for model evaluation. Given evidence, or faith, in the plausibility of the model, we could consider projecting our multiplicity of estimates into one coherent estimate of the model parameters by employing the "method of quantiles" discussed in Section 4.8.

To illustrate the estimation of such models, we may consider the Frank copula a bit further. Data was generated from the Frank model with $\delta = 8$ and both X and Y taken to be Student with eight degrees of freedom. In Figure 8.6 we compare true and estimated conditional quantile curves for this model for one realization of sample size 200. Estimation of this nonlinear-in-parameters quantile regression model is quite accurate in the interior quantiles, but in the extremes, particularly in the lower tail at $\tau = 0.01$, the error is larger. Given the sampled x values, estimation involves only one free parameter – δ – if we assumed that the parameters of F_Y^{-1} are known. If, on the other hand, we assume that F_Y is known only up to a location and scale parameter, so that

$$Q_{Y|X}(\tau|x) = \mu + \sigma F_Y^{-1}(-\delta^{-1} \log(1 + (e^{-\delta} - 1)(1 + e^{-\delta F_X(x)}(\tau^{-1} - 1)))),$$

we can estimate all three parameters of the family. Not surprisingly, the latter approach requires somewhat larger sample sizes to achieve the same precision.

See Section 4.4 and Appendix A for further details on the computation of such estimators.

8.5 HIGH-BREAKDOWN ALTERNATIVES TO QUANTILE REGRESSION

Although we know that quantile regression is quite robust to outlying response observations, it can – like other regression M-estimators – be quite sensitive to outlying covariate observations. In fact, it is easily shown that, if we are allowed to perturb one (x_i, y_i) point in a completely arbitrary fashion, we can force *all* of the quantile regression hyperplanes to pass through the perturbed point. Sometimes, of course, outlying x_i observations are highly desirable. When the linearity of the model is credible and the covariates are measured accurately, spreading the x points apart is known to be an efficient design strategy. But when these conditions are not satisfied it is prudent to seek alternative strategies that offer more robustness.

In the robustness literature, considerable attention has been devoted to proposals for high-breakdown regression estimators capable of withstanding arbitrary perturbations of a significant fraction of the sample observations without disastrous results. One of the most influential of these proposals is the least median of squares estimator considered in Rousseeuw and Leroy (1987). One could legitimately worry that such proposals are too pessimistic – sacrificing too much efficiency when the nominal model is nearly correct – but such methods have an important diagnostic role and may alert us to circumstances in which model assumptions or data reliability are suspect. The marriage of high-breakdown objectives and quantile regression methods is inherently uneasy because it is difficult, or perhaps even impossible, to be robust about estimation and inference concerning tail behavior.

There have been several proposals for "robustifying" quantile regression with respect to outlying design observations. De Jongh, de Wet, and Welsh (1988) and Antoch and Jurečková (1985) have proposed bounded influence versions of the quantile regression objective function, but unfortunately there is little experience with these approaches in applications. Recently, Rousseeuw and Hubert (1999) have proposed a new, highly design-robust variant of quantile regression based on the concept of regression depth. This approach will be briefly described in the context of bivariate regression.

Suppose we have data $Z_n = \{(x_i, y_i) : i = 1, \ldots, n\} \in \mathbb{R}^2$ and the model

$$y_i = \theta_1 x_i + \theta_2 + u_i. \tag{8.10}$$

Rousseeuw and Hubert introduce the following definitions.

Definition 8.1. *A candidate fit $\theta = (\theta_1, \theta_2)$ to Z_n is called a nonfit if and only if there exists a real number, $v_\theta = v$, that does not coincide with any x_i and such that*

$$r_i(\theta) < 0 \ \text{ for all } x_i < v \quad \text{and} \quad r_i(\theta) > 0 \ \text{ for all } x_i > v$$

or

$$r_i(\theta) > 0 \ for \ all \ x_i < v \quad and \quad r_i(\theta) < 0 \ for \ all \ x_i > v,$$

where $r_i(\theta) = y_i - \theta_1 x_i - \theta_2$.

Definition 8.2. *The regression depth of a fit* $\theta = (\theta_1, \theta_2)$ *relative to a data set* $Z_n \in \mathbb{R}^2$ *is the smallest number of observations that need to be removed to make* θ *a nonfit.*

A mechanical description of regression depth in the "primal" or data-space plot is also provided by Rousseeuw and Hubert: the existence of v_θ for any nonfit θ corresponds to a point on the line $y = \theta_1 x + \theta_2$ about which one could rotate the line to the vertical without encountering any observations. However, the geometric notion of "depth" is more clearly brought out by the fundamental concept of the dual plot.

In the bivariate regression version of the dual plot, each point (x_i, y_i) appears as a line in parameter space; that is, all the points on the line

$$\theta_2 = y_i - \theta_1 x_i$$

in (θ_1, θ_2)-space have ith residual zero, and intersections of such lines correspond to points in parameter space that have two zero residuals. Rousseeuw and Hubert observe that

> The [regression depth] of a fit θ is (in dual space) the smallest number of lines L_i that need to be removed to set θ free, i.e. so that it lies in the exterior of the remaining arrangement of lines. (p. 398)

In fact, this view brings us very close to several fascinating papers by F. Y. Edgeworth on median regression, or what he called the "plural median." Edgeworth (1888) gives an almost prescient description of the simplex algorithm for linear programming:

> The method may be illustrated thus:– Let $C - R$ (where C is a constant [and R denotes the objective function]) represent the height of a surface, which will resemble the roof of an irregularly built slated house. Get on this roof somewhere near the top, and moving continually upwards along some one of the edges, or *arrétes*, climb up to the top. The highest position will in general consist of a solitary pinnacle. But occasionally there will be, instead of a single point, a horizontal ridge, or even a flat surface. (p. 186)

Supplemented by a more explicit rule for choosing the edges at each vertex, this description would fit nicely into modern textbooks of linear programming. Edgeworth is obviously maximizing, having decided to consider $-R$, and he is simply following the edges of the constraint set toward the roof's highest point. In terms of the dual plot, this strategy can be described as starting from an arbitrary intersection corresponding to a basic feasible solution, finding the directional derivatives corresponding to all of the possible directions emanating from this point, choosing the most favorable direction, and going in this direction until the objective function stops decreasing. This turns out to be a concise description of the most commonly used algorithm for quantile regression originally developed for the median case by Barrodale and Roberts (1974) and modified by Koenker and d'Orey (1987) for general quantile regression. A more detailed discussion of this approach and its alternatives is provided in Chapter 6.

It is a curious irony that Edgeworth's long-time collaborator A. L. Bowley, in trying to describe Edgeworth's geometric method for computing the "plural median," came very close to the formulation of the maximum depth regression estimator of Rousseeuw and Hubert. Bowley (1902), speaking of the dual plot, suggests that

> we may with advantage apply Prof. Edgeworth's "double median" method and find the point, line or small area, such that, whether we proceed from it to the left, or right, or up, or down, we always intersect the same number of lines before we are clear of the network. (p. 341)

This is clearly not the same as finding the "deepest point" in the network, as formulated by Rousseeuw and Hubert; but if we interpret it a bit generously to include *all* possible directions, not just the canonical ones, we obtain something akin to their "deepest point" and this "point" corresponds to the "deepest regression line."

Unlike the conventional median regression estimator, which has a breakdown point of $1/n$ in the (x, y)-contamination model, and only marginally better breakdown properties in the fixed-x, y-contamination model, as discussed by He, Jurečková, Koenker, and Portnoy (1990) and Mizera and Muller (1999), the deepest line estimator has breakdown point $1/3$. It shares the equivariance properties of the ℓ_1-estimator but exhibits a somewhat greater tendency toward nonuniqueness. It is worth remarking in this connection that one of Theil's (1950) earliest papers also deals with a variant of this type that is usually described as the "median of pairwise slopes." It may be viewed geometrically in the dual plot by projecting all the intersections onto the axis of the "slope" parameter and then choosing the median of these projected values.

The contrast between the deepest line estimator and the usual median regression estimator is, perhaps, most clearly seen in their asymptotic behavior, which has been recently studied by He and Portnoy (1998). The deepest line may be formulated as follows:

$$\tilde{\beta}_n = \operatorname{argmin}_b \max_{x_{(1)} \leq a \leq x_{(n)}} |D_n(b, a)|,$$

where

$$D_n(b, a) = \sum \operatorname{sgn} \{(y_i - b_1 x_i - b_2)(x_i - a)\}.$$

To formulate an asymptotic theory for the maximum regression depth estimator, He and Portnoy assume that the sequence $\{x_i\}$ satisfies the following conditions:

A1. $\sum x_i^2 = O(n)$.
A2. $n^{-1}\sum x_i \operatorname{sgn}(x_i - x_{[tn]}) \to g_1(t)$ uniformly from $t \in (0, 1)$, with $g_1''(t) < 0$ for all t.
A3. The $\{u_i\}$s are iid random variables with median zero, bounded density f, $f(0) > 0$, and f is Lipschitz in a neighborhood of zero.

When the $\{x_i\}$s are iid from distribution function G with positive density on its entire support, they note that

$$g_1(t) = \int_t^1 G^{-1}(u)du - \int_0^t G^{-1}(u)du.$$

so that $g_1'(t) = -2G^{-1}(t)$ and, therefore, Condition A2 follows immediately from the Kolmogorov strong law and the monotonicity of G^{-1}. Now let $g_0(t) = 1 - 2t$ denote the limit of $n^{-1}\sum \operatorname{sgn}(z_i - z_{[nt]})$ and set $g(t) = (g_0(t), g_1(t))'$. He and Portnoy prove the following theorem.

Theorem 8.1. *Under Conditions A1–A3, $\sqrt{n}(\hat{\theta} - \theta)$ converges in distribution to a random variable whose distribution is that of the unique minimizer of the function*

$$h(\delta) = \max_t |2B(t) - B(1) + 2f(0)g(t)'\delta|,$$

where $B(t)$ is standard Brownian motion.

Unfortunately, it is rather difficult to compare the asymptotic performance of the maximal depth estimator with the more familiar median regression estimator, even in this simple iid error bivariate setting. Even under non-iid error conditions, as long as the conditional median function is linear in parameters, both approaches can be shown to be $\sqrt{n}$-consistent for the same parameter; this in itself is quite remarkable. We would expect that the improved robustness of the maximal depth estimator would come at the price of some efficiency loss under idealized Conditions A1–A3 where influential design observations are highly desirable. He and Portnoy provide a very limited evaluation of the asymptotic relative efficiency of the two estimates, showing that under iid error conditions the loss of efficiency using the deepest line rather than the median regression estimator is about 10% for uniform xs, about 15% for Gaussian xs, and nearly 40% for t_3 xs. Of course, when influential xs are highly unreliable, these comparisons may be reversed. See the discussions of Rousseeuw and Hubert (1999) and Koenker and Portnoy (2000) for consideration of an extreme example.

Given that the maximal depth estimator consistently estimates the linear conditional median function under essentially similar conditions to those required by the ℓ_1-estimator, it is natural to ask whether it is possible to estimate the parameters of other linear conditional quantile models using similar methods.

A simple reweighting of the maximal depth objective function allows us to answer this question affirmatively.

Asymmetrically reweighting positive and negative residuals suggests the quantile regression depth function

$$d_\tau(\theta) = \min_t\{\min\{\tau L^+(t) + (1 - \tau)R^-(t), \tau R^+(t) + (1 - \tau)L^-(t)\}\},$$

and essentially the same asymptotic analysis of He and Portnoy shows that the minimizer

$$\hat\theta_n(\tau) = \text{argmin } d_\tau(\theta)$$

is a $\sqrt{n}$-consistent estimator of the parameters of the linear τth conditional quantile function.

Thus, regression depth provides an alternative "influence robust" approach to quantile regression estimation that could be compared to the earlier weighting proposals of Antoch and Jurečková (1985) and de Jongh, de Wet, and Welsh (1988). Extending the regression depth idea beyond the bivariate model poses some challenges, particularly on the asymptotic and algorithmic fronts, but the basic conceptual apparatus is already provided by Rousseeuw and Hubert (1999), Van Aelst, Rousseeuw, Hubert, and Struyf (2002), and Mizera (2002). Bai and He (1999) extend the preceding asymptotic result to the general p-variate regression setting.

Adrover, Yohai, and Maronna (2004) have recently proposed another promising approach to high-breakdown quantile regression. They propose solving

$$\hat\beta(\tau) = \text{argmin}_{\beta\in\mathbb{R}^p} \max_{\gamma\in\mathbb{R}^p} L_\tau(\beta, \gamma),$$

where

$$L_\tau(\beta, \gamma) = q_\tau(R_\tau(\beta, \gamma)) + q_{1-\tau}(R_\tau(\beta, \gamma)),$$
$$R_\tau(\beta, \gamma) = \rho_\tau(r(\beta)) - \rho_\tau(r(\gamma)),$$

$r(\beta) = y - X\beta$, $\rho_\tau(u) = u(\tau - I(u < 0))$, and $q_\tau(v)$ denotes the τth sample quantile of the vector v. In simulations, this estimator performed well relative to the maximum depth estimator in contaminated situations and had fairly high efficiency relative to the ordinary quantile regression estimator in uncontaminated settings.

8.6   MULTIVARIATE QUANTILES

The search for a satisfactory notion of multivariate quantiles has become something of a quest for the statistical holy grail in recent years. Despite generating an extensive literature, it is fair to say that no general agreement has emerged. The situation is exemplified by the conflicting central notion of the multivariate median.

In contrast to the sample mean of d-dimensional vectors, there is no consensus about an appropriate notion of multivariate median. The coordinatewise median fails to satisfy basic equivariance requirements. The multivariate mean is equivariant to general nonsingular linear transformations in the sense that if $Y = AX$ for an $n \times p$ matrix of observations X, with A a nonsingular $p \times p$ matrix, then $\bar{y} = A\bar{x}$ and we can infer $\bar{x}$ from $\bar{y}$. In contrast, the coordinatewise median is equivariant to diagonal forms of A but not to more general forms of transformation. The spatial median, which goes back at least to Fermat,

$$\hat{\mu}_n = \operatorname{argmin}_{\mu \in \mathbb{R}^d} \sum_{i=1}^{n} \|y_i - \mu\|,$$

is orthogonally equivariant, but fails to be fully equivariant like the multivariate mean.

8.6.1 The Oja Median and Its Extensions

Oja (1983) introduced the affine equivariant multivariate median

$$\check{\mu}_n = \operatorname{argmin}_{\mu \in \mathbb{R}^d} \sum_{i<j} \Delta(y_{i_1}, \ldots, y_{i_d}, \mu),$$

where the summation runs over the indices $1 \leq i_1 < \cdots < i_d \leq n$, and Δ denotes the volume of the polyhedron with extreme points, $y_{i_1}, \ldots, y_{i_d}$, and μ. Thus, for example, for $d = 2$ we sum over all pairs of points and the object is to choose μ in such a way that the sum of the areas of the triangles formed by each pair of points and the point μ is minimized. Remarkably, as with the formulation of the spatial median, squaring the minimands of the Oja median yields the sample mean.

The problem of computing the Oja median can be formulated as a median regression problem and thus solved by linear programming methods. For simplicity of exposition we will consider only the bivariate case, but the generalization to higher dimensions is straightforward. Recall that the area of the triangle with vertices $y_i = (y_{i1}, y_{i2})$, $y_j = (y_{j1}, y_{j2})$, $\mu = (\mu_1, \mu_2)$ is given by

$$\Delta(y^i, y^j, \mu) = \frac{1}{2} \begin{vmatrix} 1 & 1 & 1 \\ y_{i1} & y_{j1} & \mu_1 \\ y_{i2} & y_{j2} & \mu_2 \end{vmatrix},$$

and so expanding in cofactors, we may reexpress $\hat{\mu}$ as

$$\hat{\mu} = \operatorname{argmin} \sum_{i \neq j} |y_{ij} - x_{ij1}\mu_1 - x_{ij2}\mu_2|, \tag{8.11}$$

where

$$y_{ij} = \begin{vmatrix} y_{i1} & y_{j1} \\ y_{i2} & y_{j2} \end{vmatrix}, \quad x_{ij1} = - \begin{vmatrix} 1 & 1 \\ y_{i2} & y_{j2} \end{vmatrix}, \quad x_{ij2} = \begin{vmatrix} 1 & 1 \\ y_{i1} & y_{j1} \end{vmatrix}.$$

The computation of $\check{\mu}_n$ may be formulated as a median regression in $n(n-1)/2$ pseudo-observations, which are themselves U-statistics based on the original observations. This formulation was suggested by Ninimaa, Oja, and Nyblom (1992). A remarkable fact about this formulation is that if you replace the median regression by a least-squares regression you obtain the sample mean! The question naturally arises of whether one could define quantiles other than the median along similar lines. Because the sign information contained in the determinants is suppressed by taking absolute values in the median computation, it is tempting to explore asymmetric weighting of the objective function that retains this information. Recall that the sign of the determinant is controlled by the ordering of the columns or rows. Thus, if we permute the order of the vertices of our triangles, we alter the signs of the resulting determinants. If vertices are ordered in a clockwise fashion, the determinant will be positive; if they are counterclockwise, then it will be negative.

Adopting the convention that the observations are ordered by their first coordinate and that pairs in the sum are always selected so that the index of the first vertex is greater than the second (e.g., $\{(2,1),(3,2),\ldots,(n,n-1)$, $(3,1),\ldots,(n,1)\})$, then for any orientation determining the ordering of the observations, that is, for any angle θ, we have

$$\hat{\mu}(\tau,\theta) = \operatorname{argmin}\sum_{i>j}\rho_\tau(y_{ij}(\theta) - x_{ij}(\theta)^\top\mu).$$

The pseudo-observations $(y_{ij}(\theta), x_{ij}(\theta))$ depend on θ through the ordering of the original observations according to the quantity $y_{i1}\cos\theta + y_{i2}\sin\theta$. Solving for $\theta \in (0,\pi)$ and $\tau \in (0,1)$ gives a series of nested contours as illustrated in Figure 8.7.

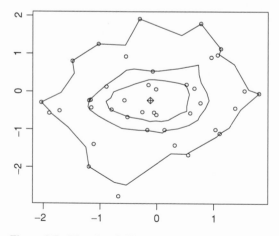

Figure 8.7. Directional Oja quantile contours. The figure illustrates the Oja median and three quantile contours $\{0.75, 0.85, 0.95\}$ as described in the text.

In this approach, pairs of observations and their associated triangles play the role of residuals and the magnitude of a residual is represented by the area of the associated triangle. This approach can be extended in a straightforward way to multivariate, or seemingly unrelated, regression problems for which the coordinates of μ are replaced by linear predictors: $(\mu_1, \mu_2) = (x_{i1}^\top\beta_1, x_{i1}^\top\beta_2)$ A fundamental difficulty with the approach is that there is no apparent way to assess the probability content of the resulting contours, except perhaps via the pseudo-observations of the quantile regression problem. Clearly, the approach presumes a unimodal nominal model and this too may be questioned in many circumstances.

This approach can be extended to multivariate regression by replacing the scalar coordinates of μ by linear parametric functions of covariates. Extensions to dimensions greater than two are also straightforward, although the resulting computational problems involve nontrivial computational effort because the number of terms in the linear model formulation of the problem is $\binom{n}{p}$. This U-statistic form of the objective function illustrates the general approach outlined by Chaudhuri (1992).

8.6.2   Half-Space Depth and Directional Quantile Regression

Tukey (1975) introduced the following notion of the centrality of a point x with respect to a distribution P.

Definition 8.3. *The half-space depth of a point $x \in \mathbb{R}^d$ with respect to a probability distribution P is*

$$D(x, P) = \inf_{\|u\|=1} P\{u^\top y \geq u^\top x, y \in \mathbb{R}^d\}.$$

Points with maximal depth constitute an alternative centering notion to the median concepts described earlier.

Laine (2001) has recently investigated the use of quantile regression methods as a means of defining directional multivariate quantiles that can be related to half-space depth. Briefly, let $Z \in \mathbb{R}^d$ be a random vector with distribution P, and let Z_α and $Z_\alpha^\perp$ denote the projection of Z onto the direction $\alpha/\|\alpha\|$ and its orthogonal complement, respectively. For any $\|\alpha\| \leq 1$, we can consider the quantile regression of Z_α on $Z_\alpha^\perp$:

$$\min_{(\beta,\gamma)\in\mathbb{R}^{d-1}\times\mathbb{R}} E\rho_{\|\alpha\|}\left(Z_\alpha - Z_\alpha^\perp\beta - \gamma\right).$$

For absolutely continuous P, we have the gradient (moment) condition

$$E\left[\|\alpha\| - I\left(Z_\alpha \leq Z_\alpha^\perp\beta + \gamma\right)\right]\begin{pmatrix} Z_\alpha^\perp \\ 1 \end{pmatrix} = 0.$$

The contribution of the "intercept" term γ requires at a solution that

$$\|\alpha\| = P\left\{Z_\alpha \leq Z_\alpha^\perp\beta(\alpha) + \gamma(\alpha)\right\},$$

and so the mass below the hyperplane $\{Z_\alpha \leq Z_\alpha^\perp \beta(\alpha) + \gamma(\alpha)\}$ is $\|\alpha\|$. For empirical measures P_n, the corresponding subgradient condition provides an analogous result via Theorem 2.2. Laine (2001) defines quantile contour sets as the intersection of these lower half-spaces and proceeds to analyze their asymptotic behavior. Computationally, parametric linear programming can be employed, but the situation poses some challenging new problems.

Chaudhuri (1996) provides a valuable survey of this literature and introduces a geometric notion of multivariate quantiles that is also related to the quantile regression paradigm. He notes that the usual quantile regression objective function may be written as

$$R_\tau(\xi) = \sum_{i=1}^{n} |y_i - \xi| + (2\tau - 1)|y_i - \xi|.$$

Viewing this objective function not as a function of $\tau \in [0, 1]$, but as a function of $u = 2\tau - 1$, in $[-1, 1]$ suggests that, for observations $Y_i \in \mathbb{R}^d$ and parameter $\xi \in \mathbb{R}^d$, we might consider minimizing

$$R_u(\xi) = \sum_{i=1}^{n} \|Y_i - \xi\| + u^\top(Y_i - \xi)$$

for $u \in B = \{u \in \mathbb{R}^d \mid \|u\| < 1\}$. The link to the spatial median corresponding to $u = 0$ is clear. Related work is reported by Koltchinskii (1997) and Serfling (2004).

8.7   PENALTY METHODS FOR LONGITUDINAL DATA

Longitudinal data pose some important new challenges for quantile regression methods. On the one hand, such data offer the possibility of tracing the dynamic consequences of covariate movements, potentially pulling aside the veil of ignorance faced in the classical randomized treatment setting. On the other hand, many of the tricks of the trade developed for Gaussian random effects models are no longer directly applicable in the context of quantile regression. In this section we will briefly sketch an interpretation of classical random effects estimation that does seem to be fruitful in the wider context of quantile regression. Some comments on the relevance of this approach for quantile growth curve estimation are made in the final subsection.

8.7.1   Classical Random Effects as Penalized Least Squares

Consider the model

$$y_{ij} = x_{ij}^\top \beta + \alpha_i + u_{ij} \quad j = 1, \ldots, m_i, \quad i = 1, \ldots, n,$$

which will be written in matrix form as

$$y = X\beta + Z\alpha + u.$$

Suppose u and α are independent random vectors with $u \sim \mathcal{N}(0, R)$ and $\alpha \sim \mathcal{N}(0, Q)$. The minimum variance unbiased estimator of β under these conditions is

$$\hat{\beta} = (X^\top (R + ZQZ^\top)^{-1} X)^{-1} X^\top (R + ZQZ^\top)^{-1} y.$$

This is immediately apparent on setting $v = Z\alpha + u$ and noting that

$$Evv^\top = R + ZQZ^\top.$$

This estimator is certainly not very appealing from a robustness standpoint, especially if elements of the matrices R and Q need to be estimated, but the optimization problem that gives rise to $\hat{\beta}$ is suggestive of a larger class of possible candidate estimators.

Proposition 8.1. $\hat{\beta}$ *solves* $\min_{(\alpha,\beta)} \|y - X\beta - Z\alpha\|^2_{R^{-1}} + \|\alpha\|^2_{Q^{-1}}$, *where* $\|x\|^2_A = x^\top A x$.

Proof. By differentiating we have the following normal equations:

$$X^\top R^{-1} X \hat{\beta} + X^\top R^{-1} Z \hat{\alpha} = X^\top R^{-1} y$$
$$Z^\top R^{-1} X \hat{\beta} + (Z^\top R^{-1} Z + Q^{-1}) \hat{\alpha} = Z^\top R^{-1} y.$$

Solving for $\hat{\beta}$ yields

$$\hat{\beta} = (X^\top \Omega^{-1} X)^{-1} X^\top \Omega^{-1} y,$$

where $\Omega^{-1} = R^{-1} - R^{-1} Z (Z^\top R^{-1} Z + Q^{-1})^{-1} Z^\top R^{-1}$. But $\Omega = R + ZQZ^\top$ (see, e.g., Rao, 1973, p. 33). ∎

This result has a long history. Robinson (1991) attributes the preceding normal equations to Henderson (1950). Goldberger (1962) introduced the terminology "best linear unbiased predictor," subsequently rendered BLUP, to describe the estimator $\hat{\beta}$ and its associated "estimator" $\hat{\alpha}$ of the random effects. The random effects estimator is sometimes described as a way to avoid estimating the α_is, and so it may come as a surprise that can be viewed as simply producing a shrunken estimate of these parameters. But this is clearly what the normal equations reveal. Lindley and Smith (1972) provided a Bayesian interpretation.

The result can also be interpreted in the light of Stein's (1956) fundamental results on the inadmissibility of the multivariate sample mean. When the dimension of α is large, it is advantageous in terms of risk based on quadratic loss to shrink the unconstrained fixed effects estimator toward the origin; this has the effect of reducing variability in exchange (presumably) for some increase in bias.

For certain (spherical) special cases, Nerlove (1971) showed how Ω^{-1} can be diagonalized, yielding simple transformations of X and y that enable ordinary least-squares computation of $\hat{\beta}$. Whereas convenient computational devices exist in the least-squares setting, these transformations do not appear to yield fruitful generalizations outside that setting.

Instead of viewing the random effects estimator as inherently tied to the normal theory of the covariance structure of additive random components, the penalty form of the random effects estimator immediately suggests a much wider domain of applicability. Altering the two components of the objective function enables one to account for possible nonnormality in both the innovations u_{ij} and the random effects α_i.

The crucial observation is that the somewhat esoteric form of the optimal weighted least-squares estimator can be banished in favor of the much simpler penalization principle. The random effects estimator, $(\hat{\alpha}, \hat{\beta})$, is just the usual fixed effect estimator *modified* so that the estimated fixed effects, $\hat{\alpha}_i$s, are all shrunken toward zero according to the penalty term. The penalty term may be viewed as data augmentation; in effect, we are simply adding m pseudo-observations. In some applications, the dimension of the resulting augmented regression may appear daunting, but the sparsity of the augmented design matrix makes the linear algebra quite manageable.

It is obviously implausible that R and Q are "known" in their entirety. In typical examples we would have at least one free scalar parameter, say λ, multiplying the penalty term that would serve to determine the degree of shrinkage. In the least-squares theory, this parameter is interpreted as a variance ratio, but more generally one requires other interpretations.

8.7.2   Quantile Regression with Penalized Fixed Effects

If we now reconsider the model

$$y = X\beta + Z\alpha + u$$

with quantile regression applications in mind, we are inclined to regard the α parameters simply as fixed effects that may need to be disciplined a little to achieve better performance in the estimation of β. Concerns about the complicated distributional properties of additive random components vanish. We are thus led to consider estimators of the form

$$(\hat{\alpha}(\tau), \hat{\beta}(\tau)) = \operatorname{argmin}_{(\alpha, \beta)} \sum_i \sum_j \rho_\tau \left(y_{ij} - x_{ij}^\top \beta - \alpha_i \right) + \lambda \sum_{i=1}^n |\alpha_i|.$$

Additivity of the penalty in the α_is reflects an assumption of independence, or perhaps exchangeability, across the cross-sectional units. In some settings it may be useful to model dependence among these units by alternative forms of the penalty. In this setting, we might regard each subject as having its own response distribution characterized by the quantile function

$$Q_{y_{ij}}(\tau|x_{ij}) = x_{ij}^\top \beta(\tau) + \alpha_i(\tau).$$

This is the usual additive decomposition of the conditional quantile functions that is imposed by the quantile regression model. It is obviously quite distinct from the additive decomposition of random variables that is usually assumed in random effects models, but it is clearly more flexible in some respects.

However, when the number of observations for each subject, m_i, is small, it may be imprudent to attempt to estimate a full distributional effect $\alpha_i(\tau)$ for each subject. In these cases we may be satisfied with the conventional assumption that the subject-specific effect degenerates into a pure location shift (i.e., $\alpha_i(\tau) \equiv \alpha_i$). Unrestricted estimators of $\alpha_i(\tau)$ could be combined over τs, or joint estimation carried out as proposed in Section 5.5.

Koenker (2004) considered estimators solving the penalized problem

$$\min_{(\alpha,\beta)} \sum_{k=1}^{q} \sum_{j=1}^{n} \sum_{i=1}^{m_i} w_k \rho_{\tau_k} \left(y_{ij} - \alpha_i - x_{ij}^\top \beta(\tau_k) \right) + \lambda \sum_{i=1}^{n} |\alpha_i|. \tag{8.12}$$

This approach pools sample information over several quantiles in an effort to improve the estimation of the individual specific estimates of the α_is.

A word is needed concerning the form of the penalty function. The ℓ_1 form of the penalty implicitly makes quite different assumptions about the αs than does the ℓ_2 penalty of the previous subsection. Tibshirani (1996) and Donoho, Chen, and Saunders (1998) have also emphasized recently that the ℓ_1 penalty acts more like a model selection device. Rather than shrinking all components of the vector α toward zero quite uniformly, as does the ℓ_2 penalty, the ℓ_1 penalty shrinks some components a lot and leaves others almost unperturbed. This reflects the implicit prior belief that, relative to the Gaussian assumptions underlying the ℓ_2 penalty, there is more mass concentrated at the origin and considerably greater probability of αs far away from zero. Whether this is plausible depends, obviously, on the application; whether it can be successfully investigated empirically remains an intriguing open question. One might consider, for example, examining the empirical distribution of the unrestricted $\hat{\alpha}_i$s.

The unweighted form of the penalty is well suited to the case of exchangeable subjects, but there are many circumstances that may suggest some form of dependence among the αs. A long-standing empirical problem in the quantile regression literature involves the analysis of repeated measurement data for biometric reference growth curves. In a typical application, we have observations $\{(y_{ij}, t_{ij}) : j = 1, \ldots, T_i, \ i = 1, \ldots, n\}$ reflecting measurements y_{ij}, say, height of individual i at time t_{ij}. The simplest analysis of such data would ignore the panel nature of the data entirely and simply estimate reference curves by solving

$$\hat{\beta}(\tau) = \operatorname{argmin}_\beta \sum_i \sum_j \rho_\tau(y_{ij} - g(t_{ij}, \beta)).$$

There are many possible ways to choose the parametric model for the reference curves, but the choice of a linear B-spline expansion (see, e.g., Hastie and

Tibshirani, 1990),

$$g(t_{ij}, \beta) = \sum_{k=1}^{p} \phi_k(t_{ij})\beta_k,$$

is likely to be satisfactory. Ignoring the dependence among the observations over time for a given subject seems foolish, however, and so we may prefer to consider models in which we allow individual specific perturbations, $\delta(t_{ij}, \alpha_i)$, of the population growth curves $g(t, \beta(\tau))$. Again penalty methods to control the variability of the $\hat{\alpha}$s would be desirable. But now the α_is are vector-valued and we would need some way to account for the dependence among coordinates. When exchangeability of the α_is over i seems plausible, it may be reasonable to estimate the structure of the dependence based on the unrestricted $\hat{\alpha}_i$s. This approach requires either a large number of observations per subject or a high signal-to-noise ratio for the individual subject measurements.

The foregoing example raises some serious questions of interpretation about the estimated reference curves. How do we distinguish the variability in the systematic part of the model represented by the $g(t, \beta(\tau))$ curves from the id-iosyncratic fixed effects represented by the $\delta(t, \alpha_i)$ effects? As we have noted earlier, we may even consider models with $\delta(t, \alpha_i(\tau))$ effects, but this would require extremely large samples on each subject. Related problems in the sim-pler context of nonlinear least-squares estimation of random effects models are discussed by Ke and Wang (2001).

To fix ideas suppose we have m repeated measurements on each of n subjects without any covariates. We adopt the quantile regression model

$$Q_i(t) = \beta(\tau) + \alpha_i(\tau).$$

The model purports to decompose the quantile functions of the n subjects into two components: one a common population quantile function and the other an idiosyncratic component for each subject. Clearly, without some further normalization, the model is unidentified. There is a variety of normalizations that could be imposed. Provisionally, suppose that we impose the condition that

$$\sum_{i=1}^{n} \alpha_i(\tau) = 0 \qquad \tau \in (0, 1),$$

so that, "on average" (across subjects), the idiosyncratic component vanishes. The model can be estimated locally for any $\tau \in (0, 1)$ by solving

$$\min \sum_{i=1}^{n} \sum_{j=1}^{m} \rho_\tau(y_{ij} - \alpha_i - \beta) + \lambda \sum_{i=1}^{n} |\alpha_i|.$$

For λ near zero, $\hat{\alpha}_i(\tau) + \hat{\beta}(\tau)$ is near the τth sample quantile of the ith subject's observation. For λ sufficiently large, $\hat{\alpha}_i(\tau) \approx 0$, and so $\hat{\beta}(\tau)$ is close to the τth sample quantile of the pooled sample. To choose λ optimally in the simplest case, where α is independent of u and $\alpha \sim \mathcal{N}(0, \sigma_\alpha^2 I)$ and $u \sim \mathcal{N}(0, \sigma_u^2 I)$, we would set $\lambda = \sigma_u/\sigma_\alpha$. In a somewhat more interesting case, suppose $\alpha \sim \mathcal{N}(\alpha_0, \sigma_\alpha^2 I)$; then we might estimate α_0 at the median and then for other quantiles and modify the objective function to

$$\sum_i \sum_j \rho_\tau(y_{ij} - \beta - \alpha_i) + \lambda \sum_i |\alpha_i - \hat{\alpha}_{0i}|,$$

where λ is still simply σ_u/σ_α. In a limiting version of this in which the αs are pure location-shift fixed effects so that $\alpha_i(\tau)$ degenerates to α_{i0}, the optimal $\lambda \to \infty$ and $\beta \to 0$. But this is observable in the sense that we would (eventually) see the degenerate behavior of the subsamples. Note that this may not be immediately obvious; we would need to have sufficient observations to be confident that the only difference among the subject-specific distributions was the location effect α_0 needed to recenter them. Similarly, if the subject-specific distributions differed in both location and scale, then we could eventually recognize this, and perhaps even test for it using the Khmaladze approach or some alternative resampling approach.

8.8 CAUSAL EFFECTS AND STRUCTURAL MODELS

The past decade has seen a vigorous revival of interest in models of causal inference in econometrics and in statistics more generally. The early history of this subject – Working (1927), Frisch (1934), Wright (1934), and Wald (1940) – and the subsequent work of the Cowles Commission focused almost exclusively on estimation and inference about mean effects in linear models. Recent work has begun to explore sources of heterogeneity in causal effects and for this task quantile regression methods offer a natural way forward. Work by Abadie, Angrist, and Imbens (2002) and Chernozhukov and Hansen (2005) has explored instrumental variable methods for estimating endogenous quantile treatment effects. In this section, we briefly consider a quantile regression approach to recursive structural equation models.

8.8.1 Structural Equation Models

The classical linear simultaneous equation model in econometrics takes the form

$$Y_1 = Y_2\alpha + X_1\beta + u_1 \equiv Z_1\gamma + u \tag{8.13}$$

$$Y_2 = X\delta + v, \tag{8.14}$$

where $X = [X_1 \vdots X_2]$. In the usual terminology of econometrics, the variables Y_1 and Y_2 are *endogenous* – that is, determined within the model by the stochastic components u and v and the *exogenous* variables X. The latter are assumed to be independent of, or at least uncorrelated with, u and v. In this simple two-equation form, the crucial identifying feature of the model is the exclusion restriction asserting that the covariates X_2 do not appear in (8.13). A necessary condition for the identification of the structural parameters $\gamma = (\alpha^\top, \beta^\top)^\top$ is that there are at least as many columns of X_2 as there are columns of Y_2. The parameter vector γ is estimable in this model, provided $P_X Z_1$ has full column rank, by the two-stage least-squares estimator

$$\hat{\gamma}_{2\mathrm{SLS}} = \left(Z_1^\top P_X Z_1\right)^{-1} Z_1^\top P_X y,$$

where $P_X = X(X^\top X)^{-1} X^\top$ is the usual least-squares projection matrix. In effect, the assumption that $E X^\top u = 0$ enables us to replace the "endogenous" variables denoted by Y_2 by their projection $\hat{Y}_2 = P_X Y_2$ onto the space spanned by X, and we thus obtain a consistent estimator of γ by least-squares regression of Y_1 on $\hat{Y}_2$ and X_1. Amemiya (1982) and Powell (1983) have considered variants of this approach for estimation of a structural conditional median model.

A somewhat less conventional interpretation of two-stage least-squares estimation reveals that the "endogeneity bias" – the bias exhibited by the ordinary least-squares estimator of γ in (8.13) – can also be viewed as an omitted variable bias. Let

$$R = Y_2 - \hat{Y}_2 = Y_2 - P_X Y_2 \equiv M_X Y_2$$

denote the residuals from the least-squares regression of Y_2 on X, and consider the least-squares estimator of γ in the model

$$Y_1 = Z_1 \gamma + R \xi + \epsilon,$$

that is,

$$\hat{\gamma}_{\mathrm{CV}} = \left(Z_1^\top M_R Z_1\right)^{-1} Z_1^\top M_R Y_1.$$

Here $M_R = I - R(R^\top R)^{-1} R^\top$ and CV stands for control variate. Adding the columns of the matrix R to the structural form of the first equation "corrects" the ordinary least-squares estimator in precisely the same manner that the two-stage least-squares estimator does; that is,

$$\hat{\gamma}_{\mathrm{CV}} = \hat{\gamma}_{2\mathrm{SLS}}.$$

To see this, it suffices to show that $Z_1^\top M_R = Z_1^\top P_X$. But because

$$M_R = I - P_R = I - P_{M_X Y_2},$$

we have

$$X_1^\top M_R = X_1^\top = X_1^\top P_X$$

and also that

$$Y_2^\top M_R = Y_2^\top (I - M_X) = Y_2^\top P_X.$$

Note that Y_2 may be multivariate in this formulation. After discussing this result, Blundell and Powell (2003), citing Dhrymes (1970), comment that it was difficult to locate a definitive early reference to the control function version of two stage least-squares. It seems plausible, however, that it is part of a quite ancient oral tradition in econometrics. Only relatively recently has it been widely recognized as a fruitful approach to more general models of endogeneity.

8.8.2 Chesher's Causal Chain Model

Clearly the classical linear structural model adheres to the location-shift view of covariate effects. What can be done for models with heterogeneity? Chesher (2003) has recently proposed an elegant generalization of the structural model that facilitates the study of heterogeneous structural effects.

Chesher's model may be viewed as an extension of the recursive causal chain models discussed by Strotz and Wold (1960). Imbens and Newey (2002) have also recently stressed the important role of recursive nonlinear structural models. The triangular structure of these models permits one to define structural effects by recursive conditioning, thus focusing on the identification of local quantile effects rather than pure location-shift effects.

A simple bivariate version of the Chesher model takes the form

$$Y = h(S, x, u, v)$$
$$S = g(x, z, v).$$

For the sake of concreteness, we will retain Chesher's interpretation of Y as the logarithm of annual earnings and S as years of education. The vector x denotes individual specific characteristics, and z denotes a vector of "instrumental variables" – covariates that are assumed to influence educational attainment but not directly influence earnings. In the conventional econometric interpretation of this model, there are two sources of randomness: v represents "ability" and is thought to influence both earnings and schooling, whereas u represents luck in the labor market. It is assumed that u and v are independent and that u is independent of (S, x) and v of (x, z). This triangularity of the error structure is essential to the recursive conditioning to be employed. Interest focuses on how schooling influences earnings, but of course one would like to estimate a structural effect while holding the effect of ability constant.

Let $Q_Y(\tau|s, x, z)$ denote the conditional quantile function of Y given the level of schooling $S = s$ and values of the covariates x and z, and let $Q_S(\tau|x, z)$ denote the conditional quantile function of S given x and z. Following Chesher, denote $\nabla_s = \partial/\partial s$ and consider the effect

$$\pi(\tau_1, \tau_2, x, z) = \nabla_s Q_Y(\tau_1|s, x, z) + \frac{\nabla_{z_i} Q_Y(\tau_1|s, x, z)}{\nabla_{z_i} Q_S(\tau_2|x, z)}, \qquad (8.15)$$

evaluating the right-hand side at $s = Q_S(\tau_2|x, z)$. This expression may be viewed as a bias-corrected version of the leading term based on the ratio of effects in the second term. The Chesher formula is most easily seen in the case of the pure location-shift effect model. In this case, one can solve for v in the schooling equation, substitute for it in the wage equation, and then see that the asymptotic bias suffered by estimating the model *conditional on S* can be canceled by adding back the second term. More generally, note that the effect is local in the sense that it depends not only on the earnings quantile τ_1 of interest and on the values of the "exogenous variables" x and z but also on the quantile chosen for the evaluation of Q_S.

8.8.3   Interpretation of Structural Quantile Effects

The structural effect $\pi(\tau_1, \tau_2, x, z)$ corresponds to a thought experiment in which we fix values of x and z and ask the following question: How would the τ_1 quantile of earnings change if we were able to alter the τ_2 conditional quantile of S? This experiment requires us to provisionally suspend belief in the operation of the equation specifying the response of schooling to exogenous forces and to imagine the effect of an exogenous shift in the distribution of schooling.

In their triptych on causal chain systems, Strotz and Wold (1960) illustrate this point with a vivid fresh water example:

> Suppose z is a vector whose various elements are the amounts of various fish feeds (different insects, weeds, etc.) available in a given lake. The reduced form
>
> $$y' = B^{-1}\Gamma z' + B^{-1}u$$
>
> would tell us specifically how the number of fish of any species depends upon the availabilities of different feeds. The coefficient of any z is the partial derivative of a species population with respect to a food supply. It is to be noted, however, that the reduced form tells us nothing about the interactions among the various fish populations – it does not tell us the extent to which one species of fish feeds on another species. Those are the causal relations among the y's.
>
> Suppose, in another situation, we continuously restock the lake with species g, increasing y_g by any desired amount. How will this affect the values of the other y's? If the system were recursive and we had estimates of the elements of B, *we would simply strike the gth equation out of the model and regard y_g, the number of fish of species g, as exogenous* – as a food supply or, when appearing with a negative coefficient as a poison (pp. 421–2, emphasis added).

By averaging over the (x, z)-space we can obtain an average derivative version of this effect, and averaging over the τ arguments yields a variety of more conventional mean effects. For example, integrating out τ_2 enables us to look at the effect of changing the mean value of schooling on the τ_1 quantile of earnings. Integrating out both τ_1 and τ_2 gives the effect of changes in mean schooling on mean earnings. Of course, in the case of the linear pure location-shift version of the structural model, π will be independent of its arguments and the fully averaged effect is exactly what we want. However, when heterogeneity of effects is suspected to be important, a more disaggregated view is desirable. In some circumstances, we may have a form of partial identification restricted to a subset of $(\tau_1, \tau_2) \in (0, 1)$, where the validity of the assumptions hold. Careful thinking about such cases is a useful discipline because it reveals the full force of classical structural equation assumptions. It also encourages a healthy skepticism about the identification of mean effects. When instruments are only effective over a limited quantile range, then mean effects are unidentified unless one makes stringent assumptions about the homogeneity of effects across quantiles (see Chesher, 2004).

8.8.4 Estimation and Inference

We have implicitly assumed, of course, that both endogenous variables, Y and S, as well as the instrumental variable z_i are continuously varying so that the specified derivatives are meaningful. Some progress can also be made with discrete instrumental variables and finite differences as shown by Chesher (2004), but discrete endogenous variables pose more of a challenge. The crucial feature of the identification strategy is the existence of the instrumental variable z_i excluded from the τ_1-conditional quantile function of earnings and having a nonzero effect on the τ_2-conditional quantile function of schooling. There may of course be several such variables and in such "overidentified" situations we will have several available estimates of the effect of interest. These estimates can be reconciled in several ways.

Consider the linear location–scale model:

$$Y_i = \alpha_0 + \alpha_1 S_i + \alpha_2 x_i + S_i(\lambda v_i + u_i) \tag{8.16}$$

$$S_i = \beta_0 + \beta_1 x_i + \beta_2 z_i + v_i. \tag{8.17}$$

Suppose that the pairs (u_i, v_i) are iid and independent of the pairs (x_i, z_i), and that $\lambda > 0$. Given the linear structure, we also need some additional conditions on the "exogenous" variables and errors that ensures that Ss take only positive values. If this is not satisfied, then there are *piecewise* linear quantile functions in this model and, not surprisingly, there will be bias from estimation methods that assume linearity.

Solving for v_i in (8.17), substituting into (8.16), and applying Chesher's formula, we are interested in the "effect":

$$\pi(\tau_1, \tau_2, x, z) = \alpha_1 + \lambda(Q_S(\tau_2|x, z) - \beta_0 - \beta_1 x_i - \beta_2 z_i) - F_u^{-1}(\tau_1), \tag{8.18}$$

or, simplifying,

$$\pi(\tau_1, \tau_2) = \alpha_1 + \lambda F_v^{-1}(\tau_2) + F_u^{-1}(\tau_1). \tag{8.19}$$

The mildly magical aspect of this purported effect arises from the willing suspension of belief in the mechanism specified in (8.17). We are asked to imagine a *gedanken* experiment in which S is manipulated independently of this relation. The model under consideration is intended to be as simple as possible while still allowing $\pi(\tau_1, \tau_2)$ to exhibit a nontrivial dependence on both τ_1 and τ_2. Various other related endogenous effects appearing in the literature – see, for example, Blundell and Powell (2003) and Imbens and Newey (2002) – may be obtained by integrating out τ_1 and/or τ_2 in $\pi(\tau_1, \tau_2)$.

Two estimators of $\pi(\tau_1, \tau_2)$ are considered by Koenker and Ma (2004). The first is based squarely on the Chesher identification strategy: it evaluates (8.15) and then averages over the empirical distribution of the exogenous covariates. This weighted average derivative estimator is shown to be consistent and asymptotically normal under quite mild regularity conditions. A drawback of this approach, especially when the model is overidentified, is that one ends up estimating a highly overparameterized model with many interaction effects that are eventually "averaged out." To control this proliferation of terms, an alternative estimation strategy is suggested based on the "control variate" ideas described earlier.

To briefly describe this control variate approach, consider the location–scale model with conditional quantile functions:

$$Q_{Y_i}(\tau_1 | S_i, x_i, z_i, v_i(\tau_2)) = \alpha_0 + \alpha_1 S_i + \alpha_2 x_i + \alpha_3 S_i v_i(\tau_2) + S_i F_u^{-1}(\tau_1)$$

and

$$Q_{S_i}(\tau_2 | x_i, z_i v_i(\tau_2)) = \beta_0 + \beta_1 x_i + \beta_2 z_i + F_v^{-1}(\tau_2).$$

Estimating

$$\hat{\beta}(\tau_2) = \operatorname{argmin}_\beta \sum_{i=1}^n \rho_{\tau_2}(S_i - \beta_0 - \beta_1 x_i - \beta_2 z_i),$$

we obtain $\hat{v}_i(\tau_2) = S_i - \hat{Q}(\tau_2 | x_i, z_i)$ and compute

$$\hat{\alpha}(\tau_1, \tau_2) = \operatorname{argmin}_\alpha \sum_{i=1}^n \rho_{\tau_1}(Y_i - \alpha_0 - \alpha_1 S_i - \alpha_2 x_i - \alpha_3 S_i \hat{v}_i(\tau_2)).$$

The resulting estimator, $\hat{\alpha}(\tau_1, \tau_2)$ of the structural effect of schooling on wages given by (8.19), is shown to be consistent and asymptotically normal. The following question naturally arises: Can the asymptotic relative efficiency of the two estimators be evaluated? An affirmative answer is provided under an appropriately weighted version of the two estimators and shows that the control variate method has a slight advantage over the weighted average derivative approach. This can be attributed to the advantage obtained by its somewhat more parsimonious parameterization. The linear location–scale form of the model is not essential; asymptotics are derived for a general nonlinear *parametric* form of the Chesher model. The methods are illustrated with an investigation of the effect of class size on the performance of students in Dutch primary schools.

8.9 CHOQUET UTILITY, RISK, AND PESSIMISTIC PORTFOLIOS

Classical mean-variance portfolio theory is built on on a Hobsonian choice: either preferences are taken to be quadratic or asset returns are taken to be Gaussian. Neither alternative is very appealing. Quadratic preferences violate basic precepts of utility theory, and asset returns are commonly observed to exhibit non-Gaussian features. Nevertheless, the mean-variance approach to portfolio selection continues to play a central role in modern finance. One reason for its enduring success is undoubtedly the tractability of the quadratic programming formulation of its decision rules. In the simplest settings without inequality constraints, portfolio weights can be estimated by ordinary least-squares regression methods. Therefore, it is naturally tempting to ask: Can quantile regression methods also play a constructive role in portfolio theory and applications?

This question is as old as quantile regression itself, but a plausible answer has emerged only quite recently. One rationalization for this long gestation period is perhaps the strong disciplinary allegiance to expected utility theory and consequent resistance to its mildly heretical alternatives.

8.9.1 Choquet Expected Utility

Consider the problem of choosing between two lotteries represented as real-valued random variables, X and Y, with distribution functions, F and G, respectively. Suppose that initial wealth, if any, is embodied in the two random variables. Comparing expected utilities, we prefer X to Y if

$$E_F u(X) = \int_{-\infty}^{\infty} u(x) dF(x) > \int_{-\infty}^{\infty} u(x) dG(x) = E_G u(Y).$$

The utility function in this formulation of the theory, u, bears the entire burden of representing the decision makers' attitudes toward risk. Changing variables, we have the equivalent formulation that X is preferred to Y if

$$E_F u(X) = \int_0^1 u(F^{-1}(t)) dt > \int_0^1 u(G^{-1}(t)) dt = E_G u(Y).$$

In effect we have transformed the original integrand into "equally likely" slices on the domain $[0, 1]$, now integrable with respect to Lebesgue measure. Expected utility theory as elaborated by Bernoulli (1738), Ramsey (1931), de Finetti (1937), von Neumann and Morgenstern (1944), Savage (1954), and many other authors is a cornerstone of the modern theory of decision making under uncertainty. And yet there have been persistent doubts expressed about the adequacy of the expected utility framework to encompass the full range of preferences over risky alternatives.

Arguably, the most successful alternative to expected utility theory has been the non-additive, Choquet, or rank-dependent utility formulation of Schmeidler

(1989), Yaari (1987), and Quiggin (1981). Schmeidler argues that the independence axiom underlying the von Neumann–Morgenstern axiomatization "may be too powerful to be acceptable" and proposed a weaker form of independence that applies only to pairwise comonotonic acts.

Recall that random variables X and Y are comonotone if there exists a random variable Z and monotone increasing functions f and g such that $X = f(Z)$ and $Y = G(Z)$ (see Section 2.6). By restricting the applicability of the independence axiom to comonotonic acts, the force of the axiom is considerably weakened. Schmeidler (1986, 1989) shows that the effect is precisely to enlarge the scope of preferences from those representable by a von Neumann–Morgenstern (Savage) utility function, u, to those representable by a pair, (u, v), consisting of a utility function and a Choquet distortion measure. In this framework, X is preferred to Y if

$$E_{v,F}u(X) = \int_0^1 u(F^{-1}(t))dv(t) > \int_0^1 u(G^{-1}(t))dv(t) = E_{v,G}u(Y).$$

(8.20)

Rather than integrating dt we are permitted to integrate $dv(t)$ with respect to some other probability measure on $[0, 1]$. Preferences are represented by a pair of functions (u, v): u transforms monetary outcomes into utility terms, whereas v transforms probability assessments. Because the change of variables has ordered the events $u(F^{-1}(t))$ and $u(G^{-1}(t))$ according to increasing desirability, the distortion v acts to inflate or deflate the probabilities *according to the rank ordering of the outcomes*. In the terminology of Choquet (1954), the distortion measure v is a capacity.

Choquet expected utility leads naturally to an interpretation of the distorting probability measure v as a reflection of optimism or pessimism. If v is concave, so that dv is decreasing, then the least favorable events receive increased weight and the most favorable events are discounted, reflecting pessimism. When v is convex the situation is just reversed: optimism prevails and the Choquet integral exaggerates the likelihood of the more favorable events and downplays the likelihood of the worst outcomes. As noted by Schmeidler (1989), distortion functions that are initially concave and then convex offer an alternative to the classical Friedman and Savage (1979) rationale for the widespread, but still puzzling, observation that many people seem to be willing to buy insurance and gamble at (nearly) the same time.

The simplest distortions are those given by the one parameter family: $v_\alpha(t) = \min\{t/\alpha, 1\}$ for $\alpha \in [0, 1]$. This family plays an important role in the portfolio application. Focusing for a moment on a single v_α, we have

$$E_{v_\alpha}u(X) = \alpha^{-1} \int_0^\alpha u(F^{-1}(t))dt,$$

and we see – relative to the usual computation of expected utility – that the probabilities of the α least favorable outcomes are inflated and the $1 - \alpha$ most favorable outcomes are discounted entirely. Compared to the "worst-case-scenario" outlook of classical maximin decision theory, this does not appear quite so extreme, but clearly it still requires a somewhat schizophrenic view of probability assessments. On the one hand, there are the objective (or subjective) distributions F and G, whereas on the other hand, there are the distorted versions of F and G that are used to compute expectations.

8.9.2   Choquet Risk Assessment

There has been considerable recent interest motivated by regulatory concerns in the financial sector in the related question of how to measure portfolio risk. An influential paper in this literature is that by Artzner, Delbaen, Eber, and Heath (1999), which provides an axiomatic foundation for "coherent" risk measures.

Definition 8.4 (Artzner, Delbaen, Eber, and Heath, 1999). *For real-valued random variables $X \in \mathcal{X}$ on $(\Omega, \mathcal{A})$, a mapping $\varrho : \mathcal{X} \to \mathbb{R}$ is called a coherent risk measure if it is:*

1. *monotone: $X, Y \in \mathcal{X}$, with $X \leq Y \Rightarrow \varrho(X) \geq \varrho(Y)$.*
2. *subadditive: $X, Y, X + Y \in \mathcal{X}, \Rightarrow \varrho(X + Y) \leq \varrho(X) + \varrho(Y)$.*
3. *linearly homogeneous: for all $\lambda \geq 0$ and $X \in \mathcal{X}$, $\varrho(\lambda X) = \lambda \varrho(X)$.*
4. *translation invariant: For all $\lambda \in \mathbb{R}$ and $X \in \mathcal{X}$, $\varrho(\lambda + X) = \varrho(X) - \lambda$.*

These requirements rule out most measures of risk traditionally used in finance. In particular, measures of risk based on second moments including variance and the standard deviation are ruled out by the monotonicity requirement, and quantile-based measures like the popular "value at risk" are ruled out by the subadditivity requirement. A measure of risk that *is* coherent and that has gained considerable recent prominence in the wake of these findings is

$$\varrho_{v_\alpha}(X) = -\int_0^1 F^{-1}(t) dv_\alpha(t) = -\alpha^{-1} \int_0^\alpha F^{-1}(t) dt,$$

where $v_\alpha(t) = \min\{t/\alpha, 1\}$. Variants of $\varrho_{v_\alpha}(X)$ have been suggested under a variety of names including expected shortfall (Acerbi and Tasche, 2002), conditional value at risk (Rockafellar and Uryasev, 2000), and tail-conditional expectation (Artzner, Delbaen, Eber, and Heath, 1999). For the sake of brevity we will call $\varrho_{v_\alpha}(X)$ the α-risk of the random prospect X. Clearly, α-risk is simply the negative Choquet v_α expected return.

Having defined α-risk in this way, it is natural to consider the following criteria: $\varrho_{v_\alpha}(X) - \lambda\mu(X)$ or, alternatively, $\mu(X) - \lambda\varrho_{v_\alpha}(X)$. Minimizing the former criterion may be viewed as minimizing risk subject to a constraint on mean return; maximizing the latter criterion may be viewed as maximizing return subject to a constraint on α-risk. Several authors, including Denneberg (1990), Rockafellar and Uryasev (2000), and Jaschke and Küchler (2001), have suggested criteria of this form as alternatives to the classical Markowitz criteria in which α-risk is replaced by the standard deviation of the random variable X. Since $\mu(X) = \int F_X^{-1}(t)dt = -\varrho_1(X)$, these criteria are special cases of the following more general class.

Definition 8.5. *A risk measure ϱ will be called pessimistic if, for some probability measure φ on $[0, 1]$,*

$$\varrho(X) = \int_0^1 \varrho_{\nu_\alpha}(X)d\varphi(\alpha).$$

To see why such risk measures are pessimistic, note that by the Fubini theorem we can write

$$\varrho(X) = -\int_0^1 \alpha^{-1} \int_0^\alpha F^{-1}(t)dt d\varphi(\alpha) = -\int_0^1 F^{-1}(t) \int_t^1 \alpha^{-1}d\varphi(\alpha)dt.$$

And so, for example, we can take φ as a finite sum of (Dirac) point masses, say, $d\varphi = \sum_{i=0}^m \varphi_i \delta_{\tau_i}$ with $\varphi_i \geq 0$, $\sum \varphi_i = 1$, and $0 = \tau_0 < \tau_1 < \cdots < \tau_m \leq 1$. Noting that

$$\int_t^1 \alpha^{-1}\delta_\tau(\alpha)d\alpha = \tau^{-1}I(t < \tau),$$

we can write

$$\varrho(X) = \int_0^1 \varrho_{\nu_\alpha}(X)d\varphi(\alpha) = -\varphi_0 F^{-1}(0) - \int_0^1 F^{-1}(t)\gamma(t)dt,$$

where $\gamma(t) = \sum_{i=1}^m \varphi_i \tau_i^{-1}I(t < \tau_i)$. If $\varphi_0 > 0$ then there is a contribution from the least favorable (worst-case) scenario. If $m = 1$ and $\tau_1 = 1$ then we are back to expected utility as a special case. Positivity of the point masses, φ_i, assures that the resulting density weights are decreasing, and so the resulting distortion in probabilities acts to accentuate the implicit likelihood of the least favorable outcomes and depress the likelihood of the most favorable ones. Such preferences are clearly "pessimistic."

We may interpret the α-risks, $\varrho_\alpha(\cdot)$, as the extreme points of the convex set of coherent risk measures, and this leads to a nice characterization result.

Theorem 8.2. *A regular risk measure is coherent if and only if it is pessimistic.*

See Bassett, Koenker, and Kordas (2003) for further details.

Example 8.1. A simple class of pessimistic ν functions is the one-parameter family

$$\nu_\theta(t) = 1 - (1 - t)^\theta \qquad \theta \geq 1.$$

Members of the family range from the perfectly equanimous at $\theta = 1$ to the profoundly pessimistic as $\theta \to \infty$. As $\theta \to \infty$, more and more weight is shifted to the least favorable outcome, and Choquet decision making eventually looks like maximin behavior.

Note that, changing variables so that $t = F(u)$, we have

$$E_{\nu_\theta} X = \int_0^1 F^{-1}(t) d\nu(t) = \int_{-\infty}^{\infty} u \, dG(u),$$

where $G(u) = 1 - (1 - F(u))^\theta$. When θ is a positive integer, say m, this Choquet expectation has a nice interpretation: $G(u)$ is the distribution function of the *minimum* of m independent realizations of the random variable X. The pessimist imagines not a single occurrence of X, but m such realizations among which he will get the worst. That favorite maxim of the cautious aunt and misanthropic uncle, "expect the worst, and you won't be disappointed," is transformed into a precise calculus of probabilities. In the process the parameter θ becomes a natural measure of the degree of pessimism.

8.9.3   Pessimistic Portfolios

We have seen that decision making based on minimizing a "coherent" measure of risk as defined by Artzner, Delbaen, Eber, and Heath (1999) is equivalent to Choquet expected utility maximization using a linear form of the utility function and a pessimistic form of the Choquet distortion function. But the question remains: Does the Choquet approach to decision making under uncertainty lead to tractable methods for analyzing complex decision problems of practical importance? Empirical strategies for minimizing α-risk lead immediately to the methods of quantile regression, as the following result shows.

Theorem 8.3. *Let X be a real-valued random variable with $EX = \mu < \infty$, then*

$$\min_{\xi \in \mathbb{R}} E\rho_\alpha(X - \xi) = \alpha(\mu + \varrho_{\nu_\alpha}(X)).$$

Proof. Because

$$E\rho_\alpha(X - \xi) = \alpha(\mu - \xi) - \int_{-\infty}^{\xi} (x - \xi) dF_X(x)$$

is minimized when $\xi_\alpha = F_X^{-1}(\alpha)$, we have

$$E\rho_\alpha(X - \xi_\alpha) = \alpha\mu - \int_0^\alpha F^{-1}(t) dt = \alpha\mu + \alpha\varrho_{\nu_\alpha}(X). \qquad \blacksquare$$

Now consider a portfolio $Y = X^\top \pi$ of assets comprising of $X = (X_1, \ldots, X_p)^\top$ with portfolio weights π. Suppose that we observe a random sample of asset returns $\{x_i = (x_{i1}, \ldots, x_{ip}) : i = 1, \ldots, n\}$ and we wish to choose a portfolio that minimizes

$$\min_{\pi} \varrho_{\nu_\alpha}(Y) - \lambda\mu(Y). \tag{8.21}$$

This is evidently equivalent to minimizing $\varrho_{\nu_\alpha}(Y)$ subject to a constraint on mean return. We will impose the additional constraint that the portfolio weights π sum to one and reformulate the problem as

$$\min_{\pi} \varrho_{\nu_\alpha}(X^\top \pi) \; s.t. \; \mu(X^\top \pi) = \mu_0, \quad 1^\top \pi = 1.$$

Taking the first asset as numeraire we can write the sample analog of this problem as

$$\min_{(\beta,\xi)\in\mathbb{R}^p} \sum_{i=1}^n \rho_\alpha \left(x_{i1} - \sum_{j=2}^p (x_{i1} - x_{ij})\beta_j - \xi \right) \; s.t. \; \bar{x}^\top \pi(\beta) = \mu_0,$$

(8.22)

where $\pi(\beta) = (1 - \sum_{j=2}^p \beta_j, \beta^\top)^\top$. This is a standard quantile regression problem. The mean return constraint can be easily imposed by augmenting the observations representing the initial sum with a single additional observation and assigning it a sufficiently large weight. It is easy to verify that the solution is invariant to the choice of the numeraire asset. At the solution, the intercept parameter $\hat{\xi}$ is an αth sample quantile of the chosen portfolio's (in-sample) returns distribution.

Although the α-risks provide a convenient one-parameter family of coherent risk measures, they are obviously rather simplistic. As has already been suggested, it is natural to consider weighted averages of α-risks,

$$\varrho_\nu(X) = \sum_{k=1}^m \nu_k \varrho_{\nu_{\alpha_k}}(X),$$

as a way to approximate general pessimistic risk measures. The weights, $\nu_k : k = 1, \ldots, m$, should be positive and sum to one. These general risk criteria can also be easily implemented empirically extending the formulation in (8.22) to obtain

$$\min_{(\beta,\xi)\in\mathbb{R}^{p+m}} \sum_{k=1}^m \sum_{i=1}^n \nu_k \rho_\alpha \left(x_{i1} - \sum_{j=2}^p (x_{i1} - x_{ij})\beta_j - \xi_k \right) s.t. \; \bar{x}^\top \pi(\beta) = \mu_0.$$

(8.23)

The only new wrinkle is the appearance of m distinct intercept parameters representing the m estimated quantiles of the returns distribution of the chosen portfolio. In effect we have simply stacked m distinct quantile regression problems on top of one another and introduced a distinct intercept parameter for each of them, while constraining the portfolio weights to be the same for each quantile. Since the ν_k are all positive, they may be passed inside the ρ_α function to rescale the argument. The statistical theory of such constrained quantile regression estimators has been discussed in Section 5.5. Because any pessimistic distortion function can be represented by a piecewise linear concave function generated as a weighted average of α-risks, this approach offers a general solution to the problem of estimating pessimistic portfolio weights.

CHAPTER 9

Conclusion

Much of the early history of social statistics, strongly influenced by Quetelet, can be viewed as a search for the "average man" – that improbable man without qualities who could be comfortable with his feet in the ice chest and his hands in the oven. Some of this obsession can be attributed to the seductive appeal of the Gaussian law of errors. Everyone, as Poincaré famously quipped, believes in the normal law of errors: the theorists because they believe it is an empirical fact, and the empiricists because they believe that it is a mathematical theorem. Once in the grip of this Gaussian faith, it suffices to learn about means. But sufficiency, despite all its mathematical elegance, should be tempered by a skeptical empiricism: a willingness to peer occasionally outside the cathedral of mathematics and see the world in all its diversity.

There have been many prominent statistical voices who, like Galton, reveled in the heterogeneity of statistical life – who resisted proposals to throw the mountains of Switzerland into its lakes. Edgeworth (1920) mocked excessive reliance on "reasoning with the aid of the *gens d'arme's* hat – from which, as from the conjuror's, so much can be extracted." Models for the conditional mean in which independently and identically distributed Gaussian "errors" are tacked on almost as an afterthought are rife throughout the realms of science. They are indispensable approximations in many settings. We have argued that it is sometimes useful to deconstruct these models, complementing the estimation of models for the conditional mean with estimates of a family of conditional quantile functions.

Under the idealized conditions of the textbook linear regression model, this step is quite superfluous. The conditional quantile functions all line up nicely parallel to one another and spaced according to the well-tabulated curve of the *gens d'armes* hat. If, however – and we have seen that this is not unusual – the quantile functions portray a less-regimented picture, then a deeper view into the data is revealed. Conditioning covariates may well shift the location, the central tendency, of the distribution of the response variable, but they may also alter its scale or change its entire shape.

Quantile regression is intended to explore these possibilities. Gradually it is evolving into comprehensive approach to estimation and inference for models of conditional quantile functions. Linear and nonlinear parametric models as well as a variety of nonparametric models have been explored. By supplementing the exclusive focus of least-squares-based methods on estimation and inference about conditional means, quantile regression offers a view beyond the average man – a way to explore the sources of heterogeneity in statistical relationships.

Having struggled with these ideas for nearly 30 years, it is very gratifying to find that they are gradually making their way into empirical applications across a wide range of scientific disciplines. There are still many unsettled questions and much unexplored territory. Completing the regression picture is an ambitious undertaking, one that can only be brought to fruition with the help of many hands. In the summer of 1959, L. J. Savage spoke to the Joint Statistics Seminar of Birkbeck and Imperial Colleges on the application of subjective probability in statistics. Savage's talk and the ensuing discussion constitute a fascinating snapshot of statistical thinking of that time. D. R. Cox (1962) concluded his contribution to the formal discussion by saying:

> A final general comment is that the discussion above is of the question of how to reach conclusions about parameters in a model on which we are agreed. It seems to me, however, that a more important matter is how to formulate more realistic models that will enable scientifically more searching questions to be asked of data. (p. 53)

I would like to think that quantile regression could contribute to this important objective.

Quantile Regression in R: A Vignette

A.1 INTRODUCTION

Beran's (2003) provocative definition of statistics as "the study of algorithms for data analysis" elevates computational considerations to the forefront of the field. It is apparent that the evolutionary success of statistical methods is to a significant degree determined by considerations of computational convenience. As a result, design and dissemination of statistical software has become an integral part of statistical research. Algorithms are no longer the exclusive purview of the numerical analyst or the proto-industrial software firm; they are an essential part of the artisanal research process. Fortunately, modern computing has also transformed the software development process and greatly facilitated collaborative research; the massive collective international effort represented by the R project exceeds the most idealistic Marxist imagination.

Algorithms have been a crucial part of the research challenge of quantile regression methods since their inception in the 18th century. Stigler (1984) describes an amusing episode in 1760 in which the itinerant Croatian Jesuit Rudjer Boscovich sought computational advice in London regarding his nascent method for median regression. Ironically, a fully satisfactory answer to Boscovich's questions only emerged with the dawn of modern computing. The discovery of the simplex method and subsequent developments in linear programming have made quantile regression methods competitive with traditional least-squares methods in terms of their computational effort. These computational developments have also played a critical role in encouraging a deeper appreciation of the statistical advantages of these methods.

Since the early 1980s I have been developing software for quantile regression: initially for the S language of Becker and Chambers (1984), later for its commercial manifestation Splus, and since 1999 for the splendid open source dialect R, initiated by Ihaka and Gentleman (1996) and sustained by the R Development Core Team (2003). Although there is now some functionality for quantile regression in most of the major commercial statistical packages, I have a natural predilection for the R environment and the software that I have developed for R. In what follows, I have tried to provide a brief tutorial introduction to this environment for quantile regression.

A.2 WHAT IS A VIGNETTE?

This Appendix was written in the Sweave format of Leisch (2003). Sweave is an implementation designed for R of the literate programming style advocated by Knuth (1992). The format permits a natural interplay among code written in R, the output of that code, and commentary on the code. Sweave documents are preprocessed by R to produce a LATEX document that may then be processed by conventional methods. Many R packages now have Sweave vignettes describing their basic functionality. Examples of vignettes can be found for many of the R packages including this one for the `quantreg` packages in the source distribution directory `inst/doc`.

A.3 GETTING STARTED

I will not attempt to provide another introduction to R. There are already several excellent resources intended to accomplish this task. The books of Dalgaard (2002) and Venables and Ripley (2002) are particularly recommended. The Comprehensive R Archive Network website link to contributed documentation also offers excellent introductions in several languages.

R is an open source software project and can be freely downloaded from the CRAN website along with its associated documentation. For UNIX-based operating systems it is usual to download and build R from source, but binary versions are available for most computing platforms and can be easily installed. Once R is running, the installation of additional packages is quite straightward. To install the quantile regression package from R one simply types

```
> install.packages("quantreg")
```

Provided that your machine has a proper Internet connection and you have write permission in the appropriate system directories, the installation of the package should proceed automatically. Once the `quantreg` package is installed, it needs to be made accessible to the current R session by the command

```
> library(quantreg)
```

These procedures provide access to an enormous variety of specialized packages for statistical analysis. As we proceed, a variety of other packages will be called upon.

Online help facilities are available in two modalities. If you know precisely what you are looking for, and would simply like to check the details of a particular command, you can, for example, try

```
> help(package = "quantreg")
> help(rq)
```

The former command gives a brief summary of the available commands in the package, and the latter requests more detailed information about a specific command. A convenient shorthand for the latter command is to type simply ?rq. More generally, one can initiate a web browser help session with the command

```
> help.start()
```

and navigate as desired. The browser approach is better adapted to exploratory inquiries, whereas the command line approach is better suited to confirmatory ones.

A valuable feature of R help files is that the examples used to illustrate commands are executable, and so they can be pasted into an R session or run as a group with a command like

```
> example(rq)
```

The examples for the basic rq command include an analysis of the Brownlee stackloss data: first the median regression, then the first quantile regression is computed, then the full quantile regression process. A curious feature of this often-analyzed data set, but one that is very difficult to find without quantile regresion fitting, is the fact the 8 of the 21 points fall exactly on a hyperplane in 4-space.

The second example in the rq help file computes a weighted univariate median using randomly generated data. The original Engel (1857) data on the relationship between food expenditure and household income is considered in the third example. The data are plotted and then six fitted quantile regression lines are superimposed on the scatterplot. The final example illustrates the imposition of inequality constraints on the quantile regression coefficients using a simulated data set.

Let's consider the median regression results for the Engel example in somewhat more detail. Executing

```
> data(engel)
> fit1 <- rq(y ~ x, tau = 0.5, data = engel)
```

assigns the output of the median regression computation to the object fit1. In the command rq() there are also many options. The first argument is a "formula" that specifies the model that is desired. In this case, we wanted to fit a simple bivariate linear model and so the formula is just $y \sim x$; if we had two covariates we could say, for example, $y \sim x+z$. Factor variables – that is, variables taking only a few discrete values – are treated specially by the formula processing and result in a group of indicator (dummy) variables.

If we would like to see a concise summary of the result, we can simply type

```
> fit1
```

```
Call:
rq(formula = y ~ x, tau = 0.5, data = engel)
```

```
Coefficients:
(Intercept)       x
 81.4822474   0.5601806
```

```
Degrees of freedom: 235 total; 233 residual
```

By convention for all the R linear model fitting routines, we see only the estimated coefficients and some information about the model being estimated. To obtain a more detailed evaluation of the fitted model, we can use

```
> summary(fit1)
```

```
Call: rq(formula = y ~ x, tau = 0.5, data = engel)
```

```
tau: [1] 0.5
```

```
Coefficients:
            coefficients lower bd  upper bd
(Intercept)   81.48225     53.25915 114.01156
x              0.56018      0.48702   0.60199
```

The resulting table gives the estimated intercept and slope in the first column and confidence intervals for these parameters in the second and third columns. By default, these confidence intervals are computed by the rank inversion method described in Section 3.5.5. To extract the residuals or the coefficients of the fitted relationship, we can write

```
> r1 <- resid(fit1)
> c1 <- coef(fit1)
```

They can then be easily used in subsequent calculations.

A.4   OBJECT ORIENTATION

A brief digression on the role of object orientation in R is perhaps worthwhile at this juncture. Expressions in R manipulate objects. Objects may be data in the form of vectors, matrices or higher order arrays, but objects may also be functions or more complex collections of objects. Objects have a class and this clsss identifier helps to recognize their special features and enables functions to act on them appropriately. Thus, for example, the function summary when operating on an object of class rq as produced by the function rq can act quite differently on the object than it would if the object were of another class, say, lm, indicating that it was the product of least-squares fitting. Summary of a data structure like a matrix or data frame would have yet another intent and outcome. In the earlier dialects of S and R, methods for various classes were distinguished by appending the class name to the method separated by a period. Thus, the function summary.rq would summarize an rq object, and summary.lm would summarize an lm object. In either case, the main objective of the summary is to produce some inferential evidence to accompany the point estimates of parameters. Likewise, plotting of various classes of R objects can be carried out by the expression plot(x) with the expectation that the plot command will recognize the class of the object x and proceed accordingly. More recently, Chambers (1998) has introduced an elegant elaboration of the class, method-dispatch framework for S and R.

Assignment of objects is usually accomplished by the operator <- and, once assigned, these new objects are available for the duration of the R session or until they are explicitly removed from the session. R is an open source language and so *all* of the source files describing the functionality of the language are ultimately accessible to the individual user, and users are free to modify and extend the functionality of the language in any way they see fit. To accomplish this, one needs to be able to find functions and modify them. This takes us somewhat beyond the intended tutorial scope of this vignette; however, suffice it to say that most of the functions of the quantreg package you will find used in the following can be viewed by simply typing the name of the function perhaps concatenated with a class name.

A.5 FORMAL INFERENCE

There are several alternative methods of conducting inference about quantile regression coefficients. As an alternative to the rank-inversion confidence intervals, one can obtain a more conventional-looking table of coefficients, standard errors, *t*-statistics, and *p*-values using the summary function:

```
> summary(fit1, se = "nid")

Call: rq(formula = y ~ x, tau = 0.5, data = engel)

tau: [1] 0.5

Coefficients:
                Value       Std.   Error t value  Pr(>|t|)
(Intercept) 81.48225   19.25066        4.23270   0.00003
x            0.56018    0.02828       19.81032   0.00000
```

The standard errors reported in this table are computed as described in Section 3.2.3 for the quantile regression sandwich formula, and using the Hall–Sheather bandwidth rule. To obtain the Powell kernel version of the covariance matrix estimate, one specifies the option se="ker" in the summary command. It is also possible to control the bandwidths employed with the bandwidth option. Another option available in summary.rq is to compute bootstrapped standard errors. This is accomplished by specifying the option se="boot". There are currently three flavors of the bootstrap available: the standard (x, y) pair bootstrap, the Parzen, Wei, and Ying (1994) version, and the Markov chain marginal bootstrap of He and Hu (2002) and Kocherginsky, He, and Mu (2004).

There is also the ability to specify m out of n versions of the bootstrap in which the sample size of the bootstrap samples is different from (typically smaller than) the original sample size. This "subsampling" approach has a number of advantages, not the least of which is that it can be considerably faster than the full n out of n version. By default, summary also produces components estimating the full covariance matrix of the estimated parameters and its constituent pieces. For further details, see the documentation for summary.rq. In the case of the bootstrap methods, the full matrix of bootstrap replications is also available.

There are several options to the basic fitting routine rq. An important option that controls the choice of the algorithm used in the fitting is method. The default is method = "br", which invokes a variant of the Barrodale and Roberts (1974) simplex algorithm described by Koenker and d'Orey (1987). For problems with more than a few thousand observations, it is worthwhile to consider method = "fn", which invokes the Frisch–Newton algorithm described by Portnoy and Koenker (1997). Rather than traversing around the exterior of the constraint set like the simplex method, the interior point approach embodied in the Frisch–Newton algorithm burrows from within the constraint set toward the exterior. Instead of taking steepest descent steps at each intersection of exterior edges, it takes Newton steps based on a log-barrier Lagrangian form of the objective function. Special forms of Frisch–Newton are available for problems that include linear inequality constraints and for problems with sparse design matrices. For extremely large problems with plausibly exchangeable observations, method = "pfn" implements a version of the Frisch–Newton algorithm with a preprocessing step that can further speed things up considerably.

In problems of moderate size where the default simplex option is quite practical, the parametric programming approach to finding the rank inversion confidence intervals can be rather slow. In such cases it may be advantageous to try one of the other inference methods based on estimation of the asymptotic covariance matrix or to consider the bootstrap. Both approaches are described in more detail following.

To provide a somewhat more elaborate visualization of the Engel example, consider an example that superimposes several estimated conditional quantile functions on the Engel data scatterplot. In the resulting Figure A.1, the median regression line appears as a solid line and the least-squares line as a dashed line. The other quantile regression lines appear in gray. Note that the plotting of the fitted lines is easily accomplished by the convention that the command abline looks for a pair of coefficients which, if found, are treated as the slope and intercept of the plotted line. There are many options that can be used to further fine-tune the plot. Looping over the quantiles is also conveniently handled by R's for syntax.

Often it is useful to compute quantile regressions on a discrete set of τs; this can be accomplished by specifying tau as a vector in rq:

```
> xx <- x - mean(x)
> fit1 <- summary(rq(y ~ xx, tau = 2:98/100))
```

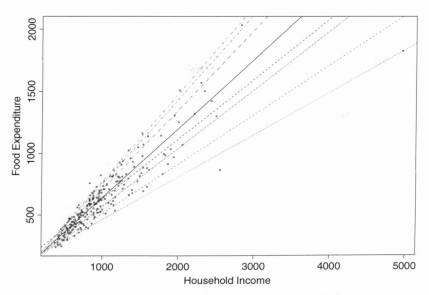

Figure A.1. Scatterplot and quantile regression fit of the Engel food expenditure data. The plot shows a scatterplot of the Engel data on food expenditure vs. household income for a sample of 235 19th century working-class Belgian households. Superimposed on the plot are the {0.05, 0.1, 0.25, 0.75, 0.90, 0.95} quantile regression lines in gray, the median fit in solid black, and the least-squares estimate of the conditional mean function as the dashed line.

```
> library(quantreg)
> data(engel)
> attach(engel)
> plot(x, y, cex = 0.25, type = "n", xlab =
    "Household Income", +   ylab = "Food Expenditure")
> points(x, y, cex = 0.5, col = "blue")
> abline(rq(y ~ x, tau = 0.5), col = "blue")
> abline(lm(y ~ x), lty = 2, col = "red")
> taus <- c(0.05, 0.1, 0.25, 0.75, 0.9, 0.95)
> for (i in 1:length(taus)) {
+   abline(rq(y ~ x, tau = taus[i]), col = "gray")
+ }
> fit2 <- summary(rq(y ~ x, tau = c(0.05, 0.25,
+   0.5, 0.75, 0.95)))
```

The results can be summarized as a plot:

```
> postscript("engelcoef.ps", horizontal = FALSE,
+   width = 6.5, height = 3.5)
> plot(fit1, nrow = 1, ncol = 2)
> dev.off()
```

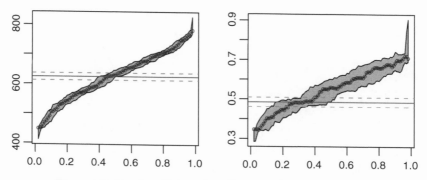

Figure A.2. Engel coefficient plots. The slope and intercept of the estimated linear quantile regression function for the Engel food expenditure data are plotted as a function of τ. Note that the household income variable has been centered at its mean value for this plot, and so the intercept is really a centercept and estimates the quantile function of food expenditure conditional on mean income.

or by producing a LaTex-formatted table.

```
> latex(fit2, caption = "Engel's Law", transpose = TRUE)
```

The `postscript` command preceding the plot tells R that instructions for the plotting should be written in encapsulated postscript format and placed in the file `engelcoef.ps`. Such files are then conveniently included in LaTeX documents, for example. The `dev.off()` command closes the current postscript device and concludes the figure. The horizontal lines in the coefficient plots of Figure A.2 represent the least-squares fit and its associated confidence interval.

In the one-sample setting, we know that integrating the quantile function over the entire domain [0,1] yields the mean of the (sample) distribution:

$$\mu = \int_{-\infty}^{\infty} x \, dF(x) = \int_{0}^{1} F^{-1}(t) dt.$$

Similarly, in the coefficient plots we may expect to see that integrating individual coefficients yields roughly mean effect as estimated by the associated least-squares coefficient. One should be cautious, however, about this interpretation in very heterogeneous situations. For the Engel data, note that the least-squares intercept is significantly above any of the fitted quantile regression curves in our initial scatterplot. The least-squares fit is strongly affected by the two outlying observations with relatively low food expenditure; their attraction tilts the fitted line so that its intercept is drawn upward. In fact, the intercept for the Engel model is difficult to interpret because it asks us to consider food expenditure for households with zero income. Centering the covariate

Table A.1. *Engels's law*

Quantiles	(Intercept)	x
0.05	124.880 (98.302,130.517)	0.343 (0.343,0.390)
0.25	95.484 (73.786,120.098)	0.474 (0.420,0.494)
0.50	81.482 (53.259,114.012)	0.560 (0.487,0.602)
0.75	62.397 (32.745,107.314)	0.644 (0.580,0.690)
0.95	64.104 (46.265,83.579)	0.709 (0.674,0.734)

observations so that they have mean zero, as we have done prior to computing `fit1` for the coefficient plot, restores a reasonable interpretation of the intercept parameter. After centering, the least-squares estimate of the intercept is a prediction of mean food expenditure for a household with mean income, and the quantile regression intercept $\hat{\alpha}(\tau)$ is a prediction of the τth quantile of food expenditure for households with mean income. In the terminology of Tukey, the "intercept" has become a "centercept." (see Table A.1).

The `latex` command produces a LATEX -formatted table that can be easily included in documents. In many instances, the plotted form of the results will provide a more economical and informative display. It should again be stressed that because the quantile regression functions and indeed all of R is open source, users can always modify the available functions to achieve special effects required for a particular application. When such modifications appear to be of general applicability, it is desirable to communicate them to the package author so that they could be shared with the larger community.

If we want to see *all* the distinct quantile regression solutions for a particular model application, we can specify a τ outside the range [0,1]; for example,

```
> z <- rq(y ~ x, tau = -1)
```

This form of the function carries out the parametric programming steps required to find the entire sample path of the quantile regression process. The returned object is of class `rq.process` and has several components: the primal solution in `z$sol`, and the dual solution in `z$dsol`. In interactive mode, typing the name of an R object causes the program to print the object in some reasonably intelligible manner determined by the print method designated for the object's class. Again, plotting is often a more informative means of display and so there is a special `plot` method for objects of class `rq.process`.

Estimating the conditional quantile functions of y at a specific values of x is also quite easy. In the following code, we plot the estimated empirical

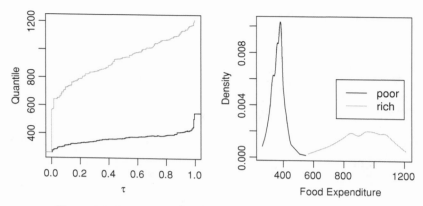

Figure A.3. Estimated conditional quantile and density functions for food expenditure based on the Engel data. Two estimates are presented, one for relatively poor households, with income of 504.5 Belgian francs, and the other for relatively affluent households, with 1538.99 Belgian francs.

quantile functions of food expenditure for households that are at the 10th and 90th percentiles of the sample income distribution (see Figure A.3). In the right panel we plot corresponding density estimates for the two groups. The density estimates employ the adaptive kernel method proposed by Silverman (1986) and implemented in the quantreg function akj. This function is particularly convenient because it permits unequal mass to be associated with the observations such as those produced by the quantile regression process.

Thus far we have only considered Engel functions that are linear in form, and the scatterplot as well as the formal testing has revealed a strong tendency for the dispersion of food expenditure to increase with household income. This is a particularly common form of heteroscedasticity. If one looks more carefully at the fitting, one sees interesting departures from symmetry that would not be likely to be revealed by the typical textbook testing for heteroscedasticity. One common remedy for symptoms like these would be to reformulate the model in log-linear terms. It is interesting to compare what happens after the log transformation with what we have already seen.

```
> x.poor <- quantile(x, 0.1)
> x.rich <- quantile(x, 0.9)
> ps <- z$sol[1, ]
> qs.poor <- c(c(1, x.poor) %*% z$sol[4:5, ])
> qs.rich <- c(c(1, x.rich) %*% z$sol[4:5, ])
> par(mfrow = c(1, 2))
> plot(c(ps, ps), c(qs.poor, qs.rich), type = "n",
+    xlab = expression(tau), ylab = "quantile")
> plot(stepfun(ps, c(qs.poor[1], qs.poor)),
   do.points = FALSE, +   add = TRUE)
```

```
> plot(stepfun(ps, c(qs.poor[1], qs.rich)),
    do.points = FALSE, +    add = TRUE,
    col.hor = "gray", col.vert = "gray")
> ap <- akj(qs.poor, qs.poor, diff(ps))
> ar <- akj(qs.rich, qs.rich, diff(ps))
> plot(c(qs.poor, qs.rich), c(ap$dens, ar$dens),
+    type = "n", xlab = "Food Expenditure", ylab = "Density")
> lines(qs.rich, ar$dens, col = "gray")
> lines(qs.poor, ap$dens, col = "black")
> legend(750, 0.006, c("poor", "rich"), lty = c(1,
+    1), col = c("black", "gray"))
> plot(x, y, log = "xy", xlab = "Household Income",
+    ylab = "Food Expenditure")
> taus <- c(0.05, 0.1, 0.25, 0.75, 0.9, 0.95)
> abline(rq(log10(y) ~ log10(x), tau = 0.5), col = "blue")
> abline(lm(log10(y) ~ log10(x)), lty = 3, col = "red")
> for (i in 1:length(taus)) {
+    abline(rq(log10(y) ~ log10(x), tau = taus[i]),
+       col = "gray")
+ }
```

Note that the flag `log="xy"` produces a plot in Figure A.4 with log-log axes, and for convenience of axis labeling these logarithms are base 10, and so the subsequent fitting is also specified as base 10 logs for plotting purposes, even though base 10 logarithms are *unnatural* and would never be used in reporting numerical results. This looks much more like a classical iid error regression model, although again some departure from symmetry is visible. An interesting exercise would be to conduct some formal testing for departures from the iid assumption of the type considered earlier.

A.6   MORE ON TESTING

Now let's consider some other forms of formal testing. A natural first question is this: Do the estimated quantile regression relationships conform to the location-shift hypothesis that assumes that all of the conditional quantile functions have the same slope parameters? To begin, suppose we just estimate the quartile fits for the Engel data and look at the default output:

```
> fit1 <- rq(y ~ x, tau = 0.25)
> fit2 <- rq(y ~ x, tau = 0.5)
> fit3 <- rq(y ~ x, tau = 0.75)
```

Recall that rq just produces coefficient estimates and `summary` is needed to evaluate the precision of the estimates. This is fine for judging whether covariates are significant at particular quantiles, but suppose that we wanted to test that the slopes were the same at the three quartiles? This is done with the

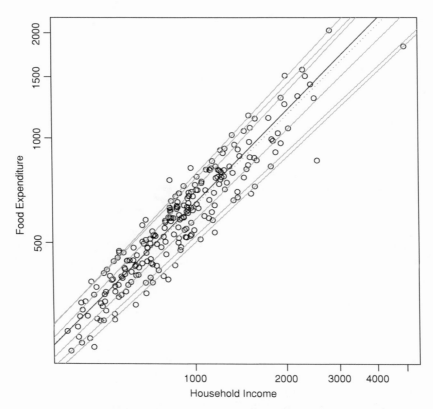

Figure A.4. Quantile regression estimates for a log-linear version of the Engel food expenditure model.

anova command as follows:

```
> anova(fit1, fit2, fit3)

Quantile Regression Analysis of Variance Table

Model: y ~ x
Test of Equality of Slopes: tau in { 0.25 0.5 0.75 }

   Df Resid Df F value   Pr(>F)
1  2    701 15.557 2.452e-07 ***
---
Signif. codes: 0 '***' 0.001 '**' 0.01 '*' 0.05 '.' 0.1 ' ' 1
```

This is an example of a general class of tests proposed by Koenker and Bassett (1982a). It may be instructive to look at the code for the command anova.rq to see how this test is carried out. The Wald approach is used and the asymptotic covariance matrix is estimated using the approach of Hendricks and Koenker (1991). It also illustrates a general syntax for testing in R adapted to the present situation.

If you have estimated two models with different covariate specifications, but the same τ, then anova(f0,f1) should test whether the more restricted model is correct. Note that this assumes that they are nested, with fits, say, f0 and f1. One needs to be careful, however, to check that the hypothesis that is intended is really the one that the anova command understands (see ?anova.rq for further details on the quantile regression version of this). A variety of other options are described in the documentation of the function anova.rq.

A.7 INFERENCE ON THE QUANTILE REGRESSION PROCESS

In least-squares estimation of linear models, it is implicitly assumed that we are able to model the effects of the covariates as a pure location shift, or somewhat more generally as a location–scale shift of the response distribution. In the simplest case of a single binary treatment effect, this amounts to assuming that the treatment and control distributions differ by a location shift or a location–scale shift. Tests of these hypotheses in the two-sample model can be conducted using the conventional two-sample Kolmogorov–Smirnov statistic, but the appearance of unknown nuisance parameters greatly complicates the limiting distribution theory. Similar problems persist in the extension of these tests to the general quantile regression setting. Using an approach introduced by Khmaladze (1981), Koenker and Xiao (2002) consider general forms of such tests. The tests can be viewed as a generalization of the simple tests of equality of slopes across quantiles described in the previous section.

In this section we briefly describe how to implement these tests in R. The application considered is the Pennsylvania reemployment bonus experiment described in Section 3.8. As Koenker and Xiao (2002), we use only the observations for the control and pooled treatment groups 4 and 6. The primary objective of the analysis is to explore the effect of a bonus payment for early reemployment on the duration of unemployment spells. The model includes indicator variables for several characteristics of the participants, and fixed effects for the quarter of enrollment in an effort to control for local labor market conditions.

To carry out the test we need to first compute the quantile regression process of the model on a moderately fine grid of taus:

```
> source("bonus/penn46.R")
> taus <- seq(0.2, 0.8, 0.002)
> formula <- log(dur) ~ treatment + female + black +
+    hispanic + ndependents + factor(quarter) +
+    recall + young + old + durable + lusd
> K <- rqProcess(formula, taus = taus, data = penn46)
```

```
> save(K, file = "K.rda")
```

This step is somewhat computationally intensive and so we save the result for future reference in the form of an R dataset. The location–scale form of the test is then conducted by the following code:

```
> load("K.rda")
> Ktest <- khmaladze.test(K)
```

The function khmaladze.test computes both a joint test that *all* the covariate effects satisfy the null hypothesis, and a coefficient-by-coefficient version of the test. In this case, the former component, Ktest$Tn, is 122.44. This test has a 1% critical value of 16.00, and so the test strongly rejects the null. The value of the joint test statistic is slightly larger than the value of 112.23 originally reported in the published paper due to an unfortunate programming error. The test statistics for the individual covariate effects are as published; for example, the test that the treatment effect is a pure location–scale shift yields 5.41.

The pure location-shift version of the test is obtained by adding the argument nullH = "location" to the invocation of the khmaladze.test command. The joint test of the null hypothesis of a pure location-shift yields a test statistic of 380.01, firmly rejecting the location shift model.

A.8   NONLINEAR QUANTILE REGRESSION

Quantile regression models with response functions that are nonlinear in parameters can be estimated with the function nlrq. For such models, the specification of the model formula is somewhat more esoteric than for ordinary linear models but follows the conventions of the R command nls for nonlinear least squares estimation.

To illustrate the use of nlrq, consider the problem of estimating the quantile functions of the Frank copula model introduced in Section 8.4. We begin by setting some parameters and generating data from the Frank model:

```
> n <- 1000
> df <- 8
> delta <- 8
> x <- sort(rt(n, df))
> u <- runif(n)
> v <- -log(1 - (1 - exp(-delta))/(1 + exp(-delta *
+    pt(x, df)) * ((1/u) - 1)))/delta
> y <- qt(v, df)
```

We plot the observations in Figure A.5, superimpose three conditional quantile functions, and then estimate the same three quantile functions and plot their estimated curves as the dashed curves:

```
> plot(x, y, pch = ".", col = "blue", cex = 3)
> us <- c(0.25, 0.5, 0.75)
```

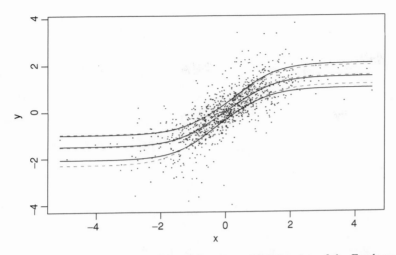

Figure A.5. Nonlinear conditional quantile estimation of the Frank copula model. The solid curves are the true conditional quantile functions and the corresponding estimated curves are indicated by dashed curves.

```
> for (i in 1:length(us)) {
+   u <- us[i]
+   v <- -log(1 - (1 - exp(-delta))/(1 + exp(-delta *
+     pt(x, df)) * ((1/u) - 1)))/delta
+   lines(x, qt(v, df))
+ }
> Dat <- NULL
> Dat$x <- x
> Dat$y <- y
> deltas <- matrix(0, 3, length(us))
> FrankModel <- function(x, delta, mu, sigma, df,
+   tau) {
+   z <- qt(-log(1 - (1 - exp(-delta))/(1 + exp(-delta *
+     pt(x, df)) * ((1/tau) - 1)))/delta, df)
+   mu + sigma * z
+ }
> for (i in 1:length(us)) {
+   tau = us[i]
+   fit <- nlrq(y ~ FrankModel(x, delta, mu, sigma,
+     df = 8, tau = tau), data = Dat, tau = tau,
+     start = list(delta = 5, mu = 0, sigma = 1),
+     trace = TRUE)
+   lines(x, predict(fit, newdata = x), lty = 2,
+     col = "green")
```

```
+    deltas[i, ] <- coef(fit)
+ }
```

A.9 NONPARAMETRIC QUANTILE REGRESSION

Nonparametric quantile regression is initially most easily considered within a locally polynomial framework. Locally linear fitting is carried out by the following function:

```
> "lprq" <- function(x, y, h, m = 50, tau = 0.5) {
+    xx <- seq(min(x), max(x), length = m)
+    fv <- xx
+    dv <- xx
+    for (i in 1:length(xx)) {
+       z <- x - xx[i]
+       wx <- dnorm(z/h)
+       r <- rq(y ~ z, weights = wx, tau = tau,
+         ci = FALSE)
+       fv[i] <- r$coef[1]
+       dv[i] <- r$coef[2]
+    }
+    list(xx = xx, fv = fv, dv = dv)
+ }
```

If you study the function a bit you will see that it is simply a matter of computing a quantile regression fit at each of m equally spaced x values distributed over the support of the observed x points. The function value estimates are returned as fv and the first derivative estimates at the m points are returned as dv. As usual you can specify τ, but now you also need to specify a bandwidth h.

Let's begin by exploring the effect of the h argument for fitting the motorcycle data. Figure A.6 illustrates four estimates of the median acceleration curve produced by the code:

```
> library(MASS)
> data(mcycle)
> attach(mcycle)
> plot(times, accel, xlab = "milliseconds",
    ylab = "acceleration")
> hs <- c(1, 2, 3, 4)
> for (i in hs) {
+    h = hs[i]
+    fit <- lprq(times, accel, h = h, tau = 0.5)
+    lines(fit$xx, fit$fv, lty = i)
+ }
> legend(45, -70, c("h=1", "h=2", "h=3", "h=4"),
+    lty = 1:length(hs))
```

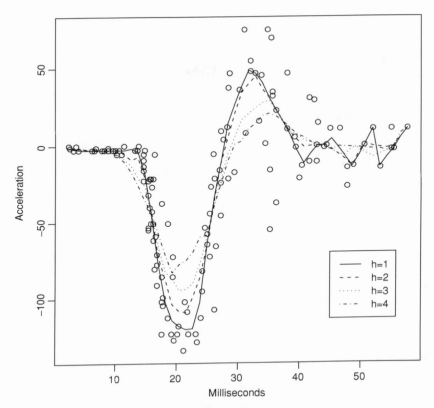

Figure A.6. Estimation of a locally linear median regression model for the motorcycle data: four distinct bandwidths.

Fitting derivatives, of course, requires somewhat larger bandwidth and larger sample size to achieve the same precision as function fitting. It is a straightforward exercise to adapt the function `lprq` so that it does locally quadratic rather than locally linear fitting.

Another simple, yet quite general, strategy for nonparametric quantile regression uses regression splines. The function `bs()` in the package `splines` gives a very flexible way to construct B-spline basis expansions. For example, you can fit a new motorcycle model like this:

```
> library(splines)
> plot(times, accel, xlab = "milliseconds",
+   ylab = "acceleration",   type = "n")
> points(times, accel, cex = 0.75)
> X <- model.matrix(accel ~ bs(times, df = 15))
> for (tau in 1:3/4) {
```

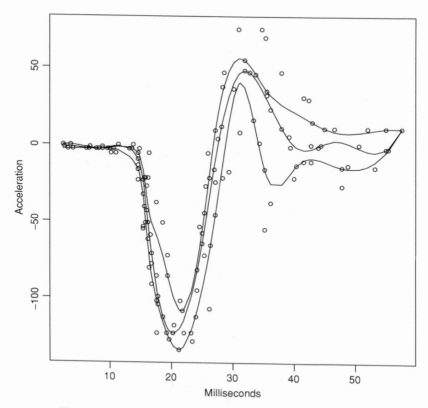

Figure A.7. B-spline estimates of the three conditional quartile functions of the motorcycle data.

```
+    fit <- rq(accel ~ bs(times, df = 15), tau = tau,
+      data = mcycle)
+    accel.fit <- X %*% fit$coef
+    lines(times, accel.fit)
+ }
```

The fitted conditional quantile functions in Figure A.7 do reasonably well except in the region beyond 50 milliseconds, where the data are so sparse that all the quantile curves want to coalesce.

This procedure fits a piecewise cubic polynomial with 15 knots (breakpoints in the third derivative) arranged at quantiles of the xs. (You can also explicitly specify the knot sequence and the order of the spline using the arguments optional to bs.) In this instance, we have estimated three quartile curves for the B-spline model; a salient feature of this example is the quite dramatic variability over the time scale. There is essentially no variability for the first few milliseconds, but quite substantial variability after the crash. One advantage of the B-spline approach is that it is very easy to add a partially linear model component. If there were another covariate, say z, it could be added as a parametric component using the usual `formula` syntax:

```
> fit <- rq(y ~ bs(x, df = 5) + z, tau = 0.33)
```

Another appealing approach to nonparametric smoothing involves penalty methods. Koenker, Ng, and Portnoy (1994) describe total variation penalty methods for fitting univariate functions; Koenker and Mizera (2004) extend the approach to bivariate function estimation. Again, partially linear models are easily adapted, and there are also easy ways to impose monotonicity and convexity on the fitted functions. In some applications it is desirable to consider models that involve nonparametric fitting with several covariates. A tractable approach that has been explored by many authors is to build additive models. This approach is available in R for least-squares fitting of smoothing spline components in the `mgcv` and `gss` packages. A prototype method for quantile regression models of this type is available using the `rqss` function of the `quantreg` package.

The function `rqss` offers a formula interface to nonparametric quantile regression fitting with total variation roughness penalties. Consider the running-speed-of-mammals example from Chapter 7. The objective is to estimate a model for the upper envelope of the scatterplot: a model that would reflect best evolutionary practice in mammalian ambulatory efficiency. In contrast to the least-squares analysis of Chappell (1989), where they are omitted, no special allowance is made for the "specials" indicated by the plotting character s or "hoppers" indicated by h. The data are plotted in Figure A.8 on a (natural) log scale, the model is fit using $\lambda = 1$ as the penalty parameter, and the fitted curve is plotted using a special plotting function that understands the structure of the objects returned from `rqss`. The estimated turning point of the piecewise linear fitted function occurs at a weight of about 40 kg.

```
> data(Mammals)
> attach(Mammals)
> x <- log(weight)
> y <- log(speed)
> plot(x, y, xlab = "Weight in log(Kg)",
+   ylab = "Speed in log(Km/hour)",   type = "n")
> points(x[hoppers], y[hoppers], pch = "h", col = "red")
> points(x[specials], y[specials], pch = "s", col = "blue")
> others <- (!hoppers & !specials)
> points(x[others], y[others], col = "black", cex = 0.75)
> fit <- rqss(y ~ qss(x, lambda = 1), tau = 0.9)
> plot(fit)
```

Bivariate nonparametric fitting using the triogram methods described in Chapter 7 can be handled in a similar manner. Consider the Cobar mining

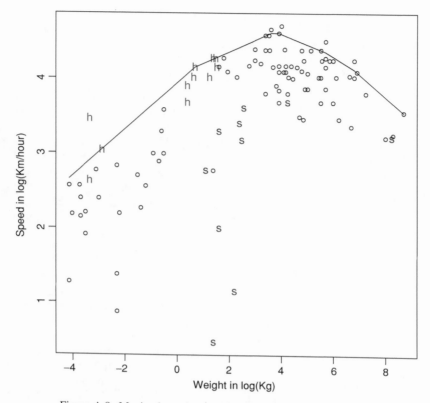

Figure A.8. Maximal running speed of terrestial mammals. The figure illustrates the relationship between adult body mass and maximal running speed for 107 species of terrestial mammals. The piecewise linear curve is an estimate of the 0.90 conditional quantile function estimated subject to a constraint on the total variation of the function gradient.

data from Green and Silverman (1994):

```
> data(CobarOre)
> fit <- rqss(z ~ qss(cbind(x, y), lambda = 0.01,
+    ndum = 100), data = CobarOre)

Loading required package: tripack

> plot(fit, axes = FALSE, xlab = "", ylab = "")

Loading required package: akima
```

The qss term in this case requires both x and y components. In addition, one needs to specify a smoothing parameter λ, and the parameter ndum may be used to specify the number of artificial vertices introduced into the fitting procedure

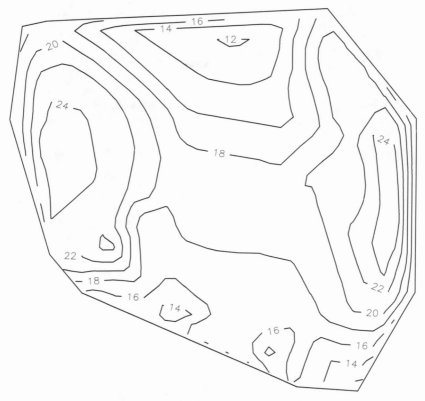

Figure A.9. Contour plot of a triogram fit of the Cobar mining data.

in addition to the actual observations. These artificial vertices contribute to the penalty term but not to the fidelity.

By default the fit is rendered as a contour plot, but there are also two forms of perspective plots. A conventional R persp plot can be obtained by passing option render = "persp" to the plot command. More adventurous R-gonauts are encouraged to explore the option render = "rgl", which produces a perspective plot in the dynamic graphics interface to the open GL library provided by the package rgl. Of course this package must be installed. A demonstration of how to create animations of rqss triogram output using rgl is available by running the command demo(cobar).

Another advantage of the penalty approach embodied in rqss is that it is straightforward to impose additional qualitative constraints on the fitted functions. Univariate functions can be constrained to be monotone and/or convex or concave. Bivariate functions can be constrained to be either convex or concave. This functionality is implemented by simply imposing nonnegativity constraints on certain linear combinations of model parameters and illustrates one of many possible applications for such constraints. An interesting open research problem involves formal inference on such constraints.

A.10   CONCLUSION

A few of the capabilities of the R quantreg package have been described. Inevitably, new applications will demand new features and reveal old bugs. In either case I hope that users will send their comments and suggestions to me. This document will be periodically updated and the current version will be made available in the R distribution of quantreg. See the R command vignette() for details on how to find and view vignettes with R.

Asymptotic Critical Values

This appendix provides critical values for the tests described in Section 3.8 of the location-shift and location–scale-shift models based on the Khmaladze approach. Like many other Kolmogorov–Smirnov-type tests (see, e.g., Andrews, 1993), the limiting distribution $\sup_{\tau \in \mathcal{T}} \|w_0(\tau)\|$ is dependent on the norm $\| \cdot \|$, the prespecified $\mathcal{T}$, and the dimension parameter q. Notice that the transformation is generally unstable in the extreme right tails, and the uniform convergence of existing estimators of the density and score ($f(F^{-1}(s))$ and $f'/f(F^{-1}(s))$) requires that $\mathcal{T}$ be bounded away from zero and one; we consider a subset of $[0, 1]$ whose closure lies in $(0, 1)$.

We calculated the 1, 5, and 10% critical values for the test statistic $\sup_{\tau \in \mathcal{T}} \|\tilde{v}_n(\tau)\|$ based on simulations where the Brownian motion was approximated by a Gaussian random walk, using a sample size $n = 2000$ and 20,000 replications. For the norm $\|\cdot\|$, we use the ℓ_1 norm for a q-dimensional vector x, $\|x\| = \sum_{j=1}^{q} |x_j|$. Tables B.1 and B.2 covers $\mathcal{T} = [\varepsilon, 1 - \varepsilon]$ for $\varepsilon = 0.05, 0.1, 0.15, 0.2, 0.25, 0.3$, and $q = 1, 2, \ldots, 20$. Although conventionally we consider symmetric intervals $\mathcal{T} = [\varepsilon, 1 - \varepsilon]$ for some small numbers ε, a much wider range of intervals $\mathcal{T}$ may be considered for the proposed tests. Critical values based other choices of the interval $\mathcal{T}$ and the dimension parameter q can be similarly calculated. These tables appeared originally as an electronic appendix to Koenker and Xiao (2002).

Table B.1. *Asymptotic critical values of the K_n statistic of Section 3.8*

	$\varepsilon = 0.05$			$\varepsilon = 0.1$			$\varepsilon = 0.15$		
p	1%	5%	10%	1%	5%	10%	1%	5%	10%
1	2.721	2.140	1.872	2.640	2.102	1.833	2.573	2.048	1.772
2	4.119	3.393	3.011	4.034	3.287	2.946	3.908	3.199	2.866
3	5.350	4.523	4.091	5.267	4.384	3.984	5.074	4.269	3.871
4	6.548	5.560	5.104	6.340	5.430	4.971	6.148	5.284	4.838
5	7.644	6.642	6.089	7.421	6.465	5.931	7.247	6.264	5.758
6	8.736	7.624	7.047	8.559	7.412	6.852	8.355	7.197	6.673
7	9.876	8.578	7.950	9.573	8.368	7.770	9.335	8.125	7.536
8	10.79	9.552	8.890	10.53	9.287	8.662	10.35	9.044	8.412
9	11.81	10.53	9.820	11.55	10.26	9.571	11.22	9.963	9.303
10	12.91	11.46	10.72	12.54	11.17	10.43	12.19	10.85	10.14
11	14.03	12.41	11.59	13.58	12.10	11.29	13.27	11.77	10.98
12	15.00	13.34	12.52	14.65	13.00	12.20	14.26	12.61	11.86
13	15.93	14.32	13.37	15.59	13.90	13.03	15.22	13.48	12.69
14	16.92	15.14	14.28	16.52	14.73	13.89	16.12	14.34	13.48
15	17.93	16.11	15.19	17.53	15.67	14.76	17.01	15.24	14.36
16	18.85	16.98	16.06	18.46	16.56	15.65	17.88	16.06	15.22
17	19.68	17.90	16.97	19.24	17.44	16.53	18.78	16.93	16.02
18	20.63	18.83	17.84	20.21	18.32	17.38	19.70	17.80	16.86
19	21.59	19.72	18.73	21.06	19.24	18.24	20.53	18.68	17.70
20	22.54	20.58	19.62	22.02	20.11	19.11	21.42	19.52	18.52

Table B.2. *Asymptotic critical values of the K_n statistic of Section 3.8*

	$\varepsilon = 0.2$			$\varepsilon = 0.25$			$\varepsilon = 0.3$		
p	1%	5%	10%	1%	5%	10%	1%	5%	10%
1	2.483	1.986	1.730	2.420	1.923	1.664	2.320	1.849	1.602
2	3.742	3.100	2.781	3.633	3.000	2.693	3.529	2.904	2.602
3	4.893	4.133	3.749	4.737	4.018	3.632	4.599	3.883	3.529
4	6.023	5.091	4.684	5.818	4.948	4.525	5.599	4.807	4.365
5	6.985	6.070	5.594	6.791	5.853	5.406	6.577	5.654	5.217
6	8.147	6.985	6.464	7.922	6.760	6.241	7.579	6.539	6.024
7	9.094	7.887	7.299	8.856	7.611	7.064	8.542	7.357	6.832
8	10.03	8.775	8.169	9.685	8.510	7.894	9.413	8.211	7.633
9	10.90	9.672	9.018	10.61	9.346	8.737	10.27	9.007	8.400
10	11.89	10.52	9.843	11.48	10.17	9.517	11.15	9.832	9.192
11	12.85	11.35	10.66	12.48	10.99	10.28	12.06	10.62	9.929
12	13.95	12.22	11.48	13.54	11.82	11.11	12.96	11.43	10.74
13	14.86	13.09	12.31	14.34	12.66	11.93	13.82	12.24	11.51
14	15.69	13.92	13.11	15.26	13.46	12.67	14.64	13.03	12.28
15	16.55	14.77	13.91	16.00	14.33	13.47	15.46	13.85	13.05
16	17.41	15.58	14.74	16.81	15.09	14.26	16.25	14.61	13.78
17	18.19	16.43	15.58	17.59	15.95	15.06	17.04	15.39	14.54
18	19.05	17.30	16.37	18.49	16.78	15.83	17.85	16.14	15.30
19	19.96	18.09	17.17	19.40	17.50	16.64	18.78	16.94	16.05
20	20.81	18.95	17.97	20.14	18.30	17.38	19.48	17.74	16.79

References

Abadie, A. (2002), "Bootstrap Tests for Distributional Treatment Effects in Instrumental Variable Models," *Journal of the American Statistical Association*, 97, 284–292.

Abadie, A., J. Angrist, and G. Imbens, (2002), "Instrumental Variables Estimates of Subsidized Training on the Quantile of Trainee Earnings," *Econometrica*, 70, 91–117.

Abreveya, J. (2001), "The Effects of Demographics and Maternal Behavior on the Distribution of Birth Outcomes," *Empirical Economics*, 26, 247–257.

Acerbi, C. and D. Tasche (2002), "Expected Shortfall: A Natural Coherent Alternative to Value at Risk," *Economic Notes*, 31, 379–388.

Adrover, J., V. J. Yohai, and R. A. Maronna (2004), "Robust Regression Quantiles," *Journal of Statistical Planning and Inference*, 120, 187–202.

Aigner, D. and S. Chu (1968), "On Estimating the Industry Production Function," *American Economic Review*, 58, 826–839.

Aigner, D. J., T. Amemiya, and D. J. Poirier (1976), "On the Estimation of Production Frontiers: Maximum Likelihood Estimation of the Parameters of a Discontinuous Density Function," *International Economic Review*, 17, 377–396.

Aitchison, J. and J. Brown (1957), *The Lognormal Distribution*, Cambridge: Cambridge University Press.

Amemiya, T. (1982), "Two Stage Least Absolute Deviations Estimators," *Econometrica*, 50, 689–712.

Andrews, D. F., P. J. Bickel, F. R. Hampel, P. J. Huber, W. H. Rogers, and J. W. Tukey (1974), *Robust Estimates of Location: Survey and Advances*, Princeton: Princeton University Press.

Andrews, D. W. K. (1993), "Tests for Parameter Instability and Structural Change with Unknown Change Point," *Econometrica*, 61, 821–856.

Andrews, D. W. K. and M. Buchinsky (2000), "A Three-Step Method for Choosing the Number of Bootstrap Repetitions," *Econometrica*, 68(1), 23–51.

——— (2001), "Evaluation of a Three-Step Method for Choosing the Number of Bootstrap Repetitions," *Journal of Econometrics*, 103(1–2), 345–386.

Angrist, J., V. Chernozhukov, and I. Fernandez (2003), "Quantile Regression under Misspecification," preprint.

Angrist, J., G. Imbens, and D. B. Rubin (1996), "Identification of Causal Effects Using Instrumental Variables," *Journal of the American Statistical Association*, 91, 444–472.

Antoch, J. and J. Jurečková (1985), "Trimmed Least Squares Estimator Resistant to Leverage Points," *Computational Statistics*, 2, 329–339.

Arcones, M. (1996), "The Bahadur–Kiefer Representation of L_p Regression Estimators," *Econometric Theory*, 12, 257–283.

Arias, O., K. Hallock, and W. Sosa-Escudero (2001), "Indidividual Heterogeneity in the Returns to Schooling: Instrumental Variables Quantile Regression Using Twins Data," *Empirical Economics*, 26, 7–40.

Arrow, K. and M. Hoffenberg (1959), *A Time Series Analysis of Interindustry Demands*, Amsterdam: North-Holland.

Artzner, P., F. Delbaen, J.-M. Eber, and D. Heath (1999), "Coherent Measures of Risk," *Mathematical Finance*, 9, 203–228.

Bahadur, R. R. (1966), "A Note on Quantiles in Large Samples," *Annals of Mathematical Statistics*, 37, 577–580.

Bai, Z.-D. and X. He (1999), "Asymptotic Distributions of the Maximal Depth Estimators for Regression and Multivariate Location," *Annals of Statistics*, 27(5), 1616–1637.

Barrodale, I. and F. Roberts (1974), "Solution of an Overdetermined System of Equations in the ℓ_1 Norm," *Communications of the ACM*, 17, 319–320.

Bassett, G., R. Koenker, and G. Kordas (2004), "Pessimistic Portfolio Allocation and Choquet Expected Utility," *Journal of Financial Econometrics*, 2, 477–492.

Bassett, G. W. and R. Koenker (1986), "Strong Consistency of Regression Quantiles and Related Empirical Processes," *Econometric Theory*, 2, 191–201.

Bassett, G. W., M.-Y. S. Tam, and K. Knight (2002), "Quantile Models and Estimators for Data Analysis," *Metrika*, 55, 17–26.

Belluzzo, W. (2004), "Semiparametric Approaches to Welfare Evaluations in Binary Response Models," *Journal of Business and Economic Statistics*, 22, 322–330.

Bennett, S. (1983), "Analysis of Survival Data by the Proportional Odds Model," *Statistics in Medicine*, 2, 273–277.

Beran, R. (1974), "Asymptotically Efficient Adaptive Rank Estimates in Location Models," *Annals of Statistics*, 2, 63–74.

Beran, R. (2003), "Impact of the Bootstrap on Statistical Algorithms and Theory," *Statistical Science*, 18, 175–184.

Beran, R. and P. Hall (1993), "Interpolated Nonparametric Prediction Intervals and Confidence Intervals," *Journal of the Royal Statistical Society, Series B*, 55, 643–652.

Becker, R. A. and J. M. Chambers (1984), *S: An Interactive Environment for Data Analysis*, Wadsworth: Pacific Grove.

Berman, A. (1973), *Cones, Matrices and Mathematical Programming*, New York: Springer.

Bernoulli, D. (1738), "Specimen theoriae novae de mensura sortis," *Commentarii Academiae Scientiarum Imperialis Petropolitanae*, 5, 175–192; trans. by L. Sommer, *Econometrica*, 22, 23–36.

Bickel, P. and A. Sakov (1999), "On the Choice of m in the m out of n Bootstrap in Estimation Problems," preprint.

———— (2000), "An Edgeworth Expansion for the m out of n Bootstrapped Median," *Statistics & Probability Letters*, 49, 217–223.

Bickel, P. J. (1975), "One-Step Huber Estimates in the Linear Model," *Journal of the American Statistical Association*, 70, 428–434.

Bickel, P. J. (1976), "Another Look at Robustness; A Review of Reviews and Some New Developments (C/R: P158-168)," *Scandinavian Journal of Statistics*, 3, 145–158.

Bickel, P. J. and D. A. Freedman (1981), "Some Asymptotic Theory for the Bootstrap," *Annals of Statistics*, 9, 1196–1217.

Bickel, P. J. and E. L. Lehmann (1975), "Descriptive Statistics for Nonparametric Models. II: Location," *Annals of Statistics*, 3, 1045–1069.

Bilias, Y., S. Chen, and Z. Ying (2000), "Simple Resampling Methods for Censored Regression Quantiles," *Journal of Econometrics*, 99, 373–386.

Bjerkedal, T. (1960), "Acquisition of Resistance in Guinea Pigs Infected with Different Doses of Virulent Tubercle Bacilli," *American Journal of Hygiene*, 72, 130–148.

Bloomfield, P. and W. S. Steiger (1983), *Least Absolute Deviations. Theory, Applications and Algorithms*, Boston: Birkhäuser.

Blundell, R. and J. Powell (2003), "Endogeneity in Nonparametric and Semiparametric Regression Models," in *Advances in Economics and Econometrics: Theory and Applications*, Cambridge: Cambridge University Press.

Bofinger, E. (1975), "Estimation of a Density Function Using Order Statistics," *Australian Journal of Statistics*, 17, 1–7.

Boneva, L., D. Kendall, and I. Stefanov (1971), "Spline Transformations: Three New Diagnostic Aids for the Statistical Data-Analyst," *Journal of the Royal Statistical Society, Series B*, 33, 1–71.

Bosch, R. J., Y. Ye, and G. G. Woodworth (1995), "A Convergent Algorithm for Quantile Regression with Smoothing Splines," *Computational Statatistics & Data Analysis*, 19, 613–630.

Bourdin, B., and A. Chambolle (2000), "Implementation of an Adaptive Finite-Element Approximation of the Mumford Shah Functional," *Numerische Mathematik*, 85, 609–646.

Bouyé, E., and M. Salmon (2002), "Dynamic Copula Quantile Regressions and Tail Area Dynamic Dependence in Forex Markets," preprint.

Bowley, A. (1902), "Applications to Wage Statistics and Other Groups," *Journal of the Royal Statistical Society*, 65, 331–342.

Breidt, F. J., R. A. Davis, and A. A. Trindade (2001), "Least Absolute Deviation Estimation for All-Pass Time Series Models," *Annals of Statistics*, 29(4), 919–946.

Brown, G. W. and A. M. Mood (1951), "On Median Tests for Linear Hypotheses," in *Proceedings of the Second Berkeley Symposium on Mathematical Statistics and Probability*, pp. 159–166, Berkeley, CA: University of California Press.

Brownlee, K. (1965), *Statistical Theory and Methodology in Science and Engineering*, New York: Wiley.

Buchinsky, M. (1994), "Changes in US Wage Structure 1963–87: An Application of Quantile Regression," *Econometrica*, 62, 405–458.

——— (1995), "Estimating the Asymptotic Covariance Matrix for Quantile Regression Models. A Monte Carlo Study," *Journal of Econometrics*, 68, 303–338.

Buchinsky, M. and J. Hahn (1998), "An Alternative Estimator for Censored Quantile Regression," *Econometrica*, 66, 653–71.

Cade, B., J. Terrell, and R. Schroeder (1999), "Estimating Effects of Limiting Factors with Regression Quantiles," *Ecology*, 80, 311–323.

Carroll, R. J. and D. Ruppert (1988), *Transformation and Weighting in Regression*, New York: Chapman & Hall.

Chamberlain, G. (1994), "Quantile Regression, Censoring and the Structure of Wages," in *Advances in Econometrics* (ed. by C. Sims), New York: Elsevier.

Chambers, J. M. (1998), *Programming with Data: A Guide to the S Language*, New York: Springer.

Chappell, R. (1989), "Fitting Best Lines to Data, with Applications to Allometry," *Journal of Theoretical Biology*, 138, 235–256.

Chaudhuri, P. (1991), "Global Nonparametric Estimation of Conditional Quantile Functions and Their Derivatives," *Journal of Multivariate Analysis*, 39, 246–269.

Chaudhuri, P. (1992), "Generalized Regression Quantiles: Forming a Useful Toolkit for Robust Linear Regression," in *Proceedings of the Second International Conference on Statistical Data Analysis Based on the L_1 Norm and Related Methods*, New York: North-Holland.

Chaudhuri, P. (1996), "On a Geometric Notion of Quantiles for Multivariate Data," *Journal of the American Statistical Association*, 91, 862–872.

Chaudhuri, P., K. Doksum, and A. Samarov (1997), "On Average Derivitive Quantile Regression," *Annals of Statistics*, 25, 715–744.

Chen, X. R., Y. Wu, and L. C. Zhao (1995), "A Necessary Condition for the Consistency of L_1 Estimates in Linear Models," *Sankhyā, Series A, Indian Journal of Statistics*, 57, 384–392.

Chernoff, H. and I. Savage (1958), "Asymptotic Normality and Efficiency of Certain Non-parametric Test Statistics," *Annals of Mathematical Statistics*, 29, 972–994.

Chernozhukov, V. (2004), "Extremal Quantile Regression," *Annals of Statistics*, forthcoming.

Chernozhukov, V. and C. Hansen (2005), "An IV Model of Quantile Treatment Effects," *Econometrica*, forthcoming.

Chernozhukov, V. and H. Hong (2002), "3 Step Censored Quantile Regression," *Journal of the American Statistical Association*, 97, 872–897.

Chesher, A. (2003), "Identification in Nonseparable Models," *Econometrica*, 71, 1405–1441.

——— (2004), "Nonparametric Identification under Discrete Variation," CEMMAP Working Paper.

Choquet, G. (1954), "Theory of Capacities," *Annales de L'Institute Fourier*, V, 131–295.

Cox, D. (1962), "Comment on L. J. Savage's Lecture 'Subjective Probability and Statistical Practice'," in *The Foundations of Statistical Inference* (ed. by G. Barnard and D. Cox), London: Methuen.

Cox, D. (1972), "Regression Models with Life Tables," *Journal of the Royal Statistical Society, Series B*, 34, 187–220.

Dalgaard, P. (2002), *Introductory Statistics with R*, New York: Springer-Verlag.

Daniels, H. (1954), "Saddlepoint Approximations in Statistics," *Annals of Mathematical Statistics*, 25, 631–650.

Dantzig, G. (1951), *Linear Programming and Extensions*, Princeton: Princeton University Press.

Davies, P. and A. Kovac (2001), "Local Extremes, Runs, Strings and Multiresolution," *Annals of Statistics*, 29, 1–65, with discussion.

Davis, R. A. and W. T. M. Dunsmuir (1997), "Least Absolute Deviation Estimation for Regression with ARMA Errors," *Journal of Theoretical Probability*, 10, 481–497.

Davis, R. A., K. Knight, and J. Liu (1992), "M-Estimation for Autoregressions with Infinite Variance," *Stochastic Processes and Their Applications*, 40, 145–180.

De Angelis, D., P. Hall, and G. A. Young (1993a), "Analytical and Bootstrap Approximations to Estimator Distributions in L^1 Regression," *Journal of the American Statistical Association*, 88, 1310–1316.

——— (1993b), "A Note on Coverage Error of Bootstrap Confidence Intervals for Quantiles," *Mathematical Proceedings of the Cambridge Philosophical Society*, 114, 517–531.

de Finetti, B. (1937), "La prévision ses lois logiques, ses sources subjectives," *Annals de l'Instutute Henri Poincaré*, 7, 1–68; trans. by H. E. Kyburg in *Studies in Subjective Probability* (ed. by H. E. Kyburg and H. E. Smokler), New York: Wiley, 1964.

de Jongh, P. J., T. de Wet, and A. H. Welsh (1988), "Mallows-Type Bounded-Influence-Regression Trimmed Means," *Journal of the American Statistical Association*, 83, 805–810.

de Jongh, P., T. de Wet, and P. van Deventer (2003), "Saddlepoint Approximations for the Distributions of Regression Quantiles," preprint.

DeLong, D. M. (1981), "Crossing Probabilities for a Square Root Boundary by a Bessel Process (Corr: V12 P1699)," *Communications in Statistics Part A, Theory and Methods*, 10, 2197–2213.

Denneberg, D. (1990), "Premium Calculation: Why Standard Deviation Should be Replaced by Absolute Deviation," *ASTIN Bulletin*, 20, 181–190.

——— (1994), *Non-Additive Measure and Integral*, Dordrecht: Kluwer Academic Publishers.

Dhrymes, P. (1970), *Econometrics: Statistical Foundations and Applications*, New York: Harper & Row.

Dickey, J. (1974), "Bayesian Alternatives to the F-Test and Least Squares Estimate in the Normal Linear Model," in *Studies in Bayesian Econometrics and Statistics* (ed. by S. Fienberg and A. Zellner), Amsterdam: North-Holland.

Dikin, I. (1967), "Iterative Solution of Problems of Linear and Quadratic Programming," *Doklady Mathematics*, 8, 674–675.

Doksum, K. (1974), "Empirical Probability Plots and Statistical Inference for Nonlinear Models in the Two-Sample Case," *Annals of Statistics*, 2, 267–277.

Doksum, K. and R. Aaberge (2002), "Lorenz, Gini, Bonferroni and Quantile Regression," preprint.

Doksum, K. and M. Gasko (1990), "On a Correspondence Between Models in Binary Regression and Survival Analysis," *International Statistical Review*, 58, 243–252.

Doksum, K. and G. Sievers (1976), "Plotting with Confidence: Graphical Comparisons of Two Populations," *Biometrika*, 63, 421–434.

Donoho, D., S. Chen, and M. Saunders (1998), "Atomic Decomposition by Basis Pursuit," *SIAM Journal of Scientific Computing*, 20, 33–61.

Donoho, D. L. and P. J. Huber (1983), "The Notion of Breakdown Point," in *A Festschrift for Erich L. Lehmann*, pp. 157–184, Belmont, CA: Wadsworth.

Durbin, J. (1973), *Distribution Theory for Tests Based on the Sample Distribution Function*, Philadelphia: SIAM.

Edgeworth, F. (1888), "On a New Method of Reducing Observations Relating to Several Quantities," *Philosophical Magazine*, 25, 184–191.

——— (1920), "The Element of Chance in Competitive Examinations," *Journal of the Royal Statistical Society*, 53, 644–663.

Efron, B. (1967), "The Two Sample Problem with Censored Data," in *Proceedings of the 5th Berkeley Symposium on Mathematical Statistics and Probability*, Berkeley: University of California Press.

——— (1982), *The Jacknife, the Bootstrap and Other Resampling Plans*, Philadelphia: SIAM.

——— (1992), "Poisson Overdispersion Estimates Based on the Method of Asymmetric Maximum Likelihood," *Journal of the American Statistical Association*, 87, 98–107.

Efron, B. and R. Tibshirani (1993), *An Introduction to the Bootstrap*, New York: Chapman & Hall.

El-Attar, R., M. Vidyasagar, and S. Dutta (1979), "An Algorithm for ℓ_1-Norm Minimization with an Application to Nonlinear ℓ_1 Approximation," *SIAM Journal of Numerical Analysis*, 16, 70–86.

El Bantli, F. and M. Hallin (1999), "L_1 Estimation in Linear Models with Heterogeneous White Noise," *Statistics and Probability Letters*, 45, 305–315.

Ellis, S. P. (1998), "Instability of Least Squares, Least Absolute Deviation and Least Median of Squares Linear Regression (Disc: P344-350)," *Statistical Science*, 13, 337–344.

Engel, E. (1857), "Die Productions-und Consumtionsver-haltnisse des Konigreichs Sachsen," *Zeitschrift des Statistischen Bureaus des Koniglich Sachsischen Misisteriums des Innern*, 8, 1–54.

Engle, R. F. (1982), "Autoregressive Conditional Heteroscedasticity with Estimates of the Variance of United Kingdom Inflation," *Econometrica*, 50, 987–1007.

Feigin, P. D. and S. I. Resnick (1994), "Limit Distributions for Linear Programming Time Series Estimators," *Stochastic Processes and Their Applications*, 51, 135–165.

——— (1997), "Linear Programming Estimators and Bootstrapping for Heavy Tailed Phenomena," *Advances in Applied Probability*, 29, 759–805.

Ferguson, T. S. (1967), *Mathematical Statistics: A Decision Theoretic Approach*, New York: Academic Press.

——— (1996), *A Course in Large Sample Theory*, New York: Chapman & Hall.

Fiacco, A. and G. McCormick (1968), *Nonlinear Programming: Sequential Unconstrained Minimization Techniques*, New York: Wiley.

Fisher, R. and L. Tippett (1928), "Limiting Forms of the Frequency Distributions of the Largest or Smallest Member of a Sample," *Proceedings of the Cambridge Philosophical Society*, 24, 180–190.

Fitzenberger, B. (1996), "A Guide to Censored Quantile Regressions," in *Handbook of Statistics* (ed. by C. Rao and G. Maddala), New York: North-Holland.

——— (1997), "Computational Aspects of Censorted Quantile Regression," in L_1-*Statistical Procedures and Related Topics* (ed. by Y. Dodge), IMS Lecture Notes-Monograph Series.

Floyd, R. and R. Rivest (1975), "Expected Time Bounds for Selection," *Communications of the ACM*, 18, 165–173.

Fox, M. and H. Rubin (1964), "Admissibility of Quantile Estimates of a Single Location Parameter," *Annals of Mathematical Statistics*, 35, 1019–1030.

Frank, I. E. and J. H. Friedman (1993), "A Statistical View of Some Chemometrics Regression Tools (Disc: P136-148)," *Technometrics*, 35, 109–135.

Friedman, J. H. and W. Stuetzle (1981), "Projection Pursuit Regression," *Journal of the American Statistical Association*, 76, 817–823.

Friedman, M. (1937), "The Use of Ranks to Avoid the Assumption of Normality Implicit in the Analysis of Variance," *Journal of the American Statistical Association*, 32, 675–701.

Friedman, M. and L. Savage (1979), "The Utility Analysis of Choices Involving Risk," *Journal of Political Economy*, 56, 279–304.

Frisch, R. (1934), *Statistical Confluence Analysis by Means of Complete Regression Systems*, Oslo: Universitetets Økonomiske Institutt.

——— (1956), "La Résolution des problèmes de programme linéaire par la méthode du potential logarithmique," *Cahiers du Séminaire d'Econometrie*, 4, 7–20.

Gál, T. (1995), *Postoptimal Analyses, Parametric Programming, and Related Topics: Degeneracy, Multicriteria Decision Making, Redundancy*, Berlin: de Gruyter.

Gauss, C. F. (1809), *Theoria Motus Corporum Celestium*. Hamburg: Perthes et Besser; translated, 1857, as *Theory of Motion of the Heavenly Bodies Moving about the Sun in Conic Sections*, trans. C. H. Davis. Boston: Little, Brown; reprinted 1963, New York: Dover.

Gill, P., W. Murray, M. Saunders, T. Tomlin, and M. Wright (1986), "On Projected Newton Barrier Methods for Linear Programming and an Equivalence to Karmarker's Projective Method," *Mathematical Programming*, 36, 183–209.

Gill, P., W. Murray, and M. Wright (1991), *Numerical Linear Algebra and Optimization*, Redwood City, CA: Addison-Wesley.

Gnedenko, B. (1943), "Sur la distribution limite du terme maximum d'une série aléatoire," *Annals of Mathematics*, 44, 423–453.

Goldberger, A. (1962), "Best Linear Unbiased Prediction in the Generalized Linear Regression Model," *Journal of the American Statistical Association*, 57, 369–375.

Goldberger, A. S. (1983), "Abnormal Selection Bias," in *Studies in Econometrics, Time Series, and Multivariate Statistics*, pp. 67–84, New York, London: Academic.

Goldie, C. M. (1977), "Convergence Theorems for Empirical Lorenz Curves and Their Inverses," *Advances in Applied Probability*, 9, 765–791.

Gonzaga, C. (1992), "Path-Following Methods for Linear Programming," *SIAM Review*, 34, 167–224.

Green, P. J. and B. W. Silverman (1994), *Nonparametric Regression and Generalized Linear Models: A Roughness Penalty Approach*, London: Chapman & Hall.

Gu, C. (2002), *Smoothing Spline ANOVA Models*, New York: Springer.

Guilbaud, O. (1979), "Interval Estimation of the Median of a General Distribution," *Scandinavian Journal of Statistics*, 6, 29–36.

Gutenbrunner, C. and J. Jurečková (1992), "Regression Quantile and Regression Rank Score Process in the Linear Model and Derived Statistics," *Annals of Statistics*, 20, 305–330.

Gutenbrunner, C., J. Jurečková, R. Koenker, and S. Portnoy (1993), "Tests of Linear Hypotheses Based on Regression Rank Scores," *Journal of Nonparametric Statistics*, 2, 307–333.

Hahn, J. (1995), "Bootstrapping Quantile Regression Models," *Econometric Theory*, 11, 105–121.

Hájek, J. (1965), "Extension of the Kolmogorov-Smirnov Test to Regression Alternatives," in *Bernoulli-Bayes-Laplace: Proceedings of an International Research Seminar* (ed. by J. Neyman and L. LeCam), New York: Springer-Verlag.

Hájek, J. and Z. Šidák (1967), *Theory of Rank Tests*, Prague: Academia.

Hall, P. and S. Sheather (1988), "On the Distribution of a Studentized Quantile," *Journal of the Royal Statistical Society, Series B*, 50, 381–391.

Hallin, M. and J. Jurečková (1999), "Optimal Tests for Autoregressive Models Based on Autoregression Rank Scores," *Annals of Statistics*, 27, 1385–1414.

Hampel, F. R. (1974), "The Influence Curve and Its Role in Robust Estimation," *Journal of the American Statistical Association*, 69, 383–393.

Hansen, M., C. Kooperberg, and S. Sardy (1998), "Triogram Models," *Journal of the American Statistical Association*, 93, 101–119.

Härdle, W. (1990), *Applied Nonparametric Regression*, Cambridge: Cambridge University Press.

Härdle, W. and T. M. Stoker (1989), "Investigating Smooth Multiple Regression by the Method of Average Derivatives," *Journal of the American Statistical Association*, 84, 986–995.

Hartigan, J., and P. Hartigan (1985), "The Dip Test of Unimodality," *Annals of Statistics*, 13, 70–84.

Hasan, M. and R. Koenker (1997), "Robust Rank Tests of the Unit Root Hypothesis," *Eonometrica*, 65, 133–161.

Hastie, T. and R. Tibshirani (1990), *Generalized Additive Models*, New York: Chapman & Hall.

Hastie, T. J. and C. Loader (1993), "Local Regression: Automatic Kernel Carpentry," *Statistical Science*, 8, 120–129.

He, X. (1997), "Quantile Curves Without Crossing," *American Statistician*, 51, 186–192.

He, X. and F. Hu (2002), "Markov Chain Marginal Bootstrap," *Journal of the American Statistical Association*, 97, 783–795.

He, X. and H. Liang (2000), "Quantile Regression Estimates for a Class of Linear and Partially Linear Errors-in-Variables Models," *Statistica Sinica*, 10(1), 129–140.

He, X. and P. Ng (1999), "COBS: Qualitatively Constrained Smoothing via Linear Programming," *Computational Statistics*, 14, 315–337.

He, X. and Q.-M. Shao (1996), "A General Bahadur Representation of M-Estimators and Its Application to Linear Regression with Nonstochastic Designs," *Annals of Statistics*, 24, 2608–2630.

He, X. and S. Portnoy (1998), "Asymptotics of the Deepest Line," in *Applied Statistical Science III: Nonparametric Statistics and Related Topics* (ed. by S. E. Ahmed, M. Ahsanullah, and B. Sinha).

He, X., J. Jurečková, R. Koenker, and S. Portnoy (1990), "Tail Behavior of Regression Estimators and Their Breakdown Points," *Econometrica*, 58, 1195–1214.

Heckman, J. J. (1979), "Sample Selection Bias as a Specification Error," *Econometrica*, 47, 153–161.

Henderson, C. (1950), "Estimation of Genetic Parameters (Abstract)," *Annals of Mathematical Statistics*, 21, 309–310.

Hendricks, W. and R. Koenker (1991), "Hierarchical Spline Models for Conditional Quantiles and the Demand for Electricity," *Journal of the American Statistical Association*, 87, 58–68.

Hercé, M. (1996), "Asymptotic Theory of LAD Estimation in a Unit Root Process with Finite Variance," *Econometric Theory*, 12, 129–154.

Hettmansperger, T. (1984), *Statistical Inference Based on Ranks*, New York: Wiley.

Hill, B. M. (1975), "A Simple General Approach to Inference about the Tail of a Distribution," *Annals of Statistics*, 3, 1163–1174.

Hjørt, N. and D. Pollard (1993), "Asymptotics for Minimizers of Convex Processes," Statistical Research Report.

Hodges, J. and E. Lehmann (1956), "The Efficiency of Some Nonparametric Competitors of the t-Test," *Annals of Mathematical Statistics*, 27, 324–335.

Hoeffding, W. (1948), "A Class of Statistics with Asymptotically Normal Distributioni," *Annals of Mathematical Statistics*, 19, 293–325.

Hogg, R. V. (1975), "Estimates of Percentile Regression Lines Using Salary Data," *Journal of the American Statistical Association*, 70, 56–59.

———— (1979), private communication.

Horowitz, J. (1992), "A Smoothed Maximum Score Estimator for the Binary Response Model," *Econometrica*, 60, 505–531.

———— (1998), "Bootstrap Methods for Median Regression Models," *Econometrica*, 66, 1327–1352.

Hotelling, H. and M. Pabst (1936), "Rank Correlation and Tests of Significance Involving no Assumption of Normality," *Annals of Mathematical Statistics*, 7, 29–43.

Huber, P. (1967), "Behavior of Maximum Likelihood Estimates under Nonstandard Conditions," in *Proceedings of the 5th Berkeley Symposium on Mathematical Statistics and Probability*, Berkeley: University of California Press.

Huber, P. J. (1964), "Robust Estimation of a Location Parameter," *Annals of Mathematical Statistics*, 35, 73–101.

——— (1973), "Robust Regression: Asymptotics, Conjectures and Monte Carlo," *Annals of Statistics*, 1, 799–821.

Hunter, D. R. and K. Lange (2000), "Quantile Regression via an MM Algorithm," *Journal of Computational and Graphical Statistics*, 9(1), 60–77.

Hyndman, R. J., D. M. Bashtannyk, and G. K. Grunwald (1996), "Estimating and Visualizing Conditional Densities," *Journal of Computational and Graphical Statistics*, 5, 315–336.

Ihaka, R. and R. Gentleman (1996), "R: A Language for Data Analysis and Graphics," *Journal of Computation and Graphical Statistics*, 5, 299–314.

Imbens, G. and W. Newey (2002), "Identification and Estimation of Triangular Simultaneous Equations Models Without Additivity," preprint.

Janas, D. (1993), "A Smoothed Bootstrap Estimator for a Studentized Sample Quantile," *Annals of the Institute of Statistical Mathematics*, 45, 317–329.

Jaschke, S. and U. Küchler (2001), "Coherent Risk Measure and Good Deal Bounds," *Finance and Stochastics*, 5, 181–200.

Jones, M. C. (1994), "Expectiles and M-Quantiles Are Quantiles," *Statistics and Probability Letters*, 20, 149–153.

Jurečková, J. (1977), "Asymptotic Relations of M-Estimates and R-Estimates in Linear Regression Model," *Annals of Statistics*, 5, 464–472.

——— (1981), "Tail-Behavior of Location Estimators," *Annals of Statistics*, 9, 578–585.

——— (1999), "Regression Rank-Scores Tests Against Heavy-Tailed Alternatives," *Bernoulli*, 5.

Jurečková, J. and B. Procházka (1994), "Regression Quantiles and Trimmed Least Squares Estimator in Nonlinear Regression Model," *Journal of Nonparametric Statistics*, 3, 201–222.

Jurečková, J. and P. K. Sen (1984), "On Adaptive Scale-Equivariant M-Estimators in Linear Models," *Statistics & Decisions Supplement Issue*, 1, 31–46.

Karmarker, N. (1984), "A New Polynomial Time Algorithm for Linear Programming," *Combinatorica*, 4, 373–395.

Ke, C. and Y. Wang (2001), "Semiparametric Nonlinear Mixed-Effects Models and Their Applications (with Discussion)," *Journal of the American Statistical Association*, 96, 1272–1298.

Kendall, M. (1938), "A New Measure of Rank Correlation," *Biometrika*, 30, 81–93.

Khmaladze, E. V. (1981), "Martingale Approach in the Theory of Goodness-of-Fit Tests," *Theory of Probability and its Applications*, 26, 240–257.

Kiefer, J. (1959), "K-Sample Analogues of the Kolmogorov-Smirnov and Cramér-von Mises Tests," *Annals of Mathematical Statistics*, 30, 420–447.

——— (1967), "On Bahadur's Representation of Sample Quantiles," *Annals of Mathematical Statistics*, 38, 1323–1342.

Kiwiel, K. (2004), "Improved Randomized Selection," preprint.

Klee, V. and G. Minty (1972), "How Good Is the Simplex Algorithm," in *Inequalities III* (ed. by O. Shisha), New York: Academic Press.

Knight, K. (1989), "Limit Theory for Autoregressive-Parameter Estimates in an Infinite-Variance Random Walk," *Canadian Journal of Statistics*, 17, 261–278.

——— (1991), "Limit Theory for M-Estimates in an Integrated Infinite Variance Process," *Econometric Theory*, 7, 200–212.

——— (1998), "Limiting Distributions for L_1 Regression Estimators under General Conditions," *Annals of Statistics*, 26, 755–770.

——— (2001), "Limiting Distributions of Linear Programming Estimators," *Extremes*, 87–103.

——— (2002), "On the Second Order Behaviour of the Bootstrap of L_1 Regression Estimators," preprint.

Knight, K. and W. Fu (2000), "Asymptotics for Lasso-Type Estimators," *Annals of Statistics*, 28, 1356–1378.

Knuth, D. E. (1992), *Literate Programming*, Center for the Study of Language and Information.

——— (1998), *The Art of Computer Programming. Volume III: Sorting and Searching.* Reading, MA: Addison-Wesley, 2 edn.

Kocherginsky, M., X. He, and Y. Mu (2004), "Practical Confidence Intervals for Regression Quantiles," *Journal of Computational and Graphical Statistics*, forthcoming.

Koenker, R. (1984), "A Note on L-Estimators for Linear Models," *Statistics & Probability Letters*, 2, 323–325.

——— (1988), "Asymptotic Theory and Econometric Practice," *Journal of Applied Econometrics*, 3, 139–147.

——— (1996), "Rank Tests for Linear Models," in *Handbook of Statistics* (ed. by C. Rao and G. Maddala), New York: North-Holland.

——— (2004), "Quantile Regression for Longitudinal Data," *Journal of Multivariate Analysis*, 91, 74–89.

Koenker, R. and G. Bassett (1978), "Regression Quantiles," *Econometrica*, 46, 33–50.

——— (1982a), "Robust Tests for Heteroscedasticity Based on Regression Quantiles," *Econometrica*, 50, 43–61.

——— (1982b), "Tests of Linear Hypotheses and l_1 Estimation," *Econometrica*, 50, 1577–1584.

——— (1984), "Four (Pathological) Examples in Asymptotic Statistics (Corr: 93V47 P88)," *American Statistician*, 38, 209–212.

Koenker, R. and Y. Bilias (2001), "Quantile Regression for Duration Data: A Reappraisal of the Pennsylvania Reemployment Bonus Experiments," *Empirical Economics*, 26, 199–220.

Koenker, R. and V. d'Orey (1987), "Computing Regression Quantiles," *Applied Statistics*, 36, 383–393.

——— (1993), "A Remark on Computing Regression Quantiles," *Applied Statistics*, 36, 383–393.

Koenker, R. and O. Geling (2001), "Reappraising Medfly Longevity: A Quantile Regression Survival Analysis," *Journal of the American Statistical Association*, 96, 458–468.

Koenker, R. and L. Ma (2004), "Quantile Regression for Recursive Structural Models," preprint.

Koenker, R. and J. Machado (1999), "Goodness of Fit and Related Inference Processes for Quantile Regression," *Journal of the American Statistical Association*, 94, 1296–1310.

Koenker, R. and I. Mizera (2004), "Penalized Triograms: Total Variation Regularization for Bivariate Smoothing," *Journal of the Royal Statistical Society, Series B*, 66, 145–163.

——— (2005), Total Variation Regularization for Density Estimation, preprint.

Koenker, R. and P. Ng (2003), "SparseM: A Sparse Linear Algebra Package for R," *Journal of Statistical Software*, 8.

——— (2004), "Inequality Constrained Quantile Regression," preprint.

Koenker, R., P. Ng, and S. Portnoy (1994), "Quantile Smoothing Splines," *Biometrika*, 81, 673–680.

Koenker, R. and B. Park (1996), "An Interior Point Algorithm for Nonlinear Quantile Regression," *Journal of Econometrics*, 71, 265–283.

Koenker, R. and S. Portnoy (1987), "*L*-Estimation for Linear Models," *Journal of the American Statistical Association*, 82, 851–857.

——— (2000), "Some Pathological Regression Asymptotics under Stable Conditions," *Statistics & Probability Letters*, 50, 219–228.

Koenker, R. and Z. Xiao (2002), "Inference on the Quantile Regression Process," *Econometrica*, 70, 1583–1612.

——— (2004), "Unit Root Quantile Autoregression Inference," *Journal of the American Statistical Association*, 99, 775–787.

Koenker, R. and Q. Zhao (1994), "L-Estimation for Linear Heteroscedastic Models," *Journal of Nonparametric Statistics*, 3, 223–235.

——— (1996), "Conditional Quantile Estimation and Interence for ARCH Models," *Econometric Theory*, 12, 793–813.

Kolmogorov, A. N. (1931), "The Method of the Median in the Theory of Errors," *Matematiceskii Sbornik*; reprinted in *Selected Works of A.N. Kolmogorov*, Vol. II (ed. by A.N. Shiryayev), Dordrecht: Kluwer.

Koltchinskii, V. (1997), "M-Estimation, Convexity, and Quantiles," *Annals of Statistics*, 25, 435–477.

Kordas, G. (2004), "Binary Regression Quantiles," *Journal of Applied Econometrics*, forthcoming.

Koul, H. and K. Mukherjee (1994), "Regression Quantiles and Related Processes under Long Range Dependent Errors," *Journal of Multivariate Analysis*, 51, 318–337.

Koul, H. and A. Saleh (1995), "Autoregression Quantiles and Related Rank Score Processes," *Annals of Statistics*, 23, 670–689.

Koul, H. L. (1992), *Weighted Empiricals and Linear Models*, Hayward, CA: Institute of Mathematical Statistics.

Laine, B. (2001), "Depth Contours as Multivariate Quantiles: A Directional Approach," Master's thesis, Université Libre de Bruxelles.

Lee, S. (2003), "Efficient Semiparametric Estimation of a Partially Linear Quantile Regression Model," *Econometric Theory*, 19, 1–31.

Lehmann, E. (1959), *Testing Statistical Hypotheses*, New York: Wiley.

——— (1974), *Nonparametrics: Statistical Methods Based on Ranks*, San Franciso: Holden-Day.

Leisch, F. (2003), "Sweave, Part II: Package Vignettes," *R News*, 3(2), 21–24.

Lindley, D. and A. Smith (1972), "Bayes Estimates for the Linear Model," *Journal of the Royal Statistical Society, Series B*, 34, 1–41.

Lustig, I., R. Marsden, and D. Shanno (1994), "Interior Point Methods for Linear Programming: Computational State of the Art with Discussion," *ORSA Journal on Computing*, 6, 1–36.

Machado, J. and J. Mata (2001), "Counterfactual Decomposition of Changes in Wage Distributions Using Quantile Regression," *Empirical Economics*, 26, 115–134.

Machado, J. and J. Santos Silva (2002), "Quantiles for Counts," preprint.

Machado, J. A. F. (1993), "Robust Model Selection and M-Estimation," *Econometric Theory*, 9, 478–493.

Major, P. (1978), "On the Invariance Principle for Sums of Independent Identically Distributed Random Variables," *Journal of Multivariate Analysis*, 8, 487–517.

Mallows, C. L. (1972), "A Note on Asymptotic Joint Normality," *Annals of Mathematical Statistics*, 43, 508–515.

Mammen, E. and S. van de Geer (1997), "Locally Adaptive Regression Splines," *Annals of Statistics*, 25, 387–413.

Mann, H. and D. Whitney (1947), "On a Test of Whether One of Two Random Variables is Stochastically Larger Than the Other," *Annals of Mathematical Statistics*, 18, 50–60.

Manning, W., L. Blumberg, and L. Moulton (1995), "The Demand for Alcohol: The Differential Response to Price," *Journal of Health Economics*, 14, 123–148.

Manski, C. (1975), "Maximum Score Estimation of the Stochastic Utility Model of Choice," *Journal of Eonometrics*, 3, 205–228.

——— (1985), "Semiparametric Analysis of Discrete Response Asymptotic Properties of the Maximum Score Estimator," *Journal of Eonometrics*, 27, 313–333.

Martin, R. D. (1982), "The Cramer-Rao Bound and Robust M-Estimates for Autoregressions," *Biometrika*, 69, 437–442.

McFadden, D. (1989), "Testing for Stochastic Dominance," in *Studies in the Economics of Uncertainty in Honor of Josef Hadar* (ed. by T. Fomby and T. Seo), New York: Springer.

Mehrotra, S. (1992), "On the Implementation of a Primal-Dual Interior Point Method," *SIAM Journal of Optimization*, 2, 575–601.

Meketon, M. (1986), "Least Absolute Value Regression," Bell Labs Technical Report.

Meyer, M. and M. Woodroofe (2000), "On the Degrees of Freedom in Shape-Restricted Regression," *Annals of Statistical*, 28, 1083–1104.

Meyer, Y. (2001), *Oscillating Patterns in Image Processing and Nonlinear Evolution Equations*, Providence, RI: American Mathematical Society.

Mizera, I. (1999), "On Continuity: Another Look at Qualitative Robustness," preprint.

——— (2002), "On Depth and Deep Points: A Calculus," *Annals of Statistics*, 30, 1681–1736.

Mizera, I. and C. H. Muller (1999), "Breakdown Points and Variation Exponents of Robust M-Estimators in Linear Models," *Annals of Statistics*, 27, 1164–1177.

Mizera, I. and J. A. Wellner (1998), "Necessary and Sufficient Conditions for Weak Consistency of the Median of Independent But Not Identically Distributed Random Variables," *Annals of Statistics*, 26, 672–691.

Mizuno, S., M. Todd, and Y. Ye (1993), "On Adaptive-Step Primal Dual Interior Point Algorithms for Linear Programming," *Mathematics of Operations Research*, 18, 964–981.

Mosler, K. (2002), *Multivariate Dispersion, Central Regions and Depth: The Lift Zonoid Approach*, New York: Springer.

Mosteller, F. (1946), "On Some Useful 'Inefficient' Statistics," *Annals of Mathematical Statistics*, 17, 377–408.

Mosteller, F. and J. Tukey (1977), *Data Analysis and Regression: A Second Course in Statistics*, Reading, MA: Addison-Wesley.

Mukherjee, K. (2000), "Linearization of Randomly Weighted Empiricals under Long Range Dependence with Applications to Nonlinear Regression Quantiles," *Econometric Theory*, 16, 301–323.

Mumford, D. and J. Shah (1989), "Optimal Approximation by Piecewise Smooth

Functions and Associated Variational Problems," *Communications on Pure and Applied Mathematics*, 42, 577–685.

Nair, V. N. (1982), "Q-Q Plots with Confidence Bands for Comparing Several Populations," *Scandinavian Journal of Statistics*, 9, 193–200.

Natanson, I. (1974), *Theory of Functions of a Real Variable*, New York: Ungar.

Nazareth, J. (1994), *The Newton-Cauchy Framework: A Unified Approach to Unconstrained Nonlinear Minimization*, New York: Springer.

Nerlove, M. (1971), "Note on Error Components Models," *Econometrica*, 39, 383–396.

Newey, W. and J. L. Powell (1987), "Asymmetric Least Squares Estimation and Testing," *Econometrica*, 55, 819–847.

Newey, W. K. and J. L. Powell (1990), "Efficient Estimation of Linear and Type I Censored Regression Models under Conditional Quantile Restrictions," *Econometric Theory*, 6, 295–317.

Ng, E. and B. Peyton (1993), "Block Sparse Cholesky Algorithms on Advanced Uniprocessor Computers," *SIAM Journal Scientific Computing*, 14, 1034–1056.

Nicholls, D. F. and B. G. Quinn (1982), *Random Coefficient Autoregressive Models: An Introduction*, New York: Springer-Verlag.

Ninimaa, A., H. Oja, and J. Nyblom (1992), "The Oja Bivariate Median," *Applied Statistics*, 41, 611–617.

Oberhofer, W. (1982), "The Consistency of Nonlinear Regression Minimizing the L_1-Norm," *Annals of Statistics*, 10, 316–319.

Oja, H. (1983), "Descriptive Statistics for Multivariate Distributions," *Statistics Probability Letters*, 1, 327–332.

Okabe, A., B. Boots, K. Sugihara, and S. Chiu (2000), *Spatial Tesselations*, New York: Wiley.

Osborne, M., B. Presnell, and B. Turlach (2000), "On the Lasso and Its Dual," *Journal of Computation and Graphical Statistics*, 9, 319–337.

Osborne, M. and G. Watson (1971), "On an Algorithm for Discrete Nonlinear 11 Approximation," *Computer Journal*, 14, 184–188.

Parzen, E. (1979), "Nonparametric Statistical Data Modeling," *Journal of the American Statistical Association*, 74, 105–121.

Parzen, M. I., L. Wei, and Z. Ying (1994), "A Resampling Method Based on Pivotal Estimating Functions," *Biometrika*, 81, 341–350.

Pfanzagl, J. (1976), "Investigating the Quantile of an Unknown Distribution," in *Contributions to Applied Statistics* (ed. by W. Zeigler), Boston: Birkháuser.

——— (1982), *Contributions to a General Asymptotic Statistical Theory*. New York: Springer.

Pollard, D. (1991), "Asymptotics for Least Absolute Deviation Regression Estimators," *Econometric Theory*, 7, 186–199.

Portnoy, S. (1984a), "Asymptotic Behavior of M-Estimators of p Regression Parameters When p^2/n Is Large. I. Consistency," *Annals of Statistics*, 12, 1298–1309.

——— (1984b), "Tightness of the Sequence of Empiric CDF Processes Defined from Regression Fractiles," in *Robust and Nonlinear Time Series Analysis* (ed. by J. Franke, W. Hardle, and D. Martin), New York: Springer-Verlag.

——— (1985), "Asymptotic Behavior of M Estimators of p Regression Parameters When p^2/n Is Large: II. Normal Approximation (Corr: 91V19 P2282)," *Annals of Statistics*, 13, 1403–1417.

——— (1989), "Asymptotic Behavior of the Number of Regression Quantile Breakpoints," *SIAM Journal of Science Statistical Computing*, 12, 867–883.

—— (1991), "Asymptotic Behavior of Regression Quantiles in Non-stationary, Dependent Cases," *Journal of Multivariate Analysis*, 38, 100–113.

—— (1997), "Local Asymptotics for Quantile Smoothing Splines," *Annals of Statistics*, 25, 414–434.

Portnoy, S. (2003), "Censored Quantile Regression," *Journal of the American Statistical Association*, 98, 1001–1012.

Portnoy, S. and J. Jurečková (1999), "On Extreme Regression Quantiles," *Extremes*, 2, 227–243.

Portnoy, S. and R. Koenker (1989), "Adaptive L-Estimation for Linear Models (Corr: V18 P986)," *Annals of Statistics*, 17, 362–381.

—— (1997), "The Gaussian Hare and the Laplacian Tortoise: Computability of Squared-Error Versus Absolute-Error Estimators, with Discusssion," *Statistical Science*, 12, 279–300.

Powell, J. L. (1983), "The Asymptotic Normality of Two-Stage Least Absolute Deviations Estimators," *Econometrica*, 51, 1569–1576.

—— (1986), "Censored Regression Quantiles," *Journal Econometrics*, 32, 143–155.

—— (1991), "Estimation of Monotonic Regression Models under Quantile Restrictions," in *Nonparametric and Semiparametric Methods in Econometrics* (ed. by W. Barnett, J. Powell, and G. Tauchen), Cambridge: Cambridge University Press.

—— (1994), "Estimation of Semiparametric Models," in *Handbook of Econometrics*, vol. 4 (ed. by R. Engle and D. McFadden), New York: North-Holland.

Quiggin, J. (1981), "Risk Perception and Risk Aversion among Australian Farmers," *Australian Journal of Agricultural Economics*, 25, 160–169.

R Development Core Team (2003), *R: A Language and Environment for Statistical Computing*, available at http://www.R-project.org

Ramsay, J. O. (1988), "Monotone Regression Splines in Action (C/R: P442-461)," *Statistical Science*, 3, 425–441.

Ramsey, F. (1931), "Truth and Probability," in *The Foundations of Mathematics and Other Logical Essays*, New York: Harcourt Brace.

Rao, C. (1947), "Large-Sample Test of Statistical Hypotheses Concerning Several Parameters with Applications to Problems of Estimation," *Proceedings of the Cambridge Philosophical Society*, 44, 50–57.

—— (1973), *Linear Statistical Inference and Its Applications*, New York: Wiley.

Reinsch, C. (1967), "Smoothing by Spline Functions," *Numerische Matematik*, 16 177–183.

Renegar, J. (1988), "A Polynomial-Time Algorithm Based on Newton's Method for Linear Programming," *Mathematical Programming*, 40, 59–93.

Ripley, B. (1996), *Pattern Recognition and Neural Networks*, Cambridge: Cambridge University Press.

Rippa, S. (1992), "Long and Thin Triangles Can Be Good for Linear Interpolation," *SIAM Journal of Numerical Analysis*, 29, 257–270.

Robins, J. M. and Y. Ritov (1997), "Toward a Curse of Dimensionality Appropriate (CODA) Asymptotic Theory for Semi-parametric Models," *Statistics in Medicine*, 16, 285–319.

Robinson, G. (1991), "That BLUP Is a Good Thing: The Estimation of Random Effects," *Statistical Science*, 6, 15–31.

Rockafellar, R. and S. Uryasev (2000), "Optimization of Conditional VaR," *Journal of Risk*, 2, 21–41.

Rockafellar, T. (1970), *Convex Analysis*, Princeton: Princeton University Press.

Rogers, A. J. (2001), "Least Absolute Deviations Regression under Nonstandard Conditions," *Econometric Theory*, 17(4), 820–852.

Ronchetti, E. (1985), "Robust Model Selection in Regression," *Statistics & Probability Letters*, 3, 21–23.

Rosenblatt, F. (1958), "The Perceptron: A Probablistic Model for Information Storage and Retrieval in the Brain," *Psychological Review*, 65, 386–408.

Rousseeuw, P. and M. Hubert (1999), "Regression Depth," *Journal of the American Statistical Association*, 94, 388–433.

Rousseeuw, P. J. (1984), "Least Median of Squares Regression," *Journal of the American Statistical Association*, 79, 871–880.

Rousseeuw, P. J. and A. M. Leroy (1987), *Robust Regression and Outlier Detection*, New York: Wiley.

Ruppert, D. and R. Carroll (1980), "Trimmed Least Squares Estimation in the Linear Model," *Journal of the American Statistical Association*, 75, 828–838.

Sacks, J. (1975), "An Asymptotically Efficient Sequence of Estimators of a Location Parameter," *Annals of Statistics*, 3, 285–298.

Savage, L. (1954), *Foundations of Statistics*, New York: Wiley.

Schmeidler, D. (1986), "Integral Representation Without Additivity," *Proceedings of the American Mathematical Society*, 97, 255–261.

––––––– (1989), "Subjective Probability and Expected Utility Without Additivity," *Econometrica*, 57, 571–587.

Schwarz, G. (1978), "Estimating the Dimension of a Model," *Annals of Statistics*, 6, 461–464.

Serfling, R. (1980), *Approximation Theorems of Mathematical Statistics*, New York: Wiley.

––––––– (2004), "Nonparametric Multivariate Descriptive Measures Based on Spatial Quantiles," *Journal of Statistical Planning and Inference*, 123, 259–278.

Shamir, R. (1993), "Probabilistic Analysis in Linear Programming," *Statistical Science*, 8, 57–64.

Sheather, S., and J. Maritz (1983), "An Estimate of the Asymptotic Standard Error of the Sample Median," *Australian Journal of Statistics*, 25, 109–122.

Shen, X. (1998), "On the Methods of Penalization," *Statistica Sinica*, 8, 337–357.

Shorack, G. R. and J. Wellner (1986), *Empirical Processes with Applications to Statistics*, New York: Wiley.

Siddiqui, M. (1960), "Distribution of Quantiles from a Bivariate Population," *Journal of Research of the National Bureau of Standards*, 64, 145–150.

Silverman, B. (1986), *Density Estimation for Statistics and Data Analysis*, New York: Chapman-Hall.

Smirnov, N. V. (1952), "Limit Distributions for the Terms of a Variational Series," *AMS Translations*, 67.

Smith, J. (1987), *From Plane to Spheroid: Determining the Figure of the Earth from 3000 BC to the 18th Century Lapland and Peruvian Survey Expeditions*, Huntington Beach, CA: Landmark Enterprises.

Smith, R. L. (1994), "Nonregular Regression," *Biometrika*, 81, 173–183.

Sonnevend, G., J. Stoer, and G. Zhao (1991), "On the Complexity of Following the Central Path of Linear Programs by Linear Extrapolation II," *Mathematical Programming*, 52, 527–553.

Spady, R. H. (1991), "Saddlepoint Approximations for Regression Models," *Biometrika*, 78, 879–889.

Spearman, C. (1904), "The Proof and Measurement of Association Between Two Things," *American Journal of the Psychology*, 15, 72–101.

Stein, C. M. (1956), "Inadmissibility of the Usual Estimator of the Mean of a Multivariate Normal Distribution," in *Proceedings of the Third Berkeley Symposium on Mathematical Statistics and Probability*, Berkeley: University of California Press.

Stevens, W. (1950), "Fiducial Limits of the Parameter of a Discontinuous Distribution," *Biometrika*, 37, 117–129.

Stigler, G. (1945), "The Cost of Subsistence," *Journal Farm Economics*, 37, 1249–1258.

Stigler, S. (1984), "Boscovich, Simpson and a 1760 manuscript note on fitting a linear relation," *Biometrika*, 71, 615–620.

Stigler, S. M. (1977), "Do Robust Estimators Work with Real Data?" *Annals of Statistics*, 5, 1055–1077.

——— (1986), *The History of Statistics: The Measurement of Uncertainty Before 1900*, Cambridge, MA: Harvard University Press.

Stone, C. J. (1975), "Adaptive Maximum Likelihood Estimators of a Location Parameter," *Annals of Statistics*, 3, 267–284.

Stone, C. J. (1977), "Consistent Nonparametric Regression, with Discussion," *Annals of Statistics*, 5, 595–645.

Stone, C. J. (1982), "Optimal Global Rates of Convergence for Nonparametric Regression," *Annals of Statistics*, 10, 1040–1053.

Strotz, R. and H. Wold (1960), "A Triptych on Causal Systems," *Econometrica*, 28, 417–463.

Stukel, T. A. (1988), "Generalized Logistic Models," *Journal of the American Statistical Association*, 83, 426–431.

Subrahmanyam, M. (1972), "A Property of Simple Least Squares Estimates," *Sankhyā, Series B, Indian Journal of Statistics*, 34, 355–356.

Theil, H. (1950), "A Rank-Invariant Method of Linear and Polynomial Regression Analysis, I–III," *Koninklijke Nederlandse Akademie van Wetenschappen, Series A*, 53, 386–402, 521–525, 1397–1412.

Thompson, S. (2004), "Robust Tests of the Unit Root Hypothesis Should Not Be Modified," *Econometric Theory*, 20, 360–381.

Tibshirani, R. (1996), "Regression Shrinkage and Selection via the Lasso," *Journal of the Royal Statistical Society, Series B*, 58, 267–288.

Tjøstheim, D. (1986), "Some Doubly Stochastic Time Series Models," *Journal of Time Series Analysis*, 7, 51–72.

Tukey, J. (1965), "What Part of the Sample Contains the Information?" *Proceedings of the National Academy of Sciences*, 53, 127–134.

——— (1975), "Mathematics and Picturing Data," in *Proceedings of the 1974 Congress of Mathematicians*, Vol. 2 (ed. by R. James), pp. 523–531. Montreal: Canadian Mathematical Congress.

Van Aelst, S., P. J. Rousseeuw, M. Hubert, and A. Struyf (2002), "The Deepest Regression Method," *Journal of Multivariate Analysis*, 81(1), 138–166.

van Eeden, C. (1970), "Efficiency-Robust Estimation of Location," *Annals of Mathematical Statistics*, 41, 172–181.

van de Geer, S. (2000), *Empirical Processes in M-Estimation*, Cambridge: Cambridge University Press.

Vanderbei, R. M. M. and B. Freedman (1986), "A Modification of Karmarkar's Linear Programming Algorithm," *Algorithmica*, 1, 395–407.

Vapnik, V. N. (1995), *The Nature of Statistical Learning Theory*, Berlin, New York: Springer.

Venables, W. and B. D. Ripley (2002), *Modern Applied Statistics with S-PLUS*. New York Springer-Verlag, 4 edn.

von Neumann, J. and O. Morgenstern (1944), *Theory of Games and Economic Behavior*, Princeton.

Wald, A. (1940), "The Fitting of Straight Lines if both Variables Are Subject to Error," *Annals of Mathematical Statistics*, 11, 284–300.

Weiss, A. A. (1991), "Estimating Nonlinear Dynamic Models Using Least Absolute Error Estimation," *Econometric Theory*, 7, 46–68.

Welsh, A. H. (1987a), "Kernel Estimates of the Sparsity Function," in *Statistical Data Analysis Based on the L_1-Norm and Related, Methods* (ed. by Y. Dodge), pp. 369–377, New York: Elsevier.

——— (1987b), "The trimmed mean in the linear model," *The Annals of Statistics*, 15, 20–36.

——— (1989), "On M-Processes and M-Estimation (Corr: V18 P1500)," *Annals of Statistics*, 17, 337–361.

Welsh, A. H. and H. L. Morrison (1990), "Robust L Estimation of Scale with an Application in Astronomy," *Journal of the American Statistical Association*, 85, 729–743.

Whittaker, E. (1923), "On a New Method of Graduation," *Proceedings of the Edinburgh Mathematical Society*, 41, 63–75.

Wiens, D. (2003), "Badly Weighted Least Squares – Solution," *Econometric Theory*, 19, 701–703.

Wilcoxon, F. (1945), "Individual Comparisons by Ranking methods," *Biometrics*, 1, 80–83.

Wood, S. (2003), "Thin Plate Regression Splines," *Journal of the Royal Statistical Society, Series B*, 65, 95–114.

Working, E. (1927), "What Do Statistical Demand Curves Show?" *Quarterly Journal of Economics*, 41, 212–235.

Wright, M. (1992), "Interior Methods for Constrained Optimization," *Acta Numerica* (ed. A. Iserles), pp. 341–407, Cambridge: Cambridge University Press.

Wright, S. (1934), "The Method of Path Coefficients," *Annals of Mathematical Statistics*, 5, 161–215.

Wu, C. F. J. (1986), "Jackknife, Bootstrap and Other Resampling Methods in Regression Analysis," *Annals of Statistics*, 14, 1261–1295.

Yaari, M. (1987), "The Dual Theory of Choice under Risk," *Econometrica*, 55, 95–115.

Ying, Z., S. H. Jung, and L. J. Wei (1995), "Survival Analysis with Median Regression Models," *Journal of the American Statistical Association*, 90, 178–184.

Yohai, V. J. and R. A. Maronna (1979), "Asymptotic Behavior of M-Estimators for the Linear Model," *Annals of Statistics*, 7, 258–268.

Zhao, L., C. Rao, and X. Chen (1993), "A Note on the Consistency of M-Estimates in Linear Models," in *Stochastic Processes* (ed. by S. Cambanis), pp. 359–367, New York: Springer.

Zhao, Q. (1999), "Asymptotically Efficient Median Regression in the Presence of Heteroscedasticity of Unknown Form," *Econometric Theory*, 17, 765–784.

Zhou, K. and S. Portnoy (1996), "Direct Use of Regression Quantiles to Construct Confidence Sets in Linear Models," *Annals of Statistics*, 24, 287–306.

Name Index

Subject Index